"Dr. Spann lends us the gift of her extensive experience in the field to improve our approach to eating disorders and enhance recovery outcomes. The importance of human connection is deftly elucidated for those of us who thought we knew how to use it, and those eager to engage with it more effectively. An indispensable resource for anyone working in eating disorder treatment."

Kate Craigen, *PhD, clinical psychologist*

"Healing happens through cultivating trust allowing connection to one's authentic self. Dr. Melissa Spann effectively demonstrates the value of a meaningful therapeutic relationship, in conjunction with personalized biopsychosocial-spiritual treatments. With over 20 years of expertise in Eating Disorders, Dr. Spann offers real world guidance to Clinicians treating complex, dynamic individuals."

Michelle Weiner, *DO MPH, Founder Neuropain Health*

"A truly necessary book. Drawing on decades of clinical leadership, Melissa Orshan Spann argues, brilliantly, that while evidence-based protocols provide essential structure, we must pivot toward genuine presence. This vital resource shows professionals how authenticity fuels the connection required for deep, transformative work in eating disorder care."

Greta Gleisner, *LCSW, author and founder of* Eating Disorder Recovery Specialists

"Dr. Spann's expertise shines through in this book! She shares her clinical experiences and humanness in ways that reflect the real-world treatment needs of individuals with eating disorders. Her recognition of the importance of utilizing evidence-based approaches, in conjunction with the importance of authentic connection in the clinician-client relationship, is of utmost importance. This book is a must-read for clinicians, seasoned and new to the field alike."

Elissa Chakoff Martinez, *PhD, LMFT*

Building and Maintaining Authentic Relationships in Eating Disorders and Body Image Therapy

This book addresses the unique interplay of interpersonal characteristics of the clinician and client, coupled with effective treatment tools, to explore how to leverage authentic therapeutic relationships to enhance treatment outcomes.

Within the field of eating disorder treatment, authentic relationships are the cornerstone to breaking through these difficult to treat diseases. A clinician's tone, affect, physical presence, appropriate use of disclosure, and embodiment of the work impact whether a client will be receptive to care. By focusing on the therapeutic relationship, rather than focusing on the disorder, this book empowers both therapists and clients to break free from harmful cycles and destructive patterns that perpetuate disordered eating and move toward self-acceptance.

By bridging the gap between relational dynamics and evidence-based practice, this book provides invaluable insights and tools for clinicians and offers a fresh perspective on the therapeutic process, emphasizing the critical role of authentic relationships in effective treatment.

Melissa Orshan Spann, PhD, MBA, CEDS-C, is a passionate clinician, educator, and leader specializing in eating disorders and body image treatment. She brings warmth, expertise, and authenticity to every aspect of her work.

Building and Maintaining Authentic Relationships in Eating Disorders and Body Image Therapy

Melissa Orshan Spann

Routledge
Taylor & Francis Group
NEW YORK AND LONDON

Designed cover image: Getty Images

First published 2027
by Routledge
605 Third Avenue, New York, NY 10158

and by Routledge
4 Park Square, Milton Park, Abingdon, Oxon OX14 4RN

Routledge is an imprint of the Taylor & Francis Group, an informa business

ISBN: 978-1-041-05255-5 (hbk)
ISBN: 978-1-041-06284-4 (pbk)
ISBN: 978-1-003-63201-6 (ebk)

DOI: 10.4324/9781003632016

Typeset in Galliard
by Taylor & Francis Books

Contents

Acknowledgments

This book would not exist without the people who have shaped me both personally and professionally.

To Archer and Violet, who continue to teach me more about love, courage, humor, and humility than any textbook ever could; thank you for grounding me in what truly matters. You are my greatest teachers, and the light you bring into my life fills me more than you know.

To Steve, whose steadfast presence, partnership, and belief in me has been a constant source of strength. Thank you believing in this project long before it even had a title. Thank you for loving me through every step along the way and holding us together in our messy, beautiful reality of lives.

To my parents and siblings, the people who shaped my earliest understandings of connection, loyalty, and becoming. Your encouragement, curiosity, and unwavering support have been the scaffolding on which I have built my life's work. I carry your voices and values with me in everything I do.

To my dear friends who have walked beside me in laughter, grief, growth, and countless conversations that reminded me who I am and what I care about. Thank you for holding space for both my ambition and my vulnerability.

To the remarkable professionals I have had the privilege to learn from: mentors who challenged and inspired me; colleagues who sharpened my thinking and expanded my vision; and trainees I have supervised, who reminded me every day that teaching is a reciprocal act. I am grateful for your brilliance, your generosity, and the ways you have each shaped my understanding of this work.

And finally, with reverence and gratitude, to every client who has trusted me enough to share their story, their fear, their hope, and their unfolding selves. Thank you for allowing me to witness your courage and for modeling what authenticity looks like in its most honest forms. You have changed me.

In all of these relationships—family, friendship, mentorship, collegiality, and the sacred space of therapy—I have been shaped, challenged, and held. It is in these connections that I have learned that who we become is inseparable from those who walk alongside us. For all of you, and for all of this, I am endlessly grateful.

About the Author

Melissa Orshan Spann, PhD, MBA, CEDS-C, is a nationally recognized clinician, educator, and leader in the field of behavioral health. With over two decades of experience, she has built a distinguished career in psychotherapy, clinical supervision, program development, and organizational leadership, specializing in the treatment of complex eating disorders, body image, and trauma.

Known for her authentic, compassionate approach, Dr. Spann is a sought-after speaker, presenter, and clinical operator who brings both heart and strategy to every level of care she leads. She holds a PhD from Drexel University, an MBA from Florida Gulf Coast University, a master's degree from the University of Miami, where she also serves as an adjunct professor, and a bachelor's degree from the University of Florida.

A lifelong learner and advocate for holistic healing, Dr. Spann is a Certified Eating Disorder Specialist and Consultant (CEDS-C), Cognitive Processing Therapy provider, and certified yoga instructor. A proud Floridian, she lives in Miami with her husband, two incredible children, and their beloved pup, where she continues to blend evidence-based practice with the art of human connection.

Introduction

Why Authenticity Matters in Eating Disorder Care

People often ask why I chose to write a book about authenticity in eating disorder treatment. The short answer is that, after more than two decades as a clinician, supervisor, and clinical leader, I have learned that technique alone is never enough. The long answer is layered: a combination of professional experiences, personal reflections, and cultural observations that have shaped my belief that healing in this field depends as much on the quality of our relationships as on the interventions we provide.

I did not begin my career with this clarity. Like many new therapists, I entered the field armed with theory, protocols, and a determination to "do it right." Early on, I believed that if I could master enough techniques, complete enough trainings, and earn enough credentials, I would be fully equipped to help anyone who walked into my office. It took real work with real people to show me that healing is rarely that linear. The lessons came quietly, in moments where my interventions failed and all I had left was my honesty. It was in the spaces between what I planned and what unfolded that I saw how essential authenticity is to therapeutic change.

One of the earliest turning points came when a client told me, "I feel like you're saying all the right things, but it doesn't matter." She didn't need a perfect cognitive reframe. She needed presence; my willingness to show up, not as a flawless expert, but as another human being sitting with her suffering. That moment planted a seed I would return to again and again: people are not transformed only by what we know, but by how we offer ourselves in relationship.

Over time, first with my own clients then in supervising clinicians for decades, this truth became even more apparent. I saw new therapists who could recite protocols flawlessly yet felt immobilized in the face of silence, tears, or anger. They clung to the manual for safety, afraid to step outside its borders, even when the room called for something more relational, bridging empathy, curiosity, and humility. I noticed that the therapists who consistently helped clients the most were not those who delivered interventions perfectly, but

DOI: 10.4324/9781003632016-1

those who cultivated trust. They were present. They were real. They recognized that evidence-based skills require a foundation of genuine connection to become meaningful.

This is not simply anecdote. Decades of research demonstrate that the therapeutic relationship is one of the strongest predictors of client outcomes across all modalities, often exceeding the specific treatment model or technique (Wampold & Imel, 2015; Norcross & Lambert, 2019). In eating disorder care, the relational factors are especially central. Eating disorders are not just clusters of symptoms; they are disorders of disconnection from the body, from identity, from community, from meaning (Piran, 2017). Shame, secrecy, and fragmentation often obstruct engagement, making the therapeutic alliance both fragile and vital. When clients struggle to trust anyone—including themselves—authentic presence becomes a living intervention (Tasca & Balfour, 2014).

Yet the training clinicians receive rarely reflects this reality. Most graduate programs offer at most a lecture or two on eating disorders. Few teach how to sit with someone who desperately wants recovery yet fears losing the only coping strategy they've ever known. Few prepare therapists for the relational complexities that show up when food becomes language, when silence becomes protection, or when compliance hides despair. Many clinicians are left to learn these lessons by stumbling through them, without mentorship, without reflection, without acknowledgment of how profoundly this work demands their full humanity.

In the years leading to this book, the question "Are eating disorders on the rise?" surfaced frequently. The answer, supported by global data, is yes. A systematic review found that between 2000 and 2018, prevalence more than doubled worldwide from 3.4% to 7.8% (Galmiche et al., 2019). In the United States, roughly 28.8 million people will experience an eating disorder in their lifetime (Galmiche et al., 2019). During the COVID-19 pandemic, hospital admissions among adolescents for eating disorders increased dramatically; in England, admissions soared 515% from 2012 to 2022 (Ward et al., 2025).

These numbers are staggering, but statistics alone cannot convey the urgency. During the height of the pandemic, outpatient practices developed months-long waitlists. Residential and partial hospitalization programs filled beyond capacity. People who had never struggled with food before found themselves spiraling into obsessive tracking or compulsive exercise in an effort to feel in control amid global uncertainty. Routine structures collapsed. Social connection dissolved. Screens became lifelines. The perfect storm was not metaphor; it was daily reality.

What stood out most was not only the clinical severity, but the profound loneliness that accompanied it. I saw people starving not only for nourishment, but for connection. Isolation, disrupted routines, financial instability, and increased social comparisons created conditions where disordered eating could take hold with alarming speed. The rise in symptoms illuminated a broader truth: eating disorders do not emerge in a vacuum. They arise within relationships, culture, identity, trauma histories, and systems that shape how people see themselves and their bodies.

This is why we cannot treat eating disorders with technique alone. These illnesses involve a deeply personal negotiation between biology, psychology, relationships, and culture. The biopsychosocial–spiritual model is not philosophical, it is practical. Treatment must reflect the complexity of the illness. Evidence-based practices, such as CBT-E, FBT, and DBT provide essential scaffolding. But even the most validated approaches require a strong therapeutic foundation to take root. Without trust, behavior change feels unsafe. Without connection, insight does not translate to action. Without authenticity, the relationship can feel hollow.

We enter the therapy room carrying more than theory.

We bring our bodies, our beliefs, our vulnerabilities, our histories, and our nervous systems.

For years, I believed that my job was to minimize the self I brought to the room. I imagined myself as a steady but neutral presence, careful not to contaminate the work with too much humanity. But clients taught me that neutrality can feel distant, even withholding. They taught me that moments of honest reflection and acknowledging uncertainty, sharing emotional reactions thoughtfully, naming what feels unspoken can deepen connection and expand what is possible. Authenticity is not self-disclosure for its own sake. It is the embodied willingness to be present and real in service of the relationship.

The world is not making authentic connection easy. The rise of digital communication has changed how people relate to one another. Technology offers convenience, but it can also dull our capacity for presence and attunement. Many clients describe feeling more isolated than ever, despite being constantly connected. Their inner lives are often shaped by comparison, performance, and fear of judgment, all forces that foster self-surveillance rather than self-acceptance. Popular thinkers today have highlighted how the collapse of in-person community and the rapid adoption of social media have fueled loneliness, anxiety, and disconnection, particularly among youth.

The cultural message is clear: curate, perform, improve. In this landscape, authenticity can feel risky. For individuals with eating disorders, it can feel nearly impossible. Many have learned to protect themselves through perfectionism, emotional suppression, secrecy, or people-pleasing. These patterns make sense in context and are often formed in response to trauma, criticism, conditional acceptance, or cultural pressures. But they also make relationships incredibly difficult.

When a client enters treatment with an eating disorder, they often have a long history of feeling misunderstood, minimized, or dismissed. They may not trust easily. They may expect rejection. They may show up with rigid defenses, testing whether the therapist can hold the truth of their pain without flinching. The eating disorder itself can become a companion, a coping mechanism, a protector, making change both desired and feared. Authenticity in therapy must honor this ambivalence, neither demanding nor rushing vulnerability.

This book exists because I have watched, again and again, how authenticity, held alongside evidence-based care, can transform treatment. Authentic presence creates safety. Safety allows for vulnerability. Vulnerability allows for connection. Connection allows for change.

I wrote this book for the clinician who has ever sat with a client and thought, "There is something happening here that is deeper than the protocol."

For the supervisor who has tried to teach what cannot be captured on a checklist.

For the therapist-in-training who knows that being human feels like both a risk and a resource.

For the seasoned clinician who senses that the most meaningful moments are the ones that break the rules a little.

I also wrote it for myself. Because I need the reminder that we grow not by perfecting ourselves and our techniques, but by enlarging our capacity to feel, to tolerate discomfort, to stay when things get hard, and to trust that our presence has value.

The chapters that follow explore how authenticity functions as a therapeutic tool, a stance, and a way of being. We will examine how relational connection intersects with evidence-based models, attachment, embodiment, family systems, rupture and repair, culture, and identity. We will look at barriers to authenticity including shame, clinician insecurity, trauma histories, stigma, and bodily discomfort, and how to navigate them. We will explore how endings hold profound opportunities for integration and how clinicians can support clients in internalizing the therapeutic relationship beyond formal treatment.

This work is not about abandoning structure. It is about infusing structure with humanity. It is about holding evidence and intuition, skill and presence, clarity and uncertainty. The research tells us that authenticity matters. The clinical experience tells us that authenticity is what allows treatment to become recovery.

Ultimately, this book is an invitation.

To show up whole.

To trust that who we are matters as much as what we do.

To believe that real connection, that is imperfect, honest, and alive, can help people find their way back home to themselves.

Let's begin.

References

Galmiche, M., Déchelotte, P., Lambert, G., & Tavolacci, M. P. (2019). Prevalence of eating disorders over the 2000–2018 period: A systematic literature review. *The American Journal of Clinical Nutrition*, 109(5), 1402–1413.

Norcross, J. C., & Lambert, M. J. (2019). What works in the psychotherapy relationship: Results, conclusions, and practices. In J. C. Norcross & M. J. Lambert (Eds.), *Psychotherapy relationships that work: Evidence-based therapist contributions* (3rd ed., pp. 631–646). Oxford University Press

Piran, N. (2017). Embodied possibilities and disruptions: The emergence of the experience of embodiment construct from qualitative studies with girls and women. *Body Image*, 20, 14–26.

Tasca, G. A., & Balfour, L. (2014). Attachment and eating disorders: A review of current research. *The International Journal of Eating Disorders, 47*(7), 710–717.

Wampold, B. E., & Imel, Z. E. (2015). *The great psychotherapy debate: The evidence for what makes psychotherapy work* (2nd ed.). Routledge.

Ward, J. L., Vázquez-Vázquez, A., Phillips, K., Settle, K., Pilvar, H., Cornaglia, F., Gibson, F., Nicholls, D., Roland, D., Mathews, G., Roberts, H., Viner, R. M., & Hudson, L. D. (2025). Admission to acute medical wards for mental health concerns among children and young people in England from 2012 to 2022: A cohort study. *The Lancet. Child & Adolescent Health*, 9(2), 112–120.

Chapter 1

Why Authenticity Matters in Eating Disorder Treatment

- *Authenticity is more than a buzzword; it is a multidimensional way of being that shapes how we show up in relationships, communities, and within ourselves.* This chapter defines authenticity in contemporary terms, weaving together perspectives from philosophy, psychology, and lived experience.
- *The therapeutic relationship becomes the crucible where authenticity is tested, nurtured, and transformed.* Far beyond technique, therapy is introduced as a relational bridge where clients can rehearse vulnerability, honesty, and connection in ways that ripple outward into all aspects of life.
- *Influential thinkers and contemporary relational theorists remind us that congruence, presence, and attunement are not just ideals but practical tools for fostering authentic connection.* Their ideas ground our understanding of what it means to be real with another human being.
- *In today's world, authenticity is under siege.* Cultural pressures, social media, secrecy, isolation, and body image struggles conspire to keep individuals disconnected from their truest selves, with eating disorders and body image disturbances serving as the most poignant examples of this rupture.
- *At its core, authenticity is the therapist's greatest instrument.* Through intentional use of self, bringing their own personality, values, and humanity into the room, clinicians foster a therapeutic alliance formed from an authentic relational way of being, that is consistently linked to healing, growth, and improved outcomes across diagnoses.

Introduction

I met Sydney on the day she arrived at the residential treatment facility where I worked. At 38, she had stopped working and moved back in with her parents as her long-term eating disorder tightened its grip. I was nearly a decade younger, a working mom with two preschoolers, juggling home life while supporting clients in crisis. On the surface, we shared some similarities—both cis-White, Jewish, and from middle-class backgrounds—but the moment she saw me, Sydney burst into tears. "I don't want to be here," she sobbed. "And I definitely don't want you as my therapist." Her reaction was immediate and fierce.

DOI: 10.4324/9781003632016-2

Sydney wasn't new to treatment. She'd been in twice-weekly outpatient psychotherapy for more than a decade but escalating restriction and weight loss led her outpatient treatment team to insist on residential care. The program she admitted to was immersive: daily individual sessions, multiple groups, and meals shared shoulder-to-shoulder. Her rejection couldn't be avoided or postponed. She rolled her eyes in groups, scoffed at meals, and shut down in our sessions. I knew her defensiveness wasn't personal; it was her armor. Sydney approached every relationship with the same question, spoken or not: What do you want from me?

Four months into her 11-month stay, I took three days of leave after my grandmother died. When I returned, Sydney refused to meet with me. To her, my absence confirmed everything she feared: that I wasn't reliable, that she didn't matter, that therapy was just another place she would be abandoned. She made her anger known to staff, peers—anyone who would listen. She accused me of abandoning her and insisted she needed a new therapist. My first instinct was to pathologize her response as the ego-syntonic nature of anorexia nervosa, emotional dysregulation, and black-and-white thinking. But, for Sydney, this wasn't about logic—it was about history. Sydney wasn't reacting to my absence; she was reacting to a pattern that had defined her relationships throughout her lifetime: people leave. People disappoint. People don't show up when they are needed the most. And unintentionally, I had stepped into that role.

Eventually, she agreed to talk with me. When we sat down, I didn't begin with clinical interpretation. I began with honesty. I acknowledged my need to be with family and how hard it was to return to her anger. Slowly, I asked what outcome she believed would happen by pushing me away. Was this a familiar pattern? Did anger keep her safe from deeper hurt? I attempted not to defend my actions or challenge her in distortion. I began to invite her into relationship with me through my disclosure of my experience with her. That conversation didn't magically repair our alliance, but it marked a shift. I stopped tiptoeing around her defenses and began naming them—gently, directly, and with genuine curiosity. It wasn't always smooth—vulnerability rarely is—but from that point on, we were doing the real work. Together.

When we first met, Sydney reported no close friends, no romantic relationships, and strained ties with family. Her support system consisted solely of her outpatient therapist and dietitian—professionals, not personal connections. She was profoundly isolated. And given how deeply her eating disorder demanded control, secrecy, and self-reliance, it made sense that vulnerability felt impossible. Eating disorders don't just damage the mind and body, they erode connection. They thrive on disconnection, on keeping others out. Sydney had learned to relate through performance and protection, not presence. So, every small moment of honesty, every shared laugh, every expression of need, became a radical act of healing.

Her recovery didn't emerge from a dramatic breakthrough, but from slow, authentic steps toward connection. Over time, we developed a rhythm. I invited her to reflect on how she experienced me, and I shared what it felt like to be in relationship with her. We used our therapeutic bond to explore what trust, repair, and acceptance could feel like, experiences that were almost entirely new to her. For Sydney, recovery was not simply about renourishment or symptom interruption. In fact, true nourishment was not possible without relational trust. It was about learning to let another person in, to risk being seen, to dare to believe she was worth staying for. That was the real work, and it was transformational.

Defining Authenticity: A Multidimensional Perspective

Authenticity, broadly speaking, refers to the alignment between an individual's internal experiences, values, and outward expressions. Authenticity in the client–clinician relationship refers to the clinician and client being genuine, transparent, and true to their experiences in therapy. Authenticity is the clinician's and client's ability to show up in the therapeutic relationship with honesty, congruence, and emotional presence. An authentic therapeutic relationship is not just a friendly rapport, it involves the clinician responding to the client in a real, attuned way rather than a rigidly "clinical" manner. By carefully, and appropriately, "removing the mask" and showing genuine care, clinicians signal to clients that they are fully present, attuned, and invested in the person, not just the disorder. This relational process is a reciprocal development: as the clinician brings authenticity, clients often feel safer to drop their own guard, discuss difficult and shameful thoughts, and engage more honestly in treatment.

In my own clinical life, I learned early that the moments that moved clients forward rarely came from flawless interventions or tightly orchestrated treatment plans. They came when I allowed myself to be human, including when I sat with discomfort, when my voice cracked, when I didn't have an answer but stayed present anyway. Over time, I found that clients were not seeking the illusion of a perfect therapist; they were seeking a real person who could meet them where they were. It is from this place of genuine connection that transformation often begins.

A Brief History of Authentic Relationships in Therapy

The therapeutic relationship provides a unique and transformative space where individuals can explore and reconnect with their authentic selves. Rooted in Carl Rogers's (1951) concept of unconditional positive regard, therapy can offer an environment of acceptance, empathy, and non-judgment, which many individuals may not have experienced in their personal lives. When clients feel truly seen and valued by their clinician, without conditions of worth or the pressure to perform, they begin to internalize a sense of self-acceptance. This process allows them to examine the ways they have suppressed their true emotions, desires, and values in order to meet external expectations. By fostering a relationship built on trust and congruence, therapy helps individuals break free from ingrained patterns of inauthenticity and instead cultivate a deeper understanding of who they truly are. This process becomes transferable, what is learned in treatment becomes applicable in life, allowing people to live authentically.

The study of authenticity within the therapeutic relationship has steadily deepened over the past several decades. Early work emphasized the therapeutic alliance itself, suggesting that when clinicians showed up as genuine, congruent humans rather than distant experts, clients were more likely to trust, disclose, and remain engaged. By the late 1990s and early 2000s, scholarship increasingly linked authenticity with outcomes tied to identity and embodiment, noting that clients struggling with body image concerns often sought not just expertise, but emotional presence, attunement, and affirmation.

Research has moved beyond acknowledging authenticity to examining how it can be intentionally cultivated, operationalized, and measured in clinical work (Miller et al., 2004; Pickard, 2017; Seligman, 2018; Sweeney & Taggart, 2018). This shift is especially relevant in the treatment of eating disorders, where shame, trauma, and internalized weight stigma often fracture the therapeutic bond. Within this landscape, clinician authenticity becomes essential—not only to establish trust, but to foster the embodied safety required for clients to explore their relationships with food, shape, and self. As the field continues to evolve, the message is increasingly clear: authenticity is not a luxury or a stylistic preference; it is a core ingredient in helping clients reclaim their bodies, their agency, and their sense of connection.

In the Beginning

Beginning in the 1950s, Abraham Maslow, in *Motivation and Personality* (1954), connected authenticity to self-actualization. Maslow proposed that individuals who reach the pinnacle of the hierarchy of needs exhibit a strong sense of self-awareness, autonomy, and integrity. Self-actualization, in his view, reflects the ongoing process of becoming one's fullest and most integrated self, living in alignment with internal values rather than external pressures. He noted that self-actualized individuals are less influenced by societal norms and more attuned to their intrinsic motivations, allowing them to act in ways that reflect their true selves. This emphasis aligns with the principle of self-determination, the idea that authentic behavior arises when people feel free, competent, and connected to others. Maslow's research suggests that authenticity is not merely a trait but a developmental achievement that emerges as individuals fulfill basic psychological and social needs. His emphasis on intrinsic motivation has been supported by modern psychological research, which highlights the role of self-determination in authentic living (Deci & Ryan, 2000). Maslow (1970) considered authentic self-expression a key feature of healthy individual and relational functioning.

Then, in the 1960s, Carl Rogers, a foundational figure in humanistic psychology, emphasized the importance of authenticity. In his seminal work *On Becoming a Person* (1961), Rogers proposed that individuals who experience congruence, meaning their self-concept aligns with their true feelings, are more likely to experience psychological well-being. He argued that external conditions of worth, such as societal expectations or familial pressures, often distort authenticity, leading individuals to conform rather than express their true selves. This notion has been expanded in contemporary psychology, with scholars exploring how authenticity correlates with mental health, wellness, resilience, and fulfillment.

Taken together, Maslow and Rogers laid the foundation for understanding authenticity as both a developmental milestone and a relational process. Maslow highlighted the internal conditions necessary for self-actualization through autonomy, intrinsic motivation, and alignment with one's values, while Rogers illuminated how relational dynamics can either support or hinder that unfolding. When individuals are offered environments of safety, acceptance, and empathic presence, they are more likely to shed external expectations and move toward greater congruence and self-expression. These humanistic principles collectively suggest that authenticity is cultivated at the intersection of inner psychological readiness and responsive, attuned relationships. This integration provides a conceptual bridge to contemporary work exploring how authenticity operates within complex clinical settings, particularly those involving eating disorders and body image, where identity, embodiment, and relational safety are deeply intertwined.

In my experience, these theoretical foundations come alive most vividly in the therapy room. Time and again, I have witnessed how clients begin to move toward their most honest selves not when they are pushed, but when they are gently accompanied. The brave act of showing up to their own inner world and to another human bearing witness often initiates shifts that no manualized intervention could spark on its own. It is here, in the subtle interplay between clinical skill and genuine relational presence, that I have seen authenticity take root and meaningful change begin.

The Influence of Positive Psychology

Positive psychology, pioneered by Martin Seligman in the late 1990s, emphasizes the study of human strengths, well-being, and optimal functioning. Unlike traditional psychology, which often focuses on pathology and mental illness, positive psychology explores factors that contribute to a fulfilling and meaningful life. One key distinction from a positive psychology lens is the perspective on authenticity in that living authentically contributes to a fulfilling life, whereas the absence of authenticity can contribute to psychological distress. In contrast to traditional models of therapy that focus on symptom reduction, positive psychology interventions aim to restore authenticity by helping individuals reconnect with their values, strengths, and intrinsic motivations.

In his pivotal work *Authentic Happiness* (2002), Seligman argues that authenticity is a crucial component of well-being, as it allows individuals to align their actions with their values and cultivate a sense of purpose. He notes the concept of the "authentic self" as a key to achieving true happiness, asserting that individuals flourish when they engage in activities that reflect their strengths and intrinsic motivations rather than external expectations.

Research by Martin Seligman and Christopher Peterson in *Character Strengths and Virtues* (Peterson & Seligman, 2004) highlights that individuals who live inauthentically are suppressing their emotions, conforming to societal expectations, or engaging in self-deception and when this happens, people are more prone to anxiety, depression, and other psychological disorders. In essence, when we lose touch with our core values and intrinsic motivations, we are more likely to experience distress, including experiences like chronic stress and emotional exhaustion or others, ultimately leading to mental health concerns.

Stephen Joseph, another leading scholar of positive psychology, expands these humanistic foundations in *Authentic: How to Be Yourself and Why It Matters* (2016). Drawing from both Maslow's self-actualization and Rogers's emphasis on congruence, Joseph argues that authenticity is central to psychological well-being and is built on three interconnected components: self-awareness, self-acceptance, and behavioral congruence. Self-awareness refers to the capacity to recognize one's internal experiences including thoughts, emotions, bodily cues, and values as they arise. Self-acceptance involves embracing these experiences with compassion rather than judgment, acknowledging both strengths and limitations without denying or distorting them. Behavioral congruence is the ability to act in alignment with one's inner world, allowing choices and behaviors to reflect personal values rather than external pressure. Joseph's work highlights the many barriers that disrupt these processes including societal expectations, early relational wounds, and entrenched self-doubt which often lead individuals to suppress or edit their true feelings in exchange for acceptance, safety, or approval. When people chronically abandon themselves in this way, he argues, they grow increasingly disconnected from their internal compass, resulting in distress such as anxiety, shame, and low self-esteem.

Joseph's empirical work reinforces these concepts, demonstrating that people who exhibit higher levels of authenticity, marked by greater self-awareness, self-acceptance, and behavioral congruence, report higher life satisfaction and lower rates of depression and anxiety. His findings underscore that authenticity is not merely a philosophical aspiration but a measurable dimension of psychological functioning with meaningful clinical implications. By emphasizing strengths rather than deficits, this perspective shifts the focus from pathology to growth, positioning authenticity as both a protective factor and a pathway toward healing.

In teaching an undergraduate course on *Psychosocial Change and Well-Being*, I had the opportunity to witness how these ideas resonate beyond the therapy room and into the lives of emerging young adults. Integrating principles of positive psychology, we explored how concepts like meaning, strengths, gratitude, and purpose intersect with the lived experience of authenticity. Early in the semester, I asked students to examine their own definitions of authenticity and to reflect on how congruence between their inner world and outward behavior shaped their sense of happiness and well-being. Their reflections were strikingly diverse, yet they all echoed a shared recognition: authenticity was not a static trait but an evolving practice, informed by culture, community, and lived experience. Many students described how striving for authenticity required vulnerability in themselves and others. These conversations reaffirmed for me that authenticity is not simply a theoretical construct; it is a deeply human process that, when nurtured, supports flourishing and fosters the type of grounded presence essential to therapeutic work.

Other Definitions of Authenticity

There are so many different definitions of authenticity; because authenticity is shaped by cultural values, personal identity, and evolving psychological perspectives on what it means to be "true" to oneself, there are multiple perspectives on defining it. Newman (2019) highlighted the ongoing ambiguity surrounding the definition of authenticity, proposing three distinct forms: historical authenticity (remaining true to origins), categorical authenticity (aligning with recognized standards or types), and values authenticity (acting in accordance with one's core beliefs). Beyond psychology and counseling, scholars across disciplines have continued to offer multidimensional perspectives on authenticity (Lehman et al., 2019). Some have conceptualized authenticity as a two-factor construct involving alignment between the inner self and outer expression (Toper et al., 2022).

Two influential cultural theorists, Lionel Trilling (1972) and Charles Taylor (1992), further advanced thinking about authenticity in modern Western life. Trilling framed authenticity as a form of moral sincerity, a complex and often conflicted effort to honor one's inner reality despite social pressure. By contrast, Taylor situated authenticity within a moral and relational framework, arguing that becoming one's "true self" requires ongoing dialogue with others and engagement with shared cultural values. While both view authenticity as alignment between internal experience and outward expression, Trilling emphasizes resistance to pretense, whereas Taylor underscores the importance of community, history, and shared meaning.

More recent efforts have adapted these broader cultural and philosophical perspectives into psychological models. Dammann et al. (2021) expanded Lehman's economics- and management-based "3C Model" of authenticity—consistency, conformity, and connection—into a "4C View," emphasizing connection to highlight authenticity as a developmental and relational process rather than a fixed state. Likewise, Maiese (2023) describes authenticity as the avoidance of pretense and the alignment of action with genuine desire, underscoring its deeply personal character. Together, these perspectives support the view that authenticity requires both resisting externally imposed expectations and cultivating a self-determined sense of identity.

While Maiese foregrounds the individual's alignment with personal values, I contend that authenticity is best understood as both intrapersonal and relational. It is enriched through responsiveness to others in meaningful relationships, echoing Rogers's (1961) concept of congruence, in which genuine self-expression invites trust and deepens therapeutic connection. This relational view is further supported by theorists who conceptualize authenticity as a dynamic process shaped through empathy, attunement, and mutual responsiveness (Dammann et al., 2021; Wilt et al., 2019). Taken together, these perspectives provide a multidimensional foundation for the framework proposed in this text that honors personal integrity while recognizing that authenticity is cultivated, expressed, and sustained in connection with others.

Authenticity Today

Recent discussions in mainstream media have highlighted the growing relevance of authenticity in the modern world. A *New York Times* article, "Authentic Social Media?" (2023), explores how the digital age has complicated the pursuit of authenticity. While social media platforms offer opportunities for self-expression, they also encourage curated personas that may not reflect individuals' true selves. Genuine self-expression correlates with higher psychological well-being, whereas excessive self-presentation can lead to anxiety and self-doubt. This aligns with Seligman's positive psychology perspective that authenticity is a foundation for sustainable happiness, as it fosters deeper connections and self-acceptance rather than dependence on external validation.

Researcher and professor Brené Brown has brought authenticity to the forefront of public discourse through her books and TED Talks. In *The Gifts of Imperfection* (2010), Brown defines authenticity as the daily practice of letting go of who we think we're supposed to be and embracing who we truly are. She emphasizes that authenticity is not something we have or don't have, but a conscious choice to show up with courage, vulnerability, and honesty. According to her, being authentic requires cultivating self-awareness and self-compassion, and it often means taking the risk to be seen, even when there are no guarantees of acceptance. Her research on vulnerability and shame underscores that authenticity requires courage and self-acceptance. Brown argues that fear of rejection often compels individuals to adopt personas that mask their true selves, preventing genuine connection with others. She emphasizes that embracing imperfection and cultivating self-compassion are critical components of authenticity, making it not just an individual pursuit but a relational one as well. Brown's voice has been especially influential in bridging academic concepts with lived experience, translating the language of vulnerability, courage, and connection into terms that resonate broadly. Her work reminds us that authenticity is not a singular moment of revelation but a continual, imperfect practice that unfolds within our relationships with self and others. In my own clinical and teaching experiences, I have seen how her message gives people permission to acknowledge the messy, unfinished parts of themselves, often the parts most often hidden beneath competence, performance, or caretaking. Yet, while Brown's work offers a powerful framework, the realities of authenticity in eating disorder and body image treatment require an even more nuanced lens that holds not only the intrapersonal experience of "being ourselves" but also the relational, cultural, and embodied contexts in which authenticity is possible or constrained.

Bridging Definitions

Ultimately, authenticity is best understood as a dynamic process rather than a fixed trait. Across literature, authenticity emerges as a complex interplay between self-knowledge, self-expression, and external influences. While Rogers and Maslow laid the theoretical groundwork in the 1950s and 1960s, contemporary thinkers such as Brown and Joseph have expanded our understanding of how authenticity operates in everyday life. The intersection of positive psychology and authenticity continues to evolve as researchers explore how authenticity influences well-being across various life domains. From Seligman's foundational theories to contemporary discussions in major news outlets, the consensus is clear: Authenticity is essential not just for functioning but for psychological flourishing as well. Whether in personal relationships, leadership, or digital self-expression, the ability to live authentically fosters deeper meaning and satisfaction. The growing body of psychological and sociological research suggests that cultivating authenticity is a lifelong endeavor that requires introspection, courage, and an ongoing commitment to personal growth. As we move forward, I offer my own working definition of authenticity: a dynamic, relational process in which individuals feel safe enough to recognize, trust, and express their inner experience in a way that aligns with their values, fosters connection, and supports growth.

Challenges in Maintaining Authenticity in Today's Culture

While social psychologists and philosophers offer many more definitions of authenticity, we can all agree that being authentic matters in our personal satisfaction, promotes psychological well-being, positive affect, and most certainly relationship quality (Goldman & Kernis, 2002; Schlegel et al., 2013; Wood et al., 2008). Maintaining authenticity in relationships today is increasingly difficult due to psychological, societal, and technological factors. One of the primary obstacles in developing authentic relationships is the fear of rejection, where individuals hesitate to reveal their true selves due to concerns about disapproval or abandonment (Firestone, 2014). This apprehension leads many people to suppress their genuine thoughts and emotions, prioritizing social acceptance over personal authenticity. Consequently, this self-censorship prevents meaningful connections, as relationships built on conformity rather than genuine self-expression tend to be less fulfilling and more fragile (Firestone, 2014).

A significant factor impacting authenticity in relationships is the prevalence of digital communication. While technology may facilitate social interactions, it has also encouraged individuals to curate idealized versions of themselves, especially through social media (Ormerod, 2022). Platforms like Instagram and TikTok often showcase selective, polished representations of people's lives, fostering unrealistic standards and superficial engagement. This constant exposure to filtered personas creates societal pressure to conform, making it more challenging for individuals to express their true selves without fear of judgment (Ormerod, 2022). As a result, digital communication often prioritizes performance over sincerity, reducing opportunities for genuine emotional connection (Turkle, 2015).

Julia's Case: Struggling With the False Veneer of Online Life

Julia was a 42-year-old mother of two who spent most of her day scrolling through social media, following fitness influencers, diet accounts, and beauty bloggers whose perfectly curated lives made her feel perpetually "not enough." Although she struggled with body image issues when she was younger, she had experienced nearly two decades of what she considered "normalcy" in her relationship with food and body image. However, with her kids now in school and constant scrolling and trolling, she began tailoring her own online identity to match what she saw: filtered selfies, rigid food tracking posts, and subtle body-checking disguised as "wellness." What began as a desire for connection and belonging quickly morphed into isolation and obsession. Her world narrowed until her only real sense of identity was constructed through likes, followers, and comparison. Feeling alone in the world and with her phone in hand, she restricted, binged, and spiraled, feeling simultaneously unseen and overly exposed. After some time, Julia's outward appearance IRL (in real life) began to shift noticeably and the once-praise she received for her appearance was now turning into stares and glares. After a school event in which Julia's husband overheard other parents' comments, questions, and concerns about the changes in Julia, her husband, who previously was not concerned, began to talk with Julia about the concerns he overheard and asked her if she should talk with someone. After her husband really saw Julia, she later expressed a sense of relief that someone noticed her, and she began therapy.

The Harms of Inauthenticity

A lack of authenticity can significantly contribute to a diminished sense of self-awareness, which in turn leads to psychological distress. When individuals suppress their true thoughts, emotions, and values in order to conform to societal or familial expectations, they lose touch with their authentic selves. This detachment creates confusion about their true identity, making it difficult to recognize their needs, desires, and emotions. As previously mentioned, self-awareness is a fundamental component of psychological well-being, as it enables individuals to make choices that align with their intrinsic values (Deci & Ryan, 2000). Without self-awareness, individuals are more likely to experience chronic dissatisfaction, internal conflict, and an increased susceptibility to external influences that dictate their self-worth. This lack of clarity can make individuals more vulnerable to mental health disorders, including depression, anxiety, and disordered eating behaviors.

A diminished sense of self-worth often emerges when individuals feel pressured to conform rather than express their true selves. When a person's value is derived from external approval such as meeting unrealistic beauty standards, achieving professional success, or adhering to rigid social norms, they may develop a fragile self-esteem that is highly dependent on outside validation. People who struggle with authenticity often feel unworthy unless they meet societal expectations, leading to chronic shame and self-criticism (Brown, 2012). In my work, I have seen how this quiet erosion of self can touch even the most high-achieving, compassionate people. Those who appear confident on the outside yet are internally burdened by the fear that who they truly are may never be "enough."

Authentic relationships are built on mutual understanding, vulnerability, and genuine self-expression. When individuals feel unable to show their true selves due to fear of rejection or societal pressure, they may experience a profound sense of loneliness and unworthiness. Disconnection from oneself is often the result of conforming to external pressures or internalized social norms at the expense of genuine self-expression, which can lead to feelings of emptiness, dissatisfaction, and distress (Kernis & Goldman, 2006). Self-alienation, or the process in which someone feels detached and disconnected from their true values, emotions, desires, and identity, leads to a lack of alignment with inner and outer expression of oneself. Self-alienation in a sense, represents that opposite of living authentically, where congruence, self-awareness, and genuine engagement with one's identity promote psychological well-being (Rae, 2010; Sutton, 2023).

A lack of authenticity is particularly linked to identity-based disorders and emotional dysregulation. Carl Rogers, in *On Becoming a Person* (1961), argued that individuals develop incongruence, defined as a psychological state where one's self-concept does not align with their true feelings, when they prioritize external validation over self-expression. This incongruence, according to Rogers, is a major factor in the development of psychological disorders such as depression, anxiety, and low self-esteem. Similarly, research has shown that individuals with persistent inauthenticity are more susceptible to conditions like borderline personality disorder and social anxiety disorder. Other research has indicated that high levels of self-alienation, can have profound psychological consequences, including increased susceptibility to depression, anxiety, identity confusion, and social withdrawal (Chaudhary & Reddy, 2025).

Seeking Therapy

Many individuals seek therapy because they experience inner conflict between their authentic self and the expectations imposed on them by family, culture, or society. Joseph (2016) suggests that therapy should help clients dismantle these external pressures and reconnect with their core values and emotions. This is particularly relevant in eating disorder therapy, where individuals often develop disordered behaviors in an attempt to control emotions, gain validation, or conform to unrealistic beauty standards (Tylka & Wood-Barcalow, 2015). Additionally, individuals may enter therapy feeling ashamed of their struggles or disconnected from their emotions due to past invalidation (Gilbert, 2017). Clinicians working within an authenticity framework help clients recognize that vulnerability is not a weakness but is instead a pathway to self-connection and meaningful relationships (Brown, 2012).

Vulnerability

Joseph (2016) indicated that embracing vulnerability and self-compassion is essential for authenticity. He argued that individuals cannot act in alignment with their true selves unless they are willing to acknowledge their imperfections, unmet needs, and emotional realities without judgment. Vulnerability creates the conditions for honest self-reflection, while self-compassion provides the safety needed to explore one's inner world with openness rather than defensiveness or shame. Together, they form the emotional scaffolding through which people can move from self-protection toward self-expression. In this view, authenticity emerges not from perfection or certainty, but from the courage to inhabit one's experience with kindness and truth.

Challenges to Authenticity

In today's clinical landscape, conversations about authenticity are inseparable from the expanding understanding of trauma and its effects on identity, embodiment, and relational safety. Trauma, particularly interpersonal, developmental, and systemic forms, can significantly impair a person's capacity for authenticity by disrupting the ability to experience, express, and act in accordance with one's true self. In environments where safety is uncertain or conditional, individuals learn to prioritize survival over self-congruence, often adopting protective strategies such as dissociation, emotional suppression, hypervigilance, or people-pleasing (Brown, 2012). These strategies, initially adaptive, can become deeply ingrained patterns that constrain self-expression and connection long after the threat has passed.

Relational trauma, especially experiences of conditional acceptance, emotional neglect, or rejection in early caregiving relationships, profoundly shapes one's ability to trust others and to reveal one's inner experience in adulthood. When expressions of one's true self were previously met with criticism or abandonment, individuals may retreat into emotional withdrawal or develop false personas to maintain attachment or avoid harm (Firestone, 2014). Over time, such protective adaptations can erode one's sense of identity and make it difficult to access internal needs and values. Research has shown that trauma disrupts self-awareness and emotional regulation, which are key components of authenticity, that contribute to identity disturbance, fear of rejection, and internalized shame (Briere & Rickards, 2007; van der Kolk, 2014). These shifts often lead survivors to distance themselves from their core self, reinforcing patterns of self-alienation.

Authenticity requires a stable and integrated sense of identity, yet trauma can fragment this coherence, leaving individuals disconnected from their internal experiences and unable to act in alignment with their true selves. Even within therapy, survivors may feel unsafe being open, fearing judgment, abandonment, or retraumatization. As trauma-informed models emphasize, rebuilding authenticity is possible but must occur within relationships characterized by safety, attunement, compassion, and choice (Pearlman & Courtois, 2005). In this sense, authenticity is not taken for granted and it is a capacity that must be nurtured, protected, and slowly reclaimed through supportive relational contexts.

Societal norms and cultural expectations play a crucial role in shaping the struggle for authenticity. Many individuals feel pressured to adhere to predefined roles such as traditional gender expectations, professional personas, or social status ideals at the expense of their personal truths (Firestone, 2014). These societal pressures can lead to a disconnect between how individuals present themselves in relationships and how they truly feel, fostering inauthenticity and emotional dissatisfaction. This phenomenon aligns with self-determination theory, which suggests that autonomy and authenticity are essential for psychological well-being and meaningful interpersonal connections (Deci & Ryan, 2000).

Social norms often encourage individuals to conform to expectations rather than embrace their true selves. This is evident in workplace dynamics that may reward emotional suppression, making individuals feel they must "perform" rather than express their true thoughts and feelings (Grandey, 2008). Finally, cultural and family expectations may discourage emotional vulnerability, particularly for men, who are often socialized to suppress emotions, or for individuals raised in environments where expressing negative emotions was seen as weakness or failure (Levant, 2011). As people navigate these external pressures, they may further detach from their authentic selves to fit in, leading to inauthentic relational patterns.

The Therapeutic Relationship as a Bridge to Authenticity in All Relationships

Authenticity is crucial in the clinician–client relationship and is the core of effective therapy, providing a foundation for trust, emotional safety, and transformative healing. Research emphasizes that authenticity helps create a therapeutic environment where clients feel seen, understood, and valued (Geller & Srikameswaran, 2006). This environment, in which clients can explore their vulnerabilities, confront deeply ingrained beliefs about their bodies, and engage in the process of recovery, is critical not just in eating disorder therapy, but is an important part of any therapeutic approach. Authenticity fosters a relational dynamic that moves beyond clinical interventions, emphasizing the therapeutic alliance as a mutual and collaborative space for growth. This relationship-centered approach has been shown to facilitate greater client engagement and deeper emotional processing (Norcross & Lambert, 2019). When clinicians model authenticity, they create a safe environment where clients feel encouraged to be open about their thoughts and emotions (Geller & Porges, 2014). This is particularly beneficial in eating disorder therapy, where clients often struggle with interpersonal trust and benefit from clinicians who demonstrate emotional honesty and presence (Costin, 2017).

Authenticity Leads to Improved Recovery

At its core, authenticity enhances the therapeutic alliance, which is consistently linked to improved outcomes across modalities and diagnoses (Norcross & Lambert, 2019). When clinicians engage with clients from an authentic stance, meaning they are emotionally attuned, transparent when appropriate, and congruent in affect, clients often report feeling safer, more validated, and more willing to explore difficult material (Farber & Doolin, 2011). Authenticity also fosters mutual recognition, a relational concept wherein both clinician and client are seen as real, feeling individuals. This mutuality shifts therapy from being a one-sided expert model to a collaborative and deeply human process (Knox & Cooper, 2015). In this space, clients begin to test and revise long-held internal working models, especially those involving trust, self-worth, and safety in relationships. These shifts are foundational to recovery, as they allow the client to internalize a new relational experience in which their emotional needs are met without distortion, control, or rejection.

Research consistently supports the idea that therapist authenticity fosters stronger therapeutic alliances and improved recovery outcomes. Research demonstrates that when clients perceive their therapists as genuine and trustworthy, they are more likely to engage deeply in the therapeutic process, which in turn strengthens motivation and accelerates recovery (Schnellbacher & Leijessen, 2009; Truax et al., 1966). In a 2024 systematic review of 38 studies, clinician authenticity, defined as the ability to intuitively respond to a client's needs beyond standard protocols, was repeatedly associated with a better therapeutic relationship and improved recovery in clients (Albano et al., 2024). Clinicians who were perceived as authentic (for instance, flexible and attuned rather than formulaic) helped clients feel understood, instilling hope for recovery. Importantly, authenticity often manifests through behaviors like appropriate clinician self-disclosure and transparency. This growing body of evidence demonstrates that authenticity creates an environment where clients feel understood and motivated, thereby accelerating the recovery process.

Authenticity and Attachment

Our capacity for authenticity is deeply shaped by early attachment experiences. As John Bowlby proposed, the bonds formed between infants and caregivers serve as the foundation for how individuals understand themselves, others, and relationships across the lifespan (Bowlby, 1969/1982, 1980). These early interactions give rise to internal working models which are deeply held, often unconscious beliefs about one's worth, lovability, and the reliability of others that significantly influence how authentically a person is able to show up in the world. Building on this work, Mary Ainsworth identified distinct attachment patterns: secure, anxious, and avoidant, and later expanded to include disorganized attachment (Ainsworth et al., 1978; Main & Solomon, 1990). When caregivers are consistently attuned and responsive, children develop secure attachment, characterized by a sense of safety, trust, and inherent worth. This foundation supports emotional expression, healthy boundary-setting, and the ability to engage in relationships with openness and authenticity. In contrast, inconsistent, rejecting, or frightening caregiving environments often lead to insecure attachment patterns. Individuals with anxious attachment may learn to prioritize others' needs and approval to maintain connection, while those with avoidant attachment may suppress emotions and distance themselves from vulnerability. Disorganized attachment, often rooted in fear-based caregiving, can disrupt a coherent sense of self and relational safety.

Over time, these adaptive strategies, although protective in early environments, can interfere with authentic living. Individuals may become disconnected from their own needs, engage in people-pleasing or emotional withdrawal, and struggle to assert themselves or establish boundaries. Insecure attachment has also been linked to increased vulnerability to internalizing symptoms such as anxiety and depression, further complicating access to a stable and authentic sense of self (Bowlby, 1980).

Importantly, attachment patterns are not fixed. Through corrective emotional experiences, particularly within the therapeutic relationship, individuals have the opportunity to revise these internal working models. Therapy provides a consistent, attuned, and nonjudgmental space where clients can safely express their genuine thoughts and feelings without fear of rejection or abandonment. Within this relational context, individuals can begin to practice new ways of being through identifying their needs, tolerating vulnerability, setting boundaries, and engaging more authentically with others.

Over time, these experiences support the development of what is often referred to as "earned secure attachment," fostering a more integrated, confident, and authentic sense of self (Siegel, 1999; Wallin, 2007). As relational safety increases, so does the capacity for authenticity which allows individuals to participate in relationships that are reciprocal, validating, and grounded in honesty. In this way, authenticity is not simply an individual trait, but a relational achievement that is shaped, reinforced, and ultimately healed through meaningful human connection.

In my clinical work, I have seen how deeply these attachment imprints shape a person's capacity for authenticity. Clients with histories of insecure attachment often describe a lifelong tension between longing for closeness and fearing that their real selves are too much or not enough. Many learned early that emotional expression came at a cost including punishment, withdrawal, or inconsistence, so they adapted by silencing needs, performing competence, or becoming hyper-attuned to the emotional states of others. In therapy, when these clients are met with steady presence, curiosity, and attuned responsiveness, something profound can occur: the possibility that relationships need not require self-abandonment. I have watched individuals tentatively test this new relational landscape in sharing a vulnerable truth, expressing anger safely, or simply saying "I don't know," and witnessed how these small acts of honesty begin to rewire long-held expectations. Over time, this earned sense of security allows clients to more fully inhabit themselves, fostering a deeper internal trust that they can show up authentically and still remain connected. Authenticity, then, becomes not just an intrapersonal achievement but a relational accomplishment, born from the courage to be seen and the assurance that one's truth will be met rather than rejected.

Authenticity Challenges Self-Limiting Beliefs

Another key element of the therapeutic relationship is its role in challenging self-limiting beliefs that reinforce inauthenticity. Many individuals develop deeply internalized narratives that limit and undermine self-worth, agency, and relational capacity. These beliefs often originate in early attachment experiences, cultural messaging, and traumatic relationships and become embedded in a client's internal world as "truths" about who they are and what they are capable of (Beutler et al., 2004; Jordan, 2018). Self-limiting beliefs often arise from relational experiences in which authenticity was unsafe, unwelcome, or punished around early attachments. For example, a child who learns that expressing anger leads to withdrawal or punishment may grow into an adult who believes that their emotions are dangerous or invalid. In an authentic therapeutic relationship, the client is met with consistent emotional presence rather than withdrawal or judgment. This fosters disconfirmation of the belief that "if I am real, I will be rejected" (Jordan, 2018).

Authenticity in Therapeutic Practice

Authentic clinician behaviors, such as naming emotional reactions, offering real-time reflections, and acknowledging power imbalances, allows clients to experience vulnerability without anticipated relational consequences. Over time, this new relational template allows clients to update long-held assumptions about themselves and others (Geller & Greenberg, 2012; Safran & Muran, 2000). When clinicians embody authenticity in the therapeutic relationship through offering congruent emotional presence, honesty, and attunement, they create a context in which these beliefs can be examined, disrupted, and ultimately transformed. This can be particularly beneficial in treating clients with eating disorders.

Clinician Use of Self

The clinician's use of self refers to the intentional and skillful application of the clinician's personality, values, and relational presence as a means to foster therapeutic change. It is a dynamic process that involves the clinician leveraging their own emotional and relational authenticity to create a meaningful connection with the client. Baldwin (2000) describes the clinician's use of self as the ability to draw upon personal experiences, emotional responses, and intuitive insights to deepen the therapeutic alliance. This approach does not mean that the clinician becomes the focus of the session but rather that their humanity serves as a bridge to understanding and healing.

Clinician's Use of Self for Clients with Eating Disorders and Body Image Issues

In the context of eating disorder and body image therapy, the clinician's use of self can be particularly impactful. Clients who struggle with these issues often experience disconnection from their own bodies and emotions, making relational authenticity a powerful tool for modeling self-acceptance and emotional regulation. By sharing appropriate levels of vulnerability or personal insights, therapists can demonstrate that imperfection is a natural and acceptable part of the human experience. This can help clients challenge their own perfectionistic tendencies and foster a more compassionate relationship with themselves.

Effective use of self also requires self-awareness. Clinicians must continuously monitor their own biases, emotional responses, and boundaries to ensure that their authenticity enhances rather than hinders the therapeutic process. Clinicians must understand their intersectional identities and the impact this has on developing relationships. Authenticity is not merely about sharing personal truths but about embodying an attitude of openness and sincerity that fosters trust and connection. Awareness and training in transference, countertransference, and ruptures in the therapeutic relationship are critical to building appropriate authentic connections.

Jessie's Case: Breaking Down a Therapeutic Wall

I remember sitting across from Jessie, a 24-year-old woman in residential treatment for anorexia nervosa. Brilliant and sharply perceptive, she held her trust like currency—rarely offered, tightly guarded. From the beginning, she made it clear that therapists were not to be believed, especially those who, in her words, "don't get it." Our early sessions felt like balancing on a wire. She engaged just enough to avoid confrontation, but whenever emotion edged into the room, she retreated into intellectual analysis—safe, distant, controlled.

One afternoon, she arrived after a particularly tense body-image group I had facilitated. Jessie sat quietly, eyes fixed on the floor, her usual composure frayed. Without looking up, she murmured, "I don't see how anyone could actually believe what you all say. About recovery. About being enough. It just feels … fake."

My instinct was to reach for familiar tools—validation, reframing, hopeful metaphors. But something in her tone widened the space between us. I felt my own self-doubt flicker—the younger version of me who had also wrestled with perfectionism, comparison, and never feeling "enough." Instead of pushing it away, I let it guide me. Gently, I said, "I hear how impossible it feels to believe that right now. And … I'll be honest—there are days I struggle with those messages too." I told her that even with years of training and practice, I still catch myself in self-criticism or comparison. "What's different now," I said, "is that I've learned how to return to myself with compassion rather than punishment."

She lifted her head, startled. "Wait—you too?"

That moment cracked something open—not because I had revealed something extraordinary, but because I had revealed something true. I hadn't shared to center myself; I shared to meet her where she felt most alone. From then on, our work shifted. Jessie began to risk more: letting herself feel, challenging the harshness of her inner critic, allowing me to accompany her into the places she tried hardest to bury.

That experience reminds me that authenticity in therapy is not about self-disclosure for its own sake, nor about having the right words. It is about showing up with congruence, presence, and care—modeling what it means to be both human and healing inside a relationship.

Rogers in Practice: Congruence, Presences, and Attunement

I now return to Carl Rogers, one of the first to write about authenticity, to examine how clinicians can develop it in the therapeutic relationship with their clients. Chapter 5 explores more in depth how congruence, presence, and attunement form the foundation of an authentic therapeutic relationship. These elements enable the clinician to move beyond the role of neutral observer and engage as a genuine partner in the client's healing journey. Authenticity requires a delicate balance of professional skill and personal vulnerability, demonstrating that the therapist is not merely applying techniques but is deeply invested in the client's growth.

Ultimately, the therapeutic relationship serves as a model for how individuals can cultivate authenticity in all relationships. As clients experience the profound impact of being accepted and valued for who they truly are, they become more willing to seek out relationships that honor their authenticity. They learn to surround themselves with people who respect their boundaries, validate their emotions, and support their personal growth. Over time, they develop the courage to show up as their true selves, no longer molding their identities to fit societal or relational expectations. In this way, therapy acts as a bridge that helps individuals move from a life of inauthenticity and disconnection to one of genuine self-expression, emotional intimacy, and deeper, more meaningful connections with others.

Congruence

Carl Rogers (1957) identified congruence, or the alignment between a clinician's inner experience and outward expression, as a cornerstone of effective therapy. Congruence allows clinicians to model honesty and emotional integrity, demonstrating a level of self-awareness that invites clients to do the same. This mutual authenticity creates a safe environment for vulnerability, which is particularly critical in addressing eating disorders and body image concerns, where shame and secrecy often play central roles.

Rogers (1957) defined congruence as the therapist's ability to be real, integrated, and transparent within the therapeutic relationship. Congruence means the clinician is not hiding behind a professional façade or pretending to be unaffected; rather, their internal experiences (feelings, thoughts, bodily sensations) are aligned with their external responses. This creates a foundation of trust and safety, allowing the client to risk being more authentic themselves.

When clinicians model authenticity, clients are invited to explore their own incongruences, or moments when their internal experiences (e.g., fear, hurt, longing) conflict with how they present themselves in relationships. Genuineness fosters a climate in which clients can challenge beliefs like "My needs are too much" or "If I speak my truth, I'll be punished" and experiment with showing up more fully (Knox & Cooper, 2014). This movement toward congruence is foundational to shifting beliefs tied to shame and unworthiness (Farber & Doolin, 2011).

Modern understandings of clinician authenticity extend Rogers's congruence to include deliberate and attuned use of selective self-disclosure, emotional transparency, and reflexive awareness. Clinician authenticity today is not simply about expressing one's feelings but about knowing when, why, and how to do so in a way that supports the client's process (Geller & Greenberg, 2012; Knox & Cooper, 2014). It is relationally responsive, not impulsive.

Presence

Presence is another essential component of authenticity in therapy. Presence involves the therapist being fully engaged and attuned to the client in the moment, offering undivided attention and deep empathy (Geller & Greenberg, 2012). It goes beyond simply being in the room; it requires the therapist to remain emotionally available and connected, even in the face of difficult emotions or resistance. This level of engagement helps clients feel seen and valued, countering the isolating effects of their struggles.

Rogers (1980) spoke of presence as a "completely attentive, deeply understanding, and sensitive companionship" (p. 129). Presence allows clients to feel emotionally held, even when they are struggling to hold themselves. This felt sense of presence becomes a corrective emotional experience, especially for clients with histories of emotional neglect or trauma.

Authentic presence incorporates concepts from mindfulness, neuroscience, and attachment theory. Authenticity today includes the therapist's embodied presence, regulated nervous system, grounded affect, and nonverbal communication, which offers clients a relational anchor and co-regulation (Geller et al., 2010). The therapist's real-time responsiveness fosters the safety needed for clients to explore difficult emotional material.

Attunement

Attunement, closely linked to presence, is the ability to sense and respond to the client's emotional state accurately. According to Stern (1985), attunement involves recognizing subtle shifts in the client's affect and responding in ways that resonate with their internal experience, creating a profound sense of being understood.

Attunement, in Rogers's (1957) framework, is the clinician's deep understanding and resonance with the client's internal world. This attunement enables empathy not as a cognitive act but as an emotional bridge. It is through attunement that clients feel seen, heard, and emotionally understood.

Relational theories build upon this, framing authenticity as something that emerges in the space between client and clinician. It is a mutual process, not just the clinician attuning to the client but also sharing and negotiating the experience of being in relationship together (Jordan, 2018). Authenticity allows for rupture and repair, where moments of disconnection can be explored and worked through rather than avoided—deepening the trust and healing potential of the relationship (Safran & Muran, 2000; Geller, 2017).

Eating Disorders, Body Image, and Authenticity

Eating disorders and body image concerns significantly impact an individual's ability to develop and maintain authentic relationships. These challenges are often accompanied by shame, secrecy, and low self-esteem, which can create emotional barriers to open communication and trust in interpersonal relationships (National Eating Disorders Association [NEDA], 2023). Individuals struggling with negative body image and disordered eating patterns may fear judgment, rejection, or conditional acceptance, leading to social withdrawal, self-objectification, and emotional disconnection (Calogero, 2012). Maiese (2024) asserted that for individuals with anorexia nervosa who view their bodies as objects, internalizing cultural ideals and expectations regarding thinness likely contributes to them struggling to gain an authentic self.

Social anxiety, a common comorbid condition with eating disorders, is a long-term and overwhelming fear of social situations (Kerr-Gaffney et al., 2018). Whether as a result of social or emotional avoidance or as a result of a history of experiences of loneliness, someone with a history of social anxiety plus eating disorder issues is likely to struggle with inauthentic social interactions, fearing that their true selves are unlovable or inadequate. This emotional disconnect can further drive unhealthy coping mechanisms, such as restrictive dieting, binge eating, or excessive exercise, as a way to regain control or achieve validation through their appearance. Ultimately, the inability to cultivate authentic connections exacerbates body image concerns and reinforces harmful patterns of self. This dynamic is particularly evident in body image concerns and the development of eating disorders. Studies suggest that individuals who feel disconnected from their authentic selves are more likely to internalize unrealistic body ideals, leading to body dissatisfaction, disordered eating patterns, and a preoccupation with weight and appearance as a means of seeking external validation (Jiotsa et al., 2021).

For me, authenticity in the therapeutic relationship is not optional, it is essential in the treatment of eating disorders. In my view, it is the relational quality of authenticity that is central to recovery because it reduces the client's sense of isolation and fosters a therapeutic environment where vulnerability is met with acceptance. Eating disorders thrive in secrecy, self-criticism, and a deep sense of disconnection from others. Clients frequently arrive in treatment feeling misunderstood, mistrustful, and burdened by external expectations about how they "should" look, eat, or live. When a therapist shows up authentically, genuine, transparent, and emotionally present, it disrupts the cycle of social anxiety and isolation. Authenticity communicates to the client: you are worthy of honesty, attunement, and real human connection. This aligns with Rogers's (1961) notion of congruence, in which genuine presence fosters trust and deepens therapeutic connection. In eating disorder therapy specifically, authenticity provides a corrective emotional experience where vulnerability can be met with acceptance rather than judgment. This makes authenticity the foundation for healing; it creates the trust needed for clients to take risks, challenge rigid beliefs, and reimagine a life not dictated by their eating disorder. In a field where protocols and weight goals can sometimes overshadow the human element, authenticity restores the heart of therapy, reminding both therapist and client that recovery is ultimately built on real relationships (Hopwood, 2021; Robertson et al., 2025).

Secrecy and Emotional Isolation Impact Authenticity

One of the most significant ways eating disorders disrupt authenticity in relationships is through secrecy and emotional isolation. The intense shame and guilt surrounding disordered eating behaviors often lead individuals to hide their struggles from loved ones, reinforcing a cycle of isolation. This secrecy prevents open and honest communication, which is essential for forming deep and meaningful connections (Arcelus et al., 2013). Research suggests that individuals with eating disorders are less likely to seek emotional support, fearing that their struggles will be misunderstood or invalidated (Linardon, 2018).

Inauthenticity Leads to Body Image Distress

Inauthenticity, defined as a misalignment between one's true self and outward behaviors, has been linked to the development of body image distress. When individuals conform to external expectations and societal beauty standards that conflict with their personal values and self-perception, they may experience heightened body dissatisfaction, leading to disordered eating behaviors (Swami et al., 2023). Research suggests that authentic self-expression plays a crucial role in fostering positive body image, while inauthenticity contributes to self-objectification, body dissatisfaction, and internalized self-criticism (Cannavò, et al., 2024).

I have found that struggles with authenticity and body image are often inseparable threads of the same story. Many clients arrive in therapy having spent years contorting themselves, not only physically, but emotionally to meet an external ideal that feels impossibly distant and fundamentally disconnected from who they are. They describe a profound sense of betrayal toward their own bodies, as if their worth is contingent on compliance with rules they never consciously chose. This internal conflict is rarely about appearance alone; it reflects a deeper longing to belong, to be seen, and to feel "acceptable." I have sat with countless individuals who realized that the pursuit of the "perfect" body was not simply about weight or shape, but about trying to earn permission to exist. As they begin to reconnect with their values, preferences, and embodied experiences, they often discover that authenticity offers a pathway back to themselves, a way of inhabiting their bodies that feels grounded in truth rather than performance. In these moments, healing becomes less about changing the body and more about honoring the self within it.

How Poor Body Image Impacts Self-Identity and Relationships

Negative body image is closely linked to self-objectification, where individuals begin to view themselves primarily as objects to be evaluated based on appearance rather than intrinsic qualities (Fredrickson & Roberts, 1997). Self-objectification leads to chronic body monitoring, social anxiety, and fear of intimacy, which can negatively affect both platonic and romantic relationships (Rodgers et al., 2021). A study by Calogero (2012) found that self-objectification is associated with lower relationship satisfaction, reduced trust, and difficulties in emotional vulnerability, particularly in romantic relationships. Individuals with heightened body dissatisfaction often struggle with intimacy and trust, fearing that their partner's affection is contingent upon maintaining a certain physical appearance (Markey & Markey, 2011).

In romantic relationships, body image dissatisfaction can lead to reduced intimacy and emotional distance. Individuals with disordered eating patterns often struggle with being vulnerable, fearing that their body is not "good enough" for their partner (Tylka & Kroon Van Diest, 2015). A study by Rodgers et al. (2021) highlighted that body dissatisfaction and disordered eating symptoms correlate with lower relationship satisfaction and fear of emotional closeness. These concerns may lead individuals to avoid physical intimacy, engage in body-checking behaviors, or withdraw emotionally, which disrupts authentic connection and trust (Linardon, 2018).

Authenticity in therapy is not a technique but rather a way of being that invites trust, safety, and meaningful change. For many clients, particularly those with histories of eating disorders, or relational wounding, authenticity is not only unfamiliar but is potentially threatening.

Summary

Eating disorders and body image concerns can foster secrecy, self-objectification, and emotional withdrawal, which often lead to difficulties in trusting others, expressing vulnerability, and forming meaningful connections, all creating significant obstacles to authentic relationships. It is through the clinician's genuine presence, emotional congruence, and willingness to engage relationally that healing becomes possible. When clinicians model authenticity with care and intention, they offer clients a new relational template where vulnerability is met with attunement, not abandonment. In this way, authenticity is both the foundation and the vehicle for therapeutic transformation, reminding clients that they are worthy of being seen, known, and accepted exactly as they are.

As her therapist, witnessing Sydney's shift was a powerful reminder of why authenticity matters so deeply in the treatment of eating disorders. Weight restoration and symptom reduction are critical, but they are not enough on their own. What ultimately sustains recovery is the ability to live in honest connection with oneself and with others. Sydney taught me that authenticity cannot be forced, but has to be nurtured, modeled, and met with safety in the therapeutic relationship. Each time she dared to show up more fully, it was my responsibility to meet her there with the same openness, creating a space where truth could be spoken and held. Her story continues to shape how I practice: reminding me that recovery is not just about food or weight, but about rediscovering the courage to be real, and finding in that realness the possibility of genuine healing and human connection.

In the following chapter, I will begin to dive deeper into understanding the complex interplay of biological, psychological, sociocultural, and spiritual factors that converge together to cause an eating disorder to emerge. This information can help a clinician apply authenticity effectively to this specific population. Later chapters will discuss how to integrate authenticity into therapy as well as discuss considerations for treating special populations and circumstances.

Key Take-Aways

- Authenticity is foundational to healing, particularly in eating disorder and body-image treatment, where shame, isolation, and mistrust often undermine engagement.
- Therapeutic relationships are powerful change agents: research consistently shows that relational factors including attunement, congruence, and genuine presence predict outcomes as strongly as, or more strongly than, specific interventions.
- Authenticity is multidimensional, involving self-awareness, self-acceptance, and behavioral congruence; it is shaped by developmental, relational, and contextual forces across the lifespan.
- Trauma, especially relational trauma, disrupts the capacity for authenticity, fragmenting identity and fostering self-protective strategies like emotional suppression, perfectionism, or people-pleasing. Rebuilding authenticity requires relational safety, compassion, and trust.
- Therapists must bring their full, grounded selves into the room, not as experts who fix, but as humans who join, modeling vulnerability, navigating rupture and repair, and co-creating space where clients can risk being seen.

References

Albano, G., Teti, A., Scrò, A., Bonfanti, R. C., Fortunato, L., & Lo Coco, G. (2024). A systematic review on the role of therapist characteristics in the treatment of eating disorders. *Research in Psychotherapy: Psychopathology, Process and Outcome*, 27(2).

Ainsworth, M. D. S., Blehar, M. C., Waters, E., & Wall, S. (1978). *Patterns of attachment: A psychological study of the strange situation*. Lawrence Erlbaum Associates.

Arcelus, J., Haslam, M., Farrow, C., & Meyer, C. (2013). The role of interpersonal functioning in the maintenance of eating psychopathology: A systematic review and testable model. *Clinical Psychology Review*, 33(1), 156–167.

Baldwin, M. (Ed.). (2000). *The use of self in therapy* (2nd ed.). The Haworth Press.

Bayır-Toper, A., Sellman, E., & Joseph, S. (2022). Being yourself for the "greater good": An empirical investigation of the moderation effect of authenticity between self-compassion and compassion for others. *Current Psychology, 41*(7), 4871–4884.

Beutler, L. E., Malik, M., Alimohamed, S., Harwood, T. M., Talebi, H., Noble, S. (2004). Therapist variables. In M. Lambert (Ed.), *Bergin and Garfield's handbook of psychotherapy and behavior change*, (5th ed., pp. 227–306). Wiley.

Bowlby, J. (1979). The Bowlby-Ainsworth attachment theory. *Behavioral and Brain Sciences*, 2(4), 637–638.

Bowlby, J. (1980). *Attachment and loss: Vol. 3. Loss: Sadness and depression.* Basic Books.

Bowlby, J. (1982). *Attachment and loss: Vol. 1. Attachment* (2nd ed.). Basic Books. (Original work published 1969.)

Briere, J., & Rickards, S. (2007). Self-awareness, affect regulation, and relatedness: Differential sequels of childhood versus adult victimization experiences. *Journal of Nervous and Mental Disease*, 195(6), 497–503.

Brown, B. (2010). *The gifts of imperfection.* Hazelden Information & Educational Services.

Brown, B. (2012). *Daring greatly: How the courage to be vulnerable transforms the way we live, love, parent, and lead.* Gotham Books.

Calogero, Rachel M. (2012). Objectification theory, self-objectification, and body image. In T. Cash (Ed.), *Encyclopedia of body image and human appearance* (pp. 574–580). Academic Press.

Cannavò, M., Cella, S., Gullo, J., & Barberis, N. (2024). Self-compassion and body shame: Observing different pathways from body surveillance to eating disorders symptoms. *Journal of Affective Disorders Reports*, 17, 100816.

Chaudhary, Aman, & Reddy, Sandeep. (2025). The phenomenology of self-alienation in people with high perfectionistic traits. *Journal of Assessment and Research in Applied Counseling*, 7, 245–254.

Costin, C. (2017). *The embodied recovery workbook: A somatic-based approach to treating eating disorders.* Routledge.

Dammann, O., Friederichs, K. M., Lebedinski, S., & Liesenfeld, K. M. (2021). The essence of authenticity. *Frontiers in Psychology, 11*, 629654.

Deci, E. L., & Ryan, R. M. (2000). The "what" and "why" of goal pursuits: Human needs and the self-determination of behavior. *Psychological Inquiry*, 11(4), 227–268.

Farber, B. A., & Doolin, E. M. (2011). Positive regard. *Psychotherapy*, 48(1), 58.

Firestone, L. (2014). Three thorny obstacles to being authentic. *Psychology Today.* Retrieved from https://www.psychologytoday.com/us/blog/intimacy-a-path-toward-spirituality/201409/three-thorny-obstacles-to-being-authentic

Fredrickson, B. L., & Roberts, T. A. (1997). Objectification theory: Toward understanding women's lived experiences and mental health risks. *Psychology of Women Quarterly*, 21(2), 173–206.

Geller, S. M. (2017). *A practical guide to cultivating therapeutic presence.* American Psychological Association.

Geller, J., & Srikameswaran, S. (2006). Treatment non-negotiables: Why we need them and how to make them work. *European Eating Disorders Review*, 14(4), 212–217.

Geller, S. M., Greenberg, L. S., & Watson, J. C. (2010). Therapist and client perceptions of therapeutic presence: The development of a measure. *Psychotherapy Research*, 20(5), 599–610.

Geller, S. M., & Greenberg, L. S. (2012). *Therapeutic presence: A mindful approach to effective therapy.* American Psychological Association.

Geller, S. M., & Porges, S. W. (2014). Therapeutic presence: Neurophysiological mechanisms mediating feeling safe in psychotherapy. *Journal of Psychotherapy Integration*, 24(3), 178–192.

Gilbert, P. (2017). *Compassion: Concepts, research and applications.* Routledge.

Goldman, B. M., & Kernis, M. H. (2002). The role of authenticity in healthy psychological functioning and subjective well-being. *Annals of the American Psychotherapy Association*, 5(6), 18–20.

Grandey, A. (2008). Emotions at work: A review and research agenda. In J. Barling, C. L. Cooper, & S. R. Clegg (Eds.), The SAGE handbook of organizational behavior (pp. 235–261). SAGE.

Hopwood, C. J. (2021). Realness is a core feature of authenticity. *Journal of Research in Personality*, 92.

Jiotsa, B., Naccache, B., Duval, M., Rocher, B., & Grall-Bronnec, M. (2021). Social media use and body image disorders: Association between frequency of comparing one's own physical appearance to that of people being followed on social media and body dissatisfaction and drive for thinness. *International Journal of Environmental Research and Public Health, 18*(6), 2880.

Jordan, J. V. (2018). *Relational–cultural therapy* (2nd ed.). American Psychological Association.

Joseph, S. (2016). *Authentic: How to be yourself and why it matters.* Piatkus.

Kernis, M. H., & Goldman, B. M. (2006). A multicomponent conceptualization of authenticity: Theory and research. *Advances in Experimental Social Psychology*, 38, 283–357.

Kerr-Gaffney, J., Harrison A., & Tchanturia, K. (2018). Social anxiety in the eating disorders: A systematic review and meta-analysis. *Psychological Medicine*, 48(15), 2477–2491.

Knox, R., & Cooper, M. (2015). *The therapeutic relationship in counselling and psychotherapy.* SAGE Publications Ltd.

Lehman, D. W., O'Connor, K., Kovács, B., & Newman, G. E. (2019). Authenticity. *Academy of Management Annals*, 13(1), 1–42.

Levant, R. F. (2011). Research in the psychology of men and masculinity using the gender role strain paradigm as a framework. *American Psychologist*, 66(8), 765.

Linardon, J. (2018). Rates of abstinence following psychological or behavioral treatments for binge-eating disorder: Meta-analysis. *International Journal of Eating Disorders*, 51(8), 785–797.

Maiese, M. (2024). Anorexia nervosa, bodily alienation, and authenticity. *Review of Philosophy and Psychology*, 15(3), 773–793.

Main, M., & Solomon, J. (1990). Procedures for identifying infants as disorganized/disoriented during the strange situation. In M. T. Greenberg, D. Cicchetti, & E. M. Cummings (Eds.), *Attachment in the preschool years: Theory, research, and intervention* (pp. 121–160). University of Chicago Press.

Markey, C., & Markey, P. (2011). Romantic partners, weight status, and weight concerns: An examination using the actor-partner interdependence model. *Journal of Health Psychology*, 16(2), 217–225.

Maslow, A. H. (1954). *Motivation and personality.* Harpers.

Maslow, A. H. (1970). New introduction: Religions, values, and peak-experiences. *Journal of Transpersonal Psychology*, 2(2), 83–90.

Miller, J. B., Jordan, J. V., Stiver, I. P., Walker, M., Surrey, J. L., & Eldridge, N. S. (2004). Therapists' authenticity. In J. V. Jordan, M. Walker, & L. M. Hartling (Eds.), *The complexity of connection: Writings from the Stone Center's Jean Baker Miller Training Institute* (pp. 64–89). The Guilford Press.

National Eating Disorders Association. (2023). https://www.nationaleatingdisorders.org/2023/

Newman, G. E. (2019). The psychology of authenticity. *Review of General Psychology*, 23(1), 8–18.

Norcross, J. C., & Lambert, M. J. (2019). What works in the psychotherapy relationship: Results, conclusions, and practices. In J. C. Norcross & M. J. Lambert (Eds.), *Psychotherapy relationships that work: Evidence-based therapist contributions* (3rd ed., pp. 631–646). Oxford University Press.

Ormerod, P. (2022). Online friendships and self-deception: How social media distorts authenticity. *The Times* UK. Retrieved from https://www.thetimes.co.uk/article/online-friendships-self-deception-catfishing-d3kdcqxh9

Pearlman, L. A., & Courtois, C. A. (2005). Clinical applications of the attachment framework: Relational treatment of complex trauma. *Journal of Traumatic Stress*, 18 (5), 449–459.

Peterson, C., & Seligman, M. E. P. (2004). *Character strengths and virtues: A handbook and classification.* Oxford University Press; American Psychological Association.

Pickard, H. (2017). Responsibility without blame for addiction. *Neuroethics*, 10(1), 169–180.

Rae, G. (2010). Alienation, authenticity and the self. *History of the Human Sciences*, 23(4), 21–36.

Robertson, A. M., Cruwys, T., Stevens, M., & Platow, M. J. (2025). Leading by example: Experimental evidence that therapist lived experience disclosures can model the path to recovery for clients. *British Journal of Psychology, 116*(2), 409–431.

Rodgers, R. F., DuBois, R. H., & Jaeger, K. (2021). The impact of self-objectification on body dissatisfaction and eating disorder symptoms: A longitudinal study. *Body Image*, 38, 175–183.

Rogers, C. R. (1951). *Client-centered therapy; its current practice, implications, and theory*. Houghton Mifflin.

Rogers, C. R. (1957). The necessary and sufficient conditions of therapeutic personality change. *Journal of Consulting Psychology*, 21(2), 95–103.

Rogers, C. (1961). *On becoming a person: A therapist's view of psychotherapy*. Houghton Mifflin.

Rogers, C. R. (1980). *Way of being*. Houghton Mifflin.

Safran, J. D., & Muran, J. C. (2000). Resolving therapeutic alliance ruptures: Diversity and integration. *Journal of Clinical Psychology*, 56(2), 233–243.

Schlegel, R. J., Hicks, J. A., Davis, W. E., Hirsch, K. A., & Smith, C. M. (2013). The dynamic interplay between perceived true self-knowledge and decision satisfaction. *Journal of Personality and Social Psychology*, 104(3), 542–558.

Schnellbacher, J., & Leijssen, M. (2009). The significance of therapist genuineness from the client's perspective. *Journal of Humanistic Psychology*, 49(2), 207–228.

Seligman, M. E. P. (2002). *Authentic happiness: Using the new positive psychology to realize your potential for lasting fulfillment.* Free Press.

Seligman, M. (2018). PERMA and the building blocks of well-being. *The Journal of Positive Psychology*, 13(4), 333–335.

Siegel, D. J. (1999). *The developing mind: How relationships and the brain interact to shape who we are.* Guilford Press.

Stern, D. N. (1985). *The interpersonal world of the infant: A view from psychoanalysis and developmental psychology*. Basic Books.

Sutton, A. (2024). Changing ourselves: How does personality change relate to well-being and authenticity? *Journal of Individual Differences, 45*(1), 1–15.

Swami, V., Barron, D., Weis, L., & Furnham, A. (2023). Social media, authenticity, and body image: The role of self-objectification in young adults. *Health Psychology Research*, 12(14), 1396.

Sweeney, A., & Taggart, D. (2018). (Mis)understanding trauma-informed approaches in mental health. *Journal of Mental Health*, 27(5), 383–387.

Taylor, C. 1992. *The ethics of authenticity*. Harvard University Press.

Trilling, L. 1972. *Sincerity and authenticity*. Harvard University Press.

Truax, C. B., Wargo, D. G., Frank, J. D., Imber, S. D., Battle, C. C., Hoehn-Saric, R., Nash, E. H., & Stone, A. R. (1966). Therapist empathy, genuineness, warmth and patient therapeutic outcome. *Journal of Consulting Psychology*, 30(5), 395–401.

Turkle, S. (2015, September 26). Stop googling. Let's talk. *The New York Times*, 27.

Tylka, T. L., & Wood-Barcalow, N. (2015). What is and what is not positive body image? Conceptual foundations and construct definition. *Body Image*, 14, 118–129.

van der Kolk, B. A. (2014). *The body keeps the score: Brain, mind, and body in the healing of trauma*. Viking.

Wallin, D. J. (2007). *Attachment in psychotherapy*. Guilford Press.

Wilt, J. A., Thomas, S., & McAdams, D. P. (2019). Authenticity and inauthenticity in narrative identity. *Heliyon, 5*(7), e02178.

Wood, A. M., Linley, P. A., Maltby, J., Baliousis, M., & Joseph, S. (2008). The authentic personality: A theoretical and empirical conceptualization and the development of the Authenticity Scale. *Journal of Counseling Psychology*, 55(3), 385.

Chapter 2

Frameworks on Eating Disorders and Body Image Development

Overview

- *The story of eating disorders is both historical and evolving, shaped by shifting cultural ideals, medical discourse, and psychological theory.* This chapter traces the roots of how these complex illnesses have been defined and understood, situating them within a broader historical and clinical context.
- *At the heart of modern understanding lies the bio-psycho-social-spiritual model, which captures the interplay between biology, environment, psychology, relationships, and meaning.* This framework recognizes that eating disorders are never caused by a single factor but emerge from the convergence of vulnerability, culture, and circumstance.
- *The environment often pulls the trigger.* Body image development, shaped by families, peers, media, and cultural messages, sets the stage for struggles with identity, belonging, and authenticity, making it clear that these disorders live at the crossroads of the personal and the societal.
- *Social media has rewritten the landscape of body image, fueling comparison, conformity, and inauthentic self-presentation.* In a culture where curated images dominate, conformity erodes authenticity and distances individuals from their truest selves.
- *Research has expanded to explore how eating disorders intersect with authenticity, interpersonal connection, and emotional well-being.* These findings highlight that healing is not just about changing thoughts but about reclaiming the capacity for genuine relationships.
- *Clinicians, too, must reflect on our own body image development.* By acknowledging the influence of their personal histories and cultural conditioning, therapists can bring greater honesty, humility, and authenticity into their work.

I grew up in a world before smartphones, Instagram, TikTok, or hashtags about recovery and body positivity. In the 1990s, eating disorders lived mostly in the shadows. The only image I carried was the stereotype: a painfully thin cis White

DOI: 10.4324/9781003632016-3

girl who didn't want to eat. It wasn't something people around me talked about—not in youth groups, not at the dinner table, not even in the health classes I sat through as a teenager. The silence felt so complete that it was easy to imagine these struggles barely existed.

The first time I heard the words eating disorder spoken with real seriousness was in college. A girl in my sorority left mid-semester to seek treatment, and suddenly the air filled with whispers—some said she was dangerously thin; others brushed it off as stress. But once I knew to look, I saw it everywhere: friends skipping meals, roommates obsessively counting calories, casual comments about "earning" food or "being bad" for eating dessert. Diet pills tucked into desk drawers. Purging passed off as the flu. So much suffering hidden behind jokes, silence, and shame. I began to realize how common disordered eating was—even when no one dared to name it.

In graduate school, eating disorders made a brief appearance in our psychopathology syllabus: one class during the review of the DSM (APA, 2013)*, a few diagnostic criteria, then on to the next topic. No one taught us how to sit with a client who hated their body, or how to respond when an eating disorder was their only coping tool. These illnesses lived on paper, not in people. I left with a degree, a diagnostic checklist, and almost no understanding of what healing might actually require.*

It wasn't until I sat across from clients—face-to-face with their grief, terror, and tenacity—that I realized how much I hadn't been taught. My experience was not unique. Most counseling programs train students well in diagnostic language and symptom clusters but spend far less time cultivating the practical, relational skills that form the backbone of effective therapy: attunement, presence, and authentic connection. When eating disorders are covered at all, it is often in a single course or a handful of lectures. New clinicians walk away with academic knowledge but little preparation for the relational work required to meet clients who arrive ambivalent, guarded, or mistrustful.

This gap leaves early-career therapists eager but unprepared for the moment-to-moment work of navigating rupture and repair, setting compassionate boundaries, and building trust with clients whose eating disorders have taught them that vulnerability is dangerous. It highlights the essential role of supervision and mentorship, the spaces where emerging clinicians learn to integrate theory with lived relational depth. Because clients with eating disorders don't simply need treatment manuals; they need therapists who can sit with their pain, honor their defenses, and build the authentic relationships that make healing possible.

Although much of this book is centered on authenticity, I felt it was essential to dedicate a chapter to the basic understanding of eating disorders because this has been the heart of my clinical work for more than two decades. These illnesses are where I have witnessed, most vividly, how struggles with authenticity take root: how clients lose their voices to external expectations, to perfectionism, to the relentless pursuit of approval. Without grounding the conversation in the fundamentals of eating disorders, it would feel incomplete to then explore how authenticity can be reclaimed. My decision to include this chapter is both professional and personal: I have seen countless clients wrestle with the tension between who they feel they are supposed to be and who they truly are, and I know that understanding the complexity of eating disorders is necessary to fully appreciate why authenticity matters so deeply in the healing process.

The Evolution of Eating Disorders

Eating disorders have been documented throughout history, with their understanding evolving over time. Historically, patterns resembling disordered eating have been observed long before modern diagnostic frameworks. For example, Crichton (1996) explored accounts of Roman emperors Claudius and Vitellius, suggesting that their reported cycles of excessive eating and purging behaviors may reflect early descriptions consistent with what we now understand as bulimia nervosa.

The origins of eating disorders as recognized medical conditions date back to the late 19th century, when Sir William Gull introduced the term "anorexia nervosa" in 1873, providing one of the earliest clinical descriptions of severe food restriction and extreme weight loss (Mayall, et al., 2025). This marked a significant shift in understanding disordered eating behaviors as medical and psychological conditions rather than simply issues of morality or self-control. More than a century later, in 1979, British psychiatrist Gerald Russell identified and formally named "bulimia nervosa," distinguishing it from anorexia by highlighting the binge–purge cycle and intense fear of weight gain (Russell, 1979). The evolving recognition of disordered eating patterns continued into the 21st century, culminating in the official recognition of binge-eating disorder (BED) in 2013 when it was classified as a distinct diagnosis in the *Diagnostic and Statistical Manual of Mental Disorders* (DSM-5). The DSM-5 is the main guide that mental health professionals use to diagnose and understand eating disorders (American Psychiatric Association, 2013). This progression reflects the growing understanding of the complexity and diversity of eating disorders, emphasizing their biological, psychological, and sociocultural underpinnings.

Alongside BED's inclusion, the DSM-5 also introduced avoidant/restrictive food intake disorder (ARFID), which accounts for individuals who limit their food intake due to sensory sensitivities, fear of choking, or lack of interest in eating, rather than concerns about body image or weight (American Psychiatric Association, 2013). Additionally, other specified feeding or eating disorder (OSFED) was created to categorize serious eating disorders that do not meet the exact criteria for anorexia, bulimia, or BED but still cause significant distress and impairment (Fairburn & Cooper, 2011). These classifications reflect the expanding understanding of eating disorders as complex conditions that extend beyond weight-focused concerns, encompassing a broad spectrum of disordered eating behaviors and psychological factors. Eating disorders are serious mental health conditions that involve disturbances in eating behaviors, thoughts, and emotions related to food, body image, and weight (American Psychiatric Association [APA], 2022).

Box 2.1 Major eating disorder diagnoses included in the DSM-5

Anorexia nervosa (AN) is characterized by:

- Extreme food restriction leading to significant weight loss or difficulty maintaining a healthy weight.
- Intense fear of gaining weight, even when underweight.
- Distorted body image, meaning the person sees themselves as overweight even when they are very thin.

In simple terms:

Anorexia nervosa is when a person severely limits how much they eat, even to the point of starvation, because they are terrified of gaining weight. They might see their body differently than others do and feel intense pressure to stay thin.

Bulimia nervosa (BN) is characterized by:

- Episodes of binge eating, meaning eating large amounts of food in a short time while feeling out of control.
- Compensatory behaviors to "undo" the binge, such as forced vomiting, excessive exercise, fasting, or using laxatives.
- Preoccupation with body shape and weight that strongly affects self-esteem.

In simple terms:

Bulimia nervosa is when someone eats a lot of food in a short time and then tries to get rid of the calories in an unhealthy way, like vomiting or over-exercising. This cycle can become very stressful and hard to break.

Binge-eating disorder (BED) is characterized by:

- Repeated episodes of binge eating, meaning eating large amounts of food in a short time while feeling out of control.
- Unlike bulimia, there is no attempt to "undo" the binge (no purging, extreme exercise, or fasting).
- Feelings of guilt, shame, and distress after binge eating.

In simple terms:

Binge-eating disorder is when a person regularly eats large amounts of food in a way that feels out of control. Unlike bulimia, they don't purge afterward, but they may feel ashamed or guilty about their eating.

Avoidant/restrictive food intake disorder (ARFID) is characterized by:

- Severe restriction of food intake, but not due to concerns about body image or weight.

- Avoiding foods due to sensory issues, fear of choking, vomiting, or a past negative experience with food.
- Can lead to serious nutritional deficiencies and weight loss.

In simple terms:

ARFID is when a person avoids eating certain foods or doesn't eat enough, not because of body image concerns, but due to fear of certain textures, choking, or other food-related anxieties. It's most common in children but can also affect adults.

Other specified feeding or eating disorder (OSFED) is characterized by:

- Eating disorder symptoms that don't fully meet the criteria for anorexia, bulimia, or binge-eating disorder but still cause serious distress and health risks.
- Can include atypical anorexia nervosa (where a person has severe food restriction but is not underweight), purging disorder (purging without binge eating), and night eating syndrome (eating excessive amounts of food at night).

In simple terms:

OSFED is when a person has disordered eating behaviors that are serious but don't exactly fit the criteria for other eating disorders. It's still very real and requires proper treatment.

The etiology of eating disorders is complex, involving an interplay of biological, psychological, and social factors. Understanding eating disorders through the biopsychosocial model highlights the necessity of comprehensive treatment approaches that address the biological, psychological, and social dimensions of these complex conditions.

In addition to an overview of eating disorders, it is important to understand how eating disorder development occurs and is maintained. There are various theoretical approaches to understanding eating disorder development; these models include neurobiological models, sociocultural models, and both prominent and novel psychosocial models as well as approaches from needs-based frameworks, schema theory, dysfunction models, and cognitive-behavioral frameworks as well as others (Munro et al., 2016). Here, I will explore the biopsychosocial–spiritual framework as a means to better understand eating disorder and body image disturbances.

How the Biopsychosocial–Spiritual Model Provides a Helpful Understanding of the Development of an Eating Disorder

The biopsychosocial–spiritual (BPS-S) model is a comprehensive approach to understanding health, illness, and human behavior by integrating the interrelated domains of biological, psychological, sociocultural, and spiritual factors.

This framework of eating disorders offers a comprehensive framework that recognizes the complex interplay between biological, psychological, and social factors in the development, maintenance, and treatment of eating disorders. Rather than attributing eating disorders and body image issues to a single cause, this model acknowledges the multifaceted and individualized nature of eating pathology.

The biopsychosocial model, first introduced by psychiatrists George Engel and John Romano in the 1970's, contrasts with the traditional biomedical model, which focuses primarily on biological causes of disease, and is known as a more holistic approach that addresses the interconnectedness of biological, psychological, and social factors' impact on health and illness. Culbert et al.'s (2015) seminal paper emphasizes that eating disorders arise from a complex interplay of these three risk factors, rather than any single cause. A rapid review synthesizing 284 studies found nine major domains of risk of eating disorder development including genetics, personality traits (e.g. emotion dysregulation), socioeconomic status, ethnicity, and body image influences, all supporting a multisystem perspective consistent with biopsychosocial thinking (Barakat et al., 2023). This research demonstrates the interacting complexities of eating disorder development. As the field has evolved, scholars have emphasized the need to include a spiritual dimension in the biopsychosocial model, and without it, the model remains incomplete in failing to fully capture the human experience of healing, resilience, and identity (Liff, 1998; Sulmasy, 2002; Saad et al., 2017; Van Denend et al., 2023; Young et al., 2024). The biopsychosocial model must include spirituality because meaning-making, purpose, values, and connection to something beyond oneself profoundly shape how individuals understand suffering, engage in coping, and sustain recovery.

To better understand this model and how it provides useful context for eating disorders, I will break down each factor and discuss it more in depth. This framework will guide clinicians in treating these conditions and illuminate pathways for building authentic therapeutic relationships, which I will explore more fully in later chapters.

Biological Factors

Biological factors refer to our physical health, genetic predisposition, abilities, neurochemistry, and immune responses. The biological component of eating disorder and body image issue development acknowledges the genetic, neurochemical, and physiological factors that contribute to vulnerability. Research has shown that individuals with a family history of eating disorders, anxiety, or depression have a higher likelihood of developing disordered eating patterns due to inherited genetic predispositions (Yilmaz et al., 2015). Family and twin studies suggest a strong heritable component for eating disorders, particularly anorexia nervosa and bulimia nervosa (Thornton et al., 2018).

Neurobiology offers another window into why some people develop eating disorders while others, exposed to similar pressures, do not. Research has shown that disruptions in neurotransmitter systems, especially serotonin and dopamine, can shape appetite, anxiety, impulse control, and mood in ways that increase vulnerability to illness. For example, altered 5-HT1A and 5-HT2A receptor functioning has been linked to both anorexia nervosa and bulimia nervosa, influencing the experience of hunger, fear, and emotional intensity (Kaye et al., 2013; Steinglass et al., 2016). Meanwhile, irregularities in dopamine pathways may help explain why many individuals with anorexia report feeling a sense of calm or even reward from food restriction, while typical eating can feel deeply aversive. Functional neuroimaging studies show that, in eating disorders, the brain's reward circuits respond differently to food cues (Frank et al., 2019; Zipfel et al., 2022).

Beyond reward learning, imaging research highlights changes in the insula, anterior cingulate cortex, and amygdala, all areas involved in tracking internal sensations, regulating emotions, and assigning meaning to experiences (Frank, 2016; Haynos et al., 2020). These shifts may contribute to the profound difficulty many clients have sensing hunger, tolerating emotional distress, or interpreting bodily cues—a challenge that often feels to them like a personal failing, but in reality reflects altered brain processing.

Biology also intersects with timing. Puberty introduces hormonal cascades, including changes in estrogen, leptin, and ghrelin, that can heighten sensitivity to stress, reward, and body image, especially among those already genetically vulnerable (Culbert et al., 2015; Nagata et al., 2022). And as weight drops, whether through dieting, illness, or restriction, metabolic changes reinforce the problem. Starvation sparks shifts in neuropeptides, like neuropeptide-Y, and alters dopaminergic firing in ways that make rigidity, anxiety, and compulsivity even more pronounced (Hildebrandt et al., 2018; Kaye et al., 2020). What begins as a coping strategy becomes biologically entrenched, creating a feedback loop that pulls people deeper into illness.

All of this reminds us that eating disorders are not simply about food, willpower, or vanity. They are complex biopsychosocial conditions shaped by neural circuitry, developmental timing, temperament, and lived experience. When clients say they "can't just eat," the science affirms that they're right: their brains, in many ways, have been rewired. Understanding this helps us meet them with more compassion and more effective care.

Samantha's Case: Illustrating Biological Factors

Samantha arrived at college eager for independence, but within her first semester, she began skipping meals and exercising compulsively. Her family history hinted at biological vulnerability: her mother and grandmother had long engaged in chronic dieting, and both were praised for their "discipline" around food, patterns later understood as possible genetic and behavioral risk markers. From childhood, Samantha had been a high achiever with a naturally anxious temperament, characteristics often linked to heritable traits associated with eating disorders and obsessive–compulsive tendencies. Genetic testing would later reveal a family history of anxiety-related disorders and obsessive–compulsive features, reinforcing the idea that she carried a biological predisposition to both anxiety and rigid behavior patterns.

Once Samantha began restricting her eating, she described experiencing a surprising "high": a sense of calm, clarity, and control that made the behavior neurologically rewarding. This reaction aligns with research showing that starvation can alter serotonin and dopamine pathways, creating a reinforcing cycle that decreases anxiety while intensifying compulsive restriction. During periods of academic stress, her symptoms escalated, suggesting that her biologically mediated stress-response system further entrenched the illness. For Samantha, anorexia did not emerge simply from dieting or social pressure; it was rooted in a constellation of biological vulnerabilities that, once activated, accelerated the disorder's onset and fueled its persistence.

Psychological Factors

Psychological factors in this model include our personality traits, behaviors, beliefs, emotions, and abilities to cope. From a psychological perspective, eating disorders and body image issues are often rooted in low self-esteem, perfectionism, emotional dysregulation, and maladaptive coping mechanisms. Cognitive distortions, such as overgeneralization ("I must be thin to be loved"), black-and-white thinking ("If I eat this, I have failed"), and catastrophizing, all fuel negative body image and compulsive behaviors related to food and weight. Many individuals struggling with disordered eating use food control to manage deeper emotional pain, trauma, or feelings of inadequacy. Psychological models also highlight the role of emotional avoidance, where individuals use restrictive eating, purging, or bingeing as a way to suppress negative emotions, which reinforces the disorder as a maladaptive coping mechanism. Trauma, particularly childhood abuse or neglect, is also recognized as a significant psychological risk factor (Monteleone et al., 2020).

Jordan's Case: Illustrating Psychological Factors

To better understand the psychological factors that influence eating disorder development, consider the case of Jordan. Jordan always felt the need to be the "good kid" growing up. He was praised for being disciplined and never causing trouble. Beneath the surface, he struggled with feelings of inadequacy and emotional vulnerability, which he never felt safe expressing at home. In graduate school, he started bingeing and purging after receiving critical feedback on his work. He later reflected that the purging offered a temporary relief from shame and self-criticism. Therapy revealed deeply rooted perfectionism and a rigid internal narrative that equated failure with worthlessness. His bulimia nervosa became a coping mechanism for regulating overwhelming emotions he had no language for. The eating disorder gave him a sense of control over the chaos inside.

Social Factors

Sociocultural factors refer to our family relationships, peers, schools and education, and social supports, while socioeconomic status influences our beliefs in shaping body image and food-related behaviors. Sociocultural influences are particularly salient in eating disorder etiology. Cultural ideals emphasizing thinness, the objectification of bodies (especially female bodies), and weight stigma contribute to body dissatisfaction and disordered eating behaviors (Himmelstein et al., 2018). Western media has long promoted thinness as an ideal standard of beauty, leading to widespread body dissatisfaction, historically focused on cisgender women, and now with increased awareness and research, we know impacts all genders. Social media and peer comparisons further amplify these pressures, especially among adolescents and young adults. Family dynamics, including parental modeling of dieting behaviors or communication patterns, also play a role (Levine & Smolak, 2021).

Social comparison theory (Festinger, 1954) tells us that people naturally evaluate themselves in relation to others, an instinct that becomes especially potent when societal standards of beauty are narrow and idealized. When appearance becomes the currency of value, these comparisons can quickly evolve into unrealistic expectations and chronic self-scrutiny. Within families, this sensitivity may be amplified: critical comments about weight, parental preoccupation with dieting, or enmeshed dynamics can communicate that worth is contingent on appearance or performance. Outside the home, peers and social environments add another layer including bullying, exclusion, and constant exposure to curated, filtered images on social media that intensify feelings of inadequacy. Together, these relational and cultural pressures reinforce a relentless cycle of comparison and self-criticism, creating fertile ground for body dissatisfaction and disordered eating to take hold.

When researchers analyzed media portrayals of eating disorders between 1981 and 2022, they found that the overwhelming majority featured heterosexual, White females under age 30, a demographic that does not accurately reflect the diversity of those impacted by these illnesses (Bassett & Ewart, 2023). This skewed representation reinforces harmful sociocultural attitudes regarding who "should" develop eating disorders and as a result, may delay recognition, diagnosis, and intervention for marginalized groups. At the same time, Common Sense Media's research demonstrates that boys are also deeply affected by body image pressures: for instance, 33–35 % of boys aged 6–8 report that their ideal body is thinner than their current body, and many young males are increasingly exposed to muscular-ideal media and diet/fitness content (Common Sense Media, 2018). These findings underscore that body dissatisfaction is not exclusively a female phenomenon and highlight the importance of inclusive media literacy and clinical attention. When media consistently presents narrow, gendered ideals and fails to reflect the full spectrum of eating disorder experiences across gender, age, race/ethnicity, and sexual orientation, that contributes not only to stigma but to real treatment gaps for individuals who do not fit the "typical" image.

Lila's Case: Illustrating Social Factors

When Lila's family moved to a new city, she was determined to fit in at her high-achieving high school. It didn't take long to notice that the social hierarchy revolved around appearance. The most popular girls curated their Instagram feeds with wellness influencers, green-juice cleanses, workout selfies, and carefully posed images of slim, toned bodies. Lila, who had always lived comfortably in her curvier frame, suddenly felt out of place. Comments from classmates like "You're so brave to wear that," landed like compliments wrapped in judgment, quietly feeding her belief that her body was a problem.

Wanting to belong, Lila started adopting the language and habits she saw around her: cutting out foods labeled "bad," skipping meals, and logging workouts obsessively. Her parents, influenced by the same wellness culture, initially praised these changes as signs she was "getting healthy." What they didn't see was that Lila was internalizing a powerful social message that thinness was the price of acceptance.

As she spent more time online, her social media feeds became an echo chamber of narrow beauty ideals and "body transformation" content. Each scroll amplified her self-criticism, reinforcing the idea that worthiness was measured in weight, waistlines, and aesthetic discipline. Restrictive eating soon became a way to manage both her longing for belonging and the shame she felt about her body. The more affirmation she received for looking smaller, likes on photos, compliments from peers, the more entrenched her behaviors became.

Lila's story reflects the sociocultural forces that shape eating disorder risk: beauty standards defined by media, peer norms that equate thinness with social value, and families who may unintentionally reinforce these pressures. Her struggle did not emerge in isolation, it was cultivated in a cultural landscape where shrinking one's body is celebrated, and the pursuit of thinness is mistaken for well-being.

Spiritual Factors

In more recent years, the dimension of spirituality was included in the BPS model (Liff, 1998; Saad et al., 2017; Sulmasy, 2002; Van Denend et al., 2022; Young et al., 2024). Within this framework, it is important to note that spirituality does not mean religiosity. In fact, spirituality may have nothing to do with religion at all. Rather, this spiritual dimension is about a sense of connection, meaning, and greater purpose in life. The spiritual dimension acknowledges the existential and meaning-based factors in eating disorder development. Many individuals struggling with eating disorders report a sense of disconnection—not only from their authentic selves but also from a greater sense of purpose or belonging. Spiritual emptiness or a lack of meaning can manifest in rigid food rituals, compulsive behaviors, and an obsession with body control as a way to seek structure or fulfillment. Some individuals with eating disorders express a need for transcendence—believing that extreme thinness or dietary restriction will lead to a sense of purity, control, or moral superiority. Conversely, spirituality and mindfulness-based interventions, such as self-compassion practices, intuitive eating, and mindful self-awareness, have been shown to help individuals heal from disordered eating by fostering a deeper connection with themselves and others. Addressing this spiritual dimension of identity can be crucial in long-term recovery, as it helps individuals cultivate self-worth beyond physical appearance and embrace their inherent value as human beings.

I once worked with a young woman in her early twenties who had struggled with anorexia for nearly a decade. While she had made progress with nutritional rehabilitation and learned cognitive strategies to challenge distorted thoughts, she often described feeling "hollow" and disconnected from any sense of meaning beyond calories and weight. She told me, "Even when I'm doing better with food, I still feel empty inside." In our work, I invited her to reflect on moments when she felt most alive or most herself, which initially felt foreign and uncomfortable. She began to reflect on times when she was with her family on vacation outdoors. She first talked about lying on the ground, laughing with her brother, staring into a starry sky, later about the feeling of sand beneath her feet with the ocean in front of her. Gradually, we experimented with small practices, stepping outside to experience being grounded then incorporating mindful walks outdoors, creative journaling about gratitude, and guided imagery that connected her to the sense of peace she found at the ocean. These interventions helped her notice and name experiences that nourished her spirit, not in a religious sense but as part of her human need for purpose, connection, and transcendence.

Integrating this spiritual dimension into her treatment allowed her to practice authenticity in new ways, including through voicing long-ignored desires, honoring her values, and reconnecting to what gave her life meaning beyond external approval. Research highlights that including spirituality as a dimension of care can deepen the healing process by addressing the often-overlooked domain of human experience (Van Denend et al., 2022). Similarly, recent work emphasizes that spirituality—understood broadly as connection, purpose, and meaning—can strengthen resilience and improve therapeutic outcomes, especially in populations struggling with identity and authenticity (Young et al., 2024). These kinds of interventions, rooted in evidence-based integrative models, demonstrate that spiritual practices can enhance coping, foster meaning-making, and support long-term recovery. For this client, embracing the spiritual aspect of the biopsychosocial model was not about prescribing practices but about creating space to explore what nourished her spirit. In doing so, she found a more authentic path to recovery that honored not just her body and mind, but also her deeper sense of self.

An Integrative Perspective

The biopsychosocial–spiritual model does not treat these domains as isolated factors but rather emphasizes their interaction. For example, a biologically vulnerable individual (e.g., with a genetic predisposition or temperament trait like high harm avoidance) might develop an eating disorder when exposed to intense sociocultural pressures and in the context of personal psychological challenges, such as poor emotion regulation or trauma. This comprehensive, multidimensional view informs personalized treatment approaches, encouraging interdisciplinary interventions that address all domains. By integrating the biopsychosocial–spiritual model with an understanding of authenticity, it becomes clear that eating disorder development is not solely about food or body image, but rather it is deeply rooted in an individual's early relational experiences, emotional regulation, and sense of self.

Amira's Case: How Many Factors Contribute to an Eating Disorder

Amira grew up in a family where food was either tightly controlled or used for comfort. Her mother had a history of bulimia, and Amira struggled with anxiety and emotional sensitivity since early childhood. In high school, Amira was sexually assaulted at a party and never disclosed it, internalizing deep shame. In college, she joined a sorority where appearance and diet culture dominated social life. She began restricting, which initially gave her a sense of strength and numbness. Over time, this spiraled into anorexia nervosa. In treatment, it became clear that her eating disorder was sustained by a mix of inherited traits, unprocessed trauma, perfectionism, and a toxic social environment. Addressing only one factor, like the symptom of food intake, was never going to be enough.

The biopsychosocial–spiritual framework helps reduce stigma by acknowledging that eating disorders are not simply driven by "media obsession" or individual weakness but emerge from systemic, interacting vulnerabilities.

Body Image Development

Body image development is a multifaceted process influenced by various psychological, sociocultural, and developmental factors. Several theoretical frameworks have been proposed to explain how individuals perceive and evaluate their bodies. For example, as noted above in the biopsychosocial framework, a sociocultural perspective on body image argues that societal standards and cultural norms significantly shape body image. Media representations, peer influences, and cultural expectations promote idealized body types, leading individuals to internalize these thin ideals and potentially experience body dissatisfaction when their own bodies do not align with these standards.

Theories on Body Image Development

The tripartite influence model of body image emphasizes the roles of media, peers, and family in transmitting appearance-related messages that individuals may internalize, shaping their sense of body image and reinforcing the impact of our sociocultural environment's impact on body image (Thompson et al., 1999). According to the model, repeated exposure to appearance ideals, particularly the thin ideal, encourages individuals to compare themselves to others, often leading to the belief that one's worth is contingent upon achieving a narrowly defined standard. When these internalized expectations are inevitably unmet, body dissatisfaction becomes more likely.

In my clinical experience, this progression often unfolds subtly. A young person may begin by mimicking the habits of admired peers or influencers such as cutting out foods, tracking calories, or celebrating weight loss without question. Meanwhile, well-intentioned comments from family members ("You look so good!" or "Are you sure you want seconds?") reinforce the belief that bodies are constantly being evaluated. Over time, these external messages become woven into a client's internal narrative: *My body is not good enough as it is.*

What stands out to me is how quickly these influences can shift from casual comparison to deep emotional conviction. Even adolescents who appear confident can absorb these ideals without awareness, shaping their self-esteem long before symptoms of disordered eating emerge. The tripartite model helps us understand that body image does not form in isolation, but it is cultivated through relationships, culture, and identity. When we view body dissatisfaction through this wider sociocultural lens, it becomes clear that prevention and intervention must include not only the individual, but also the systems and environments that shape how we learn to see and value our bodies.

A developmental perspective on body image emphasizes how perceptions and attitudes about the body evolve across the lifespan, particularly during periods of heightened physical and psychosocial change. Childhood marks the early emergence of body awareness, as children begin to internalize messages from caregivers, peers, and media about appearance and weight (Smolak, 2004). While young children may initially exhibit positive or neutral body image, exposure to weight-based teasing, critical comments, or idealized body portrayals can begin to shape negative self-evaluations. These early influences form the foundation for later body image development and may contribute to long-term dissatisfaction or disordered eating behaviors, especially when paired with temperament traits like high sensitivity or anxiety (Evans et al., 2013).

Adolescence is a particularly vulnerable period for body image disturbances due to the rapid and often uneven biological changes associated with puberty. Adolescents undergo significant physical transformations, such as growth spurts, weight gain, and the development of secondary sex characteristics, which can heighten body consciousness and social comparison. Those who experience early or late maturation relative to their peers may be at elevated risk for body dissatisfaction and psychosocial distress. For example, early maturing girls often report increased body dissatisfaction due to gaining weight and body fat earlier than their peers, while late-maturing boys may experience teasing or feel inadequate about their smaller stature (Ricciardelli & McCabe,

2001). These experiences are compounded by increased peer influence and media exposure during adolescence, both of which can reinforce appearance ideals and narrow beauty standards.

Furthermore, body image development must be understood within a broader ecological and cultural context that shapes how individuals make meaning of their bodies over time. Social identities, including gender, race, socioeconomic status, and sexual orientation, interact with developmental experiences to influence how people evaluate and relate to their bodies (Rodgers et al., 2023). For instance, adolescents from marginalized groups may contend with intersecting pressures, such as Eurocentric beauty standards or cultural expectations around body size and shape. As a result, developmental trajectories of body image are not universal but shaped by systemic factors and individual lived experiences. This complexity highlights the importance of developmentally and culturally informed prevention and intervention strategies that consider the diverse influences on body image over the course of life.

Cognitive Perspectives

From a cognitive perspective, body image development is shaped by the way individuals process, interpret, and respond to information about their appearance. Cognitive distortions such as overgeneralization, catastrophizing, and appearance-based perfectionism play a central role in the formation of negative body image. Cash's (2002) cognitive–behavioral model highlights how maladaptive thought patterns and internalized appearance standards contribute to body dissatisfaction. According to this model, individuals develop body image schemas which are core beliefs and mental representations about their bodies that influence attention, memory, and interpretation of appearance-related experiences (Cash & Smolak, 2011). For example, someone with a negative body image schema may selectively attend to perceived flaws, interpret neutral comments as criticism, or compare themselves unfavorably to others, reinforcing a cycle of negative self-evaluation.

These entrenched schemas can give rise to maladaptive behaviors such as restrictive eating, compulsive exercise, body checking, or avoidance of social situations. As these behaviors become habit, they reinforce the distorted beliefs and intensify emotional distress. This perspective emphasizes the importance of addressing internal mental processes, rather than focusing solely on external factors like media exposure or peer influence, in order to facilitate lasting change in body image and related behaviors.

Cognitive Theory in Popular Culture Illustration

Disney/Pixar's *Inside Out* (2015) and *Inside Out 2* (2024) offer powerful metaphors for how cognitive theory explains the development of core schemas, including those related to body image. In the original film, Riley's internal world is governed by the core emotions of joy, sadness, anger, fear, and disgust, which help shape her core memories and, in turn, her core beliefs about herself (e.g., "I'm a happy girl," "I'm a good daughter," "I'm great at hockey"). These core beliefs reflect early cognitive schemas, guiding how Riley interprets new experiences, such as moving to a new city or struggling to fit in socially.

In *Inside Out 2*, Riley is now entering adolescence, a critical period for body image development. The sequel introduces new emotions like anxiety, envy, and embarrassment, which highlights the increasing complexity of cognitive and emotional processing during puberty. Anxiety, in particular, plays a central role in reshaping Riley's internal narrative. When she begins to compare herself to older, more athletic, or socially accepted teammates, we see the emergence of cognitive distortions such as all-or-nothing thinking ("If I'm not the best, I'm nothing"), catastrophizing ("If I mess up, they'll all hate me"), and appearance-based overgeneralization ("They're all thinner and better than me").

These thoughts mark the formation of a negative body image schema, a mental filter that begins to guide how Riley perceives her appearance and social worth. As this schema takes shape, Riley starts seeking external validation, internalizes unrealistic standards, and distances herself from previously held core beliefs about joy, play, and authenticity. This reflects how, in real life, negative cognitive schemas related to the body often lead to maladaptive behaviors like body checking, social withdrawal, or disordered eating, especially when reinforced by peers, media, or critical self-talk (Cash & Smolak, 2011). The film creatively captures the internalization of cognitive distortions, the shift in self-concept, and the emotional intensity that shapes early body dissatisfaction.

How the Environment Pulls the Trigger

Other theories examine how the environment may contribute to negative body image development. Objectification theory posits that in cultures where individuals (particularly women in previous research) are frequently valued for their appearance and sexual appeal, they may begin to internalize this objectifying gaze and view themselves as objects to be evaluated by others (Fredrickson & Roberts, 1997). This self-objectification leads to chronic body surveillance, body shame, and heightened anxiety, which contribute significantly to negative body image and an increased risk for disordered eating and other mental health concerns.

Understanding objectification theory in both historical and modern digital contexts highlights how societal and cultural forces can shape the internal psychological experiences that drive eating disorders and related concerns. A powerful illustration of this theory in action comes from the landmark Fiji study, in which researchers found that rates of disordered eating among Fijian adolescent girls rose dramatically following the introduction of Western television programming that emphasized thin ideals and beauty norms (Becker, 2004). Prior to this exposure, disordered eating was virtually nonexistent in the region. This shift underscores how cultural objectification and media exposure can fundamentally alter body image norms and self-perception.

Closely related is social comparison theory, which suggests that individuals evaluate their own worth and appearance by comparing themselves to others. In contemporary culture, and especially with social media, this often manifests as upward comparison, where users compare themselves to idealized, filtered, and curated images of others who are perceived as more attractive or successful. These comparisons intensify self-objectification, leading individuals to assess their bodies from an outsider's perspective rather than through their own lived, embodied experience. Research shows that exposure to thin-ideal and appearance-focused content on platforms like Instagram and TikTok is significantly associated with increased body dissatisfaction and self-surveillance, particularly among adolescents and young adults (So & Kwon, 2022).

Over time, these dynamics foster a disconnection from authenticity, where individuals become preoccupied with how their bodies appear to others rather than how they feel in their bodies. This externalized self-view undermines self-compassion and reinforces a cycle of inauthentic self-presentation and body image distress. Fardouly & Holland (2018) reported that with or without the presence of disclaimer comments, viewing idealized images on social media had a negative influence on women's body image.

Social Media and Its Effects

In my experience, more often than not, body image distress is the catalyst and true first symptom in eating disorder development, and, unfortunately, the last to heal due to its deep psychological, social, and cultural roots. We are bombarded with messages and social ideals on thinness and the "need" for specific body types. Social media and the comparison culture that it creates is a breeding ground for body image dissatisfaction.

In his groundbreaking book, *The Anxious Generation: How the Great Rewiring of Childhood Is Causing an Epidemic of Mental Illness*, Jonathan Haidt (2024) argues that there are profound effects of smartphones and social media on adolescent girls, who are more susceptible to body image issues. He concludes that the constant exposure to curated and often unrealistic portrayals of beauty on platforms like Instagram and Snapchat fosters negative self-comparisons, leading to increased body dissatisfaction and related mental health challenges. Haidt further argues that the widespread adoption of these technologies has led to a significant increase in mental health issues among young people, identifying foundational harms associated with social media use: sleep deprivation, attention fragmentation, addiction, and loneliness.

Building on Haidt's (2024) assertions, a growing body of empirical research confirms the destructive impact of social media on body image, particularly among adolescent girls. Platforms like Instagram, TikTok, and Snapchat are visually driven and often saturated with idealized images that promote unattainable beauty standards. These platforms amplify appearance-based social comparison and self-objectification, both of which are linked to increased body dissatisfaction, low self-esteem, and disordered eating behaviors (Fardouly & Vartanian, 2016; Tiggemann et al., 2020). Frequent engagement with appearance-focused content such as influencer posts, selfies, or "fitspiration" has been shown to increase internalization of the thin ideal and heighten pressure to conform to narrow aesthetic norms (Perloff, 2014). Longitudinal research indicates that even brief exposure to such content can lead to measurable declines in mood and body satisfaction (Tiggemann, 2022). Moreover, algorithmic reinforcement of these images perpetuates a feedback loop, where adolescents are repeatedly exposed to and rewarded for appearance-centric behavior, deepening their investment in external validation. This digital environment cultivates an externally oriented self-concept, in which young people begin to assess their worth through likes, comments, and perceived attractiveness, distancing them from authentic self-perception and body trust.

Conformity Yields Inauthenticity

The pressure to conform to societal beauty norms can result in individuals suppressing their authentic selves, further exacerbating body image issues. Individuals who feel unable to express their true identities due to cultural expectations, social norms, or self-imposed pressures are more likely to experience self-objectification and body dissatisfaction. Chen et al. (2022) found that greater engagement with social media was linked to increased self-objectification, which can produce decreased authenticity. Individuals who frequently compared themselves to idealized online images reported greater body dissatisfaction and lower self-esteem, as they prioritized curated online personas over their authentic self-expression. This underscores that social media fosters a false sense of self, reinforcing societal beauty ideals while discouraging genuine self-acceptance. Similarly, Rodgers et al. (2023) demonstrated that self-objectification detaches individuals from their intrinsic self-worth, increasing the likelihood of negative body image and eating disorders.

Both Rodgers et al. (2023) and Swami et al. (2021) underscore the detrimental effects of inauthenticity on body image and mental health. Self-objectification, fueled by external beauty standards and social media influence, creates a disconnect from one's authentic self, resulting in heightened body dissatisfaction and disordered eating behaviors. When people lose connection with their authentic selves, they become more vulnerable to external validation and comparison, reinforcing negative body image and self-criticism. In contrast, fostering authenticity—through self-acceptance, intrinsic self-worth, and reduced reliance on external validation—can serve as a protective factor against self-objectification and body dissatisfaction. Much of this book will explore how clinicians can help clients focus more on their bodies and away from the noise of social media and other cultural messaging.

Implications for Building Authenticity

Research has now expanded the cognitive approach to include its implications for authenticity, interpersonal relationships, and emotional well-being. Negative body image schemas have been linked to difficulties in forming and sustaining intimate relationships, as individuals may fear judgment, avoid vulnerability, or suppress aspects of their true selves (Nejad et al., 2023; Orbach et al., 2023). This self-protective avoidance can limit meaningful connection and contribute to a fragmented sense of identity. Additionally, poor body image is associated with increased self-objectification and reduced self-compassion, which further distance individuals from their internal values and reinforce external validation as a primary source of worth (Rodgers et al., 2023). Understanding body image through a cognitive lens thus provides a powerful framework for recognizing how thought processes shape self-perception, behavior, and relational functioning across the lifespan.

Clinician Self-Reflection on Body Image Development

It is essential that clinicians working with individuals struggling with body image and eating disorders examine their own developmental narratives to better attune to the vulnerabilities their clients may be facing. This is true for all clinicians but should be especially pertinent for those looking to integrate authenticity into therapeutic practice. Self-reflection fosters empathy, reduces countertransference, and helps clinicians remain mindful of how their internalized beliefs about the body might subtly enter the therapeutic space. This practice of self-awareness not only strengthens the therapeutic alliance but also deepens a clinician's capacity to hold space for clients navigating the complex interplay of body, identity, and societal pressure during formative years.

Growing up as a girl surrounded by sisters, female cousins, youth-group peers, and later a sorority, I absorbed countless spoken and unspoken messages about bodies, beauty, and belonging. In these female-centered spaces, body talk was woven into everyday life through compliments about weight loss celebrated as achievement, shared anxieties normalized as bonding, and silent comparisons quietly shaping our self-worth. Even as I became a professional doing this work, and later as a mother raising a daughter, I found that body image was not a challenge one simply grows out of; it shifts, resurfaces, and evolves. My personal and clinical experiences continue to remind me that body image is not a static belief but a lifelong relationship that is influenced by culture, community, and identity, requiring ongoing curiosity, compassion, and practice.

It may be helpful for clinicians to think back to their own body image development to better understand their relationship with the topic. For example, clinicians should consider their own time of adolescent development and reflect on the physical, emotional, and social changes they experienced during that period. Questions clinicians may ask themselves include:

- How did they feel about their body as it changed?
- Were there moments of pride, shame, confusion, or comparison?
- Who or what influenced how they understood their body—family, peers, media, cultural messages?

By engaging in this kind of self-reflection, clinicians not only deepen their empathy for the developmental struggles of their clients but also become more aware of how their own body image history may shape their presence and authenticity in the therapeutic relationship. Such awareness can transform body image work from a purely clinical task into a shared human exploration.

Summary

Taken together, the research and reflections in this chapter underscore the complex, multifaceted nature of eating disorder and body image development. From inherited biological predispositions to cognitive distortions and negative body schemas to sociocultural pressures rooted in objectification and social comparison, individuals navigate a web of internal and external influences that shape how they view and treat their bodies. As digital platforms continue to promote unattainable beauty standards and encourage self-objectification, it is more critical than ever for clinicians, educators, and caregivers to cultivate protective factors like body trust, media literacy, and authentic self-expression. Integrating biopsychosocial–spiritual, developmental, cognitive, and sociocultural perspectives allows for a more comprehensive understanding of eating disorder and negative body image development and maintenance. With a clearer understanding of the factors that contribute to body image distress and eating disorder development, we can now turn our attention to treatment approaches and interventions. This next section will explore the therapeutic models, levels of care, and clinical strategies used to support recovery and promote lasting change.

At the heart of these influences lies a common thread: the struggle to remain authentic in a world that often rewards conformity, perfectionism, and self-denial. Whether through biological vulnerabilities, internalized distortions, or societal pressures, eating disorders and body image concerns frequently silence the true self in favor of external expectations. For both clients and clinicians, the path forward involves reclaiming authenticity and cultivating spaces where individuals can explore their identities without judgment, reconnect with their bodies as trustworthy guides, and practice vulnerability as a source of strength rather than shame. Framing authenticity not as an endpoint but as an ongoing practice offers hope that recovery is not simply about symptom reduction, but about living in alignment with one's genuine self. I am reminded of a client who once told me, after months of treatment, "I don't even know what I like anymore. I've only ever cared about being what others wanted me to be." Over time, as she began experimenting with small acts of honesty in therapy such as naming her hungers, her fears, and even her frustrations with me, she began to glimpse a self that felt real and worth protecting. That rediscovery of voice and agency reflected the deeper healing that authenticity makes possible. As we shift into the next section on treatment approaches, authenticity will serve as a guiding principle in examining how therapeutic relationships and interventions can foster deeper healing and sustainable change.

Key Take-Aways

- Eating disorders have a complex and evolving history, shaped by shifting cultural values, medical frameworks, and psychological theories, underscoring that our understanding of these illnesses is continually developing.
- The biopsychosocial–spiritual model offers the most comprehensive lens, recognizing that eating disorders arise from the interaction of biological vulnerability, psychological processes, relational experiences, cultural pressures, and personal meaning.
- Body image is formed at the intersection of personal and societal forces including family, peers, and media, demonstrating that sociocultural environments can activate underlying vulnerabilities and shape identity, belonging, and authenticity.
- Social media has intensified body scrutiny, amplifying comparison and inauthentic self-presentation; these forces can erode self-trust and deepen emotional struggles that contribute to disordered eating.
- Healing requires relational authenticity, not only for clients but for clinicians who must examine their own body-image histories to engage with humility, honesty, and deepened therapeutic presence.

References

American Psychiatric Association. (2013). *Diagnostic and statistical manual of mental disorders (5th ed.)*. Arlington, VA: Author.

American Psychiatric Association. (2022). *Diagnostic and statistical manual of mental disorders* (5th ed.), Text Revision. American Psychiatric Association.

Barakat, S., McLean, S. A., Bryant, E. et al. (2023). *Risk factors for eating disorders: findings from a rapid review.* Journal of Eating Disorders, 11(8).

Bassett, L. & Ewart, M. (2023). *Discrepancies between media portrayals and actual demographics of eating disorders in TV and film: Implications of representation.* Journal of Eating Disorders, 11(161).

Becker, A. E. (2004). *Television*, disordered eating, and young women in Fiji: Negotiating body image and identity during rapid social change. Culture, Medicine and Psychiatry, 28(4), 533–559.

Cash, T. F. (2002). *Cognitive-behavioral perspectives on body image.* In T. F. Cash & T. Pruzinsky (Eds.), Body image: A handbook of theory, research, and clinical practice (pp. 38–46). Guilford Press.

Cash, T. F., & Smolak, L. (2011). *Body image: A handbook of science*, practice, and prevention (2nd ed.). Guilford Press.

Chen, S., van Tilburg, W. A. P., & Leman, P. J. (2022). *Women's self-objectification and strategic self-presentation on social media.* Psychology of Women Quarterly, 47(2), 266–282.

Common Sense Media. (2018). *Boys and Body Image.* Available at https://www.commonsensemedia.org/articles/boys-and-body-image

Crichton, P. (1996). Were the Roman emperors Claudius and Vitellius bulimic? *International Journal of Eating Disorders, 19*(2), 203–207.

Culbert, K. M., Racine, S. E., & Klump, K. L. (2015). *Research review: What we have learned about the causes of eating disorders - a synthesis of sociocultural*, psychological, and biological research. Journal of Child Psychology and Psychiatry, and Allied Disciplines, 56(11), 1141–1164.

Docter, P., & Del Carmen, R. (Directors). (2015). *Inside out.* Walt Disney Studios Motion Pictures.

Engel, G. (1977). *The Need for a New Medical Model: A Challenge for Biomedicine.* Science 196, 129–136.

Evans, E., Tovee, M., Boothroyd, L., & Drewett, R. (2013). *Body dissatisfaction and disordered eating attitudes in 7 to 11-year-old girls: Testing a sociocultural model.* Body Image, 10(1), 8–15.

Fairburn, C. G., & Cooper, Z. (2011). *Eating disorders*, DSM–5 and clinical reality. The British Journal of Psychiatry, 198(1), 8–10.

Fardouly, J., & Vartanian, L. R. (2016). *Social media and body image concerns: Current research and future directions.* Current Opinion in Psychology, 9, 1–5.

Fardouly, J., & Holland, E. (2018). *Social media is not real life: The effect of attaching disclaimer-type labels to idealized social media images on women's body image and mood.* New Media & Society, 20(11), 4311–4328.

Festinger, L. (1954). A theory of social comparison processes. Human Relations, *7*, 117–140.

Frank, G. K. W. (2016). *The perfect storm - A bio-psycho-social risk model for developing and maintaining eating disorders. Frontiers in Behavioral Neuroscience*, 10, 44.

Frank, G. K. W., Shott, M. E., & DeGuzman, M. C. (2019). The neurobiology of eating disorders. *Child and Adolescent Psychiatric Clinics of North America, 28*(4), 629–640.

Fredrickson, B. L., & Roberts, T.-A. (1997). *Objectification theory: Toward understanding women's lived experiences and mental health risks.* Psychology of Women Quarterly, 21(2), 173–206.

Haidt, J. (2024). *The anxious generation: How the great rewiring of childhood is causing an epidemic of mental illness.* Penguin Press.

Haynos, A. F., Lavender, J. M., Nelson, J., Crow, S. J., & Peterson, C. B. (2020). Moving towards specificity: A systematic review of cue features associated with reward and punishment in anorexia nervosa. *Clinical Psychology Review, 79*, 101872.

Hildebrandt, T., Schulz, K., Schiller, D., Heywood, A., Goodman, W., & Sysko, R. (2018). Evidence of prefrontal hyperactivation to food-cue reversal learning in adolescents with anorexia nervosa. *Behaviour Research and Therapy, 111*, 36–43.

Himmelstein, M. S., Puhl, R. M., & Quinn, D. M. (2018). *Weight stigma and health: The mediating role of coping responses.* Health Psychology: official journal of the Division of Health Psychology, American Psychological Association, 37(2), 139–147.

Kaye, W. H., Wierenga, C. E., Bailer, U. F., Simmons, A. N., & Bischoff-Grethe, A. (2013). *Nothing tastes as good as skinny feels: The neurobiology of anorexia nervosa.* Trends in Neurosciences, 36(2), 110–120.

Kaye, W. H., Wierenga, C. E., Bischoff-Grethe, A., Berner, L. A., Ely, A. V., Bailer, U. F., Paulus, M. P., & Fudge, J. L. (2020). Neural insensitivity to the effects of hunger in women remitted from anorexia nervosa. *The American Journal of Psychiatry, 177* (7), 601–610.

Levine, M. P., & Smolak, L. (2021). *The prevention of eating problems and eating disorders: Theories*, research, and applications (2nd ed.). Routledge/Taylor & Francis Group.

Liff, Z. A. (1998). *Adding the spiritual to the biopsychosocial framework [Review of the book Textbook of Transpersonal Psychiatry and Psychology*, by B. W. Scotton, A. B. Chinen & J. R. Battista, Eds.]. Contemporary Psychology, 43(2), 144–145.

Mann, K. (Director). (2024). *Inside out* 2 [Film]. Pixar Animation Studios.

Mayall, M., Sadhu, R., & McDermott, B. (2025). *Contemporary reflections on William Gull's case studies of anorexia nervosa*, 150 years on. European Eating Disorders Review, 33(2), 199–209.

Monteleone, A. M., Marciello, F., Cascino, G., Cimino, M., Ruzzi, V., Pellegrino, F., Del Giorno, C., & Monteleone, P. (2020). *Early traumatic experiences impair the functioning of both components of the endogenous stress response system in adult people with eating disorders.* Psychoneuroendocrinology, 115, 104644.

Munro, C., Randell, L., & Lawrie, S. M. (2016). *An integrative bio-psycho-social theory of anorexia nervosa.* Clinical Psychology & Psychotherapy, 24(1), 1–21.

Nagata, J. M., Cortez, C. A., Cattle, C. J., Ganson, K. T., Iyer, P., Bibbins-Domingo, K., & Baker, F. C. (2022). Screen time use among US adolescents during the COVID-19 pandemic: Findings from the adolescent brain cognitive development (ABCD) study. *JAMA Pediatrics, 176*(1), 94–96.

Nejad, E., Shairi, M. R., & Azadfallah, P. (2023). *Body image dissatisfaction and intimacy in romantic relationships: The mediating role of self-disclosure and fear of rejection.* Body Image, 45.

Orbach, I., Gilboa-Schechtman, E., & Ben-Avi, N. (2023). *The body and the self: Negative body image*, fear of intimacy, and authenticity in relationships. Journal of Social and Personal Relationships, 40(4), 1123–1145.

Perloff, R. M. (2014). *Social media effects on young women's body image concerns: Theoretical perspectives and an agenda for research.* Sex Roles: A Journal of Research, 71 (11–12),363–377.

Ricciardelli, L. A., & McCabe, M. P. (2001). *Children's body image concerns and eating disturbance: A review of the literature.* Clinical Psychology Review, 21(3), 325–344.

Rodgers, R. F., Laveway, K., Campos, P., de Carvalho, P. H. B. (2023). *Body image as a global mental health concern.* Cambridge Prisms: Global Mental Health, 10.

Russell G. (1979). *Bulimia nervosa: An ominous variant of anorexia nervosa.* Psychological Medicine, 9(3), 429–448.

Saad, M., De Medeiros, R., & Mosini, A. C. (2017). *Are we ready for a true biopsychosocial–spiritual model?* The many meanings of "spiritual". Medicines, 4(4), 79.

Smolak, L. (2004). Body image in children and adolescents: Where do we go from here? *Body Image, 1*(1), 15–28.

So, B., & Kwon, K. H. (2022). *The impact of thin-ideal internalization*, appearance comparison, social media use on body image and eating disorders: A literature review. Journal of Evidence-Based Social Work, 20(1), 55–71.

Steinglass, J., Mayer, L., & Attia, E. (2016). Treatment of restrictive eating and low-weight conditions, including anorexia nervosa and avoidant/restrictive food intake disorder. In B. T. Walsh, E. Attia, D. R. Glasofer, & R. Sysko (Eds.), *Handbook of assessment and treatment of eating disorders* (pp. 259–277). American Psychiatric Publishing, Inc.

Sulmasy, D. P. (2002). *A biopsychosocial-spiritual model for the care of patients at the end of life*. The Gerontologist, 42 (Special Issue 3), 24–33.

Swami, V., Horne, G., & Furnham, A. (2021). *COVID-19-related stress and anxiety are associated with negative body image in adults from the United Kingdom*. Personality and Individual Differences, 170, 110426.

Thompson, J. K., Coovert, M. D., & Stormer, S. M. (1999). *Body image*, social comparison, and eating disturbance: A covariance structure modeling investigation. International Journal of Eating Disorders, 26(1), 43–51.

Thornton, L. M., Munn-Chernoff, M. A., Baker, J. H., Juréus, A., Parker, R., Henders, A. K., Larsen, J. T., Petersen, L., Watson, H. J., Yilmaz, Z., Kirk, K. M., Gordon, S., Leppä, V. M., Martin, F. C., Whiteman, D. C., Olsen, C. M., Werge, T. M., Pedersen, N. L., Kaye, W., Bergen, A. W., … Bulik, C. M. (2018). *The anorexia nervosa genetics initiative (ANGI): Overview and methods*. Contemporary Clinical Trials, 74, 61–69.

Tiggemann, M. (2022). Digital modification and body image on social media: Disclaimer labels, captions, hashtags, and comments. *Body image*, *41*, 172–180.

Tiggemann, M., Anderberg, I., & Brown, Z. (2020). #Loveyourbody: The effect of body positive Instagram captions on women's body image. *Body Image*, *33*, 129–136.

Van Denend, J., Ford, K., Berg, P., Edens, E. L., & Cooke, J. (2022). *The body*, the mind, and the spirit: Including the spiritual domain in mental health care. Journal of Religion and Health, 61(5), 3571–3588.

Yilmaz, Z., Hardaway, J. A., & Bulik, C. M. (2015). Genetics and epigenetics of eating disorders. Advances in Genomics and Genetics, *5*, 131–150.

Young, T., Rappleyea, D., Jensen, J., Sira, N., & Quagliana, H. (2024). *The current state of spirituality: A four-world view*. Journal for the Study of Spirituality, 15(1), 9–23.

Zipfel, S., Schmidt, U., & Giel, K. E. (2022). The hidden burden of eating disorders during the COVID-19 pandemic. *The Lancet. Psychiatry*, *9*(1), 9–11.

Chapter 3

Evidence, Integration, and the Art of Eating Disorder Care

Overview

- *The therapeutic landscape of eating disorders reflects the complexity of the illness itself, requiring approaches that honor biological, psychological, social, and cultural dimensions.* No single intervention is sufficient; instead, treatment unfolds through a tapestry of complementary methods.
- *Evidence-based practices (EBPs) remain the gold standard, offering robust empirical support for symptom reduction and functional improvement.* Their prominence in the field underscores the power of structured interventions yet also highlights the limits of narrowly defined protocols.
- *The history and philosophy of evidence-based practice reveal both its strengths and its blind spots.* While EBPs help establish credibility and measurable outcomes, they often overlook the nuanced, relational, and contextual realities that define the lived experience of eating disorders.
- *Integrative therapies broaden the lens of care.* Frameworks rooted in relational models offer powerful complements to more traditional, protocol-driven interventions by emphasizing meaning, history, and relationships, reminding us that healing is not merely the absence of symptoms but the presence of authentic connection.
- *The continuum of care—from outpatient therapy to inpatient treatment—requires clinicians to critically reflect on their roles, biases, and practices.* Self-reflection questions invite therapists to examine how they engage with theory, evidence, and authenticity in the treatment room and beyond.

Early in my career as a primary therapist at a higher level of care program, our entire clinical team was informed that we would be participating in a research study aimed at evaluating the effectiveness of a structured cognitive–behavioral treatment protocol. The study required us to incorporate a specific exposure-based intervention into our individual sessions, using fear hierarchies, structured meal and snack challenges, and systematic introduction of fear foods, all of which would then be bridged into a larger group therapy process. While the clinical cognitive–behavioral design sounded theoretically sound and clinically promising

DOI: 10.4324/9781003632016-4

for clients struggling with food-related anxiety, its rollout within our agency sparked intense frustration, confusion, and even quiet rebellion among us, many of whom were new to the field and still forming our professional identities. I remember the hollow feeling in my chest as an outside interventionist instructed us, step-by-step, how to conduct protocol-driven sessions, replacing ones that had once felt fluid and deeply relational. One colleague, still accruing hours toward licensure, broke the tension by saying aloud what many of us were thinking: "It feels like you're trying to kill my therapist spirit." Though a bit dramatic, the sentiment struck a nerve. For many of us, the strict protocol felt more like constraint than clarity, and it stifled our clinical curiosity, disconnecting us from the evolving sense of who we were becoming as clinicians.

Years later, in a reversal of roles, I found myself as a program administrator trying to guide clinicians across the country to follow standardized treatment protocols to ensure clinical fidelity. In one training session, I recounted that early experience for the staff, hoping my self-deprecating humor might lighten the conversation. Instead, I watched a new generation of clinicians bristle when offered structure I had once resisted. What I saw then, and continue to believe now, is that there is no substitute for clinical wisdom, curiosity, and clinician use of self. While structured, evidence-based interventions offer consistency and accountability yielding results, they must be balanced with space for creativity, personal presence, and professional growth. The real art of training lies in teaching clinicians how to hold both: to trust the map and to know when to step off the path in service of the relationship.

Eating disorders are among the most complex and multifaceted psychiatric conditions. Accordingly, treatment approaches have evolved across decades, reflecting advances in neuroscience, shifts in sociocultural understanding, and the growing recognition of embodiment, identity, and attachment in the development and maintenance of disordered eating. This chapter offers an overview of the major clinical approaches to eating disorder treatment, encompassing medical stabilization, evidence-based psychotherapies, relational and systemic models, and emerging integrative modalities. In this chapter, I offer a critical lens to some of these approaches from my experiences in the field, the experiences of others, and scholarly literature. It's unlikely that there is a one-size-fits-all approach to treating eating disorders (EDs), as they are quite nuanced and require clinicians to treat each individual and their specific needs. While standards of care are essential in health-care settings, clinicians should be able to use a variety of modalities to treat clients effectively, and that starts by developing authentic therapeutic relationships.

First Line of Treatment: Medical and Nutritional Stabilization

Regardless of the therapeutic orientation, the first priority in treating eating disorders is medical safety. Malnutrition, electrolyte imbalances, cardiac arrhythmias, and other physiological risks often require a multidisciplinary team approach, including physicians, psychiatrists, and registered dietitians.

Medical management typically includes:

- Regular labs and vitals monitoring
- Weight restoration and stabilization when necessary
- Cardiac and bone health assessment
- Refeeding protocols for clients with severe restriction or purging

Nutritional rehabilitation, guided by an eating disorder-informed dietitian, aims to normalize eating patterns, challenge food fears, and support metabolic recovery. Dietitians may use meal plans, hunger/fullness tracking, or exposure-based strategies tailored to the client's developmental stage, culture, and level of care.

This medical–nutritional phase is not separate from psychological work; it creates the foundation for clients to begin engaging in therapy. For many clients, cognitive flexibility, emotional regulation, and relational capacity improve only after medical and nutritional restoration (Redgrave et al., 2015). The end of this chapter provides recommendations for additional readings on medical management and nutritional stabilization.

The ED Therapeutic Landscape

As discussed in the last chapter and throughout this book, eating disorders (EDs) represent a complex interplay of biological, psychological, and social factors that require multifaceted treatment approaches. The therapeutic landscape for treatment often focuses on evidence-based practices (EBPs) such as cognitive behavioral therapy (CBT), enhanced cognitive behavioral therapy for eating disorders (CBT-E) and family-based therapy (FBT), which have demonstrated robust empirical support for symptom reduction and are the recommended treatment modalities to treat EDs (Fairburn, 2008; Lock & Le Grange, 2015). The following section explores the history and implementation of EBPs as well as highlighting the tension between structured EBPs and relational psychotherapy, arguing for an integrative model that targets both symptom alleviation and deeper emotional and relational concerns. It also advocates for increasing the accessibility and affordability of treatment.

EBPs in ED Treatment: History, Clinical Use, and Shortcomings

The term *evidence-based practice* (EBP) originated in the field of medicine during the early 1990s, as part of a movement to bring more scientific rigor to clinical decision-making. At its core, EBP was intended to reduce clinician reliance on anecdotal experience or personal intuition by emphasizing interventions supported by systematic research (Sackett et al., 1996). This approach quickly gained traction in allied health fields, including psychology, where concerns about treatment variability, professional accountability, and cost-effectiveness were becoming increasingly prominent. The use of evidence-based practices in mental health treatment is essential to ensure that interventions are grounded in scientifically validated methods, leading to improved patient outcomes, greater treatment consistency, and enhanced clinical accountability (American Psychological Association, 2006).

In 2006, the American Psychological Association (APA) formally defined evidence-based practice in psychology as "the integration of the best available research with clinical expertise in the context of patient characteristics, culture, and preferences" (APA Presidential Task Force on Evidence-Based Practice, 2006). This definition reflects an important nuance: EBP is not just about using the latest randomized controlled trials (RCTs) but about weaving together empirical knowledge, professional wisdom, and client values to inform care.

Despite this integrative definition, the rollout of EBPs in practice has often leaned heavily on manualized protocols, particularly those validated through randomized control trials. These manuals, often derived from cognitive–behavioral therapy (CBT) origins, became the standard for defining what "counts" as an effective treatment. In doing so, they shaped insurance reimbursement models, treatment fidelity expectations, and training curricula across clinical settings.

Within the eating disorder field, the emphasis on EBP integration led to the widespread promotion of models like family-based treatment (FBT) for adolescents with anorexia nervosa and CBT-E for adults across the diagnostic spectrum. Both are supported by a plethora of research and are recognized by guidelines such as those from the National Institute for Health and Care Excellence (2017). These protocols provide structure and guidance, particularly for newer clinicians or high-risk cases, and they have undoubtedly contributed to greater consistency in care delivery.

The next section will highlight the different treatment strategies for ED clients based on EBPs, as they are considered the standard of care. I will explore the criticisms of EBPs and their shortcomings when treating clients with EDs. It is my belief that EBPs are a very effective form of treatment, but that they should not be the exclusive approach for handling the nuanced needs of ED clients. Integrating the best available research with clinical expertise and patient preferences supports more effective, individualized care and strengthens overall quality within behavioral health systems (Substance Abuse and Mental Health Services Administration, 2018).

Cognitive Behavioral Therapy—Enhanced (CBT-E)

CBT-E is widely considered the gold-standard treatment for bulimia nervosa, binge eating disorder, and adult anorexia nervosa (Fairburn, 2008). It targets the core cognitive distortions and behavioral patterns that maintain disordered eating, including perfectionism, overvaluation of weight and shape, and avoidance of emotions.

CBT-E is structured in phases:

- Psychoeducation and behavioral regulation
- Identification of triggers and cognitive restructuring
- Addressing maintaining mechanisms (e.g., low self-esteem, body image concerns)
- Relapse prevention

While CBT-E is effective for many, its focus on cognition and behavior may be insufficient for clients with trauma histories, identity concerns, or relational dysregulation.

Family-Based Treatment (FBT/Maudsley)

Family-based treatment is the leading EBP for adolescents with anorexia nervosa and is increasingly applied to other diagnoses. Developed at the Maudsley Hospital in London, it empowers caregivers to take an active role in renourishing their child (Lock & Le Grange, 2015).

Key tenets of FBT include:

- Externalizing the eating disorder (separating the illness from the person)
- Parental control of meals (initially)
- Gradual return of autonomy to the adolescent
- Minimal focus on family pathology

FBT boasts strong efficacy in research settings but has received criticism for being overly prescriptive, culturally narrow, and limited in addressing trauma, identity development, or attachment ruptures.

Dialectical Behavior Therapy (DBT)

Originally developed for borderline personality disorder, DBT is often used for clients with binge–purge behaviors, suicidality, or emotional dysregulation (Linehan & Chen, 2005; Safer et al., 2001). DBT emphasizes mindfulness, emotion regulation, distress tolerance, and interpersonal effectiveness.

In eating disorder settings, DBT may be adapted to focus on:

- Urge surfing and distress tolerance during mealtime
- Alternatives to binge/purge behaviors
- Mindful body awareness
- Validation and containment of shame and self-hatred

DBT can be powerful in higher levels of care but may feel rigid if not integrated with deeper relational work.

Interpersonal Psychotherapy (IPT)

IPT addresses disordered eating in the context of relational patterns, grief, role transitions, and interpersonal conflict (Wilfley et al., 2002). It is especially effective for binge eating and bulimia, where emotional eating is tied to loneliness or unresolved interpersonal pain.

By focusing on how relational disruptions affect mood and behavior, IPT supports:

- Emotional regulation through connection
- Grief processing
- Role negotiation (especially during developmental transitions)
- Improved social support

Beyond the Go-To Evidence-Based Practices

While evidence-based practices (EBPs) remain central to modern eating disorder treatment supported by randomized controlled trials and endorsed by organizations such as the American Psychological Association (APA, 2006) and the National Institute for Health and Care Excellence (NICE, 2020), relying solely on manualized protocols has important limitations. These structured treatments are generally developed around "average" clinical presentations, which means they may not sufficiently account for the wide heterogeneity of eating-disorder symptoms, comorbidities, cultural identities, or neurodevelopmental differences observed in real-world practice. For example, Bryant et al. (2025) reported that standard manualized interventions demonstrated modest long-term recovery rates, with only approximately 31% of individuals with anorexia nervosa and 68% with bulimia nervosa achieving recovery at nine-year follow-up, suggesting that standardized protocols alone fail to meet the needs of a substantial portion of clients. The authors concluded that eating disorders are fundamentally heterogeneous illnesses requiring more individualized and flexible treatment models.

A growing body of literature reinforces the necessity of individualized approaches in eating disorder care. Anderson et al. (2023) argue that advancing treatment effectiveness requires a shift toward precision psychiatry, in which interventions are tailored to an individual's unique biological, psychological, and behavioral profile rather than relying solely on standardized protocols. Complementing this, Levinson et al. (2024) highlight that manualized treatments often fail to adequately account for intersecting and compounding factors such as trauma exposure, neurodevelopmental differences (e.g., autism spectrum traits and ADHD), and experiences of marginalization, which can significantly influence both symptom expression and treatment engagement.

Importantly, emerging empirical work has begun to operationalize these principles in clinical practice. Levinson et al. (2023) demonstrate that idiographic, person-specific models can be used to map individual symptom dynamics and guide tailored interventions, resulting in more precise and responsive care. In parallel, Austin and Allen (2025) suggest that routine outcome monitoring allows clinicians to adjust treatment in real time, further enhancing alignment with each patient's evolving clinical presentation. Collectively, this evidence underscores that effective eating disorder treatment must move beyond one-size-fits-all models toward flexible, data-informed, and deeply personalized approaches.

Taken together, these findings underscore that while manualized EBPs provide valuable structure, they should be understood as frameworks rather than formulas. Applied inflexibly, they risk overlooking critical client-specific variables and may inadvertently reinforce a one-size-fits-all mindset. In practice, the most effective approach blends the rigor of EBPs with a personalized, relational, and contextually attuned stance that allows clinicians to adjust pace, integrate adjunctive strategies (e.g., trauma-responsive or neurodiversity-affirming interventions), and emphasize the therapeutic alliance when standardized techniques plateau. Later in this chapter, I will offer practical strategies for integrating this precision-oriented lens into clinical work, supporting both evidence-based fidelity and individualized responsiveness.

Expanding our understanding of *evidence-based practices* (EBPs) in eating disorder treatment requires looking beyond narrowly defined, manualized interventions. While CBT and family-based therapy have long dominated the evidence base, growing research supports the effectiveness of other approaches and techniques that have growing literature to support their efficacy and use including psychodynamic, relational–cultural therapy, emotion-focused therapy, trauma-informed frameworks, and other systemic approaches. Emotion-focused models provide critical tools for addressing unconscious processes and emotional avoidance that sustain disordered eating (Zerbe, 2020; Greenberg & Watson, 2006). Relational–cultural therapy emphasizes authenticity, mutual empathy, and the impact of disconnection, all of which are central to healing for individuals whose disorders are often rooted in relational ruptures (Jordan, 2017). Trauma-informed perspectives highlight the high prevalence of trauma histories among clients with eating disorders and the importance of safety and empowerment in recovery (Treleaven, 2018). Systems approaches underscore the role of family, peers, and sociocultural contexts in shaping both risk and resilience (Eisler, 2005).

Psychodynamic Psychotherapy

Psychodynamic therapy explores unconscious conflicts, internalized relational patterns, and the symbolic meaning of eating disorder symptoms. From this view, disordered eating may serve as a defense against unbearable affect, a substitute for unmet attachment needs, or a way to assert autonomy in an enmeshed system (Gabbard, 2020).

Core techniques include:

- Interpretation of transference and resistance
- Exploration of early attachment experiences
- Understanding the function of symptoms
- Building affect tolerance and self-reflective capacity

Although often criticized for lacking empirical support, growing literature and meta-analyses show significant efficacy for psychodynamic therapy across diagnoses, including eating disorders (Shedler, 2017).

Relational–Cultural Therapy (RCT)

Relational–cultural therapy, developed by Jean Baker Miller and Judith Jordan, holds that human growth occurs in, through, and toward connection, not autonomy (Jordan, 2017). Applied to eating disorders, RCT helps clients dismantle shame, challenge perfectionism, and repair relational ruptures by fostering mutuality and authenticity in the therapeutic relationship.

RCT supports:

- Exploration of how disconnection shapes the client's relationship with food/body
- Development of mutual empathy and relational resilience
- Empowerment through connection, not compliance

This model is especially resonant with clients who have experienced cultural marginalization, relational trauma, or chronic invalidation.

Trauma-Informed Approaches

Trauma is often present in eating disorder histories, whether in the form of acute events (e.g., sexual abuse, bullying) or chronic relational wounds (e.g., emotional neglect, invalidation). Trauma-informed care recognizes that disordered eating may be a survival strategy rooted in dissociation, control, or attempts to regulate overwhelming states.

Key trauma-informed principles include:

- Safety and trustworthiness
- Choice and collaboration
- Empowerment and voice
- Attention to cultural, historical, and gendered trauma

Cognitive Processing Therapy

Cognitive processing therapy (CPT) was developed as a structured, evidence-based treatment for posttraumatic stress disorder that helps individuals identify and challenge maladaptive trauma-related beliefs ("stuck points") to promote more adaptive thinking and emotional processing. In cognitive processing therapy, an impact statement is a written reflection in which the individual describes how the traumatic event has affected their beliefs about themselves, others, and the world, helping to identify key "stuck points" that guide treatment focus. The PTSD Checklist for DSM-5 (PCL-5) is commonly used within CPT to assess symptom severity at baseline and track treatment progress over time, allowing clinicians to monitor changes in PTSD symptoms and guide clinical decision-making (Resick et al., 2017).

At a stage in my career where I was primarily focused on running treatment facilities rather than providing direct clinical care, I decided I needed to stay in touch with my direct-care roots and chose to work with Deb in applying CPT within an eating disorder HLOC setting. I did this not only to deepen my knowledge of the cognitive processing therapy (CPT) model, but also to bring my own clinical style that centered on authenticity and relational connection into the process. My goal was to learn the model from the inside out while also modeling for staff how structured, evidence-based interventions can be delivered with genuine presence, curiosity, and compassion. In doing so, I hoped to integrate the rigor of CPT with the relational authenticity that I believe is critical for both healing and for training the next generation of therapists.

Deb's Case: Not Just an Eating Disorder

From a multidisciplinary perspective, Deb's treatment plan included ongoing medical monitoring, nutritional rehabilitation with structured meals and snacks, psychopharmacological support, group therapy, individual sessions, and family therapy. My work with Deb focused on integrating her trauma treatment within the system of care she was receiving. Given her admission assessment resulted in a Post Traumatic Stress Disorder (PTSD) Checklist for DSM-5 (PCL-5) score of 49, which indicated clinical significance (Forkus et al., 2023) *we began cognitive processing therapy (CPT) alongside eating disorder interventions* (Bovin et al. 2016).

Early in treatment, Deb resisted trauma work, expressing that her eating disorder was inseparable from her trauma and fearing life without either. Her initial impact statement reflected deep self-blame and mistrust: "I don't feel safe in my body … If I trust people and if I am honest with them, they will hurt me or abandon me." Her beliefs reinforced perfectionism, mistrust, and negative body image, driving her restrictive and binge–purge cycles.

As she stabilized nutritionally and engaged in the process of therapy, Deb became increasingly open to integrating authenticity into recovery in risking vulnerability with others and expressing her needs more directly. Through the structured use of cognitive tools including Socratic dialogue, stuck point logs, and challenging thought worksheets, coupled with deep congruence, presence, and relational understanding, Deb gradually challenged her maladaptive beliefs. In one key exercise, she reframed the thought, "I will never have an identity without my ED," to "My past has been difficult, but my future can look different," shifting her emotional experience from fear and hopelessness toward hope and agency. This work reflected not only cognitive change but also an authentic reclaiming of her voice and identity beyond trauma and the eating disorder.

Over 14 weeks, her PTSD symptoms diminished, her eating stabilized, and she articulated readiness to step down in treatment with ongoing support. Her progress underscored the power of combining evidence-based trauma interventions like CPT with a relational, authenticity-focused lens in eating disorder treatment, demonstrating that healing involves not only symptom reduction but also the reclamation of self.

Integrative Systemic and Family-Oriented Approaches

A growing body of work demonstrates that integrating broader systemic frameworks into eating disorder treatment can expand the impact of traditional family-based treatment (FBT). Ecosystemic models, such as Bronfenbrenner's (1979), help clinicians contextualize eating-disorder symptoms within overlapping environments from family and peers to culture and community, highlighting that recovery is influenced by far more than the nuclear family. Other evidence-based models for family therapy, specifically for children and adolescents include attachment-based models, such as attachment-based family therapy (ABFT; Diamond et al., 2021), deepen the work by repairing relational ruptures and strengthening caregiver–child security, while multisystemic family therapy (MST; Henggler, 1998) extends intervention into schools, peers, and community settings. Relational–cultural and structural/strategic approaches further illuminate how communication, hierarchy, boundaries, and mutual empathy shape symptom maintenance and healing. Together, these perspectives remind us that eating-disorder recovery is not solely an individual or family task but a multilayered relational project supported by emotional connection, community engagement, cultural attunement, and restored attachment. By widening the therapeutic lens, clinicians can address patterns of communication, attachment, and cultural influences that shape both the development of eating disorders and the pathways to recovery. Approaches such as multisystemic therapy (Henggler et al., 2009), attachment-based family therapy (Diamond et al., 2014), and relational–cultural family therapy (Jordan, 2017) highlight how interventions can extend beyond the nuclear family to engage peers, schools, communities, and cultural contexts as integral parts of the healing process. Here, I will introduce some approaches that will be covered more in Chapter 6.

Bronfenbrenner's Ecosystemic Lens

Guided by Bronfenbrenner's ecological systems theory, an ecosystemic approach situates eating disorders within a layered network of influences from intimate caregiving relationships to cultural norms around bodies, food, and achievement (Bronfenbrenner, 1979). This lens reframes symptoms not as solely intrapsychic, but as shaped by interactions across environmental systems:

- *Microsystem:* family, peers, school, and healthcare teams
- *Mesosystem:* intersections among these relationships (e.g., parent–school collaboration)
- *Exosystem:* social institutions that indirectly affect the individual (e.g., media, insurance limits)
- *Macrosystem:* cultural values, weight stigma, gender norms, socioeconomic context
- *Chronosystem:* timing of transitions such as puberty, relocation, trauma exposure

Ecosystemic assessment allows clinicians to identify how external forces—such as school pressures, athletic culture, access to care, or cultural weight ideals—contribute to both risk and recovery. Interventions may therefore expand beyond the nuclear family to address advocacy, cultural meaning-making, and community supports as central to healing.

Attachment-Based Family Therapy (ABFT)

Diamond's attachment-based family therapy (ABFT) emphasizes repairing relational ruptures and rebuilding secure attachment between caregivers and children, with the understanding that emotional disconnection and attachment injury often underlie eating disorder symptoms (Diamond et al., 2014). ABFT prioritizes:

- Re-establishing trust and safety in the caregiver–child relationship
- Addressing relational ruptures that drive symptom function
- Increasing emotional expression and responsiveness
- Supporting adolescents in developing autonomy without disconnection

By strengthening caregiver responsiveness and co-regulation, ABFT targets the attachment needs that eating disorder behaviors may temporarily soothe. This model is especially relevant when patterns of withdrawal, perfectionism, rejection sensitivity, or secrecy are present. Emerging research suggests that attachment-based interventions can strengthen family functioning and reduce symptom severity, particularly when ambivalence and relational distress are prominent.

Multisystemic Therapy (MST)

Multisystemic therapy (Henggler et al., 2009) adopts a broad ecological stance, addressing not only caregivers but multiple systems simultaneously, including school, peers, and community. MST assumes that symptoms are reinforced across overlapping relational networks, and therefore mobilizes resources in each system to support recovery. MST interventions may include:

- Caregiver coaching and empowerment
- Integration of school supports (teachers, coaches)
- Peer-related interventions to reduce relational stressors
- Skill building in emotion regulation and problem-solving
- Community-based coordination

MST is particularly helpful with complex family structures, high-conflict environments, comorbidities, or when treatment engagement is limited. By decentralizing the work from clinic to community settings, MST increases ecological validity and continuity of support.

Relational–Cultural Approaches

Relational-cultural theory (Miller & Stiver, 1997; Jordan et al., 1991) expands systemic work to emphasize mutuality, empathy, and relational authenticity. This framework views isolation and disconnection as core drivers of psychological suffering, with healing emerging through increased relational connection. Within eating-disorder care, relational–cultural work helps families:

- Increase mutual empathy
- Reduce shame and emotional silencing
- Build communication that allows vulnerability
- Strengthen shared meaning around recovery

This approach aligns closely with the broader premise of this book: that authentic connection is itself curative.

Structural and Strategic Family Therapy

Structural and strategic family therapy approaches examine family hierarchies, roles, boundaries, and communication patterns. Eating disorders may reflect systemic enmeshment, covert conflict, or role confusion (Minuchin et al., 1978). Interventions may include:

- Realigning family subsystems
- Strengthening generational boundaries
- Interruption of symptom-reinforcement cycles

These models can be particularly useful when symptoms maintain stability or identity within family dynamics.

Emotion-Focused Family Therapy (EFFT)

Emotion-focused family therapy (EFFT; Lafrance et al., 2016, 2020) empowers caregivers to support their child's recovery by helping them coach emotional experience, address their own blocks, and repair relational ruptures (Lafrance et al., 2016, 2020). Core components include:

- Emotion coaching and caregiver empowerment
- Block processing
- Relational repair

Research suggests EFFT reduces caregiver guilt and helplessness while increasing feelings of efficacy, attunement, and alliance which are all essential in reducing dropout and increasing treatment engagement (Lafrance et al., 2020). These outcomes are particularly important in eating disorders, where caregiver burden is often high. EFFT emphasizes relationship repair between caregivers and children, which research has shown improves therapeutic alliance and reduces dropout rates in eating disorder treatment (Lafrance et al., 2016).

Why These Additional Lenses Matter

Each approach offers a distinct—but complementary—map for understanding how eating disorders function within a person's relational, developmental, and sociocultural landscape. When layered together, these frameworks:

- Expand intervention beyond the nuclear family
- Incorporate culture, community, and developmental timing
- Address attachment security and caregiver healing
- Offer multiple access points for change

Put simply: no single model captures the complexity of family involvement in eating disorder treatment. Together, these frameworks help us create more flexible, relationally attuned, and context-responsive care.

Challenges of EBPs as a Single Mode of Care

Too often, the phrase *evidence-based practice* is equated with the exclusive use of manualized cognitive behavioral therapy (CBT). While CBT and related protocols have strong empirical support, narrowing the definition of evidence-based care to one set of interventions overlooks the broader range of approaches that research has shown to be effective. Evidence-based practice, as originally defined, involves the integration of the best available research with clinical expertise and patient values (APA Presidential Task Force on Evidence-Based Practice, 2006). This definition leaves room for interventions that extend beyond traditional cognitive or behavioral frameworks, especially when clients present with complex needs, ambivalence about change, or struggles with authenticity. In eating disorder treatment, for instance, approaches that integrate spirituality and nature-based practices have emerging evidence to support their effectiveness (Van Denend et al., 2022). Mindfulness is considered evidence-based for eating disorders because systematic review findings show it is associated with improvements in disordered eating behaviors and emotional regulation, with multiple studies demonstrating "satisfactory results" and supporting its effectiveness as a promising therapeutic approach (Li, 2025; Grohmann & Laws, 2021; Wanden-Berghe et al., 2011).

Yet the dominance of EBP also ushered in a new set of challenges, particularly in the treatment of complex or marginalized populations. The methodological standards that elevate certain treatments to "evidence-based" status often exclude clients with comorbidities, diverse cultural backgrounds, or long-standing relational trauma (Wampold & Imel, 2015). This creates a paradox: while EBPs aim to increase equity and efficacy in mental health care, they may also contribute to a narrowing of what is considered valid or effective, especially in relationally intensive work such as eating disorder treatment.

Moreover, EBPs are embedded in sociopolitical structures. Funding bodies, academic institutions, and journal priorities all influence which treatments are studied and disseminated. Interventions that do not lend themselves easily to manualization, such as expressive arts therapy, somatic work, or relational approaches, are often underrepresented in the evidence, despite strong clinical support (Jordan, 2017; Malchiodi, 2007). For clinicians, understanding the history and evolution of EBPs is critical—not to reject them, but to contextualize their use. Evidence-based practices are tools and templates, not scripted interventions to be read in a therapy room. When used flexibly and responsively, they can support recovery. When applied rigidly or without cultural and relational consideration, they can alienate clients, flatten complexity, and even reinforce harm.

EBP Critique in Pop Culture

In recent years, critiques of evidence-based practices have begun to surface not only in academic journals but also across pop culture such as podcasts, and social media, spaces where people share their real experiences of therapy. Shows like *Where Should We Begin?* with Esther Perel and *Therapy Chat* hosted by Laura Reagan regularly highlight the emotional complexity, messiness, and relational depth of therapy in ways that defy standard protocols. These widely followed platforms illustrate what many clients already know: that true healing often happens not because a clinician followed a step-by-step technique but because they showed up with presence, attunement, and courage. Listeners are drawn to conversations that emphasize relational safety, emotional risk, and clinicians' authenticity, not simply symptom checklists.

On TikTok and Instagram, clinicians and clients alike have begun questioning the rigidity of EBPs, particularly CBT-based approaches that can feel invalidating when applied without interpersonal nuances. Posts with captions like "My therapist told me to challenge the thought—so I just stopped talking" or "CBT wasn't built for trauma" have gone viral, resonating with users who feel unseen within protocol-driven care. Podcasts such as *Maintenance Phase* and *The Mindful Kind* frequently address the mismatch between mainstream wellness trends and the depth of emotional healing people are seeking. Many guests describe experiences of therapy that felt overly clinical or rushed, leaving them feeling more disoriented than supported. What's emerging is a grassroots redefinition of what "effective therapy" means: not just what works in a study, but what feels connecting, co-created, and attuned in the room. These cultural critiques align closely with what eating disorder clinicians witness daily—clients who need more than technique. We all yearn to be deeply known and to experience connection and relational safety in healing.

The Fidelity and Flexibility Paradox

While the call for accountability and structure in psychotherapy is well-intentioned and important, it is critical to understand how evidence-based practice is implemented and integrated in the field. Cook et al. (2017) emphasize that the movement toward EBPs brought much-needed emphasis to measurable outcomes, clinician competence, and the integration of research into care. Yet these authors also acknowledge that this progress has not been without significant challenges. Chief among these challenges is the tension between fidelity and flexibility. In essence, the fidelity and flexibility paradox means that clinicians are often caught between following treatment manuals with precision and responding authentically to the immediate needs of their clients. This becomes especially salient in eating disorder treatment, where affect regulation, relational trauma, and identity development cannot always be captured in symptom-focused protocols.

The gap between theory and application is also evident in the lived experiences of trainees and early career clinicians. Seegan et al. (2020) explored how training programs in evidence-based practice can unintentionally promote a sense of rigidity or emotional detachment in novice clinicians. Many clinicians reported feeling pressured to prioritize technique over relationship, and to deliver "proven" interventions even when they felt clinically inappropriate. In settings such as eating disorder partial hospitalization or residential programs, where clinical acuity is high and interpersonal dynamics are central, this kind of training model can lead to burnout, therapeutic ruptures, or a reliance on compliance-based interactions.

Even well-supported evidence-based practices (EBPs) are often challenging to implement in real-world clinical settings that are constrained by limited resources, high staff turnover, and systemic inequities. Research consistently demonstrates that organizational factors such as insufficient staffing, time pressures, and lack of ongoing supervision can significantly impede the fidelity and sustainability of EBPs, even when clinicians value their use (Aarons et al., 2011; Beidas & Kendall, 2010). In these contexts, clinicians may not receive adequate training, consultation, or institutional support, which can lead to reduced confidence and inconsistent application of interventions (Aarons et al., 2011).

Moreover, systemic pressures such as productivity demands, documentation requirements, and performance metrics can shift the focus from relational, attuned care toward procedural compliance, leaving clinicians feeling compelled to "complete" interventions rather than meaningfully engage in them (Beidas & Kendall, 2010). These dynamics are further compounded in under-resourced settings, where structural inequities disproportionately affect both providers and patients, limiting access to high-quality, sustained care (Proctor et al., 2009). As a result, the gap between research and practice persists, underscoring the need for implementation strategies that prioritize not only fidelity, but also feasibility, clinician support, and the therapeutic relationship. As Seegan and colleagues (2020) argue, effective training in EBPs must be coupled with opportunities for reflective supervision, self-awareness, and the development of relational competence, not just technical mastery.

Jasmine's Case: A Novice Clinician Struggling with EBP Constraints

During my years supervising newer clinicians, one moment stands out. Jasmine, a newly licensed associate clinician working in a residential eating disorder program, entered the field passionate about eating disorders and client-centered care. But within weeks, she found herself overwhelmed by the demands of the system, including daily progress notes coded to satisfy insurance audits, strict adherence to evidence-based protocols, and constant reminders to document "measurable outcomes." Jasmine struggled to balance clinical intuition with institutional expectations. Over time, she began to doubt her effectiveness, feeling more like a compliance officer than a clinician. She relied on a manualized eating disorder protocol, to ensure she was "doing therapy right." She sat across from her client with the workbook open on her lap, reading each prompt verbatim. The client nodded politely at first, answering the questions as though they were a checklist, completing the task rather than experiencing it. But as Jasmine continued, the client's posture stiffened. Her eyes drifted to the clock. The room felt increasingly flat, more like a classroom than a therapeutic space.

Afterward, Jasime explained to me that she had worried about "doing it wrong," so she clung tightly to the script. She believed fidelity meant precision in the approach, following every step exactly as written. What she missed was the client's growing disengagement, the subtle cues that signaled boredom, discomfort, or maybe even fear. The session was technically correct, but emotionally empty.

In supervision, we explored what it meant to honor the treatment model while still leaving room for humanity. I reminded her that manuals were never meant to replace the relationship; they were tools, not lifelines. Fidelity ensures we deliver what works; flexibility ensures it works for this person, in this moment. Over time, she learned to use the protocol as a guide rather than a script and lead with listening first, responding to the client's emotional tone, and adapting the interventions to fit their lived experience. The work became less about doing therapy "right" and more about helping the client feel met, understood, and safe. That tension between staying true to the model and staying true to the person is the paradox at the heart of good clinical care.

Limitations of Eating Disorder Treatment with EBPs

In the treatment of eating disorders, where symptoms often express deeper struggles related to identity, trauma, embodiment, and relational disconnection, clinicians frequently encounter the limitations of manualized protocols. Research affirms that therapeutic alliance, authenticity, and contextual attunement are among the most powerful drivers of clinical outcomes, often eclipsing the impact of any specific technique (Geller & Greenberg, 2012; Norcross & Lambert, 2018; Jordan, 2017). The risk of narrowly adhering to what is evidence based is that we ignore what is experience based, in both the client and the clinician. The therapeutic space must allow for more than just the delivery of skills or cognitive reframing; it must invite deep emotional presence, attunement to attachment wounds, and space for identity exploration. Protocols alone cannot offer this.

Ultimately, the challenge is not to abandon EBPs but instead reclaim a fuller definition of evidence, one that includes relational nuance, clinician authenticity, and the lived experience of clients. As Cook et al. (2017) argue, the next phase of the EBP movement must prioritize integration over prescription, making room for approaches that are grounded not only in research, but also in human connection. The following sections discuss challenges that occur when the clinician or institution relies solely on EBPs to treat those with eating disorders.

Oversimplification

Standardized EBPs often promote a structured, stepwise progression designed for research clarity and treatment fidelity. However, recovery rarely (if ever) is measured in clear progressive steps that can be structured through following steps in a book and may, inadvertently, constrain clinicians from responding to the unique developmental histories, cultural contexts, and internal worlds of their clients.

Sophia & Eve: Branching Out from CBT-E

Sophia, a 22-year-old, female identifying, Latina college student in a partial hospitalization program for anorexia nervosa, had been assigned to work with Eve, a recent graduate of an excellent master's program in mental health counseling. Eve was competent, eager, and deeply committed to CBT-E. Yet after several weeks, she reported growing concern that Sophia remained disengaged, guarded, mistrustful, and emotionally flat, despite her best efforts. Session after session, cognitive restructuring and behavioral experiments were introduced as prescribed, but nothing seemed to penetrate.

As part of supervision, we routinely watched session tapes together. Reviewing tapes allows us to capture what clinicians often miss in the moment such as subtle shifts in posture, silence, or emotional tone that signal deeper needs. It also helps clinicians integrate feedback more precisely by seeing and hearing themselves in relationship, rather than relying on memory alone. When Eve and I watched her sessions, something became clear: although she was naturally warm and relational, she appeared unusually rigid in her delivery as evidenced by reading prompts closely, moving swiftly from one intervention to the next, and leaving little room for emotional exploration. Her fidelity to the model was admirable, but it came at the cost of meaningful connection.

I gently asked Eve to imagine what it might be like to momentarily pause the protocol and explore Sophia's family story. In their next session, she invited Sophia to share her background. Slowly at first, then with growing clarity, Sophia described intergenerational trauma, immigration stress, and a family culture where emotions were rarely spoken. As she spoke, her voice cracked. Eventually, she wept, something that had never happened in prior sessions. "I didn't think this place cared about that stuff," she admitted.

That moment, anchored in relational attunement rather than cognitive reappraisal, became a turning point. Sophia began engaging more fully, showing up emotionally, and slowly loosening her grip on rigid food rules. The shift did not happen because a worksheet was completed; it happened because someone made space for her humanity.

CBT-E rightly emphasizes the centrality of eating disorder symptoms, yet it may not fully address the emotional avoidance and relational disconnection that often lie beneath (Treasure & Schmidt, 2013). Eve's work with Sophia illustrates why flexibility within fidelity matters. Protocols guide us, but only authentic connection moves clients toward change.

Context Mismatch

Most evidence for EBPs comes from randomized controlled trials involving homogenous participants and ideal conditions. Real-world clients are rarely this neat. In particular, clients in higher levels of care often present with comorbid trauma, suicidality, or chronic shame, which require more nuance than a treatment manual can provide (Tasca et al., 2020).

Jared's Case: The Need for Process

Jared, a 35-year-old gay man, who identified as gay and struggled with binge eating disorder and a history of childhood sexual abuse, struggled to connect with the strategies in a DBT skills group in a binge eating disorder intensive outpatient program. "This feels like I'm being told to fix myself before I even know what's broken," he reported. Jared needed space to narrate his story, explore the emotional pain behind his binges, and examine the internalized shame rooted in years of homophobic bullying. His most profound therapeutic moments occurred not during structured skills training, but in process groups in a holding relationship where he could voice his grief. EBPs had their place and importance, but only after trust and narrative safety were established.

This illustrates how a relational foundation often precedes successful implementation of techniques. Evidence-based methods must be embedded within relationships that honor the complexity of identity, intersectionality, and developmental trauma.

Gaps in Scope

As mentioned, the historical research base for EBPs in eating disorders has primarily focused on young, White, cisgender females, leaving significant gaps in our understanding of how to treat individuals across diverse racial, gender, and size identities (Rodriguez et al., 2021). As a result, clients from marginalized groups may enter treatment already skeptical that their experiences will be seen or validated. Often, individuals from marginalized groups have experienced multiple barriers to accessing healthcare prior to the potential barriers of client–clinician interactions quality that include cultural and language differences (CDC, 2024).

Marla's Case: Importance of Cultural Factors

Marla, a 28-year-old cis-female, Black woman in a larger body, was initially diagnosed with binge eating disorder by on outpatient physician and received a referral to an IOP program. However, upon entering the program, she described feeling unheard when given a diagnosis based on her size and reported eating behaviors. It was only after several sessions that her clinician discovered Marla's long-standing restriction, history of weight-based teasing, and fear of becoming "too thin" in her community. Her presentation aligned more closely with atypical anorexia, but she had never been asked how food functioned emotionally or culturally. "I've never been thin, so no one ever thought I could be starving," she said. Marla's healing required more than symptom tracking; it required being deeply seen and a deeper exploration.

This case underscores that when EBPs are applied without contextual attunement, they may perpetuate harm, particularly for clients whose lived experiences are not represented in traditional research samples.

Quantifying Outcomes

Randomized control trials often prioritize short-term symptom reduction, excluding qualitative or relational outcomes that are more difficult to quantify. As a result, experiential therapies, embodied practices, and culturally grounded approaches are often overlooked in the EBP landscape, despite their demonstrated impact on client engagement and meaning-making (Piran, 2017; Wampold & Imel, 2015). I would often describe to caregivers and clients alike that treatment is not just about symptom reduction but about where and why the symptoms developed in the first place.

Angie's Case: Deeper Treatment Required for Long-Term Healing

Angie, a 19-year-old college student, entered residential treatment for bulimia nervosa with a primary focus on symptom interruption and medical stabilization so she could quickly return to school. Within a few weeks, her binge–purge episodes ceased, her vitals normalized, and she was completing meals; she was compliant in the program and reflected the program's benchmarks for progress. However, despite these measurable gains on paper, Leila remained emotionally disconnected and was unable to engage in deeper work to understand the onset of her bulimia. It wasn't until later in treatment, when she was introduced to therapeutic groups that were more expressive in nature, including psychodrama, that she really emerged. During a psychodrama group, Angie began to access the underlying relational wounds and shame that had fueled her eating disorder for years. Though symptom reduction was necessary and achieved early through structured protocols, meaningful change emerged only when treatment expanded beyond quantifiable outcomes to include experiential and culturally attuned approaches.

In psychodrama, clients use guided role-play to work on their personal and interpersonal problems and possible solutions through actions rather than words alone (Orkibi & Feniger-Schaal, 2019). Although having a wealth of clinical work, psychodrama has scarce research compared to other psychotherapies and is often used in residential treatment settings (Twohig et al., 2015). *Through the integration of various techniques, individuals can move beyond just symptom reduction and toward healing.*

Integrative, Embodied, and Creative Approaches

Many clients with eating disorders struggle with alexithymia, dissociation, or disembodiment, making it difficult to access or verbalize their emotional experience. Expressive, somatic, and embodiment-based interventions provide clients with experiential ways of reconnecting with their bodies, processing emotions, and fostering a more compassionate and authentic sense of self (Levine, 2015; Piran, 2017).

Somatic and Embodiment Practices

Inspired by the work of Piran (2017), these practices emphasize reconnecting clients with their bodies through nonjudgmental awareness and physical presence. Modalities may include:

- Yoga and body-based mindfulness
- Movement therapy
- Breathwork and grounding techniques

These practices can reduce body shame, enhance interoception, and support trauma recovery.

Expressive Therapies

Art, music, drama, and narrative therapies offer non-verbal ways for clients to explore identity, emotion, and relationship with food and body. They are particularly helpful when verbal processing is overwhelming or inaccessible.

Creative interventions include:

- Mandalas or collages about body image
- Journaling dialogues between the client and their eating disorder
- Sand tray explorations of family roles
- Family sculpting and sociometry activities

In another example of expanding our understanding of treatment approaches, research highlights the utility of mindfulness and spiritually oriented interventions in addressing core maintaining factors of eating disorders. Mindfulness practices, for example, have been shown to reduce perfectionism, rumination, and emotion dysregulation, often common barriers to recovery in anorexia nervosa (Dikmeer et al., 2024). Meta-analyses further demonstrate that mindfulness-based interventions significantly decrease binge eating and improve body image (Liu et al., 2025). Similarly, nature-based therapies offer promising results, with studies showing reductions in binge eating symptoms and increases in well-being and positive embodiment through structured engagement with natural environments (Corazon et al., 2019; Trangsrud et al., 2020).

The Humanistic Posture of the ED Clinician

In the context of EDs, where clients may feel misunderstood or defensive, a genuine, nonjudgmental stance by the clinician helps foster safety and trust. Research confirms that treating ED patients "requires the establishment of a strong therapeutic relationship" and that the clinician's interpersonal qualities can significantly shape treatment outcomes. These concepts are foundational from humanistic therapy traditions (e.g., Carl Rogers's person-centered approach, discussed in earlier chapters) that emphasize the clinician's genuineness, unconditional positive regard, and empathic understanding as preconditions for client growth. Humanistic approaches, such as client-centered therapy, gestalt, emotion-focused therapy, or contemporary relational therapies, likewise emphasize authenticity and the person-to-person connection. While not as common as CBT or IPT in formal ED treatment guidelines, humanistic principles permeate many effective interventions for body image. For instance, motivational interviewing, often used to enhance readiness for change in EDs, is grounded in Rogers's humanistic spirit—expressing empathy, rolling with resistance, and supporting the client's autonomy.

Clinicians practicing MI or other humanistic–integrative therapies report that adopting a non-authoritarian, authentic demeanor helps overcome the resistance and denial frequently encountered in ED patients (Fetahi, et al., 2025). Many researchers have identified that a client's belief of a supportive, non-judgmental attitude along with "genuine curiosity" were helpful across treatment (Albano et al., 2024; Li et al., 2025; Polcin et al., 2014). Even in structured treatments like CBT-E, leading clinicians have highlighted the importance of adopting a compassionate, humanistic attitude alongside the technical aspects of treatment (Russell et al., 2023). Interpersonal and humanistic frameworks remind clinicians that *how* they relate may be as important as *what* techniques they apply. Developing an authentic, empowering relationship is seen not just as aiding technique delivery but as a change mechanism in itself, especially vital for disorders rooted in shame, secrecy, and isolation.

Emerging research further affirms the value of these integrative practices. A systematic review of body-oriented therapies demonstrated promising effects in reducing eating disorder symptoms and enhancing mind–body integration (Lucas et al., 2025). Similarly, Meneguzzo et al. (2025) found that group interventions targeting body image flexibility and embodied awareness led to decreases in weight concerns and greater comfort with internal bodily sensations. Integrative approaches that combine psychological therapies with embodiment practices, such as yoga, also reveal benefits including improved mindfulness, emotional regulation, and reconnection with the body (O'Brien et al., 2023). Together, these models highlight the need for flexibility and integration rather than adherence to one narrow framework. These findings underscore that evidence-based treatment is not limited to cognitive restructuring or exposure hierarchies, but includes integrative practices that honor body, mind, and spirit. When therapists broaden their view of what counts as evidence-based, they create more authentic, holistic, and responsive spaces for clients to heal.

Levels of Care in Eating Disorder Treatment: A Continuum of Support

Eating disorders occur along a spectrum of severity and complexity, and effective treatment must be matched to the client's unique medical, psychological, nutritional, and environmental needs. To address this, the field of eating disorder treatment operates within a continuum of care, commonly referred to as levels of care. These levels are defined by national guidelines, most notably the American Psychiatric Association (APA) Practice Guidelines (APA, 2006; Crone et al., 2023) and the Eating Disorders Coalition's Level of Care Guidelines (AED, 2012; Yager et al., 2014) and are used by providers, payers, and treatment teams to determine appropriate placement and treatment planning. Insurance companies frequently use tools such as LOCUS (level of care utilization system) or InterQual® to determine medical necessity.

The level-of-care framework ensures that clients receive the least restrictive, yet most effective level of care based on safety, symptom acuity, and recovery support. While transitions between levels are often fluid and individualized, they are typically guided by a combination of clinical judgment, standardized assessment tools, and insurance requirements. I will be using many of the terms associated with the different levels of care throughout this book, so I will describe them in more detail here.

Outpatient Level of Care

Outpatient care is the least intensive level of support and is typically what people think of in terms of therapy. Outpatient treatment is suitable for individuals with mild to moderate eating disorder symptoms who are medically stable and able to function in school, work, or family life with minimal disruption. Typically, outpatient treatment includes:

- Weekly or biweekly sessions with a clinician specializing in eating disorders
- Ongoing medical monitoring by a primary care physician
- Nutritional counseling with a registered dietitian (often weekly or biweekly)
- Psychiatric care as needed

Outpatient care is often appropriate as a step down from higher levels of care or for those with strong external support systems. However, it may be insufficient for clients in early recovery with entrenched patterns of restriction, bingeing, or purging.

Intensive Outpatient Program

An intensive outpatient program is a step up from outpatient care or is a step down following a higher level of care, offering structured therapeutic and nutritional support while allowing clients to maintain school, work, or family responsibilities. Most intensive outpatient programs operate in the evenings or during after-school hours. Typically, intensive outpatient programs include:

- Programming for 3–4 hours per day, 3–5 days per week
- Supervised meals or snacks
- Individual therapy and nutrition touchpoints

An intensive outpatient program emphasizes skill development, accountability, and community support while helping clients integrate recovery into daily life. Clinically, to participate in an intensive outpatient program, an individual should be medically stable with no acute health risks and functional enough to maintain daily activities and obligations. Often individuals in an intensive outpatient program need more support with meal compliance and are struggling with eating disorder behaviors without improvement in outpatient care.

Partial Hospitalization Program/Day Treatment

Partial hospitalization (also called day treatment or PHP) is a more intensive, structured environment. It serves individuals who require daily support to manage eating disorder thoughts and behaviors, restore nutritional stability, and manage comorbid psychiatric symptoms. PHP programs typically include:

- Programming that runs 6–10 hours per day, 5–7 days per week
- Group therapy and individual sessions
- Supervised meals and snacks
- Medical and psychiatric oversight
- Family therapy and case management

Someone who is appropriate for this level of care may be medically stable but is functionally impaired by the ED, requires structured time and meals to prevent engagement in ED symptoms, is likely struggling with self-regulation of emotions, and is unable to make necessary progress in an intensive outpatient program or outpatient setting. Often, partial hospitalization is used for clients discharging from residential treatment as a step down.

Residential Treatment

Residential care provides 24/7 structured treatment in a live-in facility for clients who require continuous support but do not meet the medical necessity for inpatient hospitalization. Residential programs offer an immersive therapeutic environment designed to disrupt entrenched eating disorder patterns, support weight restoration, and address underlying psychological issues. Core treatment components of residential treatment care include:

- 24-hour nursing support and behavioral oversight
- Multiple individual and family sessions per week
- Psychiatric and medical monitoring
- Extensive group therapy support and skill building
- Meal support and nutritional rehabilitation

Clinical indicators that an individual needs residential treatment care include persistent disordered behaviors that impair functioning, an unsafe or unsupportive home environment, an inadequate response to a lower level of care, and an inability to remain safe in a lower level of care.

Residential treatment is appropriate when round-the-clock containment, community living, or distance from daily triggers is necessary for stabilization and healing. Clients often spend 30–90 days in residential care, depending on insurance and treatment progress.

Inpatient Hospitalization

Inpatient care is the most intensive and medically supervised level of care. It is reserved for clients experiencing acute medical or psychiatric crises related to their eating disorder, such as cardiac instability, electrolyte disturbances, suicidal ideation, or inability to maintain hydration or caloric intake. These programs include:

- 24/7 medical and psychiatric care
- IV hydration
- Tube feeding
- Electrolyte correction as needed
- Close monitoring of vitals, labs, and refeeding risk
- Crisis stabilization
- Short-term containment

Clinically, these individuals likely struggle with acute food refusal or rapid weight loss; suicidal ideation or severe self-injury risk; syncope, seizures, or severe dehydration; and irregular lab work and vitals (heart rate, blood pressure, and electrolyte imbalances). Inpatient stays are typically shorter term (5–14 days) and focus on stabilization rather than psychotherapy. Clients are hopefully discharged to residential or partial hospitalization programs to continue their recovery process.

Key Considerations in Level-of-Care Decisions

There are many factors that go into deciding what level of care a client needs. These include:

- Medical vs. psychological severity: clients may be medically stable but deeply entrenched in disordered behaviors or trauma symptoms requiring higher support.
- Environmental safety: home environment, family support, and triggering relationships are critical in determining whether outpatient care is viable.
- Treatment history: previous relapses or premature discharges from lower levels of care often justify admission to higher-intensity programs.
- Insurance access: unfortunately, many level-of-care decisions are influenced by coverage limitations rather than clinical best practices.

Clinicians should approach level-of-care decisions collaboratively with clients and families, helping them understand that a higher level of care is not a failure but a strategic support system designed to protect healing and promote long-term recovery.

The level-of-care continuum allows providers to match treatment intensity to clinical need, promoting safety, consistency, and hope across the recovery journey. Eating disorders demand comprehensive, individualized care that can flex with a client's changing circumstances. A comprehensive use of the level-of-care framework supports not only stabilization but transformation and long-term recovery.

For the majority of my career, I've worked exclusively in higher levels of care for eating disorders including residential, partial hospitalization programs, and inpatient settings where clients arrive in crisis, often medically compromised and emotionally raw. In these environments, I've witnessed firsthand the transformative power of structure, containment, and multidisciplinary collaboration. Clients who felt hopeless in outpatient settings were finally able to access safety, nourishment, and connection in ways that would have been impossible without the intensity and support of higher levels of care. The daily therapeutic contact, meal support, and shared community not only interrupted dangerous behaviors but also opened space for vulnerability, meaning-making, and relational healing. Time and again, I've seen that for individuals with severe or entrenched eating disorders, higher levels of care are not just helpful, they are lifesaving.

Challenges with Accessing Care

Payers commonly rely on standardized medical-necessity and placement tools such as the Level of Care Utilization System (LOCUS) and InterQual® when authorizing behavioral health care. However, regulatory and clinical reports have highlighted that these instruments were designed primarily for general psychiatric placement decisions and have notable limitations when applied to eating disorder treatment. The American Academy of Child and Adolescent Psychiatry (AACAP) white paper highlights that the LOCUS is intended to be used as part of a broader framework for determining level of care and must be supplemented by additional tools to adequately address diverse patient populations and service needs (American Academy of Child and Adolescent Psychiatry, 2023). Consistent with this, the National Association of Insurance Commissioners has noted that LOCUS does not comprehensively cover all ages or services, reinforcing that it should not be used as a standalone measure and underscoring its limited scope within clinical decision-making (National Association of Insurance Commissioners, 2021). Similarly, InterQual® released revised eating disorder criteria in 2024 to better align with the American Psychiatric Association's updated *Practice Guideline for the Treatment of Patients with Eating Disorders*, reflecting that prior versions were not fully consistent with evolving evidence-based standards (American Psychiatric Association, 2023; InterQual, 2024). Impersonal utilization review processes and rigid medical-necessity criteria often fail to capture the clinical complexity of eating disorders, resulting in barriers to appropriate care (Silber & Robb, 2002). Taken together, these critiques support concern that payer-driven tools may inconsistently apply eating-disorder-specific standards unless explicitly updated to match specialty guidelines.

Eating disorder treatment is often a prolonged process that requires involvement from multiple providers and across different levels of care, making it financially burdensome and sometimes inaccessible for patients (Accurso & Taylor, 2020). Insurance coverage is influenced not only by whether individuals have insurance but also by insurers' decisions about what they will actually cover. Too often, coverage decisions are tied to weight criteria, where patients whose weight is deemed "adequate" may be denied treatment—even when serious symptoms remain (Parliament & Treasure, 2019). This reliance on weight as the primary marker of medical necessity is deeply flawed, as it does not accurately capture the complexity of eating disorders (Accurso & Taylor, 2020). While barriers to accessing care persist, the past decade has seen some progress. Broader shortcomings in the US insurance system continue to exacerbate treatment gaps in eating disorders and other mental health conditions, highlighting the urgency of policy reform (Accurso & Taylor, 2020). Notably, the passage of the Anna Westin Act in 2016, included within the 21st Century Cures Act, marked a historic milestone as the first federal legislation addressing eating disorders and expanded insurance coverage under mental health parity (U.S. Congress, 2016).

Self-Reflection on Treatment Considerations

Manuals may offer maps, but therapy unfolds in uncharted territory. Reflection invites clinicians to pause, orient themselves, and return to the central question of what the client needs from the clinician, not just as a professional but as a person in relationship with them. The following questions are intended to be used in clinical supervision, peer consultation, or personal journaling to help clinicians explore their own thoughts on treatment modalities and approaches.

Clinician Self-Reflection Questions

- *When have I felt most effective as a clinician? What made that moment possible?*
- *In what ways do I rely on treatment manuals to feel secure or competent? How do I know when it is time to step away from the script?*
- *Have I ever continued with an evidence-based technique even when it felt misaligned with a client's emotional state or cultural experience? What might I do differently now?*
- *How do I define "progress" in therapy? Whose definition of healing am I using? Mine, a treatment manual, the client's, or an insurance chart?*
- *What implicit assumptions do I hold about which approaches are "valid" or "scientific"? How might those assumptions affect the clients I serve, particularly those from marginalized identities?*
- *Where in my current caseload do I feel torn between following an evidence-based protocol and meeting a client in their complexities and identity?*
- *How do issues of power, race, body size, or gender identity show up in your case conceptualizations? How are these considered in your use of EBP frameworks?*
- *What supports or permissions do you need to trust your clinical intuition more fully?*

Implications for the Future

In eating disorder treatment, clients often present with deeply entrenched behaviors that serve protective and symbolic functions. Restriction, bingeing, purging, or body checking are not merely behaviors to be extinguished but are strategies for emotional regulation, relational control, or self-definition. While EBPs provide valuable scaffolding, they cannot replace the relational attunement, cultural humility, and narrative exploration required to uncover deeper layers. Relational–cultural therapy, mindfulness-based approaches, and experiential modalities such as art or movement therapy offer pathways to support embodiment and authenticity (Jordan, 2017; Malchiodi, 2007). When combined with EBPs in a flexible, responsive manner, these relational methods do not detract from evidence-based care but rather deepen it to a fully integrative approach to healing.

Dr. Bruce Wampold, a leading psychotherapy researcher and author of *The Great Psychotherapy Debate*, has argued that the common factors of therapy—such as empathy, the therapeutic alliance, and the client's expectations—often have a greater impact on outcomes than any specific intervention or manualized treatment. Wampold and Imel (2015) critique the overemphasis on RCT-derived EBPs, noting that such studies can give a false impression of precision while neglecting the human elements that actually drive change. They emphasize that psychotherapy is not merely a technical procedure, but a relational and contextual endeavor: "Treatments work not because of their specific ingredients but because they provide clients with opportunities to enact new behaviors and narratives in a healing relationship" (Wampold & Imel, 2015).

Ultimately, what promotes recovery is not simply what clinicians do but how clinicians are with clients—whether clinicians are able to offer curiosity instead of control, presence instead of pressure, and collaboration instead of compliance.

Summary

There is no single approach to eating disorder treatment that works for all clients. Effective care requires a thoughtful integration of evidence-based practices, relational presence, cultural humility, and creativity. Clients bring their own histories, bodies, beliefs, and communities into treatment, and healing must be flexible enough to meet them there. As the field continues to evolve, clinicians are increasingly called to move beyond rigid models and toward integrative, compassionate, and human-centered care. That's what the rest of this book will discuss.

Medical management and nutritional stabilization suggested readings:

- Mehler, Philip S., and Arnold E. Andersen, eds. (2022). *Eating Disorders: A Comprehensive Guide to Medical Care and Complications.* Fourth edition. Baltimore: Johns Hopkins University Press.
- Herrin, M., & Larkin, M. (2013). *Nutrition counseling in the treatment of eating disorders* (2nd ed.). Routledge/Taylor & Francis.
- Tribole, E., & Resch, E. (2020). *Intuitive eating: A revolutionary anti-diet approach* (4th ed.). St. Martin's Essentials.

Key Take-Aways

- Eating disorder treatment must start with medical and nutritional stabilization, but true healing requires weaving this foundation together with psychological, relational, and systemic work.
- Evidence-based practices like CBT-E and FBT are essential but incomplete in simply reading a text; they should serve as structured frameworks, not rigid formulas, especially given the heterogeneity, trauma histories, and neurodiversity seen in real-world ED care.
- Relational, trauma-informed, and systemic approaches expand what "effective treatment" means by centering attachment, authenticity, connection, culture, and context—not just symptom reduction.
- EBPs are shaped by sociopolitical forces (funding, manuals, research standards) and invite clinicians to hold the fidelity–flexibility paradox: honoring research while adapting care to client identity, lived experience, and therapeutic relationship.
- Across levels of care, clinicians are called to move from one-size-fits-all to precision-oriented, integrative practice, using outcome monitoring, self-reflection, and authentic presence to individualize treatment and make space for clients to feel deeply seen—not just treated.

References

Aarons, G. A., Hurlburt, M., & Horwitz, S. M. (2011). Advancing a conceptual model of evidence-based practice implementation in public service sectors. *Administration and Policy in Mental Health and Mental Health Services Research, 38*(1), 4–23.

Academy for Eating Disorders. (2012). Guidelines for levels of care in the treatment of eating disorders. Academy for Eating Disorders.

Accurso, E. C., & Taylor, C. B. (2020). *Insurance coverage for eating disorders: Progress*, gaps, and challenges. Psychiatric Clinics of North America, 43(3), 473–486.

Albano, G., Teti, A., Scrò, A., Bonfanti, R. C., Fortunato, L., & Coco, G. L. (2024). *A systematic review on the role of therapist characteristics in the treatment of eating disorders.* Research in Psychotherapy: Psychopathology, Process, and Outcome, 27(2), 750.

American Academy of Child and Adolescent Psychiatry. (2023). *Toward a national standard for service intensity assessment and level of care determination.* https://www.aacap.org/App_Themes/AACAP/Docs/clinical_practice_center/23.11.13_MDI_LOCUS-White-Paper.pdf

American Psychiatric Association. (2023). *Practice guideline for the treatment of patients with eating disorders* (4th ed.). American Psychiatric Association Publishing.

American Psychiatric Association. (2006). *Practice guideline for the treatment of patients with eating disorders (3rd ed.).* American Psychiatric Publishing.

American PsychologicalAssociation PresidentialTask Force on Evidence-Based Practice. (2006). *Evidence-based practice in psychology. American Psychologist*, 61(4), 271–285.

Anderson, L. M., Lim, K. O., Kummerfeld, E., Crosby, R. D., Crow, S. J., Engel, S. G., Forrest, L., Wonderlich, S. A., & Peterson, C. B. (2023). Causal discovery analysis: A promising tool in advancing precision medicine for eating disorders. *International Journal of Eating Disorders*, 56(11), 2012–2021.

Austin, A., & Allen, K.L. (2025). Personalized and precision mental health in eating disorders: Why routine outcome measurement is key. *Journal of Eating Disorders*, **13**, 135.

Beidas, R. S., & Kendall, P. C. (2010). Training therapists in evidence-based practice: A critical review of studies from a systems-contextual perspective. *Clinical Psychology: Science and Practice, 17*(1), 1–30

Bovin, M. J., Marx, B. P., Weathers, F. W., Gallagher, M. W., Rodriguez, P., Schnurr, P. P., & Keane, T. M. (2016). Psychometric properties of the PTSD Checklist for Diagnostic and Statistical Manual of Mental Disorders–Fifth Edition (PCL-5) in veterans. *Psychological Assessment, 28*(11), 1379–1391.

Bronfenbrenner, U. (1979). The ecology of human development: Experiments by nature and design. Harvard University Press.

Bryant, E., Marks, P., Griffiths, K. et al. Treating the individual: Moving towards personalised eating disorder care. *Journal of Eating Disorders*, **13**, 63 (2025). doi:10.1186/s40337-025-01246-6

Centers for Disease Control and Prevention. (2024). *What is health equity?* Retrieved July 31, 2025. www.cdc.gov/health-equity

Cook, S. C., Schwartz, A. C., & Kaslow, N. J. (2017). *Evidence-based psychotherapy: Advantages and challenges.* Neurotherapeutics, 14(3), 537–545.

Corazon, S. S., Sidenius, U., Poulsen, D. V., Gramkow, M. C., & Stigsdotter, U. K. (2019). Psycho-physiological stress recovery in outdoor nature-based interventions: A systematic review of the past eight years of research. *International Journal of Environmental Research and Public Health, 16*(10), 1711. doi:10.3390/ijerph16101711

Crone, C., Fochtmann, L. J., Attia, E., Boland, R., Escobar, J., Fornari, V., Golden, N., Guarda, A., Jackson-Triche, M., Manzo, L., Mascolo, M., Pierce, K., Riddle, M., Seritan, A., Uniacke, B., Zucker, N., Yager, J., Craig, T. J., Hong, S.-H., & Medicus, J. (2023). The American Psychiatric Association practice guideline for the treatment of patients with eating disorders. *The American Journal of Psychiatry, 180*(2), 167–171.

Diamond, G. S., Diamond, G. M., & Levy, S. A. (2014). *Attachment-based family therapy for depressed adolescents.* American Psychological Association.

Diamond, G., Diamond, G. M., & Levy, S. (2021). Attachment-based family therapy: Theory, clinical model, outcomes, and process research. *Journal of Affective Disorders, 294*, 286–295. doi:10.1016/j.jad.2021.07.005

Dikmeer, N., Ersöz Alan, B., & Foto Özdemir, D. (2024). The role of mindfulness on the psychological aspects of anorexia nervosa. *Clinical Child Psychology and Psychiatry, 29*(1), 15–29. doi:10.1177/13591045231190675

Eisler, I. (2005). *The empirical and theoretical base of family therapy and multiple family day therapy for adolescent anorexia nervosa.* Journal of Family Therapy, 27, 104–131.

Fairburn, C. G. (2008). *Cognitive behavior therapy and eating disorders.* Guilford Press.

Fetahi, E., Søgaard, A. S., & Sjögren, M. (2022). *Estimating the effect of motivational interventions in patients with eating disorders: A systematic review and meta-analysis.* Journal of Personalized Medicine, 12(4), 577.

Forkus, S. R., Raudales, A. M., Rafiuddin, H. S., Weiss, N. H., Messman, B. A., & Contractor, A. A. (2023). The Posttraumatic Stress Disorder (PTSD) Checklist for DSM-5: A systematic review of existing psychometric evidence. Clinical Psychology, 30(1), 110–121.

Gabbard, G. O. (2020). *Psychodynamic psychiatry in clinical practice (5th ed.).* APA Publishing.

Geller, S., & Greenberg, L. (2012). *Therapeutic presence: A mindful approach to effective therapy.* American Psychological Association.

Greenberg, L., & Watson, J. (2006). *Emotion-focused therapy for depression.* American Psychological Association.

Grohmann, D., & Laws, K. R. (2021). Two decades of mindfulness-based interventions for binge eating: A systematic review and meta-analysis. *Journal of Psychosomatic Research, 149*, 110592. doi:10.1016/j.jpsychores.2021.110592

Henggler, S.W. (1998). Multisystemic treatment of antisocial behavior in children and adolescents. (Treatment manuals for practitioners.) Guilford Press; 1998.

Henggler, S. W., Schoenwald, S. K., Borduin, C. M., Rowland, M. D., & Cunningham, P. B. (2009). *Multisystemic therapy for antisocial behavior in children and adolescents* (2nd ed.). Guilford Press.

InterQual. (2024). *InterQual® behavioral health criteria: Eating disorders.* Change Healthcare.

Jordan, J. V. (2017). *Relational–cultural Therapy.* American Psychological Association.

Jordan, J. V., Kaplan, A. G., Miller, J. B., Stiver, I. P., & Surrey, J. L. (1991). Women's growth in connection: Writings from the Stone Center. Guilford Press.

Lafrance Robinson, A., Dolhanty, J., Stillar, A., Henderson, K., & Mayman, S. (2016). *Emotion-focused family therapy for eating disorders across the lifespan: A pilot study of a 2-day transdiagnostic intervention for parents.* Clinical Psychology & Psychotherapy, 23(1), 14–23. doi:10.1002/cpp.1933

Lafrance, A., Henderson, K. A., & Mayman, S. (2020). *Emotion-focused family therapy: A transdiagnostic model for caregiver-focused interventions.* American Psychological Association .

Levine, P. A. (2015). *Trauma and memory: Brain and body in a search for the living past.* North Atlantic Books.

Levinson, C. A., Williams, B. M., Christian, C., Hunt, R. A., Keshishian, A. C., Brosof, L. C., Vanzhula, I. A., Davis, G. G., Brown, M. L., Bridges-Curry, Z., Sandoval-Araujo, L. E., & Ralph-Nearman, C. (2023). Personalizing eating disorder treatment using idiographic models: An open series trial. *Journal of Consulting and Clinical Psychology, 91*(1), 14–28.

Levinson, J. A., Kinkel-Ram, S., Myers, B., & Hunger, J. M. (2024). A systematic review of weight stigma and disordered eating cognitions and behaviors. *Body Image, 48*, 101678.

Li, B. (2025). Mindfulness-based programs for eating disorders: A review of effectiveness, mechanisms, and limitations. Theoretical and Natural Science, 121, 60–66.

Li, E., Kealy, D., Aafjes-van Doorn, K., McCollum, J., Curtis, J. T., Luo, X., & Silberschatz, G. (2025). "*It felt like I was being tailored to the treatment rather than the treatment being tailored to me*": Patient experiences of helpful and unhelpful psychotherapy. Psychotherapy Research, 35(5), 695–709.

Liu, J., Tynan, M., Mouangue, A., Martin, C., Manasse, S., & Godfrey, K. (2025). Mindfulness-based interventions for binge eating: An updated systematic review and meta-analysis. Journal of Behavioral Medicine, 48(1), 57–89.

Linehan, M. M., Chen, E. Y. (2005). Dialectical behavior therapy for eating disorders. In A. Freeman, S. H. Felgoise, C. M. Nezu, A. M. Nezu, M. A. Reinecke (Eds.), Encyclopedia of cognitive behavior therapy. Springer.

Lock, J., & Le Grange, D. (2015). *Treatment manual for anorexia nervosa: A family-based approach.* Guilford Press.

Lucas, G., Sin, J., Cini, E., & Röhricht, F. (2025). *Body-oriented therapies for the treatment of eating disorders: A systematic review.* Complementary Therapies in Clinical Practice, 60, 101997.

Malchiodi, C. A. (2007). *The art therapy sourcebook.* McGraw-Hill.

Meneguzzo, P., Cazzola, C., Buscaglia, F. *et al.* (2025). Body image flexibility and embodiment in eating disorders: a mixed-methods approach combining network analysis and pilot exposure protocol. Journal of Eating Disorders, 13, 64.

Miller, J. B. & Stiver, I. P. (1997). The healing connection: How women form relationships in therapy and in life. Beacon Press.

Minuchin, S., Rosman, B., & Baker, L. (1978). *Psychosomatic families: Anorexia nervosa in context.* Harvard University Press.

National Association of Insurance Commissioners. (2021). *Mental health parity and addiction equity issues: LOCUS and level of care tools.* National Association of Insurance Commissioners.

National Institute for Health and Care Excellence. (2017). *Eating disorders: Recognition and treatment (NICE guideline NG69).* https://www.nice.org.uk/guidance/ng69

National Institute for Health and Care Excellence. (2020). https://www.nice.org.uk/guidance

Norcross, J. C., & Lambert, M. J. (2018). *Psychotherapy relationships that work* III. Psychotherapy, 55(4), 303–315.

O'Brien, J., Evans, S., McIver, S., & O'Shea, M. (2023). *A scoping review of integrated yoga and psychological approaches for the treatment of eating disorders.* Journal of Eating Disorders, 11(1), 152.

Orkibi, H., & Feniger-Schaal, R. (2019). *Integrative systematic review of psychodrama psychotherapy research: Trends and methodological implications.* PloS one, 14(2), e0212575.

Parliament, K., & Treasure, J. (2019). *Barriers to accessing evidence-based treatment for eating disorders: A review of the literature.* Journal of Eating Disorders, 7(1), 3.

Piran, N. (2017). *Embodied possibilities and disruptions: The emergence of the experience of embodiment construct from qualitative studies with girls and women.* Body Image, 20, 14–26.

Polcin, D., Mericle, A., Howell, J., Sheridan, D., & Christensen, J. (2014). Maximizing social model principles in residential recovery settings. *Journal of Psychoactive Drugs, 46*(5), 436–443. doi:10.1080/02791072.2014.960112

Polcin, D. L., Sterling, J., Brown, T., Brown, M., Buscemi, R., & Korcha, R. (2015). *Client and therapist views about intensive and standard motivational interviewing.* Journal of Contemporary Psychotherapy, 45(3), 167–176.

Proctor, E. K., Landsverk, J., Aarons, G., Chambers, D., Glisson, C., & Mittman, B. (2009). Implementation research in mental health services: An emerging science with conceptual, methodological, and training challenges. *Administration and Policy in Mental Health, 36*(1), 24–34. doi:10.1007/s10488-008-0197-4

Redgrave, G. W., Coughlin, J. W., Schreyer, C. C., Martin, L. M., Leonpacher, A. K., Seide, M., ... & Guarda, A. S. (2015). *Refeeding and weight restoration outcomes in anorexia nervosa: Challenging current guidelines.* International Journal of Eating Disorders, 48(7), 866–873.

Resick, P. A., Monson, C. M., & Chard, K. M. (2017). *Cognitive processing therapy for PTSD: A comprehensive manual.* Guilford Press.

Rodriguez, M., Lemoine, J. E., & Johnson, C. (2021). *Beyond the stereotype: Eating disorders in diverse populations.* Current Psychiatry Reports, 23(9), 58.

Russell, H., Aouad, P., Le, A., Marks, P., Maloney, D., National EatingDisorder Research Consortium, Touyz, S., & Maguire, S. (2023). *Psychotherapies for eating disorders: Findings from a rapid review.* Journal of Eating Disorders, 11(1), 175.

Sackett, D. L., Rosenberg, W. M. C., Gray, J. A. M., Haynes, R. B., & Richardson, W. S. (1996). *Evidence based medicine: What it is and what it isn't.* BMJ, 312(7023), 71–72.

Safer, D. L., Telch, C. F., & Agras, W. S. (2001). *Dialectical behavior therapy for bulimia nervosa.* The American Journal of Psychiatry, 158(4), 632–634.

Seegan, P. L., Miller, L., Young, A. S., Parrish, C., Cullen, B., & Reynolds, E. K. (2020). *Enhancing quality of care through evidence-based practice: Training and supervision experiences.* Academic Psychiatry, 44, 533–539.

Shedler, J. (2017). *Where is the evidence for "evidence-based"* therapy? The Journal of Psychological Therapies in Primary Care, 4, 47–59.

Silber, T. J., & Robb, A. S. (2002). Eating disorders and health insurance understanding and overcoming obstacles to treatment. Child and Adolescent Psychiatric Clinics of North America, 11(2), 419–428.

Substance Abuse and Mental Health Services Administration. (2018). https://www.samhsa.gov/

Tasca, G. A., Gallop, R., Ritchie, K., et al. (2020). *Change in interpersonal problems in group psychodynamic interpersonal psychotherapy and group cognitive behavioral therapy for binge eating disorder.* International Journal of Eating Disorders, 53(4), 561–570.

Trangsrud, L. K. J., Borg, M., Bratland-Sanda, S., & Klevan, T. (2020). Embodying experiences with nature in everyday life recovery for persons with eating disorders. *International Journal of Environmental Research and Public Health, 17*(8), 2784. doi:10.3390/ijerph17082784

Treasure, J., & Schmidt, U. (2013). *The cognitive-interpersonal maintenance model of anorexia nervosa revisited: A summary of the evidence for cognitive*, socio-emotional, and interpersonal predisposing and perpetuating factors. Journal of Eating Disorders, 1, 13.

Treleaven, D. A. (2018). *Trauma-sensitive mindfulness: Practices for safe and transformative healing.* W. W. Norton & Company.

Twohig, M. P., Bluett, E. J., Cullum, J. L., Mitchell, P. R., Powers, P. S., Lensegrav-Benson, T., & Quakenbush-Roberts, B. (2015). *Effectiveness and clinical response rates of a residential eating disorders facility.* Eating Disorders, 24(3), 224–239.

U.S. Congress. (2016). *21st Century Cures Act, Pub. L. No. 114–255.* (Includes the Anna Westin Act provisions). https://www.congress.gov/114/plaws/publ255/PLAW-114publ255.pdf

Van Denend, J., Ford, K., Berg, P., Edens, E. L., & Cooke, J. (2022). The body, the mind, and the spirit: Including the spiritual domain in mental health care. *Journal of Religion and Health, 61*(5), 3571–3588.

Wampold, B. E., & Imel, Z. E. (2015). *The great psychotherapy debate: The evidence for what makes psychotherapy work (2nd ed.).* Routledge.

Wanden-Berghe, R. G., Sanz-Valero, J., & Wanden-Berghe, C. (2011). The application of mindfulness to eating disorders treatment: A systematic review. *Eating Disorders, 19*(1), 34–48.

Wilfley, D. E., Welch, R. R., Stein, R. I., Spurrell, E. B., Cohen, L. R., Saelens, B. E., Dounchis, J. Z., Frank, M. A., Wiseman, C. V., & Matt, G. E. (2002). *A randomized comparison of group cognitive-behavioral therapy and group interpersonal psychotherapy for the treatment of overweight individuals with binge-eating disorder.* Archives of General Psychiatry, 59(8), 713–721.

Yager, J., Devlin, M. J., Halmi, K. A., Herzog, D. B., Mitchell, J. E., Powers, P., & Zerbe, K. J. (2014). *Guideline watch: Practice guideline for the treatment of patients with eating disorders (3rd ed.).* Focus, 12(4), 416–431.

Zerbe, K. J. (2020). *Integrated treatment of eating disorders: Beyond the body betrayed.* Routledge.

Chapter 4

What All Therapies Have in Common

Overview

- *At the heart of all therapeutic approaches lies the common factors framework, which highlights the core elements shared across modalities.* These non-specific factors remind us that beyond techniques and protocols, what heals most consistently is the quality of human connection.
- *The therapeutic alliance stands out as the most critical of these factors, a concept shown to predict positive outcomes across diagnoses, including eating disorders.* In this chapter, we explore why the alliance matters so deeply and how it shapes the trajectory of treatment.
- *The alliance itself is influenced by numerous variables including the client's attachment history and readiness for change to the therapist's presence, empathy, and ability to manage power dynamics.* These forces either deepen trust or create ruptures that must be skillfully navigated.
- *Assessment and measurement tools offer clinicians valuable ways to track and strengthen the alliance, particularly in the context of eating disorder treatment.* Used thoughtfully, these tools can transform vague impressions into concrete strategies for improving care.
- *Attachment theory provides a powerful lens for understanding the alliance, revealing how early relational patterns are re-enacted in therapy.* Adolescents and adults bring different challenges and opportunities to the therapeutic bond, requiring clinicians to adapt their stance with developmental sensitivity.
- *Ultimately, the therapeutic alliance is the bridge through which authenticity can emerge.* When clients feel seen, safe, and empowered, they move beyond compliance into genuine connection, a process that is both profoundly healing and deeply human.

For nearly a year, Erin worked as a therapist in a residential eating disorder program. Her shelves overflowed with manuals including CBT-E, FBT, DBT, and she could quote Fairburn verbatim. Staff affectionately called her the "protocol queen." Her notes were meticulous, her interventions precise, and her fidelity checklists always flawless.

DOI: 10.4324/9781003632016-5

Despite doing everything "by the book," some clients stalled. A few even seemed to slip backward. Erin noticed a pattern: clients responded early to structure that included meal support, cognitive work, body image skills, but then plateaued or emotionally withdrew. When conflicts arose such as resistance to weight goals, frustration with directives, Erin leaned harder into the models, leaving little space for the relationship. Sessions became efficient … but distant.

During a professional development talk on therapeutic alliance, I shared the research: that across all modalities, the greatest drivers of change aren't specific techniques but common factors, a strong therapeutic relationship, empathy, shared meaning, and the therapist's authentic presence. Afterward, Erin asked to meet. She confessed she cared deeply about her clients but realized she had been hiding behind the manual. Somewhere along the way, she had equated good therapy with keeping herself out of the room.

Erin began to step outside of the box. She slowed down. She made room for clients' stories instead of racing to worksheets. She asked what they needed not only from treatment, but from her. Something shifted. Clients opened. Ruptures became repairable. Erin felt more grounded, more connected, more effective. Manuals remained tools, but no longer the engine. She discovered what nearly every seasoned therapist eventually learns: what heals is not the protocol alone, but the person delivering it is the vehicle for change: the relationship, the presence, the humanity.

This chapter focuses on defining concepts that are the cornerstone of effective, authentic care, highlighting common factors that contribute to successful outcomes. The idea of authenticity in therapy, which is characterized as the therapist's sincere, open, and compassionate interaction with the client—is central to fostering a supportive environment for healing. Drawing from common factors literature (e.g., Norcross & Lambert, 2018, Wampold & Imel, 2015), this chapter explores the building of the therapeutic relationship through the therapeutic alliance, the process of building trust and rapport, and the use of empathy.

The therapeutic alliance is widely recognized as a key predictor of treatment success, particularly in psychotherapies for eating disorders (Wampold, 2015; Norcross & Lambert, 2018). Additionally, this chapter introduces how power dynamics influence the therapeutic relationship, highlighting how therapists can navigate imbalances with sensitivity and care to empower clients (Duncan et al., 2010). Overall, this chapter will provide readers with the understanding of how to form and sustain authentic relationships in therapy to ultimately promote positive treatment outcomes with clients.

How Do Clients Change?

There are many different types of therapy, hundreds at least. There are many papers and books published on the efficacy of various therapeutic models. And yet, while many of these therapies were developed with thoughtful theoretical explanations on how to do therapy, there is less evidence on the actual scientific knowledge regarding what brings about change (Cuijpers et al., 2019). Two different paradigms are used to explain the effectiveness of therapy: (1) specific theories and (2) common factors (Hyland, 2020). Research indicates that several therapeutic approaches produce roughly similar results (Norcross, 1995; Wampold 2001). This common factor perspective of change purports that the positive effects of therapies are actually a result of "nonspecific" or common factors in therapy.

What Are Common Factors?

Common factors, which may also be known as non-specific factors, are the things that all therapies have in common. The common factor approach recognizes that specific techniques and particular models are often not the key to success in therapy. According to Norcross and Lambert (2018) common factors in psychotherapy refer to elements that are present across different therapeutic approaches and are considered key contributors to positive outcomes, such as a strong therapeutic alliance, therapist empathy, positive regard, client expectations for improvement, collaboration, goal consensus, and the ability to manage countertransference.

Saul Rosenzweig first introduced the idea of common factors in 1936 using an analogy from Lewis Carroll's *Alice's Adventures in Wonderland* in which the dodo bird suddenly announces at the end of the race that "everybody has won and all must have prizes." This premise, later deemed the dodo bird verdict, asserts that all therapies have comparable effects and are really not all that different from each other. For nearly a century, other scholars have built on this concept. Wampold (2001) and later Sprenkle and Blow (2004) framed common factors within the contextual model of psychotherapy. This perspective emphasizes that the effectiveness of therapy is driven more by the shared elements across different approaches rather than by the unique mechanisms of specific therapeutic modalities. Wampold (2001), in *The Great Psychotherapy Debate*, challenged the traditional medical model of psychotherapy, which focuses on diagnosing and treating specific symptoms with targeted interventions. Instead, Wampold proposed that the benefits of therapy arise from contextual or relational factors present in any therapeutic encounter, rather than from the specific techniques of different modalities. Sprenkle and Blow (2004) expanded on this idea in the context of couple and family therapy, highlighting the shared processes that facilitate change across different therapeutic systems, which will be explored more in a later chapter.

The Contextual Model of Common Factors

In 2015, Budge and Wampold presented the contextual model of common factors, which identifies three primary pathways through which therapy fosters improvement: (1) the real relationship, (2) expectations and hope, and (3) engagement in therapeutic tasks. To begin any effective clinician–client relationship, Wampold argues that an initial therapeutic bond is needed. In his 2015 paper, Wampold states,

> The formation of the initial bond is a combination of bottom-up and top-down processing. Humans make a very rapid determination (within 100 ms [milliseconds]), based on viewing the face of another human, of whether the other person is trustworthy or not, suggesting that patients make very rapid judgments about whether they can trust their therapist.
>
> (p. 270)

He continues that in the initial therapeutic encounter, a true meeting of strangers, a client is making quick impressions based on many factors including: the office and therapist physical presentation; things that you think, feel, see, and smell when you enter into a new space. These observations tie in with the statistic I often quote to my colleagues: the most common number of therapy sessions an individual attends is one, which means that if there is not an initial connection, there will likely not be another opportunity. Therefore, it is essential that a clinician consider the three pathways Budge and Wampold (2015) present to effectively treat their clients.

1 The Real Relationship

The real relationship is defined as genuine, authentic connection between clinician and client, characterized by trust, mutual respect, and a sense of collaboration. Budge and Wampold (2015) argued that techniques serve primarily to engage the client in the therapeutic process and to demonstrate the therapist's credibility, while the healing context created by the common factors drives most of the improvement. In today's culture of loneliness, now more than ever, the therapeutic relationship can serve as a deep human connection that combats isolation and provides support. Relationships are "real" through the authentic experience of being seen, feeling valued, and being known by oneself and others.

This is especially critical in eating disorder treatment, where secrecy, shame, and bodily distrust often leave clients profoundly disconnected from themselves and others. A real relationship offers a corrective emotional experience: clients learn that their worth is not contingent on weight, compliance, or perfection, and that their most vulnerable parts can be welcomed rather than hidden. In this context, authenticity is not an abstract ideal, it is an active ingredient in helping clients rebuild trust in their bodies, their needs, and their capacity for connection.

2 Expectations and Hope

Expectations and hope refer to the client's belief in the therapeutic process and the expectation that positive change is possible. This factor, often conceptualized as expectancy, mastery, or self-efficacy, reflects the client's confidence that recovery can be achieved. Importantly, it also includes the clinician's belief in the client, which is an essential contributor to the therapeutic atmosphere. Clients draw meaning not only from the techniques offered, but from the therapist's conviction that these efforts are worthwhile. In this way, the therapist's clear explanation of the treatment approach, transparency about goals, and confidence in its efficacy help reinforce a shared expectation of progress.

These effects are particularly relevant in eating disorder treatment. Many clients have a long history of symptoms, multiple failed treatment attempts, or comorbid depression and anxiety, all of which can erode motivation and hope (Zaitsoff et al., 2008). Low weight, malnutrition, cognitive rigidity, and hopelessness may further diminish a client's belief that recovery is possible. In this context, setting realistic, values-aligned goals and celebrating incremental progress can strengthen agency and reinforce change. When a therapist communicates hope that is genuine, consistent, and without minimizing the client's suffering, it provides a counterweight to the internal voices of doubt, perfectionism, and shame that often accompany eating disorders.

Hope is not naïve optimism; it is a shared commitment to possibility. The belief that change can happen is, in itself, a catalyst for change.

3 Engagement in Therapeutic Tasks/Goals (Specific Ingredients)

In the fields of psychotherapy and eating disorder treatment, a big debate is how and what specific therapy techniques actually help people feel better. Engagement in therapeutic tasks refers to the collaborative effort between the clinician and client to identify goals and engage in meaningful therapeutic activities. Therapeutic tasks refer to the structured, collaborative activities and interventions that align with agreed-upon treatment goals. The contextual model suggests that techniques work not just because of what they do directly but also because they help clients expect that therapy will help, which leads people to take healthier actions.

In eating disorder therapy, these tasks often include structured interventions such as meal planning, cognitive restructuring of disordered beliefs, and monitoring behaviors. However, it is critical for a clinician to include an integrative set of tasks with their clients, including things such as working to improve relationships with others and themselves and exploring emotions. Effective engagement in these tasks builds the client's sense of agency and helps them reconnect with their body's natural cues.

All these actions support healing. And, in order to do any of this well, the client and clinician need a strong relationship. Without trust and shared goals, it's hard for clients to try new techniques that could help them. So, according to the contextual model, any therapy that helps a client take action can be effective. This is different from the view that only specific techniques are what make therapy work.

The Therapeutic Alliance Is the Key Common Factor Across All Approaches

While many authors have attempted to define what common factors are, here I will focus on the common factor that is likely the most prominent in all research: the therapeutic alliance. Wampold and Flückiger (2023) reported at the time of their publication, a search for "alliance" in the PsychINFO database produced around 5,000 publications! Alliance is often defined through Bordin's (1979) tripartite model, which asserts that alliance is the clinician and client's: (1) agreement on the goals of treatment; (2) agreement on the tasks of treatment; (3) the bond between the client and clinician (the relationship). In Bordin's conceptualization of alliance, he asserts the didactic nature of the relationship in that it occurs between the two people. Although it may be perceived differently with each person, alliance is created through the dynamics between both the client and the clinician.

Once a client and a clinician have made the commitment to work together, the building of the relationship is key. The therapeutic alliance, often referred to as the relationship between clinician and client, is a cornerstone of effective therapy and a key predictor of positive treatment outcomes (Wampold, 2015; Norcross & Lambert, 2018). A meta-analysis by Norcross and Lambert (2018) found that the strength of the therapeutic alliance is a more consistent predictor of positive outcomes than specific therapeutic techniques. Cuijpers et al. (2019) also found that a stronger alliance is associated with better therapeutic outcomes in more than 200 studies.

The therapeutic relationship provides the client with a connection to someone who cares. This is why it is the cornerstone of the common factors approach, which consistently predicts treatment outcomes across various mental health conditions, including eating disorders. Research shows that a strong alliance facilitates trust, fosters client engagement, and enhances motivation for change (Graves et al., 2017). In the context of eating disorders, this is particularly significant because clients often struggle with ambivalence toward treatment (Abbate-Daga et al., 2013). The ability of therapists to establish a collaborative, empathetic, and validating relationship is a key component of fostering adherence to treatment and addressing the complex emotions tied to disordered eating behaviors.

Real Relationships Versus Therapeutic Alliance

While the "real relationship" and the therapeutic alliance are not synonymous, they are closely related. Gelso (2014) identified differences in that the real relationship has a specific focus on personal connection while alliance relates to the collaborative work that occurs, with bond being the factor between them. Vaz et al. (2024) identified the real relationship and working alliance as "sister concepts" and aimed to examine these as two distinct constructs through a replication of a previous meta-analysis. While attempting to differentiate between concepts as they relate to outcomes, their findings suggested a significant association. The authors noted that both the real relationship and the working alliance are both common factors and can be seen as significant contributors of successful treatment, regardless of theoretical approach. Therefore, moving forward in this chapter, I will use the terms alliance, working alliance, therapeutic alliance, helping alliance, the real relationship, relationship, and therapeutic relationship mostly interchangeably.

The Importance of the Therapeutic Alliance in Eating Disorder Treatment

In eating disorder and body image treatment, the therapeutic alliance has a unique and important role. The relationship between client and clinician serves as a buffer against the challenges of addressing deeply ingrained behaviors and beliefs, providing a secure foundation for clients to confront and reframe their experiences. The therapeutic alliance is cultivated by active listening, self-disclosing appropriately, establishing clear boundaries, addressing transference and countertransference, and working through ruptures, all indicators of the building blocks to authentic relationships.

Developing a strong therapeutic alliance is crucial when working with individuals facing body image disturbances and eating disorders, as it significantly influences treatment outcomes. The therapeutic alliance plays a critical role in treating eating disorders. Research has consistently shown that the therapeutic alliance is a reliable predictor of treatment outcomes across various disorders, including eating disorders (Bordin, 1979; Flückiger et al., 2018). In a systematic review, Jenkins et al. (2021) found that a strong alliance not only fosters engagement in treatment but also reduces treatment dropout rates, a significant concern in eating disorder therapy. Similarly, Keski-Rahkonen and Tozzi (2005) demonstrated that clients who perceive their therapists as warm, empathic, and collaborative report higher levels of treatment adherence and symptom improvement. Overall, a strong therapeutic alliance predicts positive treatment outcomes across different therapeutic approaches and client populations (Flückiger et al., 2018).

However, the impact of the therapeutic alliance in eating disorder treatment appears to vary by diagnosis, age, and individual treatment settings. The therapeutic alliance's impact is stronger in young clients and those with anorexia (Graves et al., 2017). Two meta-analyses indicated that early eating disorder symptom reduction predicted stronger alliance (Graves et al., 2017; Vrabel et al., 2015). For all eating disorder treatments, building a robust therapeutic alliance can be challenging due to the ambivalence and resistance inherent to these disorders, yet it remains essential for improving treatment retention and outcomes (Brauhardt et al., 2014).

Eating Disorder Diagnostic Differences

In anorexia nervosa, the ego-syntonic nature of the disorder and resistance to weight gain often complicate establishing shared therapeutic goals. Clients may struggle to reconcile the necessity of weight restoration with their deep-seated fears and self-conceptualization tied to being thin (Brauhardt et al., 2014). The therapeutic alliance can be hindered by misunderstandings or misalignments regarding treatment tasks, such as dietary changes or the reduction of compulsive behaviors. This is often an ongoing challenge in eating disorder treatment. Many relational ruptures occur between therapists, dieticians, and medical providers when treatment teams attempt to make significant changes with meal plans and medications. Despite the desire for significant relationships, many clients with anorexia nervosa struggle with the ongoing ambivalence regarding change, particularly as it relates to weight gain, and as a treatment team attempts to push change, it can paralyze a client's ability to continue to connect. Lev Ari et al. (2025) identified a significant theme that clients often experience: while they deeply desire a supportive relationship, they also fear disappointment and pain, often leading to ambivalence or rejection of their therapist.

In a qualitative metasynthesis of adult client experiences with anorexia nervosa, therapeutic alliance was a significant finding (Conti et al., 2020). More specifically, respect, being treated as a person not an illness, and being emotionally held were critical to clients' experiences. Additionally, other aspects that impact the therapeutic relationship included the therapists' hope and trust in the person in recovery as well as taking their concerns seriously. The themes of trust, hope, and respect emerge consistently in research as well as in clinical practice.

For bulimia nervosa, while the ambivalence regarding change is less pronounced than in anorexia nervosa, the fear of weight gain is still significant as well as the cyclical nature of binging and purging behaviors, which create barriers to a therapeutic alliance. Clients with bulimia nervosa may find task agreements, such as reducing purging or introducing regular eating patterns, emotionally challenging (Treasure et al., 2007). Studies suggest that while the therapeutic alliance positively predicts treatment outcomes, its role in bulimia nervosa may be less pronounced compared to anorexia nervosa, potentially due to differing levels of motivation and symptom presentation (Graves et al., 2017). Despite this, an effective therapeutic alliance, built on mutual understanding and a strong therapeutic bond, has been shown to enhance client engagement and improve adherence to cognitive behavioral therapy, the standard treatment for bulimia nervosa.

Barr et al. (2024) asserted that binge eating disorder and bulimia nervosa were associated with higher dependency and a greater client-driven contribution to a strong therapeutic alliance. In their investigation of the therapeutic alliance in face-to-face versus remote self-help guided treatment for binge eating disorder, Jenkins and Wake (2024) indicated that clients rated alliance higher than clinicians. Additionally, aligned with other studies, face-to-face treatment yielded consistently higher therapeutic alliance ratings. Although limited in findings given low response at the later data collection points, this research did conclude that early alliance was not associated with treatment completion or post-treatment abstinence from binge eating. While other research discussed here supports the theory that early symptom change and therapeutic alliance support positive treatment outcomes, that did not appear to be the case in the individuals with binge eating disorder who were part of the study.

Factors That Impact the Therapeutic Alliance

The therapeutic alliance is built upon trust, empathy, and collaboration between the clinician and client. Across all eating disorders, age and treatment setting play crucial roles in determining the strength and impact of the therapeutic alliance. Developing alliance involves several key components. Bordin (1979) initially conceptualized the therapeutic alliance as a collaborative and dynamic relationship between a clinician and a client, including agreement on goals, collaboration on tasks, and bond. The emotional connection and trust between the therapist and client form the foundation of the therapeutic alliance, the bond. This bond is characterized by mutual respect, trust, empathy, and understanding. It creates a safe environment where the client feels comfortable sharing their experiences and emotions. The recognition of therapist factors, such as empathy, authenticity, and cultural competence, as well as client factors, such as readiness for change and trust in the therapist, play a significant role in the development of alliance.

Client Factors

Client factors, such as readiness for change, resilience, and support systems, are also critical in the common factors framework. Prochaska and DiClemente's (1983) stages of change model highlights the importance of tailoring interventions to the client's motivational stage, particularly in eating disorders, where denial or ambivalence about the need for change is common and can impact alliance development. While it is well established that strong alliance is linked with positive treatment outcomes, what is less established in the field are the client factors that influence the therapeutic alliance (Barr et al., 2024). Literature has looked toward interpersonal patterns, attachment history, personality traits, and early life experiences to better understand client factors.

I have often spoken to clients, families, and training clinicians about the importance and challenges of understanding motivation and stages of change. With eating disorders, most individuals do not move through the stages of change in a linear fashion. Rather, if I could visually depict change, it would be in a three-dimensional, multi-pronged tapestry of weaves. For most individuals struggling with an eating disorder, they can be committed to one aspect of change while simultaneously feeling paralyzed in another. For example, in a client struggling with bulimia nervosa, they may be in an action phase of change for discontinuing purging behaviors but in a pre-contemplation phase as it relates to weight gain. These two aspects of recovery can occur at the same time, however, but are in conflict with each other, impacting the ability of movement. Through the therapeutic relationship, a clinician may be able to aid a client in the discovery of this intrapersonal conflict.

Therapist Factors

Therapist factors, including empathy, cultural competence, and self-awareness, are integral to the common factors approach and development of alliance. Additionally, therapist factors such as experience, confidence, and degree of engagement certainly influence the development of the alliance. It is very possible that some therapists are better able to form alliance than others. In this case, therapist factors have more of an impact on alliance development.

Therapists treating eating disorders must balance validating the client's experiences with challenging maladaptive beliefs about food, weight, and body image. Research underscores the importance of therapist authenticity and nonjudgmental attitudes in creating a safe environment for clients to explore vulnerabilities (Ramjan & Fogarty, 2019). By focusing on relational dynamics and the universal principles of effective therapy, the common factors approach offers a flexible, client-centered framework for addressing the multifaceted challenges of eating disorders.

Family and Age-Related Factors

In their qualitative assessment of change processes in eating disorder family therapy, Cripps et al. (2024) remarked on the impact of the therapeutic relationship in treatment. Their findings supported the need for clinicians to hold and contain both a client and family's distress. They remarked that trust and engagement should be a priority from the onset of treatment. One remark from a client in the study exemplified how the therapeutic relationship is a vehicle for authenticity: "An important part of the turnaround was when I invited her into my feelings .... I started to trust her [therapist]" (Cripps et al., 2024, p. 13).

Adolescents

For adolescents with eating disorders, family-based therapy introduces an additional layer of complexity, requiring a balance between an individual therapeutic alliance and parental involvement. Parental alliance has been shown to influence treatment outcomes, particularly in weight restoration for adolescents (Forsberg et al., 2013). In looking at the alliance with adolescents with anorexia nervosa and comparing treatment approaches of family-based therapy and adolescent focused therapy, Forsberg et al. (2013) found that while a strong therapeutic alliance may be important in contributing to treatment success, it is not sufficient on its own to produce meaningful clinical change. These researchers assessed alliance after session four to allow for meaningful relationship development while also measuring it prior to symptom change occurring. These findings highlight that although often a difficult population to navigate as a clinician (adolescents with anorexia nervosa), a strong alliance is possible.

In a recent study published in the *American Journal of Psychotherapy*, Ruzicka et al. (2024) examined the impact of the therapeutic relationship on treatment outcomes for adolescent girls experiencing loss-of-control eating. The findings indicated that those who experienced greater connection ("emotional bond") experienced a reduction in symptoms, and it was also a predictor of positive treatment outcomes. This suggests that a strong emotional connection between the clinician and client is crucial. Interestingly, this study looked at adolescent girls, an often tricky subpopulation to treat. By placing a focus on connection and trust, clinicians can positively influence treatment trajectory.

Adults

Meanwhile, for adults, particularly those with chronic anorexia nervosa, building a therapeutic alliance may be critical for treatment retention and addressing deep-seated ambivalence (Brown et al., 2013). The bidirectional relationship between therapeutic alliance and symptom change further underscores the importance of early intervention and regular assessment of therapeutic alliance to foster a positive feedback loop throughout treatment (Accurso & Garland, 2015). The therapeutic alliance is an essential yet complex component of eating disorder treatment, with its effectiveness influenced by client-specific factors, such as diagnosis, age, and severity. While the challenges in building a strong therapeutic alliance are significant, especially in anorexia nervosa due to its ego-syntonic characteristics, tailored approaches that prioritize empathy, collaboration, and flexibility can improve outcomes. A comprehensive meta-analysis of adult psychotherapy found that the therapeutic alliance is a reliable and significant predictor of treatment outcomes, demonstrating that the quality of the collaborative relationship between therapist and adult client plays a central role in therapeutic effectiveness across modalities and settings (Flückiger et al., 2018).

In their 2024 study published in *Frontiers in Psychology*, Muzi et al. explored the direct and indirect effects of psychological well-being and the early therapeutic alliance on treatment outcomes in individuals with eating disorders. The research aimed to assess how various dimensions of psychological well-being and the quality of the initial therapeutic relationship influence clients' responses to therapy. Findings revealed that dimensions of psychological well-being—specifically autonomy, positive relations, and self-acceptance—were significantly associated with clinically significant change. Additionally, personal growth and self-acceptance were linked to reliable change. The early therapeutic alliance demonstrated both direct and indirect effects on therapy outcomes, predicting clinically significant and reliable symptom reduction. These results underscore the importance of fostering both psychological well-being and a robust therapeutic alliance in the treatment of eating disorders. Interventions that enhance clients' autonomy, ability to form positive relationships, and self-acceptance may contribute to more favorable therapy outcomes. Moreover, building a strong therapeutic alliance early in the treatment process appears crucial, as it not only directly influences outcomes but also amplifies the beneficial effects of clients' psychological well-being on their recovery.

Adolescent vs. Adult Considerations

Adolescents with eating disorders present unique relational challenges. Developmentally, teens may be more sensitive to issues of autonomy and may initially view the therapist with suspicion or resistance, especially given the ego-syntonic nature of illnesses like anorexia. The therapist must often form an alliance not only with the young client but also in family-based treatments with the parents. Research has shown that a strong early therapeutic alliance can significantly improve adolescent outcomes. For example, in a cohort of teens with anorexia, those who reported a better early alliance with their therapist achieved weight restoration more quickly and were over two times more likely to reach target weight goals (Bourion-Bédès et al., 2013). This is a powerful reminder that engaging the adolescent in a trusting, collaborative bond can accelerate recovery. In practice, clinicians should balance being authoritative and empathic, instilling hope and motivation, while also respecting the adolescent's need for control and independence.

In adult eating disorder therapy, alliance formation may hinge on addressing long-standing interpersonal schemas; many adult patients with eating disorders have histories of attachment trauma or invalidation. Here, too, the therapist's consistent empathy, reliability, and non-judgmental stance can gradually disconfirm the patient's expectations of criticism or abandonment, thereby strengthening the alliance. In the reverse scenario, if alliance struggles or fails to develop, insecurely attached clients may be prone to disengage or drop out of treatment. A strong alliance through an attachment lens is key to improving engagement and retention in care (Berry & Danquah 2020).

How to Know If There Is an Alliance

There are multiple reliable ways to determine whether a strong therapeutic alliance has been established—it does not need to be left to intuition alone. Alliance can be systematically assessed using validated measures completed by clients, clinicians, or independent observers at various points throughout treatment, allowing for ongoing monitoring and adjustment of care (Horvath & Bedi, 2002; Flückiger et al., 2018). These tools provide a structured way to evaluate the collaborative and relational aspects of therapy that are strongly linked to outcomes.

Building on this, Saxler et al. (2024) identified five core themes consistently reflected across therapeutic alliance measures: (1) therapist self-disclosure and authenticity, (2) agreement on therapeutic goals, (3) client participation and motivation, (4) trust and a sense of secure attachment, and (5) attunement to the client's individual needs and capacities. Together, these elements capture both the relational depth and collaborative nature of effective therapy, reinforcing that alliance is not a static construct but an evolving, measurable process that can be intentionally strengthened to improve treatment engagement and outcomes.

Therapeutic alliance is commonly assessed using validated instruments such as the working alliance inventory (WAI), which measures key components of the relationship including emotional bond, agreement on treatment goals, and collaboration on therapeutic tasks (Horvath & Greenberg, 1989). Evidence suggests that these alliance ratings, particularly when assessed early and monitored throughout treatment, are strong predictors of psychotherapy outcomes, supporting their use as ongoing clinical tools to inform treatment planning and enhance patient engagement (Flückiger et al., 2018; Ardito & Rabinowitz 2011).

Assessment and Measurement Tools Available for Eating Disorder Clinicians

Research on the therapeutic alliance has consistently shown that a majority of alliance–outcome studies rely on a small set of well-established post-session measures, most commonly the Working Alliance Inventory (WAI), California Psychotherapy Alliance Scale (CALPAS), Helping Alliance Questionnaire (HAQ), and Vanderbilt Psychotherapy Process Scale (VPPS) (Horvath & Bedi, 2002). In clinical practice, the WAI is most frequently utilized due to its strong psychometric properties and its alignment with core alliance constructs of bond, goals, and tasks.

There are a variety of tools to evaluate the therapeutic alliance. Alliance assessments offer an opportunity to look at alliance from different perspectives including client-rated, therapist-rated, observer-rated. Selection of the appropriate alliance measure depends on treatment modality (individual vs. family-based), age group, and clinical goals, with alliance tracking increasingly viewed as a component of best practice in eating disorder care (Zaitsoff et al., 2015; Geller & Srikameswaran, 2006). Incorporating alliance measurement into clinical practice encourages therapist reflexivity, supports rupture repair, and ultimately contributes to a more attuned, responsive therapeutic process. Here are some tools that clinicians can use with clients.

Working Alliance Inventory

The WAI assesses alliance dimensions through both client and therapist ratings. The WAI has demonstrated strong psychometric properties and is adaptable to various clinical populations, including individuals with eating disorders and other complex presentations (Horvath & Greenberg, 1989).

The California Psychotherapy Alliance Scale

CALPAS has been used in studies exploring psychodynamic or relational therapy for eating disorders. This tool measures client involvement, therapist warmth, and agreement on goals and tasks. Additionally, CALPAS has been applied to understand alliance rupture and repair processes in eating disorder treatment (Gaston, 1991).

The Helping Alliance Questionnaire

HAQ is a self-report measure assessing the strength and quality of the alliance from both client and therapist perspectives. This tool measures trust, collaboration, and perceived helpfulness, which are particularly important when clients have ambivalence toward recovery or fear of weight restoration (Alexander & Luborsky, 1986).

The Vanderbilt Psychotherapy Process Scale

VPPS differs from other instruments in that it is an observer-rated measure designed to assess alliance behaviors from recorded sessions. This tool has been used in eating disorder studies, especially in family-based treatment settings, to evaluate therapist behaviors that foster collaboration. It focuses on warmth, empathy, and client participation, which are critical in working with adolescents with anorexia nervosa (Shelef & Diamond, 2008).

Session Rating Scale

For a picture of a client's perception of alliance in real time at the end of a session, the session rating scale (SRS) can be used. The SRS offers a practical, user-friendly tool for routine outcome monitoring, which allows therapists to address alliance ruptures promptly and collaboratively (Duncan et al., 2003).

The Family-Based Therapy Alliance Scale (FBT-TAS)

This was specifically developed for use in family-based treatment for adolescents with anorexia nervosa. This tool evaluates the alliance between parents and therapist, recognizing the central role of caregivers in treatment. The FBT-TAS can be helpful to track parental engagement and trust in the therapeutic process (Accurso et al., 2020).

Attachment and Alliance

Forming the therapeutic relationship can be complicated by attachment styles, the characteristic ways clients (and therapists) relate in close relationships. While secure attachment tends to predict positive therapeutic alliances in eating disorders, insecure attachment has been the opposite, interfering with positive therapeutic alliance development (Castonguay et al., 2013; Folke et al., 2015). Research shows that individuals with eating disorders exhibit significantly higher rates of insecure attachment as compared to community controls (Jewell et al., 2023). Attachment insecurity is associated with greater difficulty developing trust and collaboration in therapy. Bonds or perceived bonds with caregivers and exposure to adverse childhood experiences may have a significant influence on adult attachment and interpersonal styles, and are therefore relevant and important in context of the therapeutic relationship and alliance (Barr et al., 2024). In other words, clients who are anxiously preoccupied or avoidantly detached based on childhood experiences and are now experiencing these within their adult relationships may struggle to fully engage with a therapist, potentially straining the alliance and relationship development. This is especially relevant in eating disorder and body image treatments, where issues of control, self-worth, and trust are central. Recognizing the interplay between attachment and alliance is thus critical for clinicians working with both adults and adolescents with eating disorders.

Research supports observations about attachment and alliance. Three meta-analyses have been conducted on the attachment–alliance relation (see Diener et al., 2009; Diener & Monroe, 2011; Bernecker et al., 2014). In all three of these studies, significant correlations were found between the two factors. Notsu et al. (2024) performed an updated meta-analysis looking at adult attachment and alliance. They note that two dimensions are often investigated when looking at attachment insecurity, attachment anxiety, and attachment avoidance, noting that both attachment and anxiety have been related to poor working alliance. These authors offered adapted definitions of attachment anxiety as "preoccupation with being close to an attachment figure and heightened anxiety in the face of abandonment or separation" and attachment avoidance as an "effort to keep one's emotional and behavioral distance from relationship partners, as well as a general disbelief of others' good intentions."

Client Attachment

An emerging evidence base confirms that client attachment style correlates with the quality of the working alliance. In an updated meta-analysis, Notsu et al. (2024) found that higher attachment anxiety and attachment avoidance in adult clients were each associated with weaker client-rated alliances (Notsu et al., 2024). This study suggests, not surprisingly, that insecurely attached clients tend to have more difficulty forming strong therapeutic bonds. For example, an anxiously attached client might fear rejection or crave reassurance, while an avoidantly attached client might be uncomfortable with emotional closeness—both scenarios can hinder collaboration and trust in therapy.

Clients with attachment anxiety are often hypersensitive around real or imagined signs of abandonment. Unfortunately, this perception can include a clinician's vacation or, even in higher levels of care, leaving for the weekend. In higher levels of care, clinical directors are recommended to run process group on Monday mornings in an effort to start off the work week rebuilding interpersonal relationships with clients after a weekend without their primary staff "caregivers." The threat of abandonment also becomes a significant issue around the holidays and traditional vacation times. Clinicians should pay particular attention to a client's needs and attend to relational fears around these times.

Clients with attachment avoidance may present as more "oppositional" in treatment, putting up walls to a therapist's attempts at alliance development. Understanding client attachment styles is critical for clinicians in the early stages of relational formation in therapy.

Therapist Attachment

Notably, therapist attachment style also matters. Bucci et al. (2016) observed that therapists with insecure attachment styles had more trouble building alliances, particularly when treating highly symptomatic clients. In this study, certain therapist–client pairings were especially challenging; one report noted that an avoidant therapist working with an avoidant client was "most demanding" in terms of establishing trust and was prone to alliance ruptures. Similarly, an anxiously attached therapist may become overinvolved or struggle with boundaries. A systematic review by Degnan et al. (2016) concluded that therapist attachment styles (and their interaction with client styles) can influence the alliance and treatment outcomes. The key message is that therapists should be aware of their own attachment-related tendencies and how these might interact with the client's style (Degnan et al., 2016). By reflecting on and managing our own attachment reactions (with supervision or in their own therapy), clinicians can provide a more consistent and secure therapeutic presence.

Clinical Implications

Insecure attachments are not only common in eating disorder populations, but they also have direct clinical implications. One longitudinal study of adults with anorexia or bulimia found that attachment insecurity predicted a poorer treatment trajectory over one year of enhanced cognitive behavioral therapy (Rossi et al., 2022). Clients with higher attachment insecurity showed less improvement in eating pathology, which in turn maintained greater body image distress. These findings underscore that unaddressed attachment issues can undermine the effectiveness of eating disorder treatments and perpetuate a negative body image. Clinically, this suggests that integrating an attachment-informed perspective into eating disorder treatment can be beneficial.

How Therapeutic Alliance Promotes Authenticity

The influence of the therapeutic alliance in promoting authenticity cannot be understated. Research suggests that a strong alliance fosters an environment where authenticity is not only welcomed but encouraged, allowing clients to navigate their challenges more effectively. The intertwining of authenticity with relational dynamics offers rich implications for therapeutic practices addressing eating disorders and body image issues. This nuanced understanding emphasizes the importance of fostering authentic relationships in clinical settings, suggesting that these relationships are essential for effective intervention and client growth.

Miri's Case: Fostering Change Between the Techniques and Interventions

When Miri first entered the partial hospitalization program (PHP) I worked at early in my career, she made it clear she was not there to make friends—and that included me. A 27-year-old client with a history of binge eating disorder and alcohol misuse, who had been previously given a diagnosis of borderline personality disorder, Miri was fiercely guarded. She rolled her eyes in group therapy; did not interact with others in milieu downtime, stating she "needed space"; and met any hint of emotional vulnerability with sarcasm. Most of all, she distrusted the very idea of connection—and me.

As a young therapist, relatively new to the PHP setting, I was assigned as Miri's primary therapist. Miri was sharp and rough around the edges. She had experienced more life than I had, and we both intrinsically knew it, although never spoke it out loud. Still early on in my career, I was focused on "doing the right thing," which meant using evidence-based treatments, primarily DBT and CBT-E. Even then, adherence to strict protocols didn't feel like the "real me." I was overly concerned with not overstepping professional boundaries so did not reveal much of myself in sessions. As a newer therapist, a structured approach felt safe. Miri responded to me with detachment. "You're just like the rest of them," she'd mutter. "Smiling like you care but waiting for me to mess up."

One afternoon, Miri entered session angry after an interpersonal issue in a process group in which another group member commented on her presentation. She was spiraling, frustrated by a peer "calling her out" about her lack of progress and ongoing disengagement with others. Instead of jumping to de-escalation techniques or challenging cognitive distortions, I paused, took a deep breath, and responded: "You know, I'm sitting here and I'm feeling a little stuck too. I want you to know I do care. I don't have all the answers on recovery. But I'm not leaving. I'm here." Miri appeared surprised. She stated no one had said that to her before without an alternative goal behind it like getting her to eat.

From that point on, our sessions shifted. Miri remained reactive but also gradually began sharing pieces of her story. The childhood neglect. The nights she binged and drank until she passed out. The fear that if she trusted anyone, she'd be abandoned all over again. I did not try to fix her. I listened and stayed steady.

This was the power of the therapeutic alliance. As our relationship evolved, so did Miri's capacity for authenticity with me, and ultimately with others. She began naming her feelings and exploring her shame, loneliness, hope. She challenged food rituals with more consistency and acknowledged struggles before acting on them. In group, she no longer sat in opposition or silence; instead, she advocated for herself and even offered support to others.

Miri's healing was not just about her meal plan or use of coping skills. It was the space between all the techniques and interventions. When there was a rupture, we worked to repair. Through this, Miri felt seen and heard, which allowed her to be present with herself and others. Through this authentic connection, Miri experienced what she never had before: a relationship grounded in trust, emotional safety, and realness.

As we prepared for discharge, Miri was still a work in progress, but the difference was clear. She had a voice, she had a plan, and most importantly, she had a sense of herself.

As the clinician, I felt profoundly impacted from Miri's treatment too—not because I followed "the rules" of a manual but because I learned that authenticity is not a detour from therapy, it is the therapy.

Relational–cultural theory (Jordan, 2017) emphasizes that growth-fostering relationships are built through mutual empathy and authenticity. Applying this model in eating disorder treatment highlights the importance of relational repair, particularly when clients struggle with emotion dysregulation or personality disorders that challenge consistent engagement. Through an extended and authentic therapeutic relationship, clients learn to experience their emotions without resorting to disordered behaviors and to trust that they can be seen and accepted in their vulnerability.

Fostering authenticity might involve naming relational ruptures, inviting meta-dialogue about the therapy process itself, and holding a non-defensive stance when clients express distrust or ambivalence (Safran & Muran, 2000). Such moments, when navigated with transparency and empathy, not only strengthen the alliance but also teach clients that relationships can withstand conflict and still remain intact, which is an essential insight for recovery from eating disorders, which often thrive in secrecy and isolation.

Developing authenticity within this alliance requires the therapist to cultivate self-awareness, engage in reflective practice, and sometimes judiciously self-disclose in ways that affirm the client's experience and reduce power differentials (Aponte & Kissil, 2016). Therapists must remain attuned to their own emotional reactions and embodiment in the therapeutic space, especially when working with clients who may project their internalized shame or body image distress onto the therapist (Costin, 2007). This attunement enables therapists to respond in ways that validate clients' lived experiences rather than reinforcing disconnection or stigma.

Authenticity in eating disorder therapy is not merely a personal quality of the therapist but is a dynamic process facilitated through the therapeutic alliance. When therapists bring their full human selves into the room, they create the conditions for clients to rediscover their own authentic selves and build the relational capacity necessary for long-term recovery.

Critiques of the Therapeutic Relationship

While I have explored the benefits of the therapeutic relationship in effectively treating eating disorder clients, it does have its challenges and shortcomings. One prominent issue is the difficulty in defining and operationalizing the therapeutic alliance. Bordin's (1979) conceptualization remains widely used, but variations in interpretation across studies lead to inconsistencies in findings (Flückiger et al., 2018). Multiple critiques of this have been written and it is likely time for a research-backed update. Critics of the common factors/contextual model argue that it underemphasizes the importance of specific evidence-based interventions for certain disorders. Earlier debate in the field suggested that perhaps alliance is not important in eating disorder treatment (Brown et al., 2013). More recently, Flückiger et al. (2018) reported on alliance–outcome correlations for various diagnosis. Specific to eating disorders, the alliance–outcome correlation was smaller than it was generally (r =.15 vs. r =.28 in general). However, the model's focus on relational dynamics and the therapeutic environment has been widely acknowledged as central to successful therapy, regardless of modality.

Challenges in Understanding the Therapeutic Alliance

Studying the therapeutic alliance is a bit like studying any meaningful relationship: there are many moving parts, and not all of them are easy to tease apart. Alliance doesn't form in a vacuum; it develops between two people, each bringing their own histories, assumptions, and ways of relating. Research suggests that therapist qualities such as empathy, communication style, and cultural responsiveness shape how safe and understood clients feel (Ackerman & Hilsenroth, 2003). At the same time, client factors, like readiness for change or attachment style, can influence how open they are to connection and collaboration (Levy et al., 2018). When these variables intersect, the process gets complicated. Two equally skilled therapists might have very different experiences with the same approach simply because the clients in front of them need very different things.

Another challenge is figuring out what causes what. We know that strong alliances are linked to better outcomes, but we don't know exactly which comes first. Does a strong alliance help people improve, or do clients who start feeling better naturally perceive the relationship as stronger? Zilcha-Mano (2017) describes this as a chicken-and-egg puzzle. Longitudinal studies hint that it's probably both: people feel safer when therapy is helping, and they make more progress when they feel safe. But these kinds of studies are hard to conduct, especially in eating disorder treatment, where dropout is common (Graves et al., 2017).

Even measuring alliance can get messy. Most tools like the Working Alliance Inventory (WAI) or the Helping Alliance Questionnaire (HAQ) rely on self-report, which means we're left interpreting how clients and therapists feel about their relationship. Those two perspectives don't always match (Horvath et al., 2011). Some therapists think things are going great just as a client is quietly slipping away, or vice versa. Future research may benefit from more independent or third-party evaluations to help sort out these discrepancies.

There's also the issue of who is represented in the research. Much of what we know about alliance comes from Western, educated, and relatively privileged samples (Henrich et al., 2010). Joseph Henrich et al. (2010) introduced the concept of "WEIRD" populations (Western, Educated, Industrialized, Rich, and Democratic), highlighting that much of psychological research—including constructs like the therapeutic alliance—has been derived from relatively privileged and non-representative samples. That means we have limited understanding of how alliance unfolds across different cultural backgrounds, marginalized identities, or treatment contexts. Norcross and Lambert (2019) argue that we need more diverse and real-world studies, not just controlled research, to know how alliance functions in everyday clinical practice.

Finally, therapeutic relationships aren't static. Like any relationship, they change over time. Many studies measure alliance only once or twice, which gives researchers just a snapshot. But snapshots don't tell the full story. Newer models try to capture both the trait-like aspects of alliance (some people simply have an easier or harder time trusting others) and the state-like changes that happen as therapy unfolds (Barr et al., 2024). These distinctions can help us understand why some clients bond quickly while others take more time, and why ruptures aren't failures but natural parts of a dynamic process.

Altogether, these challenges don't diminish the importance of alliance; they simply remind us how complex, human, and context-dependent it really is. Understanding these nuances helps us continue to refine how we study, teach, and nurture strong therapeutic relationships, especially in eating disorder care, where trust and connection are often fragile but profoundly transformative.

Synthesizing the Therapeutic Alliance in Eating Disorder Treatment

Across the psychotherapy literature, the therapeutic alliance consistently predicts treatment outcomes, and eating disorder care is no exception. Although meta-analytic findings show a small but reliable positive association between therapeutic alliance and symptom improvement, this relationship appears particularly meaningful for some subgroups. A systematic review by Werz et al. (2022) concluded that alliance may have its strongest effects among adolescents, regardless of diagnosis, and among adults with anorexia nervosa. This makes intuitive sense: developmental needs for relational safety in youth, and the ego-syntonic nature of anorexia in adults, may heighten the importance of trust, collaboration, and emotional connection in treatment.

While the research base is still growing, and often limited by small samples, homogenous populations, and inconsistent methodology, the overall pattern points to a clear conclusion: the therapeutic relationship matters. Eating disorders are inherently relational illnesses, often characterized by shame, secrecy, ambivalence about recovery, and disconnection from self and others. A strong alliance provides a corrective emotional experience by offering safety, attunement, and non-judgmental presence, which can soften resistance and enhance engagement with behavioral change.

My own experiences as a therapist, supervisor, and program leader over two decades affirm what the data suggest. Even when using structured, manualized approaches, client progress stalls if they do not feel seen, understood, or emotionally held. Conversely, when clients experience genuine connection, when the therapist shows up with empathy, curiosity, flexibility, and belief in their capacity for change, movement becomes possible, even in the face of profound ambivalence.

Overall, the alliance is not simply a backdrop to "real" treatment; it is an active therapeutic ingredient. Its power lies in helping clients tolerate discomfort, take risks, repair ruptures, and imagine a future self no longer governed by the eating disorder. As research continues to evolve, the consistent message remains: effective eating disorder treatment requires not only the right interventions, but the right relationship in which to deliver them.

Power Dynamics in Therapeutic Relationships

A broader understanding of the therapeutic alliance must also account for the inherent power dynamics embedded within the therapy relationship. Psychotherapy is not a neutral interaction; rather, it involves an inherent imbalance in which the clinician holds professional, relational, and institutional power that can shape both the process and outcomes of treatment (Boyd, 1996; Fors, 2021). These dynamics are further influenced by broader sociocultural factors—including race, gender, socioeconomic status, and identity—which intersect with clinical authority and can impact trust, engagement, and perceived safety within the therapeutic space (Fors, 2021; van Mens-Verhulst, 1991). For individuals with eating disorders who may struggle with shame, secrecy, and resistance to treatment, a strong therapeutic alliance can create the safety needed to engage fully in the process of recovery. In the context of eating disorder therapy, where clients often face deep-seated struggles and vulnerabilities, the therapeutic alliance becomes even more critical. As a result, the dynamics of power within the therapeutic relationship are another critical piece of building alliance that can be a challenge. When power remains unexamined, it may contribute to misattunement or disengagement; however, when clinicians intentionally acknowledge and share power through collaborative, transparent, and patient-centered approaches, the therapeutic alliance is strengthened and more equitable, effective care can be achieved (Boyd, 1996; Fors, 2021).

In a systematic review, Albano et al. (2024) examined therapist characteristics that influence the treatment of eating disorders. Analyzing 38 studies from 1980 to July 2023, the review highlighted perspectives from both clients and therapists. From a client perspective, several therapist traits were identified that positively impacted treatment. These included demonstrating warmth and empathy, having a supportive attitude, having an expertise in eating disorders, and appropriate sharing/self-disclosure. Conversely, negative traits such as lack of empathy, judgmental attitudes, and insufficient expertise were associated with poorer treatment outcomes.

In the same review (Albano et al., 2024), the authors also investigated what clinicians themselves thought were characteristics that contributed to treatment outcomes. Clinicians reported that their own empathy, supportiveness, optimism, and prior experience with eating disorders positively influenced treatment. However, the therapists also reported factors like clinician anxiety, judgmental attitudes, and lack of objectivity were seen as potential hindrances to effective therapy. This review underscored the importance of specific therapist characteristics —that stand up outside of treatment models—in enhancing the therapeutic process and outcomes for individuals with eating disorders.

Addressing Power Dynamics

Power dynamics are inherent in the clinician–client relationship. Clinicians hold a position of authority by virtue of their training and role, which can create imbalances. While this power can be used to guide and support clients, it must be navigated with sensitivity to avoid exacerbating feelings of helplessness or dependency (Duncan et al., 2010). For clients with eating disorders, who often experience a loss of control in their lives, sensitivity to power imbalances is particularly important. Clinicians can empower clients by involving them in decision-making, respecting their autonomy, and fostering a sense of agency. Strategies for addressing power dynamics include humility, shared decision-making, and collaborative goal-setting. Humility involves acknowledging the client's expertise in their own experiences, while shared decision-making ensures that the therapeutic process respects the client's preferences and values. For example, a therapist might invite the client to co-create a treatment plan, saying, "What do you feel would be the most helpful to focus on in our work together?"

In Summary

A common factors or contextual approach to treatment are the key elements that are present across different therapeutic approaches and are considered key contributors to positive treatment outcomes. The most significant common factor is the therapeutic alliance. A strong therapeutic alliance is fundamental to building and fostering authentic relationships in therapy. The foundation of a strong therapeutic alliance is rooted in the same factors that build authenticity. This includes trust and safety, open communication, collaboration on goals, empathy, validation, and mutual respect. The alliance has been found to be a factor associated with positive treatment outcomes. These factors collectively produce a collaborative approach that enhances motivation and commitment to treatment, which are essential for individuals dealing with eating disorders and body image distress.

Key Take-Aways

- Wampold's (2001) and Sprenkle & Blow's (2004) work on common factors has inspired a shift toward prioritizing tailored, client-centered approaches that leverage universal aspects of human relationships to promote healing.
- Budge and Wampold (2015) offer the contextual model of common factors that identifies three primary pathways through which therapy fosters improvement: the real relationship, expectations and hope, and engagement in therapeutic tasks.
- With more than 5,000 papers written on therapeutic alliance, it is often cited as the most significant common factor.
- Bordin's (1979) tripartite model reflects that alliance consists of agreement on the goals of treatment, agreement on the tasks of treatment, and the bond between the client and therapist (the relationship).
- The relationship between a client and clinician is impacted by many contextual factors, including attachment histories.
- Like any relationship, the therapeutic relationship may be perceived differently by each person and is dynamic throughout different points in time and the dynamics both people bring.
- A strong therapeutic alliance is fundamental to building and fostering authentic relationships in therapy. The foundation of a strong therapeutic alliance is rooted in the same factors that build authenticity. This includes trust and safety, open communication, collaboration on goals, empathy, validation, and mutual respect.

References

Abbate-Daga, G., Amianto, F., Delsedime, N., De-Bacco, C., & Fassino, S. (2013). *Resistance to treatment and change in anorexia nervosa: A clinical overview*. BMC Psychiatry, 13(1), 294.

Accurso, E. C., & Garland, A. F. (2015). Child, caregiver, and therapist perspectives on therapeutic alliance in usual care child psychotherapy. *Psychological Assessment, 27*(1), 347–352. doi:10.1037/pas0000031

Ackerman, S. J., & Hilsenroth, M. J. (2003). *A review of therapist characteristics and techniques positively impacting the therapeutic alliance*. Clinical Psychology Review, 23(1), 1–33.

Accurso, E. C., Le Grange, D., & Graham, A. K. (2020). Attitudes Toward Family-Based Treatment Impact Therapists' Intent to Change Their Therapeutic Practice for Adolescent Anorexia Nervosa. *Frontiers in psychiatry, 11*, 305.

Albano, G., Teti, A., Scrò, A., Bonfanti, R. C., Fortunato, L., & Lo Coco, G. (2024). *A systematic review on the role of therapist characteristics in the treatment of eating disorders*. Research Psychotherapy, 27(2), 750.

Alexander, L. B., & Luborsky, L. (1986). *The Penn Helping Alliance Scales*. In L. S. Greenberg & W. M. Pinsof (Eds.), The psychotherapeutic process: A research handbook (pp. 325–366). Guilford Press.

Aponte, H. J., & Kissil, K. (2016). *The person of the therapist training model: Mastering the use of self*. Routledge.

Ardito, R. B., & Rabellino, D. (2011). Therapeutic alliance and outcome of psychotherapy: Historical excursus, measurements, and prospects for research. *Frontiers in psychology, 2*, 270. doi:10.3389/fpsyg.2011.00270

Barr, B. L., McIntosh, V. V., Britt, E. F., Jordan, J., & Carter, J. D. (2024). *Clinical factors and early life experiences associated with therapeutic alliance development in treatment for depression or binge eating*. Psychotherapy Research, 34(1), 4–16.

Bernecker, S. L., Levy, K. N., & Ellison, W. D. (2014). *A meta-analysis of the relation between patient adult attachment style and the working alliance*. Psychotherapy Research, 24(1), 12–24.

Berry, K., & Danquah, A. N. (2020). *Attachment theory*, the therapeutic alliance, and treatment engagement. In A. Hadler, S. Sutton, & L. Osterberg (Eds.), The Wiley handbook of healthcare treatment engagement: Theory, research, and clinical practice (pp. 159–171). Wiley.

Bordin, E. S. (1979). *The generalizability of the psychoanalytic concept of the working alliance*. Psychotherapy: Theory, Research & Practice, 16(3), 252–260.

Bourion-Bédès, S., Baumann, C., Kermarrec, S., Ligier, F., Feillet, F., Bonnemains, C., Guillemin, F., & Kabuth, B. (2013). *Prognostic value of early therapeutic alliance in weight recovery: A prospective cohort of 108 adolescents with anorexia nervosa*. Journal of Adolescent Health, 52(3), 344–350.

Boyd, J. (1996). Power, empowerment, and psychotherapy: The importance of understanding power dynamics in the therapeutic relationship. Journal of Counseling & Development, 74(4), 368–373.

Brauhardt, A., de Zwaan, M., & Hilbert, A. (2014). *The therapeutic process in psychological treatments for eating disorders: A systematic review*. International Journal of Eating Disorders, 47(6), 565–584.

Brown, A., Mountford, V.A., Waller, G. (2013). Is the therapeutic alliance overvalued in the treatment of eating disorders? International Journal of Eating Disorders, 46, 779–782.

Bucci, S., Seymour-Hyde, A., Harris, A., & Berry, K. (2016). *Client and therapist attachment styles and working alliance.* Clinical Psychology & Psychotherapy, 23(2), 155–165.

Budge, S. L., Wampold, B. E. (2015). *The relationship: How it works.* In O. Gelo, A. Pritz, B. Rieken (Eds.), Psychotherapy research. Springer.

Castonguay, L. G., Constantino, M. J., & Holtforth, M. G. (2006). The working alliance: Where are we and where should we go? *Psychotherapy: Theory, Research, Practice, Training, 43*(3), 271–279.

Conti, J. E., Joyce, C., Hay, P.et al. (2020). "Finding my own identity": A qualitative metasynthesis of adult anorexia nervosa treatment experiences. *BMC Psychol* 8, 110.

Costin, C. (2007). *The eating disorder sourcebook: A comprehensive guide to the causes,* treatments, and prevention of eating disorders (3rd ed.). McGraw-Hill Education.

Cripps, S., Serpell, L., & Pugh, M. (2024). Processes of change in family therapies for anorexia nervosa: A systematic review and meta-synthesis of qualitative data. *Journal of Eating Disorders, 12*(1), 104. doi:10.1186/s40337-024-01037-5

Cuijpers, P., Reijnders, M., & Huibers, M. J. H. (2019). *The role of common factors in psychotherapy outcomes.* Annual Review of Clinical Psychology, 15, 207–231.

Degnan, A., Seymour-Hyde, A., Harris, A., & Berry, K. (2016). The role of therapist attachment in alliance and outcome: A systematic literature review. Clinical Psychology & Psychotherapy, 23(1), 47–65.

del Río Olvera, F.J., Rodríguez-Mora, Á., Senín-Calderón, C., & Rodríguez-Testal, J. F. (2022). *The first session is the one that counts: An exploratory study of therapeutic alliance.* Frontiers in Psychology, 13, 1016963.

Diener, M. J., Hilsenroth, M. J., & Weinberger, J. (2009). A primer on meta-analysis of correlation coefficients: The relationship between patient-reported therapeutic alliance and adult attachment style as an illustration. *Psychotherapy Research, 19*(4-5), 519–526. doi:10.1080/10503300802491410

Diener, M. J., & Monroe, J. M. (2011). *The relationship between adult attachment style and therapeutic alliance in individual psychotherapy: A meta-analytic review.* Psychotherapy, 48(3), 237–248.

Duncan, B. L., Miller, S. D., Sparks, J. A., Claud, D. A., Reynolds, L. R., Brown, J., & Johnson, L. D. (2003). *The session rating scale: Preliminary psychometric properties of a "working"* alliance measure. Journal of Brief Therapy, 3(1), 3–12.

Duncan, B. L., Miller, S. D., Wampold, B. E., & Hubble, M. A. (2010). *The heart and soul of change: Delivering what works in therapy.* American Psychological Association.

Flückiger, C., Del Re, A. C., Wampold, B. E., & Horvath, A. O. (2018). The alliance in adult psychotherapy: A meta-analytic synthesis. *Psychotherapy, 55*(4), 316–340.

Folke, S., Daniel, S. I. F., Poulsen, S., & Lunn, S. (2015). *Client attachment security predicts alliance in a randomized controlled trial of two psychotherapies for bulimia nervosa.* Psychotherapy Research, 26(4), 459–471.

Fors, M. (2021). The power of the therapist: A critical analysis of power in psychotherapy. International Journal of Psychoanalysis, 102(3), 457–473.

Forsberg, S., LoTempio, E., Bryson, S., Fitzpatrick, K. K., Le Grange, D., & Lock, J. (2013). Therapeutic alliance in two treatments for adolescent anorexia nervosa. *The International Journal of Eating Disorders, 46*(1), 34–38. doi:10.1002/eat.22047

Gaston, L. (1991). Reliability and criterion-related validity of the California Psychotherapy Alliance Scales—patient version. *Psychological Assessment: A Journal of Consulting and Clinical Psychology, 3*(1), 68–74.

Geller, J., & Srikameswaran, S. (2006). Treatment non-negotiables: Why we need them and how to make them work. *European Eating Disorders Review, 14*(4), 212–21.

Gelso, C. (2014). A tripartite model of the therapeutic relationship: Theory, research, and practice. *Psychotherapy Research*, 24(2), 117–131.

Graves, T. A., Tabri, N., Thompson-Brenner, H., Franko, D. L., Eddy, K. T., Bourion-Bedes, S., … & Thomas, J. J. (2017). *A meta-analysis of the relation between therapeutic alliance and treatment outcome in eating disorders.* International Journal of Eating Disorders, 50(4), 323–340.

Henrich, J., Heine, S. J., & Norenzayan, A. (2010). The weirdest people in the world? *Behavioral and Brain Sciences, 33*(2–3), 61–83.

Horvath, A. O., & Greenberg, L. S. (1989). *Development and validation of the working alliance inventory.* Journal of Counseling Psychology, 36(2), 223–233.

Horvath A. O., & Bedi R. P. (2002). The alliance. In J. C. Norcross (Ed.), *Psychotherapy relationships that work: Therapist contributions and responsiveness to patients* (pp. 37–69). Oxford University Press.

Horvath, A. O., Del Re, A. C., Flückiger, C., & Symonds, D. (2011). *Alliance in individual psychotherapy.* Psychotherapy, 48, 9–16.

Hyland, M. E. (2020). *A reformulated contextual model of psychotherapy for treating anxiety and depression.* Clinical Psychology Review, 80, 101890.

Jenkins, P. E., Hoste, R. R., Meyer, C., & Blissett, J. M. (2021). *The therapeutic alliance in eating disorder treatment: A systematic review.* Clinical Psychology Review, 87, 102033.

Jenkins, P. E., & Wake, S. (2024). *Therapeutic alliance in two forms of guided self-help for binge eating.* Clinical Psychology & Psychotherapy, 31(1), e2959.

Jewell, T., Apostolidou, E., Sadikovic, K., Tahta-Wraith, K., Liston, S., Simic, M., Eisler, I., Fonagy, P., & Yorke, I. (2023). *Attachment in individuals with eating disorders compared to community controls: A systematic review and meta-analysis.* International Journal of Eating Disorders, 56(5), 888–908.

Jordan, J. V. (2018). *Relational–cultural therapy* (2nd ed.). American Psychological Association.

Keski-Rahkonen, A., & Tozzi, F. (2005). *The process of recovery in eating disorder sufferers: The role of the therapeutic alliance and experiences of treatment.* European Eating Disorders Review, 13(6), 394–401.

Lev Ari, H. S., Tuval-Mashiach, R., Hay, D. E., Bernstein, Z. L., Kagan, L., Kivity, Y., & Gilboa-Schechtman, E. (2025). *A meta-analysis of client–therapist perspectives on the therapeutic alliance: Examining the moderating role of eating disorders versus anxiety disorders*, treatment orientation, and measurement time points. Journal of Psychotherapy Integration. Advance online publication.

Levy, K. N., Kivity, Y., Johnson, B. N., Gooch, C. V. (2018). *Adult attachment as a predictor and moderator of psychotherapy outcome: A meta-analysis.* Journal of Clinical Psychology, 74.

Muzi, L., Carone, N., Mirabella, M., Franco, A., Rugo, M. A., Mazzeschi, C., & Lingiardi, V. (2024). *Direct and indirect effects of psychological well-being and therapeutic alliance on therapy outcome in eating disorders.* Frontiers in Psychology, 15, 1392887.

Norcross, J. C. (1995). *Dispelling the dodo bird verdict and the exclusivity myth in psychotherapy.* Psychotherapy: Theory, Research, Practice, Training, 32(3), 500–504.

Norcross, J. C., & Lambert, M. J. (2018). *Psychotherapy relationships that work* III. Psychotherapy, 55(4), 303–350.

Norcross, J. C., & Lambert, M. J. (2019). Evidence-based psychotherapy relationships: The third task force. In J. C. Norcross & M. J. Lambert (Eds.), *Psychotherapy relationships that work: Evidence-based therapist contributions* (3rd ed., pp. 1–23). Oxford University Press.doi:10.1093/med-psych/9780190843953.003.0001

Notsu, H., Blansfield, R. E., Spina, D. S., & Levy, K. N. (2024). *An updated meta-analysis of the relation between adult attachment style and working alliance.* Psychotherapy Research. Advance online publication.

Prochaska, J. O., & DiClemente, C. C. (1983). *Stages and processes of self-change of smoking: Toward an integrative model of change.* Journal of Consulting and Clinical Psychology, 51(3), 390–395.

Ramjan, L., & Fogarty, S. (2019). *Clients' perceptions of the therapeutic relationship in the treatment of anorexia nervosa: Qualitative findings from an online questionnaire.* Australian Journal of Primary Health, 25(1), 37–42.

Rossi, E., Cassioli, E., Martelli, M., Melani, G., Hazzard, V. M., Crosby, R. D., Wonderlich, S. A., Ricca, V., & Castellini, G. (2022). Attachment insecurity predicts worse outcome in patients with eating disorders treated with enhanced cognitive behavior therapy: A one-year follow-up study. International Journal of Eating Disorders, 55(8), 1054–1065.

Ruzicka, E. B., Shomaker, L. B., Pyle, L., Bakalar, J. L., Shank, L. M., Crosby, R. D., … & Tanofsky-Kraff, M. (2024). *Effects of therapeutic alliance in interpersonal psychotherapy among adolescent girls with loss-of-control eating.* American Journal of Psychotherapy, 77(1), 7–14.

Safran, J. D., & Muran, J. C. (2000). *Negotiating the therapeutic alliance: A relational treatment guide.* Guilford Press.

Saxler, E., Schindler, T., Philipsen, A., Schulze, M., & Lux, S. (2024). *Therapeutic alliance in individual adult psychotherapy: A systematic review of conceptualizations and measures for face-to-face-and online-psychotherapy.* Frontiers in Psychology, 15, 1293851.

Shelef, K., & Diamond, G. M. (2008). *Revised Vanderbilt therapeutic alliance scale–short form (VTAS-R)* [*Database record*]. APA PsycTests.

Sprenkle, D. H., & Blow, A. J. (2004). *Common factors and our sacred models.* Journal of Marital and Family Therapy, 30(2), 113–129.

Treasure, J., Sepulveda, A. R., Whitaker, W., Todd, G., Lopez, C., & Whitney, J. (2007). *Collaborative care between professionals and non-professionals in the management of eating disorders: A description of workshops focused on interpersonal maintaining factors.* European Eating Disorders Review 15(1), 24–34.

van Mens-Verhulst, J. (1991). Feminist perspectives on psychotherapy and power relations. Women & Therapy, 11(3–4), 45–58.

Vaz, A. M., Ferreira, L. I., Gelso, C. & Janeiro, L. (2024) *The sister concepts of working alliance and real relationship: A meta-analysis.* Counselling Psychology Quarterly, 37(2), 247–268.

Vrabel, K. R., Ulvenes, P. G. and Wampold, B. (2015). *Alliance and symptom improvement in inpatient treatment for eating disorder patients: A study of within-patient processes.* International Journal of Eating Disorders, 48: 1113–1121.

Wampold, B. E. (2001). *The great psychotherapy debate: Models*, methods, and findings. Lawrence Erlbaum Associates Publishers.

Wampold, B. E. (2015). *How important are the common factors in psychotherapy?* An update. World Psychiatry, 14(3), 270–277.

Wampold, B. E., & Imel, Z. E. (2015). *The great psychotherapy debate: The evidence for what makes psychotherapy work.* Routledge.

Wampold, B. E., & Flückiger, C. (2023). The alliance in mental health care: Conceptualization, evidence and clinical applications. World Psychiatry, *22*(1), 25–41.

Werz, J., Voderholzer, U., & Tuschen-Caffier, B. (2022). *Alliance matters: but how much?* A systematic review on therapeutic alliance and outcome in patients with anorexia nervosa and bulimia nervosa. Eating and Weight Disorders, 27(4), 1279–1295. doi:10.1007/s40519-021-01281-7

Zaitsoff, S. L., Celio Doyle, A., Hoste, R. R., & le Grange, D. (2008). *How do adolescents with bulimia nervosa rate the acceptability and therapeutic relationship in family-based treatment?* International Journal of Eating Disorders 41: 390–398.

Zaitsoff, S. L., Pullmer, R., Cyr, M., & Aime, H. (2015). The role of the therapeutic alliance in eating disorder treatment outcomes: A meta-analytic review. *International Journal of Eating Disorders*, 48(1), 1–9.

Zilcha-Mano, S. (2017). *Is the alliance really therapeutic?* Revisiting this question in light of recent methodological advances. American Psychologist, 72(4), 311–325.

Chapter 5

Authenticity in Action

Techniques for Relational Healing

Overview

- *This chapter moves from theory to practice, offering concrete tools for creating an authentic therapeutic alliance with eating disorder clients.* Drawing on Rogers's core concepts of presence, congruence, and attunement, authenticity becomes a lived experience in the therapy room.
- *Techniques such as active listening, establishing trust, reflection, summarizing, and clarifying questions serve as the foundation of authentic dialogue.* These relational practices help therapists move beyond surface interactions into deeper, more genuine exchanges.
- *Mindfulness and embodiment approaches expand the clinician's toolkit, anchoring both client and therapist in the present moment.* Attunement, empathy, and rapport are not abstract ideals but skills that can be practiced and refined.
- *Integration of model-specific methods is included in this chapter to demonstrate how authenticity can be woven into different frameworks.* These adaptations keep therapy both structured and deeply human.
- *Creative and expressive therapies add another dimension, using movement, art, metaphor, and role play to bypass defenses and foster authentic expression.* Such approaches offer clients alternative routes to connect with themselves and others.
- *At its core, authenticity is not a single intervention but a stance that infuses every technique with meaning.* By applying these tools with presence and integrity, clinicians model what it means to be genuine, creating space for clients to reclaim their own authenticity.

I still remember my first client as a primary therapist in an eating-disorder treatment center. Her name was Sam. From the moment she walked in, it was clear she knew far more about eating disorders than I did. I had just finished my master's program and was deep into my doctorate, but no class had prepared me for what I was about to encounter.

DOI: 10.4324/9781003632016-6

Clipboard in hand, it was 2005, after all, I began the intake, relying on the same scripted questions I'd learned in graduate school. Sam answered in clipped, flat phrases, giving me nothing to hold onto. I left the room feeling discouraged. Looking back, I imagine she felt the same: frustrated to be placing her life in the hands of someone who still felt more like a student than a therapist.

In supervision the next day, I nervously suggested she needed a higher level of care, or maybe just a different clinician. The site director listened quietly, then invited me to take a breath. "Just keep showing up," she said. "Start just being there."

Two days later, I sat with Sam again, and this time, she came out swinging. She described, in clinical detail, how to assemble a homemade enema from whatever materials were available. Then came stories of stealing and hoarding food, binge drinking, anonymous unprotected sex, all while functioning on fewer calories than I'd had for breakfast. I remember sitting frozen, my face telegraphing every ounce of shock.

Sam saw it. She pushed further.

What I couldn't name at the time, but understand now, was that none of this was simply confession. It was a test:

Can you handle the truth of my life? Will you stay? Can I trust you?

I failed that test more times than I care to admit. I was new and overwhelmed. I didn't yet understand that eating disorders live in the shadows of shame and secrecy and that exposure is terrifying. I didn't know that my steadiness mattered more than my technique.

There are moments in a career that follow us. Some we carry with pride; others, we wish we could rewrite. My work with Sam is one I would have revised in so many ways. And yet, two decades later, I still talk about her in supervision and training. Not because I handled it well, but because that experience changed me.

It taught me about the power of showing up, the necessity of humility, and the truth that expertise is not simply what we know, it's how we sit with what we don't.

Chapter 5 begins here: with the lessons we learn not from getting it right, but from recognizing how much more there always is to learn.

Creating an Authentic Connection

Authentic connection in therapy is central to creating a space where healing and growth can occur. For clinicians working with clients who struggle with eating disorders and body image concerns, fostering this connection is particularly crucial, as these issues often stem from deep emotional wounds and a lack of trust both in oneself and others. Authentic connection is rooted in Rogers's key concepts of being fully present, demonstrating congruence, and attuning to the client's experiences (Rogers, 1951). In the following section, I will highlight the application of these concepts with techniques on how we can do it.

First, Table 5.1 provides an overview to help break down the concepts.

Table 5.1 Roger's Core Concepts of Being Fully Present

Rogers's Core Concept	*Definition*	*Key Techniques*
Presence	Full emotional availability and grounded awareness in the here and now.	Establishing trust, active listening, non-judgmental awareness, embodiment practices, mindfulness, co-regulation.
Congruence	Genuineness and internal consistency in thoughts, emotions, and behavior.	Developing rapport, clinician self-disclosure, model techniques: values, context, externalization, somatic practices.
Attunement	Emotional resonance and accurate understanding of the client's experience.	Expressing empathy, rupture and repair, metaphors, attachment-informed work, creative approaches, reflective listening, person-of-the-therapist work.

Presence

Being fully present involves the therapist's ability to give undivided attention to the client, creating a sense of being truly seen and heard. Presence is not a passive state; it requires active engagement and mindfulness. Techniques such as grounding exercises and pre-session rituals can help therapists cultivate presence. For instance, taking a few deep breaths or engaging in a brief mindfulness practice before a session can center the therapist's focus. Practicing non-judgmental awareness during sessions, as described by Kabat-Zinn (1990), allows therapists to remain attuned to the client's narrative without being distracted by their own internal thoughts or external distractions.

When therapists are fully present, they create a therapeutic environment characterized by trust and emotional safety. This is especially critical for clients with eating disorders, who may have experienced significant invalidation or judgment in their lives. Presence conveys to the client that they are worthy of attention and care, helping to counteract feelings of shame or unworthiness. Research by Geller and Greenberg (2012) highlights the role of therapeutic presence in fostering a secure attachment, which is a predictor of positive treatment outcomes.

Presence is connected to Arrien's (1993) principles of "show up" and "pay attention." Clients struggling with eating disorders often experience avoidance and disconnection, both from their emotions and from meaningful relationships (Costin & Grabb, 2016). Therapists working from this perspective encourage clients to engage actively in their recovery by facing difficult emotions, challenging their disordered thoughts, and committing to treatment even when it feels uncomfortable. This principle also applies to therapists, who must cultivate presence and authenticity in their interactions with clients, modeling what it means to "show up" with integrity and commitment. Many individuals with eating disorders struggle with self-criticism and disconnection from their own needs and desires. "Paying attention" brings a mindful perspective and teaching of self-compassion into therapy. By helping clients tune into what truly matters to them—whether it's relationships, creativity, or self-expression—therapists can guide them toward a recovery path that is not just about food but about reclaiming a meaningful life. The clinician's role is to foster self-compassion and encourage clients to reconnect with their authentic selves rather than the rigid rules and external validation that often drive disordered eating behaviors.

Establishing Trust

Establishing trust is a cornerstone of effective therapy, as it creates a safe space for clients to share their thoughts and feelings without fear of judgment. Carl Rogers (1957), a pioneer in humanistic psychology, emphasized the importance of unconditional positive regard, empathy, and genuineness in building trust. These core conditions allow clients to feel valued and understood, fostering a sense of safety and openness. For instance, a therapist working with a client recovering from trauma might demonstrate trustworthiness by consistently respecting the client's boundaries and affirming their experiences without minimizing their pain. Studies support Rogers's principles, showing that therapists who exhibit authentic empathy and congruence significantly enhance trust and therapeutic outcomes (Norcross & Lambert, 2018). Trust also develops over time as therapists maintain confidentiality and exhibit reliability, further deepening the therapeutic alliance. Being genuine is a significant factor to authentic relationships and establishing trust. An example of genuineness would be acknowledging a client's courage in seeking help or expressing genuine interest in their experiences, which can signal care and respect. Another factor in developing trust is keeping commitments and following through. Simple examples of this that are meaningful include keeping appointments consistent and if assigning "homework" always following up on it. Establishing trust early in the therapeutic relationship is essential.

Active Listening

There are many techniques associated with active listening. Active listening is crucial for building authentic relationships with both the client and the clinician because it fosters genuine connection, self-awareness, and trust. Authentic relationships thrive when people feel safe to be themselves, and active listening creates that safety (Brown, 2012). When you truly listen to someone without interrupting, judging, or planning your response, you show them they matter. This kind of presence builds trust, emotional intimacy, and mutual respect. It signals: *"I see you. I hear you. You matter."* Active listening isn't just outward-facing; it also helps you listen inwardly. By tuning into your own thoughts, emotions, and needs without defensiveness or distraction, you build a more honest and compassionate relationship with yourself. In personal relationships in life—whether with partners, friends, or family—most conflict stems from not feeling heard or understood. Active listening defuses defensiveness and helps you respond rather than react. When people feel listened to, they're more likely to listen in return, creating a cycle of mutual authenticity and respect (Rogers, 1961). This happens through reflection, summarizing, and clarifying, which I break down in more detail below.

REFLECTION OF CONTENT AND EMOTION

This technique helps the client feel heard and validated, and it mirrors their internal experience to promote insight and compassion. Here is an example of how this might work between a clinician and a client.

CLIENT: "I just couldn't eat breakfast again this morning. I kept staring at the food and thinking I didn't deserve it."

THERAPIST: (reflecting): "It sounds like eating felt impossible, and there was a lot of self-judgment behind that moment."

By reflecting both the client's content and underlying emotion, the therapist fosters safety and validation, deepening the client's self-awareness while modeling compassion toward their struggle.

SUMMARIZING KEY THEMES

Summarizing, although it perhaps sounds simple, is actually very important. It helps organize and clarify complex emotions while showing the clinician is tracking the narrative. For example:

CLIENT: "My mom watches everything I eat. I'm either eating too much, or not enough. Then I end up hiding food, and I hate that I do that."

THERAPIST: (summarizing): "You're caught in a cycle where feeling scrutinized leads to hiding food, which then brings on guilt and shame."

Summarizing allows the clinician to distill complex experiences into a clear, coherent theme, helping the client feel understood while also illuminating patterns that may otherwise feel overwhelming or confusing. It validates the client's struggle and offers a foundation for deeper exploration.

ASKING CLARIFYING QUESTIONS

Clarifying questions deepen the conversation and communicate interest in the client's internal world, promoting self-awareness and trust. Here is a way this could come up in a session:

CLIENT: "Sometimes I feel like the eating disorder is the only thing I have control over."

THERAPIST: (clarifying): "Can you tell me more about what it feels like to have that control? What does it give you?"

Asking clarifying questions signals genuine curiosity and attunement, encouraging the client to articulate and explore their inner experience more fully. This deepens insight, strengthens the therapeutic alliance, and fosters greater self-understanding.

Embodiment

An essential pathway to cultivating authenticity in therapy, particularly with individuals recovering from eating disorders, is through the practice of embodiment. Embodiment refers to therapeutic approaches that help clients reconnect with their physical selves through enhancing awareness of bodily sensations, emotions, and intuitive needs as integral aspects of the self (Piran, 2017). Rather than viewing the body as an object to control or perfect, embodiment invites clients to experience the body as a source of wisdom, presence, and relational meaning. This reconnection supports clients in becoming more attuned to hunger and fullness cues, emotional states, and somatic responses, ultimately strengthening their capacity to live authentically and compassionately within their bodies (Cook-Cottone, 2015b). Somatic therapy for eating disorders refers to body-centered interventions that emphasize attunement to internal sensations, awareness of the body's signals, and regulation of the nervous system to promote recovery (Cook-Cottone, 2015b). These approaches recognize that eating disorders often involve a disconnection from or conflict with the body, and healing requires re-establishing a compassionate, embodied relationship with oneself. In my own view, somatic therapies provide a critical complement to cognitive and behavioral interventions because they address what words alone cannot: the lived experience of the body. By focusing on interoception, grounding techniques, and trauma-informed practices, clients can gradually reclaim safety in their bodies, which in turn reduces reliance on restrictive, bingeing, or compensatory behaviors as coping mechanisms. For many clients, this process not only decreases symptoms but also enhances their capacity for self-compassion and authentic self-expression (Brown et al., 2020).

Recent research underscores the importance of integrating somatic awareness into eating disorder treatment. Studies have found that interventions aimed at enhancing embodiment, such as yoga or mindful movement, contribute to improved emotional regulation, body image, and treatment engagement (Cook-Cottone, 2020; Piran, 2019). I believe this is particularly important given that traditional therapies often focus heavily on cognition, while somatic therapies honor the body as both a source of wisdom and a site of healing.

In the context of eating disorder treatment, there is an overlap with embodiment-based interventions, somatic techniques, and mindfulness such as mindful movement, yoga, body scans, meditation, and somatic experiencing. These have shown promise in fostering self-regulation and healing relational disconnection from the body (Piran, 2017; Keyte et al., 2020). Somatic therapies help surface emotions stored in the body that may be difficult to articulate verbally, allowing for deeper therapeutic integration. Joseph (2019) concludes that authenticity emerges not only through cognitive or verbal self-expression, but also through embodied presence, by inhabiting one's body with greater honesty, acceptance, and awareness. Therapists who incorporate these practices help clients move from self-surveillance and shame toward self-trust and embodied authenticity.

Mindfulness

Siegel (2007) describes mindfulness as paying attention, on purpose and with openness, to the unfolding of one's moment-to-moment experience, fostering integration of mind, brain, and relationships. My perspective is that mindfulness in therapy is the practice of helping clients bring gentle, nonjudgmental awareness to their thoughts, emotions, and bodily sensations in the present moment, creating space for choice and self-compassion. Mindfulness techniques can be powerful tools for promoting authenticity in therapy by helping clients develop present-moment awareness, reduce self-judgment, and reconnect with their internal experiences. Practices such as mindful breathing, body scans, and grounding exercises foster greater emotional regulation and support clients in observing their thoughts, emotions, and bodily sensations without immediately reacting to them (Kabat-Zinn, 2003). This non-reactive stance cultivates self-acceptance and encourages clients to respond to life in ways that align more closely with their values and true selves (Germer et al., 2016). In the context of eating disorder treatment, mindfulness can help clients shift from controlling or dissociating from the body to becoming more attuned to internal cues and needs (Cook-Cottone, 2015a). Witnessing a client soften their perfectionist tendencies through ongoing use of mindfulness techniques is powerful to witness; I have seen individuals learn to notice self-critical thoughts without judgment and gradually embrace self-compassion and allow space for being imperfect yet whole. By integrating mindfulness into therapy, clinicians create space for clients to explore who they are beneath patterns of avoidance, performance, or perfectionism to support a more authentic and compassionate engagement with the self.

One morning, I found myself rushing through breakfast, half-reading emails on my phone while mentally reviewing the day's to-do list. I caught myself swallowing bites of food without even tasting them, my body going through the motions while my mind spun three steps ahead. In that moment, I paused—just long enough to put my phone down, notice the warmth of the coffee in my hand, and take a real breath. It wasn't a perfect meditation or a long mindful practice, but it was a reminder that even a small pause could anchor me back into the present. For me, mindfulness has never been about mastering stillness; it's about catching glimpses of presence in the middle of the chaos and learning to honor those moments as enough. As much as I believe in the power of mindfulness, I'll admit it doesn't always come easily to me. Like so many people, my days are often crammed with responsibilities, and my mind tends to race ahead, jumping from one task to the next. Slowing down feels almost unnatural, like I'm fighting against my own momentum. But that struggle has also taught me something important: mindfulness isn't about perfection, but about practicing presence even when it feels messy, incomplete, or fleeting.

In addition to general mindfulness practices, mindful eating exercises encourage clients to slow down and notice the texture, taste, and internal satiety signals of their food, which helps disrupt automatic patterns and challenge dissociation often present in eating disorders. Mindful eating practices involve bringing intentional, nonjudgmental awareness to the act of eating, focusing on sensory experience, hunger and satiety cues, and the emotional context of food, rather than relying on external rules or rigid expectations (Kristeller & Wolever, 2011). By fostering present-moment awareness, these practices promote greater interoceptive sensitivity and reduce reliance on external rules or perfectionistic standards to dictate eating (Kristeller & Wolever, 2014).

This approach overlaps with the principles of *Intuitive Eating* (Tribole & Resch, 2020), which emphasize attunement to internal body signals and rejecting diet culture as a means to restore a trusting and compassionate relationship with food. Other treatment approaches similarly advocate for mindful awareness. Research further suggests that mindfulness-based interventions can improve emotional regulation and self-compassion, both of which are critical in loosening the grip of rigid perfectionism and fostering a more flexible, embodied relationship with food (Sala et al., 2020).

In my perspective, mindful eating is not just a technique but a corrective experience: it allows clients to encounter food in a new way, free from judgment and fear, while also building self-compassion. By practicing presence with food, clients can gradually break cycles of restriction, bingeing, or compensatory behaviors, and instead cultivate a sense of trust in their bodies and choices. Mindfulness and intuitive eating are deeply meaningful to me, not only as a clinician but also in my own life; these practices ground me, remind me to slow down, and connect me to a more compassionate and authentic relationship with my body and well-being. Learning intuitive eating, in particular, transformed my own relationship with food by shifting me away from external rules and "shoulds" and toward an attunement to my body's cues, allowing eating to become an act of nourishment rather than judgment. This personal integration strengthens my ability to model and guide clients toward recovery in an authentic way.

INCORPORATING MINDFULNESS INTO TREATMENT SESSIONS

Here are some approaches a clinician can take to bring mindfulness into treatment sessions with eating disorder clients:

- *Mindful breathing.* The clinician uses this technique to help clients anchor in the present moment, increasing awareness of internal states and reducing automatic, defensive responses.
- *Body scan meditation.* In this technique, the clinician encourages clients to notice bodily sensations with curiosity and compassion, fostering reconnection with the body and disrupting patterns of dissociation or control (Cook-Cottone, 2015a).
- *Name and notice practice.* A clinician guides clients to "name" emotions or thoughts as they arise without judgment (e.g., "I'm noticing anxiety"), promoting self-awareness and emotional honesty (Kabat-Zinn, 2003).
- *Five senses grounding exercise.* Here, the clinician is developing presence by focusing attention on what the client can see, hear, touch, taste, and smell—strengthening connection to real-time experience and authentic expression. This is a go-to favorite of mine that is applicable for all disciplines to use.
- *Values-based visualization.* The clinician uses guided imagery centered on values and identity to help clients envision and reconnect with their authentic self (Germer et al., 2016).

Co-Regulation

Presence enhances the therapist's ability to detect subtle shifts in the client's emotions, allowing for timely and appropriate responses, which is known as co-regulation. For example, noticing a fleeting expression of sadness in a client's face and gently acknowledging it can validate their feelings and encourage deeper exploration. This responsiveness reinforces the therapeutic alliance and builds the foundation for meaningful change. Consider this emotional awareness the start to co-regulation in therapy; this is the process by which a therapist helps a client regulate their emotional and physiological states through attuned, supportive, and calming relational interactions. It is a neurobiologically informed and relational concept, grounded in attachment theory and interpersonal neurobiology, where one person's stable nervous system helps to calm and stabilize another's (Porges, 2011, Carreño, 2013; Schore 2014).

From a relational perspective, co-regulation, similar to the building of the therapeutic alliance, is didactic, meaning it occurs between two people. The therapist's grounded presence and emotional attunement can influence the client's autonomic nervous system, reducing activation related to fear, shame, or trauma (Porges, 2011). Co-regulation is particularly important for clients who have experienced relational trauma or disrupted early attachment, as it builds the capacity for later self-regulation (Siegel, 2012). An important note is that therapists must remain emotionally regulated themselves to offer effective co-regulation. A dysregulated therapist cannot model or provide calm and safety; it is critical for therapists to understand their own bodies' triggers and responses and develop a practice of personal awareness.

Co-regulation fosters trust, emotional safety, and attunement, which are prerequisites for clients to show up authentically. It creates a relational container where clients feel safe enough to risk vulnerability, explore disowned parts of the self, and integrate emotional experiences that are key components of authentic living.

From an attachment perspective, co-regulation is the foundation of safety in attachment repair and authenticity. Therapists can use a calm, grounded presence to regulate emotional intensity, employ somatic cues (e.g., breath work, grounding exercises) to model emotion regulation, or tune into nonverbal signals (posture, tone, facial expression) and respond accordingly.

A simple idea to try co-regulation is to begin sessions with one minute of shared breath or grounding to anchor clients in their bodies with the therapist.

Congruence

Congruence, or the alignment of a therapist's internal experience and external expression, is a core component of authenticity. To embody congruence, therapists must cultivate self-awareness, regularly reflecting on their own biases, discomfort, and emotional reactions. Supervision and personal therapy are invaluable tools for identifying unconscious biases or unresolved issues that could affect the therapeutic relationship (Rogers, 1957).

For example, a therapist who feels discomfort discussing a client's body image concerns must explore the roots of this discomfort to avoid projecting their own insecurities or beliefs. Journaling, mindfulness practices, and peer consultation can also support therapists in maintaining clarity about their internal states, ensuring that these do not interfere with the client's progress.

Modeling congruence helps clients develop their own sense of authenticity. When clinicians align their words, actions, and feelings, they demonstrate that it is possible to be honest and vulnerable while maintaining strength and professionalism. For instance, if a clinician feels sadness in response to a client's story, they might express this by saying, "I feel deeply moved by what you're sharing. It sounds incredibly painful." This transparent acknowledgment of emotions validates the client's experience and reinforces the clinician's genuineness.

Developing Rapport

Developing rapport involves creating a warm, collaborative, and supportive relationship that encourages clients to engage actively in therapy. A meta-analysis by Flückiger et al. (2018) found that strong rapport, characterized by mutual understanding and positive regard, significantly predicts therapeutic success across various modalities. By tailoring interventions to the client's unique needs and preferences, clinicians not only build rapport but also reinforce the client's sense of agency, contributing to lasting change. Rapport starts from the moment a client interacts with you (whether in person or virtually through your website or social media) and can be established with simple language and gestures. Examples of developing rapport include:

- Using the client's name directly when speaking with them
- Maintaining appropriate eye contact
- Listening attentively to their concerns
- Using appropriate disclosure to ease client anxiety
- Incorporating humor when appropriate and authentic to you
- Acknowledging when mistakes or missteps occur

For example, if a clinician inadvertently interrupts a client or misinterprets their feelings, they can openly address this with a comment such as "I realize I may have cut you off; I'm sorry for interrupting. Please continue." This type of acknowledgment can strengthen the relational bond. This openness fosters an environment of mutual respect and encourages clients to engage in honest self-reflection. Developing rapport in the first session is particularly important, and research has demonstrated that the alliance is initially stable within the first session and remains so through the fifth session (del Río Olvera et al., 2022). In my view, these small but intentional moments of repair set the tone for trust and safety early in treatment. They demonstrate that authenticity and humility are not weaknesses in the therapeutic relationship but powerful tools for modeling respect, accountability, and genuine connection. I believe the foundation of a strong alliance is laid in the very first session, when clients are often testing whether they can trust the process and the person in front of them. Showing warmth, curiosity, and openness from the start helps clients feel safe enough to take the vulnerable step of sharing their inner world.

Clinician Self-Disclosure (Thoughtful and Intentional)

Clinician self-disclosure, when used intentionally and ethically, can be a powerful tool for fostering authenticity in the therapeutic relationship. Authenticity thrives in spaces where vulnerability is modeled and mutual humanity is acknowledged. By appropriately sharing aspects of their own experiences, values, or emotional reactions, clinicians can help demystify the therapeutic process and reduce the power differential, particularly with clients who struggle with trust, shame, or relational trauma (Hill & Knox, 2002). Self-disclosure can communicate empathy, enhance the therapeutic alliance, and demonstrate that emotional struggles are part of the shared human experience, which are key elements in promoting client authenticity (Audet & Everall, 2010). This can be particularly meaningful in eating disorder treatment, where clients often feel isolated and misunderstood and may benefit from knowing their therapist understands the complexity of their emotional world.

While I was in my doctoral program, I visited another therapist's office space. I recall asking her questions about the artwork hanging up, books she had available for clients to see, and other artifacts lying around. It was very evident to me that all these items and objects were in clear disclosure of her religious orientation. She was not a clinician who intentionally served a particular religious community, nor did she practice from a faith-based perspective. I was bewildered at how much disclosure was represented through her office space. The clinician, who was about three decades my senior, told me that her office represented her, and that was part of who she was as a therapist. Still confused with her response at the time, I remember her smiling and saying, "I can't wait to see who you are in 30 years."

Now, 20 plus years later, I wear disclosure as pride rather than confusion. Back then, I worried that revealing too much of myself might somehow dilute the therapeutic frame, but I have since learned that authenticity is one of the most powerful tools I bring into the room. The artifacts, stories, and even the subtle ways I allow myself to be seen are not barriers to the work, they are bridges. Clients often tell me that these glimpses of my humanity give them permission to show up more fully as themselves. What once felt risky now feels essential, a reminder that therapy is not just about techniques and theories but about two people daring to meet each other with openness and presence. In many ways, this echoes Carl Rogers's concept of congruence with the alignment of one's inner and outer experience (Rogers, 1961) and resonates with relational–cultural theory, which emphasizes the healing power of authentic connection (Jordan, 2018; Miller et al., 2004). My own evolution as a therapist has taught me that disclosure, when thoughtful and intentional, is not a distraction but an embodiment of authenticity, and it transforms the therapeutic alliance into a truly mutual and healing relationship.

However, effective self-disclosure requires careful consideration of intentionality and boundaries. The primary question should always be: *Is this disclosure in service of the client's growth?* Therapists must avoid using disclosure to meet their own emotional needs or to shift focus away from the client (Zur, 2007). Ethical self-disclosure is time limited, relevant, and always grounded in clinical benefit. It also requires a solid foundation of self-awareness; clinicians must be attuned to their own motivations, countertransference, and the potential impact of disclosure on the client. Maintaining professional boundaries ensures that the relationship remains safe, contained, and focused on the client's therapeutic goals (Barnett, 2011). When approached thoughtfully, therapist self-disclosure can be a relational act of congruence in aligning words, presence, and intention to cultivate trust and model what it means to show up authentically.

Model Techniques: Values, Somatic Practices, Emotion-Focused, Attachment

Borrowing from acceptance and commitment therapy, somatic, narrative, and existential therapies, there are several techniques that foster congruence.

ACT/VALUES CLARIFICATION

Techniques from acceptance and commitment therapy help clients explore core values, life purpose, and identity. Acceptance and commitment therapy (ACT) is a promising approach in the treatment of eating disorders by helping clients cultivate psychological flexibility, reduce experiential avoidance, and develop a more compassionate stance toward difficult thoughts and emotions (Hayes et al., 2011). Rather than directly challenging maladaptive cognitions, ACT emphasizes acceptance strategies, mindfulness practices, and values-based action, which can be particularly effective for clients whose rigid perfectionism or avoidance patterns maintain disordered behaviors (Juarascio et al., 2013). Recent evidence highlights that ACT interventions are associated with reductions in eating disorder symptomatology, improvements in quality of life, and greater alignment with personal values (Berman et al., 2022; Manlick et al., 2013. Integrating ACT into treatment offers clients a pathway to build a life not defined by food or weight but by meaningful engagement and self-compassion. These types of techniques support alignment between actions and deeply held beliefs, which is key to authentic living (Hayes et al., 2011).

NARRATIVE THERAPY/RE-AUTHORING CONVERSATIONS

Narrative therapy has been increasingly applied in the treatment of eating disorders, offering clients an alternative to the dominant problem-saturated stories that often define their lives. These techniques help clients externalize problems and reclaim authorship of their identity. Reflections can invite clients to think about how they want to live and relate, not just what they want to "fix" (White & Epston, 1990). By separating the eating disorder from the self, individuals are empowered to challenge the cultural and social narratives that sustain disordered eating, such as the thin-ideal or perfectionism (Matusek et al., 2004). Recent work further suggests that narrative therapy enhances agency, self-compassion, and relational connection, positioning recovery as an ongoing process of rewriting one's story rather than eradicating symptoms alone (Lock, 2020). For many clients, this approach shifts the focus from pathology to possibility, creating a richer and more authentic sense of self. These techniques help clients externalize problems and reclaim authorship of their identity. Reflections can invite clients to think about how they want to *live and relate*, not just what they want to "fix" (White & Epston, 1990).

EMOTION FOCUSED FAMILY THERAPY/EMOTION COACHING

Emotion-focused family therapy (EFFT), developed by Adele Lafrance and colleagues, is grounded in humanistic and experiential traditions that emphasize the centrality of emotion in psychological well-being and relational healing (Lafrance Robinson et al., 2016). Drawing from emotion-focused therapy and attachment theory, EFFT integrates the principles of emotion coaching, relationship repair, and caregiver involvement to address the emotional underpinnings of mental health concerns, including eating disorders. The EFFT framework views eating disorder behaviors as relational signals and responses to attachment insecurity, emotional invalidation, or unmet relational needs (Lafrance & Miller, 2020). Therapists adopt a non-expert, collaborative, and emotionally attuned stance, acting as a secure base and modeling safety, responsiveness, and nonjudgmental curiosity (Lafrance Robinson et al., 2016). When therapists attune to both adolescent and parent attachment needs, they create a bridge for reparation and reconnection which are core ingredients for authentic engagement. EFFT creates real-time, emotionally corrective moments in therapy by re-experiencing a previously painful interaction and then building new emotional awareness and a different response (Strahan et al., 2017). For example, a teen may disclose feeling alone in their struggle with body image, and a previously distant parent, now guided by the therapist, responds with genuine care and regret for missed attunement. This type of emotional shift reorients the family toward relational safety and connection, fostering repair of attachment ruptures and encouraging authenticity between family members.

Attunement

Attunement in therapy refers to a therapist's ability to be fully present, emotionally responsive, and deeply connected to a client's experience. It involves perceiving and validating a client's emotions, thoughts, and needs in a way that fosters safety and trust (Geller & Porges, 2014). Especially in eating disorder treatment, where shame, secrecy, and self-criticism are often central, attunement provides a corrective emotional experience. By staying nonjudgmental, emotionally present, and attuned to both verbal and nonverbal cues, therapists create the conditions necessary for authentic self-expression and healing.

Expressing Empathy

Empathy is a cornerstone of effective therapy and a critical component of the therapeutic alliance. According to Elliott et al. (2011), empathy enhances the therapeutic relationship by fostering a deeper connection and encouraging clients to explore their vulnerabilities. Rogers's (1957) concept of empathy is relevant in that it allows the therapist to truly "step into the client's shoes," validating their emotions and experiences. Empathic listening involves not only hearing what clients say but also understanding their emotional experiences and reflecting them back with validation.

In practice, empathic attunement includes the following techniques for clinicians to employ when treating clients with eating disorders:

- *Practice reflective listening.* Mirror the client's feelings and content to validate their experience without judgment. This promotes attunement and emotional safety, key factors in eating disorder recovery (Geller & Greenberg, 2012). For example, "It sounds like you're feeling overwhelmed and alone in this struggle."
- *Use open-ended questions.* Encourage narrative expression to deepen understanding of the client's internal world. This helps access the meaning behind behaviors, especially important for clients with anorexia or binge eating disorder (Schmidt & Treasure, 2006). For example, "Can you tell me more about what that meal was like for you?"
- *Employ accurate empathic attunement.* Attend to both verbal and nonverbal cues, recognizing discrepancies that may indicate distress or disconnection. This is essential in building trust, especially when clients experience ambivalence or shame.
- *Use nonverbal communication.* Maintain open posture, appropriate eye contact, and grounded presence. These gestures signal safety and reduce perceived judgment—critical for clients navigating body image sensitivity (Piran, 2017).
- *Hold space for ambivalence.* Allow clients to voice conflicting feelings about food, recovery, or their body without the pressure to resolve them. This facilitates authenticity and supports motivational readiness (Vitousek et al., 1998).
- *Name shame and vulnerability gently.* Normalize difficult emotions by identifying and empathizing without minimizing. Shame resilience is key in eating disorder treatment (Brown, 2006; Geller & Srikameswaran, 2006). For example, "It makes sense that you feel exposed sharing this—thank you for trusting me."
- *Validate the protective function of the eating disorder.* Acknowledge how the eating disorder may have served a purpose, rather than focusing solely on pathology. This strengthens the alliance and reduces resistance (Skårderud, 2007).
- *Use silence and pausing.* Allow space for clients to reflect, feel, and respond, especially when processing distressing topics. This supports emotional processing and self-awareness (Farber & Doolin, 2011).
- *Employ clinician self-regulation.* Monitor your own emotional responses to stay present and attuned. This is critical for co-regulation and avoiding enactments, particularly when working with high-conflict or trauma-related eating disorders (Geller & Greenberg, 2012).

- *Affirm strengths and values.* Reflect back on moments of resilience, connection, or insight. This reinforces agency and promotes identity beyond the eating disorder (Piran, 2017). For example, "You showed a lot of courage by staying in the room when things got hard."

Attachment-Informed Work

A substantial body of research demonstrates that attachment insecurity plays a critical role in both the development and treatment outcomes of eating disorders, influencing affect regulation, interpersonal functioning, and engagement in care. Foundational work by Tasca and colleagues (Tasca & Balfour, 2014; Tasca et al., 2011) highlights that insecure attachment, particularly anxious and avoidant patterns is associated with difficulties in emotion regulation, heightened interpersonal sensitivity, and maladaptive coping strategies that maintain eating disorder symptoms. Empirical studies further show that attachment insecurity predicts poorer treatment outcomes, including less improvement in eating disorder psychopathology and body image disturbance following evidence-based interventions such as CBT-E (Rossi et al., 2022), as well as increased depressive symptoms over the course of treatment (Keating et al., 2015). Additionally, insecure attachment has been linked to mechanisms such as maladaptive perfectionism and interpersonal problems, which mediate and exacerbate eating disorder symptom severity (Dakanalis et al., 2014; Carfagno et al., 2024).

When clinicians respond with sensitivity and reliability, clients begin to internalize a sense of safety that supports authentic self-expression. Clinicians attuned to attachment histories are better able to understand emotional responses, defenses, and relational needs, all key ingredients in fostering authenticity in the therapeutic relationship. This is especially crucial in the treatment of eating disorders, where issues of trust, control, and self-worth often stem from early relational ruptures. Applying an attachment-informed framework supports clients in moving beyond protective strategies like avoidance, perfectionism, or compliance and toward more authentic self-expression and connection.

A secure therapeutic relationship can begin to reverse internalized beliefs such as "I am too much," "I am not enough," or "My needs are a burden." For example, a client with a history of emotional neglect may test the therapist by canceling sessions or downplaying distress. A secure base response involves staying steady and open, expressing curiosity rather than frustration, and validating the client's fears of being let down.

Importantly, this literature underscores the need for clinicians to integrate attachment-informed approaches into treatment planning. Techniques that target affect regulation, interpersonal functioning, and relational safety are particularly relevant, including fostering a secure therapeutic alliance, explicitly addressing attachment-related "stuck points," and supporting patients in developing more adaptive emotion regulation strategies (Tasca et al., 2011;

Keating et al., 2015). Overall, incorporating an attachment lens allows clinicians to move beyond symptom-focused care toward a more comprehensive, relationally attuned approach that can improve engagement, reduce comorbid distress, and enhance long-term recovery outcomes.

Attachment has also become deeply personal for me, not just in my clinical work but in my own life as a parent, friend, and partner. Semester after semester, as I teach attachment theory to my university students, I am reminded of its profound relevance across the lifespan. I often watch their faces light up as they connect Bowlby's foundational ideas of secure and insecure attachment to their own relationships (Bowlby, 1988) or recognize Ainsworth's (1978) descriptions of caregiving patterns reflected in their family dynamics. Those moments remind me that attachment is not simply an abstract theory; it is a lived, relational truth that shapes how we show up with others. For me, integrating attachment into my work with clients is more than explaining secure, anxious, or avoidant styles, it is about modeling, through my own presence, what safety and responsiveness look like. Both in the therapy room and the classroom, as well as in my own life, I see how authenticity flourishes when people feel held in secure connection, and I feel honored to be part of facilitating that recognition (Mikulincer & Shaver, 2019). In my work with eating disorders, this attachment lens reminds me that beneath symptoms often lies a longing for safety and attunement, making the therapeutic relationship itself a powerful intervention (Illing & Tasca, 2022).

Mirroring Clients' Affect

Affective mirroring allows clients to feel emotionally "seen," which strengthens self-awareness and trust. This is done by reflecting the emotional tone, not just using the right words (e.g., "I notice your smile, but your eyes seem concerned, what's that like inside?"). Another way the clinician can do this is by naming and validating the emotional experience (e.g., "It makes sense that you feel both relieved and scared").

Understanding How Attachment Styles Influence Vulnerability and Trust

Each client's attachment style shapes their openness to authentic expression. Helping clients reflect on how their attachment history shows up in the therapy relationship itself, and how that awareness can lead to new, authentic ways of relating can be a powerful tool. For example, clients with anxious attachment style may test boundaries to gauge therapist loyalty or seek frequent reassurance but distrust it. Techniques to work through this attachment style would include offering consistent validation and containment while clarifying the boundaries and structure of the relationship to build trust. As another example, for avoidant clients who may minimize distress or avoid emotional conversations, strategies to overcome the limitations of the attachment style may include respecting their autonomy while gently inviting emotional exploration.

Authenticity as a Byproduct of Felt Safety

When therapists provide sensitive, consistent, and attuned responses, clients internalize relational safety and gradually shift from protective strategies to genuine self-expression. Authenticity becomes possible because the therapeutic relationship becomes a rehearsal space for real-world vulnerability, boundaries, and belonging. Attachment-informed approaches are not just about insight but about creating a lived experience of a safe, healing connection that fosters the courage to be one's true self.

Creative and Expressive Therapies

Not all clients can access authenticity through words alone. Brief, embodied, and creative methods such as metaphor, guided imagery, art, music, dance, or somatic movement offer alternative pathways to attunement (Liu, et al., 2020; Malchiodi, 2018; Siegel, 2010). These methods provide clients with alternative channels to express emotion, release internalized shame, and reconnect with the body in meaningful and reparative ways. For individuals who struggle with alexithymia, dissociation, or rigid cognitive control—all common features in eating disorders, creative approaches can bypass defenses and activate deeper emotional and sensory awareness.

Art therapy, in particular, creates a safe container for clients to explore inner conflicts, relational wounds, and body image distress through symbols, color, and form. As Lisa Hinz (2009) articulated in *Drawing from Within*, the creative process itself becomes a mirror and a metaphor, revealing unconscious material, promoting integration, and fostering a sense of agency. Hinz's text has been an incredible resource for me over the years.

Movement-based interventions like dance or somatic experiencing further support embodiment and emotional regulation, allowing clients to develop a more compassionate and present relationship with their physical selves. These creative modalities also enhance the therapist's attunement to subtle shifts in posture, energy, and mood, deepening the therapeutic alliance and modeling authenticity beyond words.

Creative and Expressive Therapies in Action

I spent years running "expressive" groups in eating disorder treatment facilities. It was my joy to take clients out of the facility and gather on the sandy shorelines of Miami in front of the calm, glistening bay. In one particular session, I laid out large sheets of poster paper across the beach. Each participant sat cross-legged in the sand. The group began with a few moments of deep, intentional breathing—with each inhale inviting safety and each exhale releasing judgment. We continued to ground ourselves by bringing our attention and awareness to our surroundings. I encouraged everyone to feel the soft pressure of the sand beneath us and the warm sun shining down on us while listening to the rhythmic sound of lapping waves. I introduced them to the creative process that we were to engage in. Using oil pastels and colored pencils, each person was to draw their own mandala.

Mandala is an ancient word meaning "sacred circle" in Sanskrit. While its origins are in Eastern religions and philosophies such as Buddhism, Carl Jung further developed the use of mandalas as an integrative mind–body psychotherapy training and since has demonstrated effectiveness with various populations in reducing anxiety and depression (Flett et al., 2017).

Clients were challenged to allow shapes, colors, and patterns to emerge from within without the pressure of perfection, beginning with a central image that represented the experience of grounding themselves in the moment. After creating the central image, the clients were to add around it colors, shapes, lines, or symbols until it felt complete.

Some drew spirals; others created floral motifs or abstract symbols of struggle and hope. After reflecting on their mandalas, the group came together and joined their mandalas. Each client connected the edges of their mandala with lines to others they felt connected to, ultimately creating a shared tapestry of recovery. The simple act of connecting their mandalas symbolized the strength of community and the uniqueness of each voice in the healing process. As the wind moved softly around them, clients spoke about what their mandala represented; themes ranged from resilience, hunger for freedom, and the return to self.

We ended the group in a circle again centering ourselves with breath and gratitude, everyone's hands resting lightly on the edge of the connected artwork. For that moment, the group existed as a community of healing and support, witnessing each other, grounded by sand and sky.

Person-of-the-Therapist Training Model

The person-of-the-therapist training (POTT) model emphasizes the importance of the therapist's own history, identity, and emotional awareness in shaping the therapeutic relationship. By exploring their own blind spots and relational patterns, clinicians can remain more attuned and congruent with their clients (Aponte & Kissil, 2016). Clinicians who engage in ongoing self-reflection and supervision are better equipped to use themselves authentically and responsively in the therapy room.

I was fortunate to be introduced to the POTT model in my doctoral program. Dr. Harry Aponte, who was then teaching and supervising students, created this model and piloted programs at Drexel University while I was receiving my degree. Aponte & Kissil (2016) asserted that "the personal self who is the therapist is an essential element of the therapeutic process, because it is the human relationship with clients that is the medium through which the work of therapy is done" (p. 136). His concepts of bringing our full selves to therapy were very scary when I initially learned about them. Coming from a master's degree program where there was an emphasis on learning and practicing from a cognitive–behavioral lens, Aponte's work seemed a little "out there" to me during those early days. As I continued through the program, I became acquainted with the common factors approach (discussed in Chapter 4), which aligned with the POTT training model in that regardless of a specific model, it was important for clinicians to work through their human vulnerabilities. Self-awareness and self-mastery of the clinician (the person) in the therapeutic process is the primary goal of training within the POTT framework (Aponte, 2022). Additionally, POTT includes sociocultural and political perspectives and values that impact a therapists' life such as gender, race, ethnicity, which allows for exploration of marginalized identities. These concepts allow a clinician to position themselves within the larger cultural environment, which further aligned with my perspectives.

POTT GOALS

One concept from POTT that resonated with me first as a trainee and later as I trained clinicians was that we are who we are at a specific moment in time. In the context of learning how to be a therapist, it is important to remember that clients that we are seeing know us now, not in the "future selves" we might hope to be. We can use the tools we have at our disposal in the current moment when we are working with that individual or family. New therapists are in a continuous state of attempting to figure out what will work with their clients. A goal of POTT is for trainees to both identify with their clients while also simultaneously analyzing the "self" of the therapist as they are training to manage the process of therapy.

POTT FOR EDS

The POTT model offers a powerful framework for preparing therapists to work more authentically and effectively with clients who have eating disorders. The emphasis on the clinician's self-awareness and use of their own life experiences as clinical tools are an essential skillset when addressing the relational, emotional, and identity-based complexities of eating disorders.

As eating disorders often emerge in the context of attachment disruptions, trauma, perfectionism, shame, and control, it can often (and frequently does) evoke strong reactions from clinicians, especially related to food, body image, identity, and familial roles. The POTT model trains therapists to examine how their personal history, values, and emotional wounds may unconsciously shape their therapeutic responses. For example:

- A therapist with a history of body shame or food restriction may unknowingly collude with restrictive clients or avoid addressing weight-related topics.

- A clinician raised in a family system that avoided conflict may struggle with addressing family dynamics or resistance in ED treatment.
- Conversely, a therapist who has worked through similar vulnerabilities may model attuned, regulated presence and authentic engagement that fosters client trust and openness.

Through structured self-exploration, guided reflection, and supervised enactment, POTT helps therapists turn their inner worlds into sources of clinical wisdom rather than interference (Aponte & Kissil, 2016). This is especially relevant in ED work, where authentic relational connection, attunement to nonverbal cues, and emotional tolerance are crucial for alliance-building and rupture repair.

POTT ETHICAL BOUNDARIES AND CULTURAL RESPONSIVENESS

POTT does not promote self-disclosure for its own sake but encourages intentional and bounded authenticity. This is vital in ED work, where clients often test relational boundaries and bring high sensitivity to therapist identity (e.g., body size, food behaviors, gender). Therapists trained in POTT are better equipped to manage these dynamics ethically and empathetically, using their presence and their personal narratives to promote healing.

When Attunement Is a Miss

Therapeutic attunement is not about perfection—it's about responsiveness. Addressing moments of misattunement openly can strengthen the alliance and model relational repair (Safran & Muran, 2000). Key components include:

- Naming when the client feels unseen, misunderstood, or disconnected
- Taking responsibility as the therapist when missteps occur
- Inviting the client to express their experience of the rupture
- Co-constructing meaning from the rupture to restore trust and relational authenticity

Misattunement repairs build resilience and model relational authenticity by acknowledging when a response missed the mark such as, "I think I misunderstood what you were trying to say, can we go back to that?" or through inviting feedback, such as "Was that how you hoped I would respond?" Repair work affirms that conflict doesn't have to lead to disconnection. Instead, it can deepen trust and model authenticity as a relational process. I will discuss more on ruptures and repairs in a later chapter.

By practicing empathic responsiveness, honoring their own emotional presence, integrating attachment insights, and creating space for verbal and nonverbal expression, clinicians promote a climate of attunement where authenticity can emerge and flourish. In my own journey, I have found that this kind of attunement has become more natural with time and practice; what once felt like a deliberate effort now flows more intuitively. The more I leaned into authenticity in my work, the more comfortable I became trusting that genuine presence, rather than perfectly chosen words, was what truly created safety and healing (Safran & Muran, 2000; Norcross & Lambert, 2018).

Sam's Case: Lessons Learned

I want to go back to the example I opened this chapter with to give you some thoughts on what I learned from Sam as a novice clinician and how those lessons helped shape future interactions with clients.

They say everything you need to know you learned in kindergarten—how to listen, how to share, how to show up for others. In many ways, my early experience with Sam was my kindergarten lesson in therapy:it was a foundational moment that taught me the importance of presence, humility, and the power of authentic connection.

The first lesson I learned from Sam was simple but profound: put down the pen and paper. In the rush to complete a Columbia Suicide Severity Rating Scale (C-SSRS) within 24 hours of admit or finalize a biopsychosocial within three days to ensure compliance, it's easy to forget as a clinician that we're sitting across from a human being and not a checklist. I'm not suggesting that clinical standards and documentation don't matter. They do. In fact, I believe we need even stronger standards to ensure clients receive the right care at the right level. But what I've come to understand is that good therapy requires a dialectic, holding the tension between system demands and the relational needs of the person in front of us. This is especially true for clients with eating disorders who often carry histories of secrecy, shame, and relational rupture; we must remember that authenticity is the foundation of trust. If that means spending an extra 15 minutes with a client in the first session, do it. Ask real questions not because the form requires it but to learn more about how a client lives, who they are, and what brought them here. And offer something real in return. Clients deserve to know who we are, too: this is not about our credentials but is instead about the reasons we show up.

The second lesson was about the indispensable value of supervision. I sought support after that initial session with Sam, and my supervisor, a skilled clinician who was overseeing 50 clients and more than 10 therapists, did what she could. She offered encouragement, told me it would work out. But her response fell short of what I needed. What I've since learned, and teach often, is this: if you're concerned about a client, say something clearly and make sure you're heard. Don't minimize what your intuition is telling you. Whether you're working toward licensure or have been in the field for decades, seek consultation and training that sharpens your clinical instincts. The work we do is too complex and too sacred to do alone. For outpatient therapists especially, peer supervision or consultation groups aren't optional luxuries. They're lifelines.

Sam also taught me to trust my gut. Over the span of just one week in outpatient care, her behaviors escalated quickly. The more I learned about her history of suicidal gestures and medical risk, the more alarmed I became. When she failed to show up to program one day, I called in a wellness check. It wasn't a dramatic gesture but was a necessary one. Sam needed a higher level of care, and I had to advocate for that, even though I didn't have the language yet to do so. That moment cemented my understanding of the importance of matching clinical care to client acuity and advocating for client safety, even when it's uncomfortable.

But the most enduring lesson Sam gave me was this: people want you to show up for them. Especially clients with eating disorders, who have often lived with silence, shame, and relational mistrust. They don't need perfection. They don't need you to know everything. But they do need to know that when they speak—even if it's to shock you or test you—you'll stay. They need to believe you can bear witness to the hard stuff and still see them as worthy of care. Authenticity isn't just a therapeutic tool; it's a human necessity. In therapy, as in life, the relationships that heal are the ones where both people dare to be real.

Clinical Reminders for Fostering Authenticity

Building authenticity with clients is nuanced and may or may not develop right away or over time, but clinicians can begin to create the authentic relationship with a few simple principles. Here are some of the ones I use in practice and in trainings:

- Slow down (especially the initial intake sessions). Make space for relationships before information.
- Be real, but boundaried. Congruence requires internal awareness and intentional sharing.
- Listen with your whole self. Let the client feel felt.
- Trust your instincts. Use supervision, but don't silence your internal red flags.
- Be embodied. Ground yourself in presence to help clients reconnect with their own.

Summary

This chapter shifts from conceptual grounding to practical application, offering clinicians concrete tools for cultivating an authentic therapeutic relationship with clients struggling with eating disorders. Building on Rogers's core principles of presence, congruence, and attunement, the chapter emphasizes authenticity as something therapists *do* and *embody*, an active way of being in the room. Core relational skills such as active listening, trust-building, reflection, summarizing, and clarifying questions help move conversations beyond surface-level exchanges into deeper emotional truth. Mindfulness and embodiment practices further support both client and clinician in staying grounded and connected, strengthening empathy and rapport. The chapter also illustrates how authenticity can be integrated across different treatment models, allowing therapy to remain structured while deeply relational. Creative and expressive modalities including art, movement, metaphor, and role play offer alternative avenues for clients to access and express their inner experience when words feel insufficient. Ultimately, the chapter highlights that authenticity is not a single intervention but a therapeutic stance that infuses every technique with presence and integrity, modeling genuine connection and inviting clients to rediscover their own authentic voice.

Key Take-Aways

- Presence, congruence, and attunement help clinicians build authentic therapeutic connections.
- When clients feel genuinely seen, heard, and valued, they are more willing to explore vulnerabilities and pursue change.
- Effective therapy is grounded not only in technique but in the therapist's authentic way of being.
- The therapeutic relationship becomes a collaborative partnership in healing, rather than a one-sided intervention.
- Embodying authenticity supports deeper transformation and more enduring therapeutic outcomes.

References

Ainsworth, M. D. S. (1978). *Patterns of attachment: A psychological study of the strange situation.* Lawrence Erlbaum.

Aponte, H. J. (2022). *The Soul of Therapy: The Therapist's Use of Self in the Therapeutic Relationship.* Contemporary Family Therapy. 44, 136–143.

Aponte, H. J., & Kissil, K. (2016). *The person of the therapist training model: Mastering the use of self.* Routledge.

Arrien, A. (1993). *The Four-Fold Way: Walking the Paths of the Warrior*, Teacher, Healer, and Visionary. HarperOne.

Audet, C. T., & Everall, R. D. (2010). *Therapist self-disclosure and the therapeutic relationship: A phenomenological study from the client perspective.* British Journal of Guidance & Counselling, 38(3), 327–342.

Barnett, J. E. (2011). *Psychotherapist self-disclosure: Ethical and clinical considerations.* Psychotherapy, 48(4), 315–321.

Berman, M. I., Park, J., Kragenbrink, M. E., & Hegel, M. T. (2022). *Accept yourself!* A pilot randomized controlled trial of a self-acceptance-based treatment for large-bodied women with depression. Behavior Therapy, 53(5), 913–926.

Bowlby, J. (1988). *A secure base: Parent-child attachment and healthy human development.* Basic Books.

Brown, B. (2006). *Shame resilience theory: A grounded theory study on women and shame.* Families in Society, 87(1), 43–52.

Brown, B. (2012). *Daring greatly: How the courage to be vulnerable transforms the way we live*, love, parent, and lead. Gotham Books.

Brown, T. A., Vanzhula, I. A., Reilly, E. E., Levinson, C. A., Berner, L. A., Krueger, A., ... & Wierenga, C. E. (2020). *Body mistrust bridges interoceptive awareness and eating disorder symptoms.* Journal of Abnormal Psychology, 129(5), 445.

Carreño, T. (2013). Healing moments in psychotherapy.: Daniel J. Siegel and Marion Solomon, Eds. (2013) New York. *The Journal of Nervous and Mental Disease*, 202 (12), 894. December 2014.

Carfagno, M., Barone, E., et al. (2024). Mediation role of interpersonal problems between insecure attachment and eating disorder psychopathology. Eating and Weight Disorders, 29(1), 43.

Cook-Cottone, C. (2015a). *Mindfulness and yoga for self-regulation.* Springer.

Cook-Cottone, C. P. (2015b). *Incorporating positive body image into the treatment of eating disorders: A model for attunement and mindful self-care.* Body Image, 14, 158–167.

Cook-Cottone, C. P. (2020). *Embodiment and the treatment of eating disorders: The body as a resource in recovery.* Body Image, 33, 223–231.

Costin, C., & Grabb, G. (2016). 8 Keys to Recovery from an Eating Disorder: Effective Strategies from Therapeutic Practice and Personal Experience. W. W. Norton & Company.

Dakanalis, A., Clerici, M., et al. (2014). Attachment insecurities, maladaptive perfectionism, and eating disorder symptoms: A latent mediated and moderated structural equation modeling analysis across diagnostic groups. Psychiatry Research, 215(1), 45–52.

del Río Olvera FJ, Rodríguez-Mora Á, Senín-Calderón C and Rodríguez-Testal JF (2022) *The first session is the one that counts: An exploratory study of therapeutic alliance.* Frontiers in Psychology.

Elliott, R., Bohart, A. C., Watson, J. C., & Greenberg, L. S. (2011). *Empathy.* Psychotherapy, 48(1), 43.

Farber, B. A., & Doolin, E. M. (2011). *Positive regard.* Psychotherapy, 48(1), 58.

Flett, J. A. M., Lie, C., Riordan, B. C., Thompson, L. M., Conner, T. S., & Hayne, H. (2017). *Sharpen your pencils: Preliminary evidence that adult coloring reduces depressive symptoms and anxiety.* Creativity Research Journal, 29(4), 409–416.

Flückiger, C., Del Re, A. C., Wampold, B. E., & Horvath, A. O. (2018). *The alliance in adult psychotherapy: A meta-analytic synthesis.* Psychotherapy, 55(4), 316.

Geller, J., & Srikameswaran, S. (2006). *Treatment non-negotiables: Why we need them and how to make them work.* European Eating Disorders Review, 14(4), 212–217.

Geller, S. M., & Greenberg, L. S. (2012). *Therapeutic presence: A mindful approach to effective therapy.* American Psychological Association.

Geller, S. M., & Porges, S. W. (2014). *Therapeutic presence: Neurophysiological mechanisms mediating feeling safe in psychotherapy.* Journal of Psychotherapy Integration, 24(3), 178–192. doi:10.1037/a0037511.

Germer, C., Siegel, R. D., & Fulton, P. R. (Eds.). (2016). *Mindfulness and psychotherapy.* Guilford Publications.

Hayes, S. C., Strosahl, K. D., & Wilson, K. G. (2011). *Acceptance and commitment therapy (2nd ed.).* Guilford Press.

Hill, C. E., & Knox, S. (2002). *Self-disclosure.* Psychotherapy: Theory, Research, Practice, Training, 39(4), 413–417.

Hinz, L. D. (2009). *Drawing from within: Using art to treat eating disorders.* Jessica Kingsley Publishers.

Illing, V., Tasca, G.A., Balfour, L., & Bissada, H. (2010). Attachment insecurity predicts eating disorder symptoms and treatment outcomes in a clinical sample of women. *The Journal of Nervous and Mental Disease, 198*, 653–659.

Jordan, J. V. (2018). *Relational-cultural therapy.* Dar El Kalema Publishing House.

Joseph, S. (2019). *Authentic: How to be yourself and why it matters.* Little, Brown Book Group.

Juarascio, A., Shaw, J., Forman, E., Timko, C. A., Herbert, J., Butryn, M., … & Lowe, M. (2013). *Acceptance and commitment therapy as a novel treatment for eating disorders: An initial test of efficacy and mediation.* Behavior Modification, 37(4), 459–489.

Kabat-Zinn, J. (1990). Full catastrophe living: Using the wisdom of your body and mind to face stress, pain and illness. Delacorte.

Kabat-Zinn, J. (2003). *Mindfulness-based stress reduction (MBSR).* Constructivism in the Human Sciences, 8(2), 73.

Keating, L., Tasca, G. A., & Bissada, H. (2015). Pre-treatment attachment anxiety predicts change in depressive symptoms in women who complete day hospital treatment for anorexia and bulimia nervosa. Psychology and Psychotherapy: Theory, Research and Practice, 88(1), 83–98.

Keyte, R., Egan, H., & Mantzios, M. (2020). *How does mindful eating without non-judgement*, mindfulness and self-compassion relate to motivations to eat palatable foods in a student population? Nutrition and Health, 26(1), 27–34.

Kristeller, J. L., & Wolever, R. Q. (2011). Mindfulness-based eating awareness training for treating binge eating disorder: The conceptual foundation. *Eating Disorders, 19* (1), 49–61. https://doi.org/10.1080/10640266.2011.533605

Kristeller, J., Wolever, R. Q., & Sheets, V. (2014). *Mindfulness-based eating awareness training (MB-EAT) for binge eating: A randomized clinical trial.* Mindfulness, 5(3), 282–297.

Liu, C., Chen, H., Liu, C. Y., Lin, R. T., & Chiou, W. K. (2020). *Cooperative and individual mandala drawing have different effects on mindfulness*, spirituality, and subjective well-being. Frontiers in Psychology, 11, 564430.

Lafrance, A., & Miller, A. P. (2020). *What to say to kids when nothing seems to work: A practical guide for parents and caregivers.* Routledge.

Lafrance Robinson, A., Dolhanty, J., Stillar, A., Henderson, K., & Mayman, S. (2016). *Emotion-focused family therapy for eating disorders across the lifespan: A pilot study of a 2-day transdiagnostic intervention for parents.* Clinical Psychology & Psychotherapy, 23(1), 14–23.

Lock, A. (2020). *Narrative therapy as an approach in eating disorder treatment: Working with meaning and identity.* Journal of Eating Disorders, 8(1), 1–7.

Malchiodi, C. A. (2018). Creative arts therapies and arts-based research. In P. Leavy (Ed.), *Handbook of arts-based research* (pp. 68–87). The Guilford Press.

Manlick, C. F., Cochran, S. V., & Koon, J. (2013). *Acceptance and commitment therapy for eating disorders: Rationale and literature review.* Journal of Contemporary Psychotherapy, 43(2), 115–122.

Matusek, J. A., Wendt, S. J., & Wiseman, C. V. (2004). *Dissonance thin-ideal and didactic healthy behavior eating disorder prevention programs: Results from a controlled trial.* International Journal of Eating Disorders, 36(4), 376–388.

Mikulincer, M., & Shaver, P. R. (2019). Attachment orientations and emotion regulation. *Current Opinion in Psychology, 25*, 6–10.

Miller, J. B., Jordan, J. V., Stiver, I. P., Walker, M., Surrey, J. L., & Eldridge, N. S. (2004). Therapists' authenticity. In J. V. Jordan, M. Walker, & L. M. Hartling (Eds.), *The complexity of connection: Writings from the Stone Center's Jean Baker Miller Training Institute* (pp. 64–89). The Guilford Press.

Norcross, J. C., & Lambert, M. J. (2018). *Psychotherapy relationships that work* III. Psychotherapy, 55(4), 303–350.

Piran, N. (2017). *Journeys of embodiment.* Academic Press.

Piran, N. (2019). *Handbook of positive body image and embodiment: Constructs*, protective factors, and interventions. Oxford University Press.

Porges, S. W. (2011). *The polyvagal theory: Neurophysiological foundations of emotions*, attachment, communication, and self-regulation. Norton.

Rogers, C. (1951). *Client-centered therapy: Its current practice*, implications and theory. Constable.

Rogers, C. R. (1957). *The necessary and sufficient conditions of therapeutic personality change.* Journal of Consulting Psychology, 21(2), 95–103.

Rogers, C. R. (1961). *On becoming a person: A therapist's view of psychotherapy.* Houghton Mifflin.

Rossi, E., Cassioli, E., et al. (2022). Attachment insecurity predicts worse outcome in patients with eating disorders treated with enhanced cognitive behavior therapy: A one-year follow-up study. International Journal of Eating Disorders, 55(10), 1402–1412.

Safran, J. D., & Muran, J. C. (2000). *Resolving therapeutic alliance ruptures: Diversity and integration.* Journal of Clinical Psychology, 56(2), 233–243.

Sala, M., Rochefort, C., Lui, P. P., & Baldwin, A. S. (2020). *Trait mindfulness and health behaviors: A meta-analysis.* Health Psychology Review, 14(3), 345–393.

Schore, A. N. (2014). *The right brain is dominant in psychotherapy.* Psychotherapy, 51 (3), 388.

Schmidt, U., & Treasure, J. (2006). *Anorexia nervosa: Valued and visible.* A cognitive-interpersonal maintenance model and its implications for research and practice. British Journal of Clinical Psychology, 45(3), 343–366.

Skårderud, F. (2007). *Shame and pride in anorexia nervosa: A qualitative descriptive study.* European Eating Disorders Review, 15(2), 81–97.

Siegel, D. J. (2007). *The mindful brain: Reflection and attunement in the cultivation of well-being.* W. W. Norton & Company.

Siegel, D. J. (2010). The mindful therapist: A clinician's guide to mindsight and neural integration. W. W. Norton & Company.

Siegel, D. J. (2012). *The developing mind: How relationships and the brain interact to shape who we are* (2nd ed.). The Guilford Press.

Strahan, E. J., Stillar, A., Files, N., Nash, P., Scarborough, J., Connors, L., … & Lafrance, A. (2017). *Increasing parental self-efficacy with emotion-focused family therapy for eating disorders: A process model.* Person-Centered & Experiential Psychotherapies, 16(3), 256–269.

Tribole, E., & Resch, E. (2020). *Intuitive eating.* St Martin's Press.

Tasca, G. A., Ritchie, K., & Balfour, L. (2011). Implications of attachment theory and research for the assessment and treatment of eating disorders. Psychotherapy, 48(3), 249–259.

Tasca, G. A., & Balfour, L. (2014). Attachment and eating disorders: A review of current research. International Journal of Eating Disorders, 47(7), 710–717.

Vitousek, K., Watson, S., & Wilson, G. T. (1998). *Enhancing motivation for change in treatment-resistant eating disorders.* Clinical Psychology Review, 18(4), 391–420.

White, M., & Epston, D. (1990). *Narrative means to therapeutic ends.* WW Norton & Company.

Zhang, M. Q., Liu, X., & Huang, Y. (2024). *Does mandala art improve psychological well-being in patients?* A systematic review. Journal of Integrative and Complementary Medicine, 30(1), 25–36.

Zur, O. (2007). *Boundaries in psychotherapy: Ethical and clinical explorations.* American Psychological Association.

Chapter 6

Authenticity Through Intersectional Lenses

Overview

- *Authenticity cannot be understood apart from identity.* This chapter explores how intersectional identities—shaped by race, ethnicity, gender, sexuality, class, ability, and more—profoundly influence how clients experience themselves and show up in relationships.
- *Traditional therapeutic models often fall short for clients with marginalized identities.* Barriers to access, cultural mismatch, and systemic inequities make it clear that effective treatment must be responsive, flexible, and rooted in cultural humility.
- *Frameworks such as cultural humility, implicit bias, intersectionality, and the minority stress model provide essential lenses for clinicians.* These theories help explain why authenticity can be difficult to achieve when power, privilege, and oppression are at play in the therapy room.
- *Body image development is deeply impacted by intersectional identities.* Clients navigating multiple layers of marginalization often face conflicting cultural messages about appearance, belonging, and self-worth, complicating their ability to connect authentically with themselves and others.
- *Clinicians can cultivate authenticity by integrating techniques that center lived experience, ask hard questions, and validate the complexity of identity.* Practical strategies for assessment, dialogue, and reflection create space for clients to bring their whole selves into therapy.
- *Relational authenticity becomes the cornerstone of this work.* When therapists acknowledge and engage with intersectional realities, they model the possibility of genuine connection across difference, fostering deeper trust and transformative healing.

I was working as the clinical supervisor with a therapist, Alice, who had recently completed her master's program and she presented a case for review with me. The client, Cassandra, was a 54-year-old Black woman who entered treatment for the first time for binge eating disorder. Cassandra, having never been in any outpatient therapy previously, found the treatment center online after searching for

DOI: 10.4324/9781003632016-7

help with what she considered "out of control" eating and "weight management." She completed an online assessment, found the facility worked with her insurance, submitted paperwork to her employer, and started treatment within one week, a very quick turnaround time for the program's standards.

After her first day in the intensive outpatient program (IOP), Alice sent me an email asking to meet outside of our regularly scheduled time. After listening to the initial case presentation, Alice described her perception of Cassandra's upset upon meeting her and the other clients in the program. Alice, a White, 25-year-old mental health trainee was nearly 30 years Cassandra's junior, and the milieu make up ranged from 18–20-year-olds, all cisgender, White-presenting females in average-sized bodies. Cassandra could not see herself relating to the clinician or the other clients.

In the haste to admit Cassandra to treatment, little of what to expect was reviewed with her. Cassandra had been unaware that most of the program was spent in groups. Additionally, receiving authorization for IOP meant that she did not need to take time off from work, a hardship for her and her family as the program was run in the evenings, another misunderstanding in the rapid entry to treatment.

After several days in the program, Cassandra continued to feel like it was not the right fit for her. As a program supervisor, I decided to meet with Cassandra myself. It was important to acknowledge all of the misses in her start to treatment. Cassandra's decision to seek treatment was a very powerful one; she was in an action phase of stages and change (Prochaska & Norcross, 2002). *After struggling with an eating disorder, never having been diagnosed or referred to care, I believed we could help, but we needed to acknowledge where we were, our limitations, and our biases as providers first.*

There were several important factors that the multidisciplinary treatment team needed to consider in Cassandra's treatment. Our work included challenging and evaluating our stereotypes and bias around race, age, and eating disorders; educating ourselves about inclusive treatment approaches; and recognizing the power and privilege that we held and how this influenced the therapeutic process.

Intersectional identities, or the many factors that make someone who they are, influence an individual's development of authenticity, and that will impact the therapeutic process. A therapist may encounter challenges with their client when authenticity has been compromised by systemic forces. This chapter offers strategies for therapists to create a space where clients feel safe enough to explore and reclaim their true selves. By fostering an awareness of privilege, power, and lived experience, therapists can deepen their capacity for relational authenticity, ensuring that the therapeutic relationship is not another space where a client must perform, mask, or shrink parts of who they are.

How Intersectional Identities Shape Authenticity

Authenticity does not exist in a vacuum; it is shaped by the complex intersections of race, gender, class, sexuality, ability, religion, and other sociocultural identities. From an early age, we receive messages about who we are allowed to be, what is acceptable, and what parts of ourselves must be hidden to ensure safety, belonging, or success. For many, the process of developing self-authenticity is disrupted by systemic oppression, cultural expectations, and family dynamics that reinforce the need to conform rather than embrace one's full, unfiltered self. Those with marginalized identities often navigate a world that imposes rigid definitions of worth, beauty, and normalcy—forcing them to mask or silence parts of their identity to survive. This learned inauthenticity becomes internalized, shaping self-perception and impacting relationships, including the therapeutic relationship.

Within the therapeutic space, both the client and therapist bring their histories, experiences, and identities into the relationship—whether consciously or unconsciously. The power dynamics of therapy cannot be separated from the societal structures that have historically dictated who holds authority, whose voices are heard, and whose experiences are validated. Clients with intersectional identities may enter therapy carrying a history of being misunderstood, dismissed, or even harmed by healthcare systems, making trust difficult to establish. Additionally, therapists who have not examined their own positionality may unintentionally reinforce these patterns, creating barriers to authenticity within the therapeutic alliance. For true healing to occur, both therapist and client must engage in a process of mutual awareness, understanding how personal histories and cultural narratives shape the ways authenticity is expressed, withheld, or adapted in relationships.

Taylor's Case: A Hidden Identity

Intersectional identities are not always obvious, so they need to be considered for every client. Here's a story about Taylor and how a part of herself emerged during ED treatment that she had not recognized before.

Nearly a decade prior to the pandemic, I was introduced to Taylor when she arrived for residential treatment. Other program staff told me I was "lucky" to be assigned to work with her. On paper, it appeared as though Taylor had an eating disorder. Just an eating disorder. Perhaps some anxiety peppered in there. It seemed like an "easy" case.

Taylor was from a rural town in central Texas and was 19 years old. She presented herself with all of her Texas charm—including her long, wavy blond hair, blue eyes, and smaller body—but she was struggling with binging and purging. It was between her sophomore year and junior year of college when Taylor made the decision to come to treatment. Initially, she cited the pressure she felt from her parents advising her to major in business and her resulting struggle with the course content as the main reasons for her eating disorder.

However, after conducting an extensive psychosocial history and noticing some nuances in group therapy, the team recommended Taylor complete full psychological testing, which her parents supported. From the battery of assessments, it was determined that Taylor struggled with learning disabilities that had been undiagnosed throughout her life. Schooling has been painful for her, and she experienced shame around the difficulties she had with education. Despite her challenges with formal education, Taylor flourished with a talent for creativity. She was a creator, a painter, and even had started an Etsy shop to sell her creations.

Discovering reasons for Taylor's academic struggles and encouraging her to embrace her creativity appeared to be the main breakthroughs that would contribute to her treatment. After working with Taylor and having challenging conversations with her parents around continuation of formal education in the arts rather than business, her treatment appeared to be progressing beautifully. I thought we had hit the therapeutic jackpot: we had a "reason" for why Taylor's ED had taken center stage and we were working through it.

Taylor progressed well through both residential and partial ED programs; however, toward the end of her time in the partial hospitalization program (PHP), she really started struggling. Taylor had been hiding food, lying about her intake, and engaging again in purging behaviors. She appeared not only unable to use any coping skills she had developed, but she was also unable to reflect on her new (old) struggles.

Around this time, some of the other clients in the program were exploring outside relationships and beginning to date—though this was not recommended while they were in treatment it was happening, nonetheless. A staff member noticed Taylor's quiet and cool distancing from the barrage of dating discussions. When I brought it up to her in our next individual session, she responded in tears refusing to talk about it more. Several sessions went by with Taylor's continued protest to explore her increase in symptom engagement. When I circled back to her intimate relationship history, Taylor had previously reported dating her high school boyfriend for a year, breaking up when they attended different colleges, and going to sorority date functions with men during her freshman year in college, while maintaining high school friendships and meeting new people in college.

One day, after a particularly distressing family session where her parents demanded she "just eat," Taylor was once again tearful and unable to identify why she was spiraling. I asked Taylor to think about what she wanted her life to look like in five years. I asked her to consider what it would feel like to wake up in the morning knowing that she was recovered and to explore what it felt like to experience contentment. Where would she be? What and who would be around her? What would she be doing? While her eyes were closed when I asked her this miracle question (a technique from solution-focused brief therapy), I saw Taylor's face soften. Upon opening her eyes, while tears poked out, she was not crying, but rather, she was smiling. She began to giggle, then to guffaw. Watching her regain her composure, then experiencing some shock, Taylor said when she pictured herself in five years in recovery, she woke up in bed next to a friend from her sorority. Finding this confusing, we began exploring Taylor's sexual identity development. It turns out that Taylor had been having feelings for girls from a young age. She recalled experiencing shame, feeling this was "bad" growing up, ignoring when the feelings occurred, and surrounding herself with a boyfriend. Through continued exploration, Taylor realized that the heightened symptom engagement that landed her in treatment followed sorority date functions where she felt pressure to partner with men sexually.

As we started to explore these feelings more, I asked Taylor why she thought this had not been discussed in our therapeutic work up to that point. Two significant things stood out that I will never forget. First, Taylor told me that I did not "look" like I would be able to explore this topic with her. By presenting as a cisgender, feminine, heterosexual woman, she was concerned that I would not be able to explore topics around gender and sexual identity. The second point she made struck me hard—she simply stated that I had not asked about her sexuality.

I had generally considered myself a therapist who did not take the easy way out and asked the hard questions. However, I realized stereotypes had impacted my work with Taylor. I had not opened myself and my identities enough to Taylor to the extent that she felt comfortable enough voicing her innermost thoughts around her identity.

Stereotypes, defined by the American Psychological Association (APA, n.d.), are "a set of cognitive generalizations about the qualities and characteristics of the members of a group or social category." Stereotypes and biases inhibit our abilities to see people for who they truly are if they do not align with our preconceived perceptions and judgments. In the best-case scenario, stereotypes in therapy are a barrier to building authentic relationships in that they oversimplify predetermined ideas about who someone really is. This was certainly the case in my work with Taylor. I had made assumptions based on her presenting as a cisgender, sorority-loving, college-aged Texan. I was focused on therapeutic red herrings versus diving deeper into her background and constructs without asking questions.

Through our continued work, therapy became an opportunity for both Taylor and me to challenge internalized narratives, break down stereotypes, and work for her to develop a more integrated and empowered sense of self.

Traditional Therapeutic Models May Miss the Mark

Traditional therapeutic models often fail to fully address the needs of Black, Indigenous, and People of Color (BIPOC) and LGBTQ+ individuals because they were largely developed within a Eurocentric, cisnormative, and heteronormative framework that does not account for the unique lived experiences of marginalized populations (Sue et al., 2019). Many standard therapeutic approaches emphasize individual pathology while neglecting the systemic and structural factors such as racism, homophobia, transphobia, and socioeconomic barriers, that contribute to mental health struggles in marginalized communities (Hatzenbuehler & Pachankis 2016). Additionally, diagnostic criteria for mental health conditions, including eating disorders, have historically been based on research samples that primarily included White, cisgender individuals, leading to underdiagnosis or misdiagnosis in BIPOC and LGBTQ+ populations (Goetz, 2022). Moreover, many therapeutic models lack cultural humility and fail to incorporate the intersectional stressors that shape identity-based trauma, resulting in treatment that does not feel affirming or relevant to clients with marginalized identities (Singh & Moss, 2016).

A growing body of research highlights significant disparities in the prevalence, recognition, and treatment of eating disorders across diverse populations. For example, Marques et al. (2011) found that while eating disorders occur across all racial and ethnic groups, minority populations are less likely to access treatment despite experiencing comparable levels of impairment. Similarly, Sonneville and Lipson (2018) demonstrated that individuals from racial/ethnic minority backgrounds, higher-weight groups, and lower socioeconomic status are less likely to receive a diagnosis or treatment, even when symptoms are present. These disparities are further compounded by clinician bias, as Gordon et al. (2006) found that client race can influence the likelihood of accurate eating disorder detection, contributing to underdiagnosis in marginalized groups.

Systemic and structural factors also play a critical role. Acle et al. (2021) emphasized the importance of culturally responsive care, noting that standard treatment approaches often fail to account for cultural differences in symptom expression, help-seeking behaviors, and stigma. In addition, Jennings Mathis et al. (2020) identified a lack of workforce diversity within eating disorder treatment settings, which may limit culturally competent care and reduce patient engagement. These concerns are particularly salient in the context of an increasingly diverse U.S. population (Jensen, 2023), underscoring the urgent need for more inclusive, equitable, and culturally attuned approaches to eating disorder assessment and treatment.

Diagnostic Misses

When I ask, "what does an eating disorder look like," often people have a mental picture that is formed. Often, a picture of a thin or emaciated White teenage cis-female appears. For individuals who identify as part of the LGBTQ+ community, eating disorders can often be layered on experiences of gender dysphoria, internalized homophobia, and societal pressures regarding masculinity, femininity, and body ideals. Similarly, individuals identifying in a BIPOC community face unique challenges related to body image, influenced by cultural beauty norms, racism, and the underrepresentation of their experiences in eating disorder research and treatment. These factors combined have contributed to the underdiagnosis and misdiagnosis of eating disorders in marginalized groups, which further complicates the therapeutic relationship (Goetz, 2022).

There are often significant racial disparities in the diagnosis and treatment of eating disorders, emphasizing that individuals from minority ethnic groups are frequently underdiagnosed and undertreated. Eating disorders have historically been perceived as predominantly affecting young, affluent, White females, leading to a lack of recognition and research concerning their prevalence in diverse populations (Gordon et al., 2002). This perception often contributes to delayed diagnoses and inadequate treatment for BIPOC individuals, as healthcare providers may not readily identify eating disorder symptoms in these populations. There is a need for increased awareness and culturally sensitive diagnostic criteria to ensure timely and effective interventions across all racial and ethnic groups.

Access to Care

Individuals who identify as BIPOC and/or LGBTQ+ often encounter significant barriers to accessing appropriate medical and mental health care, leading to underutilization of services and increased risk of misdiagnosis. Systemic discrimination and implicit biases within healthcare settings contribute to these disparities. For instance, a study published in the *Journal of General Internal Medicine* found that implicit bias among healthcare providers adversely affects patient–provider interactions, resulting in lower quality of care and poor health outcomes for BIPOC and LGBTQ+ individuals (FitzGerald & Hurst, 2017). The National Alliance on Mental Illness highlights that provider bias and a lack of cultural competency can lead to misdiagnosis and inadequate treatment for Black individuals, ultimately contributing to mistrust of mental health professionals (Desai et al., 2021). These biases can lead to the dismissal of legitimate health concerns, fostering mistrust and reluctance among these populations to seek necessary care. Moreover, if referrals to higher levels of care of treatment are made by these primary care providers, it is likely patients' experiences are being dismissed and therefore not being referred to receive the appropriate care.

Socioeconomic factors often exacerbate challenges in accessing treatment. According to the Human Rights Campaign (n.d.), more than one quarter (28%) of LGBTQ+ adults of color lack health insurance coverage, compared to 8% of all adults. This disparity limits access to both preventive and acute medical services. Cachelin et al. (2001) found that barriers to access to care included financial difficulties, lack of insurance, a belief that others could not help, fear of being labeled, and not knowing about resources.

A substantial body of research demonstrates that systemic barriers significantly contribute to disparities in eating disorder treatment, with individuals from marginalized and minority populations facing reduced access to care due to socioeconomic constraints, limited availability of culturally competent providers, and structural inequities within healthcare systems (Striegel-Moore et al., 2005; Fitzsimmons-Craft et al., 2019). These disparities are further compounded by under-recognition of eating disorders in diverse populations and biases in diagnosis and referral patterns, ultimately limiting timely intervention and contributing to poorer outcomes (Fitzsimmons-Craft et al., 2019).

Research examining eating disorders among individuals of Black/African and Indigenous heritage highlights important disparities in prevalence, risk factors, and treatment access within BIPOC communities. Studies suggest that environmental stressors including acculturative stress, discrimination, and systemic inequities may contribute to the onset and maintenance of eating disorders in these populations (Acle et al., 2021; Marques et al., 2011). Despite comparable levels of impairment, Black individuals, particularly Black women, are significantly less likely than their White counterparts to seek or receive treatment for conditions such as binge eating disorder and are more likely to disengage from clinical trials and treatment settings (Marques et al., 2011; Sonneville & Lipson, 2018). These findings underscore the need for culturally responsive, accessible, and inclusive approaches to eating disorder care that better address the unique experiences of Black, Indigenous, and other marginalized populations.

Sonneville and Lipson (2018) found that in a college sample compared to White students, students of color were significantly less likely to receive an eating disorder diagnosis and significantly less likely to get treatment. Collectively, these factors create substantial obstacles for BIPOC and LGBTQ+ individuals in receiving accurate diagnoses and effective treatments, underscoring the need for systemic changes to promote equity in healthcare.

Tamara's Case: Feeling Out of Place in Treatment

I was working as the clinical supervisor with a therapist, Alice, who had recently completed her master's program and she presented a case for review. Tamara was a 54-year-old Black woman who entered treatment for the first time for binge eating disorder. Tamara, having never been in any outpatient therapy previously, found the treatment center online after searching for help with what she considered "out of control" eating and "weight management." She completed an online assessment, found the facility worked with her insurance, submitted paperwork to her employer, and started treatment within one week, a very quick turnaround time for the program's standards.

After her first day in the intensive outpatient program (IOP), Alice sent me an email asking to meet outside of our regularly scheduled time. After listening to the initial case presentation, Alice described her perception of Tamara's upset upon meeting her and the other clients in the program. Alice, a White, 25-year-old mental health trainee was nearly 30 years Tamara's junior, and the milieu make up ranged from 18–20-year-olds, all cisgender, White-presenting females in average-sized bodies. Tamara could not see herself relating to the clinician or the other clients.

In the haste to admit Tamara to treatment, little of what to expect was reviewed with her. Tamara had been unaware that most of the program was spent in groups. Additionally, receiving authorization for IOP meant that she did not need to take off from work, a hardship for her and her family as the program was run in the evenings, another misunderstanding in the rapid entry to treatment.

After several days in the program, Tamara continued to feel like it was not the right fit for her. As a program supervisor, I decided to meet with Tamara myself. It was important to acknowledge all of the misses in her start to treatment. Tamara's decision to seek treatment was a very powerful one; she was in an action phase of stages and change (Prochaska & Norcross, 2002). After struggling with an eating disorder, never having been diagnosed or referred to care, I believed we could help, but we needed to acknowledge where we were, our limitations, and our biases as providers first.

There were several important factors that the multidisciplinary team needed to consider in Tamara's treatment. Our work included challenging and evaluating our stereotypes and bias around race, age, and eating disorders; educating ourselves about inclusive treatment approaches; and recognizing the power and privilege that we held and how this influenced the therapeutic process.

Effective Treatment for All

One of the first issues with providing effective treatment for all clients is that the assessments and criteria for diagnosing eating disorders and body image issues are rooted in cisgender White individuals. Small and Fuller (2020) reported that many research studies presented mixed results when attempting to compare eating disorders in Black and White women. They argued, however, that it is likely the nature of the assessments being used that are not accurately reflecting how eating disorders and body image distress show up in Black women. Small and Fuller state, "If body dissatisfaction and restrictive eating are the two variables chosen as instrument measures, and Black women score low on it, the implication is that they may not have EDs, when in fact they may" (p. 4). Eating disorder assessments and inventories tend to focus on items that may not be relevant for Black women. As a result, Black women may be less likely to be diagnosed with an eating disorder, less likely to receive a referral, and, ultimately, less likely to receive the needed treatment for recovery. Alexander et al. (2024) assert that new assessments are needed to evaluate ED symptoms holistically that include identity-based cultural factors contributing to the emergence, maintenance, and presentation of ED symptoms.

Treatment itself needs to be approached through a lens of cultural humility and deeper understanding of how intersectional identities including all facets of identity—race, cultural background, gender identity, sexual orientation, body size, and so forth—impact eating disorder onset and development (Acle et al., 2021). While individual practitioners must work and learn through training, supervision, and personal reflection, treatment centers have an additional layer of responsibility around inclusive care. Comprehensive strategies for health care systems to provide more inclusive care should be mandatory and not "extras" for a monthly training as I have experienced. There are significant opportunities to advance more inclusive eating disorder care, including increasing diversity in research samples, improving cultural competence training among providers, and developing community-based, culturally tailored interventions to better meet the needs of diverse populations (Acle et al., 2021; Jennings Mathis et al., 2020; Sonneville & Lipson, 2018). By addressing systemic issues, we can attempt to provide more equitable and effective care for eating disorders.

Watson (cited in Small & Fuller, 2020) argued that "one of the unspoken but valuable experiences gained in treatment centers is having access to peers who are experiencing similar issues" (p.146). In Tamara's case study, she had concern about not seeing herself reflected in those around her, and this was a significant issue throughout her treatment. If there is a lack of appropriate diagnosis and assessment, and therefore referral to higher level of care, then it is less likely that minorities will see themselves represented by peers in a treatment environment.

In addition to not seeing herself represented in the client population based on race, age, and diagnoses, all significant issues in treatment facilities, Tamara also did not see herself reflected in the center's staff; there was not one therapist of color on the payroll. This is an ongoing issue in this field. Small and Fuller (2020) assert that while diversity is on the rise in the United States population, racial and ethnic minorities account for a smaller proportion of US mental health-care providers. As a result of this imbalance, Small and Fuller (2020) suggest that individuals from minority groups seeking mental health care are likely to receive treatment from providers whose cultural or ethnic backgrounds differ from their own. This was certainly the case in Tamara's environment.

Cultural Humility and Implicit Bias

Yeager and Bauer-Wu (2013) define cultural humility as the process of self-reflection and discovery to build honest and trustworthy relationships. Cultural humility speaks to the therapists' effort to learn about their clients' background and experiences rather than relying on the therapist's own perception or conclusion. Cultural humility is an active practice for providers in which it is important to recognize that there are things they do not know.

An important self-reflection practice I have had the opportunity to engage with is around understanding implicit bias. Implicit bias refers to the attitudes or stereotypes we have that affect our understanding, actions, and decisions in an unconscious manner. I have had opportunities over time to take assessments around implicit biases and always come out of the experience learning something about myself.

For providers interested in engaging in an implicit association test (IAT), Harvard has a wonderful resource, Project Implicit, where a person can take a variety of IATs including those associated with race, gender, size, and ethnicity, among other topics. I strongly encourage those providing ED care to clients to engage in this kind of professional development.

Intersectionality theory (Crenshaw, 1989) and the minority stress model (Meyer, 2003) provide critical frameworks for understanding how overlapping marginalized identities contribute to compounded stigma, discrimination, and societal pressure, particularly in the context of eating disorders and mental health treatment.

Intersectionality Theory

Intersectionality theory asserts that individuals experience oppression in multifaceted ways based on intersecting identities such as race, gender, sexual orientation, socioeconomic status, and ability. For BIPOC and LGBTQ+ individuals with eating disorders, these intersecting identities create unique challenges that mainstream eating disorder research and treatment models often overlook.

Eating disorder symptoms in BIPOC individuals are often overlooked or misdiagnosed due to persistent stereotypes that these conditions primarily affect White, cisgender women, which can bias clinical recognition and delay appropriate diagnosis and treatment (Gordon et al., 2006).

Minority Stress Model

The minority stress model (Meyer, 2003) further explains how chronic stressors related to discrimination, social rejection, and internalized stigma contribute to the development and maintenance of eating disorders in marginalized populations. The model highlights how individuals with minority identities experience additional stress beyond general life challenges due to systemic oppression and social exclusion. For example, LGBTQ+ individuals face higher rates of body dissatisfaction and disordered eating due to the compounded effects of societal pressure to conform to heteronormative standards and intracommunity expectations regarding body aesthetics (Brewster et al., 2019). Additionally, BIPOC individuals, particularly Black women, experience unique pressures to resist White-centered beauty standards while also navigating cultural expectations surrounding body size and food consumption (Rodgers et al., 2022). These intersecting stressors often manifest as disordered eating behaviors used as coping mechanisms for trauma, discrimination, and identity-based stress.

In therapy, clinicians must recognize these layers of stress and oppression to provide culturally competent and affirming care that acknowledges both the systemic and personal factors influencing a client's disordered eating behaviors. Without this nuanced understanding, therapy risks reinforcing the very structures of oppression that contribute to eating disorders in the first place. To provide truly effective care, mental health professionals must adopt culturally responsive, intersectional, and trauma-informed approaches that validate and center the lived experiences of BIPOC and LGBTQ+ individuals in therapy.

How Clients Develop Learned Inauthenticity

Individuals with multiple marginalized identities often develop learned inauthenticity concerning body image and self-perception due to pervasive societal pressures and systemic discrimination. Societal norms frequently uphold narrow standards of beauty that exclude diverse body types, skin tones, and physical features, leading individuals from marginalized groups to internalize negative perceptions of their bodies. This internalization can result in a disconnection from one's authentic self, as individuals may feel compelled to conform to unattainable ideals to gain acceptance or avoid prejudice. Research indicates that such internalized stigma is linked to body dissatisfaction and disordered eating behaviors, as individuals strive to align with societal expectations at the expense of their well-being (National Eating Disorders Association, n.d.).

Individuals from marginalized groups may often experience an inability to safely express their full selves in relationships because dominant cultural narratives render their bodies and experiences as "too much," "not normal," or "invalid." In her powerful memoir, *Hunger*, Roxanne Gay (2017) describes how her trauma and fatness shaped her sense of safety in relationships; she learned to shrink emotionally even as she physically resisted shrinking through weight loss. Her need for self-protection made honesty and vulnerability difficult, especially when society punished her for existing in a fat, Black, queer body.

The media plays a significant role in reinforcing these unrealistic beauty standards, often underrepresenting or misrepresenting marginalized bodies. This lack of representation can lead to feelings of invisibility or pressure to alter one's appearance to fit dominant ideals. As a result, people may adopt behaviors and attitudes that are incongruent with their true selves, perpetuating a cycle of learned inauthenticity.

Dalie Kinsey, a registered dietitian, emphasizes that for BIPOC and queer individuals, authenticity is often a survival negotiation. Being true to oneself in environments steeped in racism, homophobia, and fatphobia can lead to social, economic, and physical harm. In *Decolonizing Wellness: A QTBIPOC-Centered Guide to Escape the Diet Trap, Heal Your Self-Image, and Achieve Body Liberation* (2022), Kinsey argues that the existing mainstream media messages do not account for intersectional identities and the challenges of colorism, homophobia, transphobia, and generational trauma that have significant impact on body image and wellness.

Societal expectations exert considerable pressure on BIPOC communities to conform to Eurocentric beauty ideals, often leading to the marginalization of diverse body types and features. These pressures can result in individuals feeling compelled to alter their appearance or suppress aspects of their identity to align with dominant cultural norms. Such conformity not only perpetuates learned inauthenticity but also reinforces systemic biases that devalue the inherent diversity within BIPOC communities.

One of the books that was recommended to me in the spring of 2020 that I have read, referenced, and used with clients as a therapeutic tool is *Fearing the Black Body* (Strings 2019). Strings (2019) traces how anti-Blackness and fatphobia were institutionalized to uphold White supremacy. She makes the argument that authenticity has been inaccessible for Black woman whose bodies have historically been labeled as deviant or excessive. Strings argues that individuals from marginalized groups are taught that their bodies are inherently flawed, which fosters internalized shame and disconnects them from embodied, relational authenticity.

Body Image Development in Clients with Intersectional Identities

There are unique challenges associated with body image development in marginalized groups such as LGBTQ+, BIPOC, and other minority populations (Rodgers 2016). For example, while Black women have long been underrepresented in ED literature due to stereotypes that EDs mainly afflict White women, they still experience body image concerns shaped by both gendered beauty norms and racial context (Small & Fuller, 2020). Cultural ideals around body shape can differ. Many Black and other ethnic minority communities have historically valued curvier or larger body types more than the Western "thin ideal," which was believed to be a potential buffer for some women of color against body dissatisfaction. However, pervasive exposure to Western beauty standards and the stresses of racism, discrimination, and acculturative pressure can erode this protection, contributing to ED development (Small & Fuller, 2020; Acle et al., 2021).

Studies show that racism-related stress is a significant risk factor to eating disorder development: perceived racial discrimination has been linked to higher binge-eating symptoms among African Americans (with particularly strong effects in women), and similar patterns are seen in other marginalized groups (Assari, 2018; Clark & Winterowd, 2012). This underscores that intersectional experiences shape body image by compounding societal pressures and trauma that can trigger eating disorders.

Schuyler Bailar (n.d.), the first openly transgender athlete to compete in NCAA Division I men's swimming, provides a personal perspective on these challenges. Throughout his journey, Bailar grappled with body image issues, eating disorders, and gender dysphoria. He has shared that his struggles were deeply intertwined with societal expectations and the internal pressures of aligning his physical appearance with his gender identity. Bailar's experiences underscore the unique and multifaceted body image challenges faced by LGBTQ+ individuals, highlighting the need for inclusive and affirming support systems within both healthcare and community settings.

Bailar, an author and activist, is a passionate leader and educator around mental health awareness, trans inclusion, and body acceptance. I am honored to have had the unique privilege of learning from Bailar over the past decade. We have presented together nationally on topics around gender, identity, eating disorders, and body image development over half a dozen times. With each opportunity, I have learned something about who I am, my therapeutic style, and the type of authentic person I hope to be. I have profound gratitude for the work he continues to do.

Sexual and gender minority identities further intersect with race and gender to influence body image and ED risk. LGBTQ+ individuals may experience body image concerns rooted in both societal beauty norms and expectations within their own communities regarding gender expression and desirability (Kalash, et al., 2023). These layers of marginalization make it more difficult for individuals to access affirming and effective treatment, perpetuating cycles of untreated or misdiagnosed eating disorders.

Societal norms frequently promote narrow definitions of attractiveness, emphasizing ideals such as thinness or muscularity, which can marginalize those who do not conform to these standards. For LGBTQ+ individuals, these pressures are compounded by community-specific ideals. For instance, gay men may encounter expectations to maintain a lean and toned physique to align with certain subcultural aesthetics, while transgender individuals might feel compelled to modify their bodies to better reflect their gender identity, sometimes leading to body dissatisfaction or disordered eating behaviors (Brewster et al., 2019).

Research indicates that gay and bisexual men have markedly elevated rates of body dissatisfaction and eating disorders compared to heterosexual men, likely due to a cultural emphasis on leanness/muscularity in male-attracted communities and minority stress related to sexual orientation (Diemer et al., 2015; Menon et al., 2024). Among women, lesbian and bisexual individuals may face slightly less pressure to be ultra-thin from male gaze standards, but they are by no means immune; societal fatphobia and stress from homophobia can still foster body image issues and unhealthy eating behaviors. In fact, sexual orientation discrimination in adolescence has been linked to increased weight/shape concerns and later ED symptoms, showing how minority stress around identity can disrupt healthy body image development (Menon et al., 2024). Transgender and gender-diverse individuals are another high-risk group; one national study found transgender youth had the highest prevalence of disordered eating behaviors, likely stemming from gender dysphoria-related body dissatisfaction and societal marginalization (Diemer et al., 2015).

Importantly, these factors do not act in isolation: a queer person of color, for instance, may navigate both racism and anti-LGBTQ bias, compounding their stress and potentially intensifying body image distress. Such an intersectional lens recognizes that a Black lesbian woman's experience with body image is not simply the sum of being Black + female + lesbian but is a unique interplay of cultural standards and oppressions that shape how she sees and treats her body.

Overall, intersectional identities significantly impact body image development and the trajectory of eating disorders. Individuals with multiple marginalized identities often face compounded social pressures and stressors that can fuel disordered eating. For example, simultaneous exposure to racial stigma and unrealistic beauty ideals, or the dual pressures of sexism and homophobia (Small & Fuller, 2020; Menon et al., 2024). At the same time, research suggests that many transdiagnostic psychological processes underlying EDs (e.g. internalized beauty ideals, body dissatisfaction, emotion dysregulation) remain influential across all groups.

In a clinical sample of BIPOC with EDs, common factors like anxiety sensitivity, and difficulty coping with emotions significantly predicted ED severity, indicating that general risk mechanisms operate in these populations as well (Emelianchik-Key et al., 2023). This means that while the cultural expression of an ED might differ (for instance, differing weight ideals or symptom presentation), the core struggles with self-image and affect regulation are shared. Consequently, experts emphasize culturally responsive approaches that address both the universal and culture-specific aspects of ED pathology. Incorporating intersectional insights—such as acknowledging how racism, sexism, and heteronormative beauty standards collectively influence a person's body image—is crucial for effective prevention and treatment (Acle et al., 2021; Emelianchik-Key et al., 2023). Body image ideals are racialized and gendered. By understanding how race, gender, and sexual orientation intersect to mold one's relationship with food and body, practitioners can better support diverse individuals in developing a healthier body image and recovering from eating disorders.

The Importance of Authenticity When Treating an ED Client With Intersectional Identities

In therapeutic settings, it is essential for clinicians to recognize the impact of societal pressures on clients from marginalized backgrounds. Therapists should strive to create a safe and inclusive space that acknowledges and validates the unique experiences of all individuals. By understanding the cultural and societal factors that contribute to learned inauthenticity, therapists can better support clients in exploring and embracing their true selves. This approach not only enhances the therapeutic alliance but also empowers clients to challenge internalized stigma and develop a more positive self-perception.

Unfortunately, in clinical spaces, oppressive dynamics can be replicated rather than repaired. Traditional therapeutic frameworks that are grounded in White, Western, weight-normative values frequently invalidate the lived experiences of marginalized clients and force them to perform versions of themselves that align with dominant expectations. As a result, building authenticity in relationships, particularly therapeutic relationships, requires systemic repair. This includes validating the experiences of those who have been historically silenced.

Authenticity in therapy is crucial for providing truly effective care, particularly when working with BIPOC and LGBTQ+ individuals, as it fosters trust, safety, and a sense of belonging in the therapeutic space. Traditional mental health models often emphasize neutrality and professional detachment, yet research has shown that clients from marginalized backgrounds benefit from therapists who demonstrate cultural responsiveness, self-awareness, and genuine engagement (Singh & Moss, 2016). When therapists bring authenticity into their work, by acknowledging power dynamics, sharing their own positionality when appropriate, and engaging in active listening, they validate the lived experiences of their clients. This authenticity signals that therapy is not just a clinical process but a collaborative and affirming relationship, where clients do not have to perform or suppress parts of their identities to receive care. Without this level of engagement, therapy risks reinforcing the very patterns of inauthenticity and marginalization that clients have been forced to navigate in broader society.

A culturally responsive, intersectional, and trauma-informed approach ensures that authenticity is not merely performative but deeply integrated into the therapeutic process. Culturally responsive care requires clinicians to recognize the impact of systemic oppression, understand the influence of historical and ongoing trauma on BIPOC and LGBTQ+ communities, and actively examine and challenge both personal and systemic biases within mental health practice (Sue et al., 2007).

Intersectionality, as introduced by Crenshaw (1989), emphasizes that individuals experience layered and interconnected forms of oppression, meaning that therapy must address not just individual experiences but the social, cultural, and structural forces shaping mental health. Trauma-informed care, in turn, recognizes how chronic discrimination, racial trauma, and gender-based violence impact emotional regulation and self-worth, making authenticity a key component in building resilience. When therapists approach their work with this understanding, they create spaces where clients feel empowered to engage in self-exploration without fear of judgment, rejection, or retraumatization.

Techniques for Developing Authenticity in Therapy

The information-gathering necessary during the initial sessions of therapy can be daunting. It is important to remember that there is an opportunity to create authentic connection throughout the therapeutic process, including the assessment period. Asking questions and facilitating open discussions around hard topics can also be part of building rapport. Some examples of questions or topics to explore include:

Questions grounded in intersectionality theory (Crenshaw, 1989) and the understanding that eating disorders are shaped by complex social identities (Small & Fuller, 2020):

- "Can you tell me about the identities that are most important to you (e.g., cultural background, race, gender identity, sexual orientation)?"
- "How do these identities influence how you feel in and about your body?"

Exploration of body image, recognizing the dissonance between cultural body ideals and dominant (Western, thin, White) standards of beauty (Acle et al., 2021; Piran, 2017):

- "What kinds of messages did you grow up hearing about bodies, food, and health in your family or community?"
- "How do you think mainstream beauty standards match or conflict with your own cultural or gender identity?"

Exploration of oppression, stigma, and discrimination that may contribute to disordered eating in BIPOC and LGBTQ+ individuals (Emelianchik-Key et al., 2023; Velez et al., 2020):

- "Have you experienced racism, homophobia, or transphobia in medical, school, or community settings? If so, how has that impacted your relationship with food or your body?"
- "Do you ever feel that others make assumptions about your health, eating habits, or body based on your race, size, or gender presentation?"

Including trauma-informed approaches to body-based assessment and safety in one's body:

- "Do you feel safe or at home in your body? What helps you feel more connected or disconnected from it?"
- "Are there times when being in your body feels uncomfortable or like something to avoid?"

Discussion surrounding cultural values around food and appearance are often embedded in family and community dynamics and should be explored non-judgmentally (Cheng et al., 2019):

- "What role does your family or community play in your relationship with food, body, or gender identity?"
- "Have you received support or pressure from loved ones around how you should look, eat, or identify?"

Exploration of prior therapy experiences and alliance and affirming clients' experiences of marginalization builds trust and acknowledges systemic inequities (Comas-Díaz, 2012; Singh, 2013):

- "Have you had past experiences in therapy or healthcare where you felt misunderstood or stereotyped because of your identity?"
- "What would make this space feel safer or more supportive for you?"

Investigating objectification experiences and screening for minority stressors such as racial and sexual discrimination, safety, and body awareness as well as the media's impact on a client's version of themselves (Hunter et al., 2021):

- "In what ways do outside messages—like media images, cultural expectations, or experiences of racism, sexism, or discrimination—affect how you see yourself and your body?"
- "Are there particular situations or messages that make you feel more judged, pressured, or disconnected from who you know yourself to be?"

Exploration of transgenerational trauma and inherited coping mechanisms related to systemic oppression, colonization, and racialized family narratives (Mohatt et al., 2014; Comas-Díaz, 2016):

- "Have you ever felt that your relationship with food, body image, or emotional expression has been shaped by what your parents, grandparents, or community went through—such as racism, displacement, or having to "stay strong" or silent about pain?"

Adapted from ASES and microaggression literature, this question identifies everyday experiences of stigma, including racial or gender-based microaggressions, and their emotional or embodied impact. These moments often contribute to internalized shame, disconnection from the body, and identity-based stress (Sue et al., 2007; Nadal et al., 2011):

- "Can you tell me about a time when you felt dismissed, judged, or invisible because of your race, gender identity, or sexual orientation—even if it seemed subtle? How did that experience affect the way you felt about yourself or your body?"

Owning Our Stories

One powerful technique for fostering authenticity in therapy with BIPOC and LGBTQ+ clients is narrative therapy, which allows clients to reclaim their personal stories and separate their identities from the oppressive societal narratives imposed upon them. Narrative therapy offers a powerful framework for supporting individuals with intersectional identities by helping them reclaim agency over their experiences and identities in a sociocultural context that often marginalizes them.

Developed by White and Epston (1990), narrative therapy is based on the idea that people create meaning in their lives through stories and that problems are often socially constructed rather than inherently located within the individual. For clients with intersectional identities—those who experience overlapping systems of oppression related to race, gender, sexuality, body size, and other factors—narrative therapy can deconstruct dominant cultural narratives (e.g., Eurocentric beauty standards, gender norms, racial stereotypes) that have been internalized and contributed to distress, body image issues, and disordered eating (Combs & Freedman, 2012).

Many marginalized individuals have been conditioned to internalize dominant cultural messages that invalidate their experiences or devalue their identities (Singh & Moss, 2016. Through externalizing conversations, therapists can help clients reframe their narratives, emphasizing resilience, agency, and the richness of their lived experiences.

Externalization, or separating the person from the problem, is when therapists help clients view challenges like body dissatisfaction or eating disorders as external forces influenced by broader societal pressures, rather than as personal failures (White & Epston, 1990). This is particularly important for clients whose intersectional identities mean they experience layered marginalization; naming the societal and cultural forces (such as racism, fatphobia, or heteronormativity) that contribute to their struggles fosters empowerment and reduces self-blame (Combs & Freedman, 2012; White, 2007). For example, a therapist might ask, "What messages about your identity did you receive growing up, and how have they shaped how you see yourself today?" This allows clients to critically examine and challenge harmful societal constructs while affirming their authentic experiences.

Narrative therapy also emphasizes the reauthoring of personal stories, encouraging clients to articulate preferred narratives that reflect resistance, resilience, and the richness of their multiple identities. For example, a queer woman of color dealing with eating disorder recovery can work to reclaim narratives of bodily worth, cultural pride, and self-acceptance, countering the dominant narratives that have marginalized her experiences (Morgan, 2000).

Writing exercises, such as journaling or letter-writing to their past selves, can also help clients identify and reauthor their personal stories in a way that aligns with their authentic self-perception. By acknowledging the client's social, cultural, and political contexts, therapists can avoid pathologizing responses to oppression and instead honor survival strategies (Combs & Freedman, 2012; White, 2007). In working with intersectional identities, therapists using narrative therapy can cultivate spaces where clients experience agency, dignity, and recognition of their complex lived realities.

Mindfulness and Embodiment Practices

Another effective method for clinicians to use is identity-affirming mindfulness and embodiment practices, which help clients reconnect with their bodies and emotions in a world that often forces them to dissociate from their authentic selves. Research indicates that body image concerns and disordered eating behaviors are significantly shaped by intersecting experiences of racism, heteronormativity, and minority stress, placing BIPOC and LGBTQ+ individuals at increased risk for body dissatisfaction and related pathology (Markey et al., 2018; Pearl et al., 2020).

A potential method for clinicians is the use of identity-affirming mindfulness and embodiment practices, which support clients in reconnecting with their bodies and emotional experiences in environments that often promote disconnection or self-surveillance. Mindfulness-based interventions have been shown to improve interoceptive awareness, reduce body dissatisfaction, and decrease disordered eating behaviors by fostering nonjudgmental awareness of internal experiences (Kristeller & Wolever, 2011; Wanden-Berghe et al., 2011). When adapted through a culturally responsive and identity-affirming lens, these practices can also help counter the effects of minority stress and internalized stigma, particularly among BIPOC and LGBTQ+ individuals, by promoting self-compassion, safety within the body, and a more integrated sense of identity (Hatzenbuehler, 2009; Neff, 2003).

Importantly, embodiment-focused approaches—such as grounding exercises, somatic awareness, and gentle movement—can help clients shift from externalized, appearance-based evaluations of the body toward internal experiences of sensation, agency, and presence. This is particularly relevant in eating disorder treatment, where disconnection from bodily cues and emotions is common. By integrating mindfulness with identity-affirming practices, clinicians can create a therapeutic space that not only supports symptom reduction but also fosters reconnection, empowerment, and a more authentic relationship with the self (Kristeller & Wolever, 2011; Hatzenbuehler, 2009). Techniques such as guided visualization and grounding exercises can help clients develop self-compassion and a more authentic relationship with their bodies. For example, therapists can guide clients in a body scan meditation that focuses on gratitude for what their body allows them to do rather than how it conforms to societal expectations.

Piran (2017) defines embodiment not simply as having a body but as living in and through the body. According to Piran, embodiment encompasses how individuals experience, relate to, and inhabit their bodies within social and cultural contexts. It includes feeling agency, safety, and connection through the body as well as being able to express desires and engage fully in physical and emotional life without objectification or shame. Piran emphasizes that embodiment is shaped by intersecting social forces, including gender, race, and sociocultural oppression. Positive embodiment develops when individuals have access to experiences of social power, connection, and body ownership, whereas negative embodiment often results from experiences of objectification, marginalization, and disconnection from bodily agency—common among those with eating disorders.

Embodiment-based approaches have been identified as particularly meaningful for Black queer women, as they create space to reconnect with the body in ways that counter the historical and ongoing impact of racialized and sexualized objectification, marginalization, and disembodiment. These approaches often integrate mindfulness, somatic awareness, movement, and culturally grounded practices to support healing, identity integration, and empowerment (Hargons et al., 2018; Utsey et al., 2015). Research suggests that for Black women and especially those with intersecting queer identities embodiment practices that are identity-affirming and culturally responsive can reduce internalized oppression, increase body agency, and support emotional regulation by fostering a sense of safety and ownership within the body (Hargons et al., 2018).

"Sacred space" in psychotherapy refers to an environment, both physical and relational, where clients feel deeply respected, witnessed, and free from judgment or objectification. It invites a sense of emotional sanctuary where clients' experiences with their bodies, identities, and pain are treated with reverence (Jordan, 2017). This space is where authenticity lives. Establishing this space involves therapist presence, attunement, authenticity, and cultural humility, recognizing the intersectional influences—such as race, gender, and systemic oppression—that shape embodiment (Piran, 2017).

Mindfulness-based activities complement embodiment by cultivating non-judgmental awareness of the present moment, including bodily experiences, emotions, and thoughts. Mindfulness interventions for body image and eating disorder recovery often involve guided meditations focusing on breath, sensory awareness, and compassion practices aimed at softening body judgment (Kristeller & Wolever, 2011). Importantly, in clients with intersectional identities, mindfulness practices must be culturally adapted and trauma-informed to acknowledge how societal oppression, racism, and body-related trauma impact the body's felt sense of safety (Germer & Neff, 2019).

Together, sacred and authentic therapeutic space, embodiment work, and mindfulness interventions support a profound shift in body image recovery: moving from objectification and control toward presence, compassion, and agency in one's lived bodily experience.

Relational Authenticity

All the techniques described above contribute to the goal of relational authenticity. Relational authenticity exercises are crucial for helping clients practice expressing their true selves in relationships. Many individuals with intersectional identities have learned to mask their emotions or adapt their behavior to fit into dominant cultural spaces, leading to inauthentic interpersonal patterns (Matsuno & Israel, 2018).

Malebo Sephodi (n.d.), a writer and researcher, emphasizes the importance of self-expression free from external constraints, stating, "The voice of a Black woman should always be HERSELF. No edits—no erasure—no pressure—no expectations—no additions—no intruders." This sentiment underscores the necessity for individuals, particularly those from marginalized communities, to reclaim their narratives and embrace their authentic selves. By challenging societal norms and rejecting imposed standards, individuals can begin to heal from internalized stigma and develop a healthier self-perception rooted in authenticity.

Therapists can use role-playing exercises to help clients explore different ways of asserting their needs and boundaries in a safe space. For instance, a therapist might guide a client through a role-play where they practice setting a boundary with a family member who dismisses their gender identity or racial experiences. Another relational technique is the use of mirroring and validation, where therapists model authentic emotional expression, share their own cultural humility journey when appropriate, and affirm the client's experiences without pathologizing them. Through these exercises, clients not only develop the courage to show up authentically in relationships but also gain tools to navigate the world with greater self-acceptance and confidence.

Bridging Resources

It is critical as providers to seek continued education experiences and to learn from others. During the time I was working with Taylor, whose story I shared earlier in this chapter, while I felt capable of having explorative conversations around sexuality, I did not feel I had all the resources or skills Taylor needed and deserved. I was so fortunate to have an incredible resource in my area to connect with: the Yes Institute (n.d.). in Miami. This is an organization whose mission is "to prevent suicide and ensure the healthy development of all youth through powerful communication and education on gender and orientation." The Yes Institute was able to provide Taylor with support groups to explore her identity. I was thrilled to have partnered with them to provide staff trainings for the organization as well.

By my reaching out to an outside resource, Taylor found a community she didn't even know existed. In fact, three months later while she was still living in Miami and in the outpatient level of care, when her parents came for parents' weekend, she decided to bring them to a parent educational seminar at the institute. The ability to break through her deeply held beliefs around gender norms was life changing. Taylor was able to step into her authentic self in a way that she never thought was possible, and it was remarkable to witness. As a clinician, it is important to know enough to know when you don't know. Not everyone can be an expert on all things. The Yes Institute was an invaluable partner in bridging treatment with community resources, and there are a wealth of organizations out there that can be pieces of the therapeutic puzzle for a client, especially one with an intersectional identity.

In my work with Tamara, I knew enough to know that I did not know. The foundation of our work together was acknowledging this. The staff worked together to bring in resources and provide treatment through a cultural humility lens. For Tamara, a significant part of our nutritional work was designing a meal plan that was reflective of the foods that her family ate. Learning more about culturally preferred foods was critical to provide preferred food options that were based on cultural identities for longer-term recovery. The traditional peanut butter and graham cracker snack of treatment facilities was bizarre in this context. We connected with treatment professionals who identified as experts in treating eating disorders in women of color to help us design a treatment plan. However, the treatment plan would have been ineffective if the team had not been committed to doing the work on themselves as well.

I urge clinicians to find outside resources and engage with their community. In a traditional outpatient setting, a clinician spends one hour per week with a client. There are 168 hours per week. Meaning, there is a whole lot of time that a client is not sitting in your office. As clinicians, we need to attempt to arm our clients with resources so that they can connect to a deeper part of themselves—one that is not rooted with a pathology and eating disorder identity but rather one that is filled with interpersonal relationships and engagement in the community around them.

Summary

Ultimately, authenticity in therapy creates the conditions necessary for clients to heal in a way that is sustainable and affirming of their identities. When therapists model authenticity, they encourage clients to develop a more authentic relationship with themselves—one that is not shaped by external expectations but by a deep understanding of their own values, needs, and truths. This is particularly vital for BIPOC and LGBTQ+ individuals who often face societal pressures to conform or suppress parts of themselves to be accepted. Through an authentic therapeutic relationship, clients can learn to reclaim their voices, challenge internalized oppression, and build self-compassion. By integrating authenticity into culturally responsive, intersectional, and trauma-informed care, therapists do more than provide treatment; they create a transformative space where healing is rooted in empowerment, connection, and the full acknowledgment of each client's lived reality. This chapter is not meant to be an exhaustive review of the literature on marginalized populations and eating disorders. There are many additional research articles, books, and personal stories I would encourage you to read, engage in, and learn more about.

Key Take-Aways

- Individuals with marginalized identities are navigating a world that imposes rigid definitions of body image standards and beauty ideals that are rooted in systemic oppression, racism, stereotypes, and biases, which can lead to inauthenticity with self and others.
- Although eating disorders and body image disturbances occur at similar or even higher rates in marginalized groups, eating disorders continue to go undiagnosed and undertreated because of heteronormative and racial-biased assessments, provider biases, and access to care.

- Clients with intersectional identities may enter therapy carrying a history of being misunderstood, dismissed, or even harmed by healthcare systems, making trust difficult to establish. Marginalized groups are underrepresented in treatment environments and as providers of eating disorder care.
- Culturally sensitive care includes approaching treatment with cultural humility, an understanding of intersectional identities and minority stressors, a bridging of community and professional resources, and a commitment to recognizing our own privilege and biases.
- Authentically driven care includes advocacy to fight discrimination, systemic oppression, and stigma, advance research, and provide increased access to care for marginalized groups.
- The power dynamics of therapy cannot be separated from the societal structures that have historically dictated who holds authority, whose voices are heard, and whose experiences are validated.
- Providing authentic treatment requires both clinician and client engage in open dialogue that includes asking hard questions to better understand how personal histories and cultural narratives have shaped their identities and the ways authenticity is expressed.

Additional Resources

I do not represent the marginalized voices of providers and recovered individuals, so I am offering some of the voices that I have referenced and learned from.

People

- Alishia McCullough @blackandembodied
- Dr. Jenny Tzu-Mei Wang @asiansformentalhealth
- Dr. Kelli Rugless @dr.kellirugless
- Dr. Kera Nyemb-Diop @black.nutritionist
- Dr. Sand Chang @heydrsand
- Sabrina Strings @yoginiblack
- Schuyler Bailor @pinkmantaray

Organizations

- Brown Girl Therapy @browngirltherapy
- Therapy for Black Girls @therapyforblackgirls
- The Trevor Project @trevorproject
- Asian Mental Health Collective @asianmentalhealthcollective
- Project Implicit | Projectimplicit.net
- Anti Racism and Equality | Antiracisimandequity.com

Recommended Reading

- *Treating Black women with eating disorders: A clinician's guide.* (Small & Fuller, 2020)
- *A clinician's guide to gender-affirming care: Working with transgender and gender nonconforming clients.* (Chang et al., 2020)

References

Acle, A., Cook, B., Siegfried, N., & Beasley, T. (2021). *Cultural considerations in the treatment of eating disorders among racial/ethnic minorities: A systematic review.* Journal of Cross-Cultural Psychology, 52(5), 468–488.

Alexander, T., Burnette, C. B., Cory, H., McHale, S., & Simone, M. (2024). *The need for more inclusive measurement to advance equity in eating disorders prevention.* Eating Disorders, 32(6), 798–816.

American Psychological Association. (n.d.). *Stereotypes.* Retrieved May 25, 2025, from https://dictionary.apa.org/stereotype

Assari, S. (2018). *Perceived discrimination and binge eating disorder; gender difference in African Americans.* Journal of Clinical Medicine, 7(5), 89.

Brewster, M. E., Velez, B. L., Breslow, A. S., & Geiger, E. F. (2019). *Unpacking body image concerns and disordered eating for transgender women: The roles of sexual objectification and minority stress.* Journal of Counseling Psychology, 66(2), 131–142.

Cachelin, F. M., Rebeck, R., Veisel, C. (2001). *Barriers to treatment for eating disorders among ethnically diverse women.* International Journal of Eating Disorders, 30, 269–278.

Cachelin, F. M., Shea, M., Phimphasone, P., Wilson, G. T., Thompson, D. R., & Striegel, R. H. (2014). *Culturally adapted cognitive behavioral guided self-help for binge eating: A feasibility study with Mexican Americans.* Cultural Diversity & Ethnic Minority Psychology, 20(3), 449–457.

Chang, S. C., Singh, A. A., & Dickey, L. M. (2020). *A clinician's guide to gender-affirming care: Working with transgender and gender nonconforming clients.* Context Press.

Cheng, Z. H., Perko, V. L., Fuller-Marashi, L., Gau, J. M., & Stice, E. (2019). *Ethnic differences in eating disorder prevalence*, risk factors, and predictive effects of risk factors among young women. Eating Behaviors, 32, 23–30.

Clark, L. & Winterowd, C. (2012). *Correlates and predictors of binge eating among Native American women.* Journal of Multicultural Counseling and Development, 40(2), 117–127.

Comas-Díaz, L. (2012). *Multicultural care: A clinician's guide to cultural competence.* American Psychological Association.

Comas-Díaz, L. (2016). *Racial trauma: Theory*, research, and healing. American Psychologist, 74(1), 1–15.

Combs, G., & Freedman, J. (2012). *Narrative*, poststructuralism, and social justice: Current practices in narrative therapy. The Counseling Psychologist, 40(7), 1033–1060.

Crenshaw, K. (1989). *Demarginalizing the intersection of race and sex.* University of Chicago Legal Forum, (1), 139–167.

Desai, M. U., Paranamana, N., Restrepo-Toro, M., O'Connell, M., Davidson, L., & Stanhope, V. (2021). Implicit organizational bias: Mental health treatment culture and norms as barriers to engaging with diversity. *The American Psychologist, 76*(1), 78–90.

Diemer, E. W., Grant, J. D., Munn-Chernoff, M. A., Patterson, D. A., & Duncan, A. E. (2015). *Gender identity*, sexual orientation, and eating-related pathology in a national sample of college students. Journal of Adolescent Health, 57(2), 144–149.

Emelianchik-Key, K., Labarta, A. C., & Gill, E. (2023). *The mediating role of transdiagnostic factors in a clinical sample of Black*, Indigenous, and people of color with eating disorders. Journal of Mental Health Counseling, 45(4), 340–358.

FitzGerald, C., & Hurst, S. (2017). *Implicit bias in healthcare professionals: A systematic review*. BMC Medical Ethics, 18(1), 19.

Fitzsimmons-Craft, E. E., Balantekin, K. N., Graham, A. K., Smolar, L., Park, A., Mysko, C., & Wilfley, D. E. (2019). Barriers to treatment for eating disorders: Findings from a large online sample. International Journal of Eating Disorders, 52 (10), 1074–1082.

Gay, R. (2017). *Hunger: A memoir of (my) body*. HarperCollins.

Germer, C. K., & Neff, K. D. (2019). *Teaching the mindful self-compassion program: A guide for professionals*. Guilford Press.

Goetz, J. L. (2022, August 1). Eating disorders in minority and marginalized populations. *Psychiatric Times*. https://www.psychiatrictimes.com/view/eating-disorders-in-minority-and-marginalized-populations

Gordon, K. H., Perez, M., & Joiner, T. E., Jr. (2002). The impact of racial stereotypes on eating disorder recognition. *International Journal of Eating Disorders, 32*(2), 219–224.

Gordon, K. H., Brattole, M. M., Wingate, L. R., & Joiner, T. E., Jr. (2006). The impact of client race on clinician detection of eating disorders. Behavior Therapy, 37 (4), 319–325.

Hargons, C. N., Mosley, D. V., Stevens-Watkins, D., & Mance, G. A. (2018). "Studying Black sexualities": Where are we now? Journal of Black Sexuality and Relationships, 5(1), 1–19.

Hatzenbuehler, M. L. (2009). How does sexual minority stigma "get under the skin"? A psychological mediation framework. Psychological Bulletin, 135(5), 707–730.

Hatzenbuehler, M., & Pachankis, J. (2016). *Stigma and minority stress as social determinants of health among lesbian*, gay, bisexual, and transgender youth: Research evidence and clinical implications. Pediatric Clinics of North America, 63(6), 985–997.

Human Rights Campaign. (n.d.). *QTBIPOC Mental health and well-being*. Retrieved May 25, 2025 from https://www.hrc.org/resources/communities-of-color

Hunter, J., Butler, C., & Cooper, K. (2021). Gender minority stress in trans and gender diverse adolescents and young people. *Clinical Child Psychology and Psychiatry, 26*(4), 1182–1195.

Jennings Mathis, K., Anaya, C., Rambur, B., Bodell, L. P., Graham, A. K., Forney, K. J., Anam, S., & Wildes, J. E. (2020). Workforce diversity in eating disorders: A multi-methods study. Western Journal of Nursing Research, 42(12), 1068–1077.

Jensen, E. (2023, October 11). The chance that two people chosen at random are of different race or ethnicity groups has increased since 2010. United States Census Bureau.

Jordan, J. V. (2017). *Relational resilience in girls*. In J. V. Jordan (Ed.), Relational-cultural therapy (2nd ed., pp. 143–164). American Psychological Association.

Kalash, N., Harb, H., Zeeni, N., El Khoury, M., & Mattar, L. (2023). *Determinants of body image disturbance and disordered eating behaviors among self-identified LGBTQ individuals*. Journal of Eating Disorders, 11(1), 87.

Kinsey, D. (2022). *Decolonizing wellness: A queer*, trans, and BIPOC-centered guide to escaping diet culture and reclaiming your health. North Atlantic Books.

Kristeller, J. L., & Wolever, R. Q. (2011). Mindfulness-based eating awareness training for treating binge eating disorder: The conceptual foundation. Eating Disorders, 22 (1), 49–61.

Markey, C. H., August, K. J., & Markey, P. M. (2018). The impact of sexual orientation on body image and eating behaviors. Current Opinion in Psychology, 9, 11–16.

Marques, L., Alegría, M., Becker, A. E., Chen, C. N., Fang, A., Chosak, A., & Diniz, J. B. (2011). Comparative prevalence, correlates of impairment, and service utilization for eating disorders across U.S. ethnic groups: Implications for reducing ethnic disparities in health care access for eating disorders. International Journal of Eating Disorders, 44(5), 412–420.

Matsuno, E., & Israel, T. (2018). *Psychological interventions promoting resilience among transgender individuals: Transgender resilience intervention model (TRIM).* The Counseling Psychologist, 46(5), 632–655.

Nagata, J. M., Diep, T., Helmer, C. K., Domingue, S. K., Al-Shoaibi, A. A., Raney, J. H., Ganson, K. T., Testa, A., He, J., Brindis, C. D., & Baker, F. C. (2024). Sexual orientation discrimination and eating disorder symptoms in early adolescence: A prospective cohort study. *Journal of Eating Disorders, 12*(1), 196.

Meyer, I. H. (2003). *Prejudice*, social stress, and mental health in lesbian, gay, and bisexual populations: Conceptual issues and research evidence. Psychological Bulletin, 129(5), 674–697.

Mohatt, N. V., Thompson, A. B., Thai, N. D., & Tebes, J. K. (2014). *Historical trauma as public narrative: A conceptual review of how history impacts present-day health.* Social Science & Medicine, 106, 128–136.

Morgan, A. (2000). *What is narrative therapy?* An easy-to-read introduction. Dulwich Centre Publications.

National Eating Disorders Association. (n.d.). *What is body image?* Retrieved May 25, 2025 from https://www.nationaleatingdisorders.org/body-image-and-eating-disorders/

Nadal, K. L., Wong, Y., Griffin, K., Davidoff, K., & Sriken, J. (2011). *The adverse impact of racial microaggressions on college students' self-esteem.* Journal of College Student Development, 52(5), 461–474.

Neff, K. D. (2003). Self-compassion: An alternative conceptualization of a healthy attitude toward oneself. Self and Identity, 2(2), 85–101.

Pearl, R. L., Wadden, T. A., Tronieri, J. S., & Berkowitz, R. I. (2020). Sexual minority status and weight stigma: Implications for body image and eating behaviors. Obesity, 28(5), 891–897.

Piran, N. (2017). *Journeys of embodiment at the intersection of body and culture: The developmental theory of embodiment.* Academic Press.

Prochaska, J. O., & Norcross, J. C. (2002). *Stages of Change.* In J. C. Norcross (Ed.), Psychotherapy relationships that work: Therapist contributions and responsiveness to patients (pp. 303–313). Oxford University Press.

Rodgers, R. F., & Melioli, T. (2016). The relationship between body image concerns, eating disorders and Internet use, Part I: A review of empirical support. *Adolescent Research Review, 1*, 95–119.

Rodgers, R. F., Fischer, L. E., Murray, S. B., & Franko, D. L. (2022). Integrating fear of fatness into sociocultural models of body image and eating concerns. *Eating Behaviors, 46*, 101653.

Sephodi, M. (n.d.). https://about.me/malebogololo. Retrieved May 25, 2025 from https://www.goodreads.com/author/quotes/16901206.Malebo_Sephodi

Singh, A. A. (2013). *Transgender youth of color and resilience: Negotiating oppression and finding support.* Sex Roles, 68(11), 690–702.

Singh, A. A. & Moss, L. (2016). *Using relational-cultural theory in LGBTQQ counseling: Addressing heterosexism and enhancing relational competencies.* Journal of Counseling & Development, 94(4), 398–404.

Small, C., & Fuller, M. (Eds.). (2020). *Treating Black women with eating disorders: A clinician's guide.* Routledge.

Sonneville, K. R., & Lipson, S. K. (2018). *Disparities in eating disorder diagnosis and treatment according to weight status,* race/ethnicity, socioeconomic background, and sex among college students. International Journal of Eating Disorders, 51(6), 518–526.

Striegel-Moore, R. H., Franko, D. L., & Thompson, K. J. (2005). Health services research in eating disorders: A review of the literature. International Journal of Eating Disorders, 37(1), 1–13.

Strings, S. (2019). *Fearing the Black body: The racial origins of fat phobia.* NYU Press.

Sue, D. W., Capodilupo, C. M., Torino, G. C., Bucceri, J. M., Holder, A. M., Nadal, K. L., & Esquilin, M. (2007). *Racial microaggressions in everyday life*: Implications for clinical practice. American Psychologist, 62(4), 271–286.

Sue, D. W., Alsaidi, S., Awad, M. N., Glaeser, E., Calle, C. Z., & Mendez, N. (2019). *Disarming racial microaggressions: Microintervention strategies for targets,* White allies, and bystanders. American Psychologist, 74(1), 128.

Utsey, S. O., Adams, E. P., & Bolden, M. A. (2015). Development and initial validation of the Africultural coping systems inventory. Journal of Black Psychology, 26(2), 194–215.

Velez, B. L., Cox, R., Polihronakis, C. J., & Moradi, B. (2020). *Beauty and body image concerns among sexual minority women of color: A qualitative investigation.* Psychology of Women Quarterly, 44(2), 204–219.

Wanden-Berghe, C., Sanz-Valero, J., & Wanden-Berghe, R. G. (2011). The application of mindfulness to eating disorders treatment: A systematic review. Eating Disorders, 22(1), 34–48.

White, M. (2007). *Maps of narrative practice.* Norton.

White, M., & Epston, D. (1990). *Narrative means to therapeutic ends.* Norton.

Yeager, K.A., & Bauer-Wu, S. (2013). *Cultural humility: Essential foundation for clinical researchers.* Applied Nursing Research, 26(4), 251–256.

Yes Institute. (n.d.). https://yesinstitute.org

Chapter 7

Weight Stigma

The Hidden Barrier to Authentic Healing

Overview

- *Weight stigma is one of the most pervasive and overlooked barriers in eating disorder treatment.* This chapter defines weight stigma and weight bias, examining how these forces show up not only in society but within healthcare systems and even the diagnostic process itself.
- *The impact of weight stigma is profound and multifaceted.* Clients experience physical, emotional, and social harms, from heightened health risks to diminished self-worth, often compounded by stigma within workplaces, families, and friendships.
- *Weight bias also infiltrates treatment settings through assumptions about weight goals, assessment practices, and the instruments clinicians rely on.* Without awareness, providers may unintentionally reinforce the very biases that sustain disordered eating.
- *Psychoeducation, open dialogue, and structured discussion points are essential tools for clinicians and families.* By normalizing conversations about weight stigma and de-shaming the experience of living in a stigmatized body, therapy becomes a safer and more inclusive space.
- *Creating therapeutic environments that welcome all bodies requires intentional practice.* Normalizing diverse body experiences, deconstructing internalized stigma, and fostering relational authenticity are central to undoing harm and promoting healing.
- *Clinicians, too, must engage in self-reflection, training, and supervision to confront their own biases.* By examining personal experiences and assumptions, therapists model humility and authenticity, paving the way for more ethical, compassionate, and effective care.

My first job in the eating disorder field was covering weekend groups on an inpatient unit. For anyone interested in working with those affected by eating disorders, I would not advise this type of position as the place to begin a career. Clients are often escalated on the weekends as they have not seen primary staff in multiple days. Weekends tend to have less programmatic structure and may

DOI: 10.4324/9781003632016-8

include family visitations. All put together, weekends are a breeding ground for stressful situations for those with eating disorders and the staff who treats them.

On one of the early days that I was on the unit, I was running a body image group in which clients flipped through glossy women's magazines (yes, it was so long ago we actually had magazines) to consider how the media's messages impacted their views on their bodies. While I was preparing for this group session, I was jazzed. I was anticipating a creative group session that would engage clients and lead to thoughtful discussions around body image. However, it became clear rather quickly that my plan was too idealistic for the setting.

The group sat on the floor of a room that reminded me of one in a library. I watched Dana sit down and attempt to get comfortable as I outlined the group objectives and activity. Dana, the only client in a larger body on the unit, proceeded like the others to flip through the magazines. While the other clients trimmed words and images out of the magazines, creating collages, Dana dismissively continued to thumb through the content laid out on the floor. When we came back as a larger group for individual shares, Dana said she did not feel connected to the activity. I recall nodding gently and thanking her for her honesty, not wanting to make Dana uncomfortable by pushing exploration of body image with her. I moved to the next person, thereby dismissing Dana and her thoughts and feelings.

Retrospectively, moving on to the next client was less about Dana's discomfort and more about mine. At that time, I was not equipped to facilitate the type of conversation that was clearly needed. It became evident that Dana had more to say. As the next person began to speak, Dana spoke up with her voice cracking, "You don't get it, no one does. Everyone here talks about being afraid of being fat. I'm not afraid of being fat—I am fat. And this whole group just reminded me I'm not supposed to exist, even in treatment."

I recall feeling panicked by this candid statement; my fight-or-flight response kicked in. I had created upset and discomfort in a client, and it spilled to the larger group. I was unsure and ill-equipped to hold Dana's anger, grief, and truth. Dana continued, "There's no one who looks like me in here." For Dana, it may have been the first time she dared say aloud what she had been thinking all along. Even within the treatment facility, she felt invisible and unseen. At the time, I did not know what to do or say to help Dana.

Weight Stigma and Authenticity

There are too many people that have had experiences similar to Dana's at treatment facilities, doctors' offices, workplace environments, and in their own homes and relationships. Weight stigma can be conceptualized as discrimination, social rejection, devaluation, or stereotyping of people who do not comply with dominant culture's social norms of appropriate body weight and shape (Tomiyama et al., 2018). Within healthcare, this refers to the negative attitudes, beliefs, and judgments that clinicians may hold about patients with higher body weight. Biases around weight show up in many different ways and can be both subtle and overt.

Individuals who experience weight stigma often internalize negative societal messages, leading to diminished self-esteem and self-worth (World Obesity Federation, 2023). This internalization can manifest in social withdrawal or selective isolation, where individuals avoid certain environments to escape potential stigma and judgment. As a result, relationships may lack depth and authenticity, as individuals may feel compelled to hide aspects of themselves to conform to societal expectations. The fear of rejection based on body size fosters relational anxiety, preventing individuals from engaging in vulnerable and meaningful connections.

To foster authentic therapeutic relationships, clinicians must actively recognize and challenge weight stigma within their practice. This includes creating an environment of unconditional positive regard, where clients feel safe to express themselves without fear of judgment (Rogers, 1951). Therapists should engage in self-reflection to identify and address their own biases, ensuring that their interventions are inclusive and supportive rather than prescriptive. By acknowledging the pervasive impact of weight stigma and committing to an approach rooted in empathy and acceptance, therapists can strengthen the therapeutic alliance, encouraging more authentic and meaningful engagement from their clients. Through this relational approach, therapy can become a space for individuals to reclaim agency over their identities, heal from internalized stigma, and cultivate authenticity in their broader relationships.

Understanding Weight Stigma

The landmark 1961 paper *Cultural Uniformity in Reaction to Physical Disabilities* (Richardson et al., 1961) revealed a striking consistency across diverse cultural groups in their negative perceptions of individuals with visible physical disabilities, highlighting the powerful role of societal values in shaping stigma. In the study, children (ages 10 and 11) were shown pictures of other children and were asked to rank the images in order of which one they "liked best" based on physical appearance. Children in the study consistently ranked those with physical differences (e.g., those who had missing limbs or facial disfigurement) least favorably, suggesting an early internalization of cultural ideals around body norms and desirability.

This foundational work continues to have profound implications for understanding weight stigma today, as it underscores how deeply embedded physical appearance standards are in socialization processes. The biases found in the Richardson et al. (1961) study can also be applied to individuals whose weight does not fall into what is considered "normal" or "acceptable" in society. Size and weight are often perceived as a moral or personal failing, despite growing evidence that weight is influenced by complex genetic, environmental, and structural factors. The uniformity in stigmatizing responses across groups highlights the need for interventions that challenge normative beauty standards and reframe body diversity as natural rather than abnormal.

Biases related to weight are everywhere, and young children internalize these messages from a very young age, and they later impact their worldview. I experienced this firsthand when I volunteered to participate in career day at my daughter's elementary school when she was in second grade, which was less than a decade ago. I introduced myself as a "doctor of feelings" to the group of 30 second graders (who were 7 and 8 years old) and read the children a story (my personal go-to; *Shapesville*, Mills & Osborn, 2003). Afterward, I asked them to practice their breathing, handing out bubbles to each child for a fun activity. I was on a roll. I then asked them to think about things they like to do with their bodies to make themselves feel good. Hands shot up in the air, and I felt myself smiling with the excitement of their participation. A young boy said, "I like to play football with my big brothers." Another kid said, "I like to run the fastest." Another student, a girl sitting next to my daughter, burst out, "You can go on a diet!" The look on my face must have dramatically shifted upon hearing this suggestion, and my gaze went to my own daughter who looked at the beginning of a panic imagining what my response to her classmate would be. Even though I had worked in the field of eating disorders for more than a decade at that time, I was still dumbfounded that a 7-year-old's response to "something you can do to feel good in your body" was diet. I wanted to scream from the rooftops. To me and other practitioners, diet is a four-letter word. It should not be in the vocabulary of a second grader. Diets do not make people feel good about themselves. After freezing from the initial shock of this suggestion, I paused and asked my daughter's classmate to think about what she did the day prior that helped her feel good and strong. I wanted to redirect her so she could consider alternative ideas.

Research shows that as young as in preschool, kids may begin to develop weight stigma, with ideas solidifying through elementary school (Charsley et al., 2018; Harrison et al., 2016; Lehmkuhl et al., 2010). Anti-fat attitudes in young children are developed through their learning from teachers, caregivers, parents and peers (Puhl & Latner, 2007). As it relates to perceptions of themselves, a widely referenced statistic in the eating disorder community is that by 10 years old, 81% of kids are afraid of being fat (Mellin et al., 1992). While I do not believe that this statistic should be extrapolated in the way it often is, it is clear our beliefs about body size and shape develop at a young age.

Weight Bias in Healthcare

It is not just individual people in everyday life who carry biases about people's weight. Weight bias also occurs in settings like healthcare, where clients who do not fit an ideal weight experience different medical treatment than their peers. In a systemic review and meta-analysis that looked at weight bias among healthcare professionals, Lawrence et al. (2021) analyzed 41 studies based on all different fields (medical doctors, nurses, psychologists, etc.) and concluded that healthcare professionals have both implicit and/or explicit weight-biased attitudes toward people in larger bodies. They report that these biases include behaviors such as using disrespectful language, making negative assumptions about a patient's lifestyle, or even avoiding physical touch and eye contact with higher-weight patients (Lawrence et al., 2021). Additional research in this area has found that some physicians stereotype patients in larger bodies as lazy or lacking self-discipline and consequently report less desire to help them than they do thinner patients (Hebl & Xu, 2001; Puhl & Brownell, 2006).

Other studies support the weight bias in healthcare. One study discussed the staggering numbers of weight-based discrimination in medical settings: in one survey of nearly 2,500 individuals defined as "with obesity," 69% of women (and a significant portion of men) reported experiencing weight bias from doctors, making healthcare providers one of the most frequent sources of weight stigma (Puhl & Brownell, 2006). These biases and stigma are so significant that in 2020, a multidisciplinary group of international experts gathered to develop a joint statement on the harms of weight stigma and to provide recommendations to eliminate weight bias (Rubino et al., 2020). This group of over 35 experts reported that weight stigma and discrimination are "pervasive and cause significant harm to affected individuals." They continue to indicate that the misleading information that "obesity" is a personal responsibility only reinforces weight stigma and weight-based stereotypes.

Weight stigma can detrimentally impact client care and overall health outcomes in several ways. Provider biases may lead to substandard care; for example, clinicians might spend less time with higher-weight patients, offer fewer preventive interventions, or attribute every health complaint to the patient's weight without proper investigation. A comprehensive review by Phelan et al. (2015) found that many healthcare providers hold implicit and explicit negative stereotypes about people with obesity, and these attitudes can influence their judgment, interpersonal behavior, and medical decision-making. This essentially means weight-biased attitudes may result in clinicians overlooking symptoms or providing less compassionate care, thereby reducing the quality of care individuals in need of help receive.

On the client side, those who experience stigma or anticipate judgment often react in ways that negatively impact their health. Phelan et al. (2015) also reported that patients who feel stigmatized may develop mistrust in doctors, have reduced adherence to treatments, and even avoid or delay seeking medical care altogether. This avoidance of healthcare due to fear of humiliation or past negative experiences is a major concern, as it can lead to missed early diagnoses and poorer management of chronic conditions. For individuals seeking care, a wide body of evidence indicates that individuals who face weight-based discrimination often engage in coping strategies that paradoxically harm their health. Research indicates that people who encounter weight stigma frequently are more likely to doctor shop or change providers often and avoid or delay medical appointments (both routine and screenings; Rubino et al., 2020).

The healthcare field must take steps to combat weight stigma in the field. This can be achieved through educational, regulatory, and legal initiatives to debunk inaccurate and unproven assumptions and misconceptions that are promoted by the media, through politicians, and in public health campaigns related to weight bias. The current weight stigma in healthcare can "result in discrimination, and undermine human rights, social rights, and the health of afflicted individuals" (Rubino et al., 2020). In short, weight stigma is a well-documented problem in healthcare that can undermine the quality of patient interactions and care.

Weight Stigma in Healthcare Related to Eating Disorders

With the proliferation of weight stigma in healthcare and our culture, clinicians treating people with eating disorders are also vulnerable to these limiting beliefs. Garcia Moreno et al. (2025) investigated weight bias in the diagnosis of eating disorders among healthcare professionals. They indicated that both laypeople and health professionals were less likely to identify an eating disorder when the individual was described as having a higher weight, even if their behaviors and symptoms were consistent with anorexia. Furthermore, healthcare providers showed lower confidence in diagnosing "atypical" anorexia compared to a classic anorexia case, suggesting that an overweight body can bias clinical judgment about disordered eating. This underdiagnosis or skepticism means many people with EDs in larger bodies do not receive timely and appropriate interventions. Some are even praised for weight loss or advised to continue losing weight when in fact they are suffering from a dangerous eating disorder, a clear example of how stigma can lead to inappropriate or harmful care.

While research on weight bias in general healthcare settings is well documented (Puhl & Suh, 2015), fewer studies have specifically addressed how the weight of a therapist influences client perceptions, trust, and engagement in ED treatment. In a study aimed at investigating weight bias in eating disorder professionals, Puhl et al. (2014) found that the majority (56%) of those surveyed had observed other ED professionals making negative comments regarding clients in larger bodies. Additionally, like those in the medical profession in general, this study found that practitioners with stronger weight biases reported frustrations and negative attitudes regarding individuals in larger bodies as well as having a perception of poorer treatment outcomes for these individuals. Interestingly, while most providers endorsed positive attitudes towards clients in larger bodies, this finding was inconsistent with what they reported attitudes were in the field. Reasons for this could include social desirability and self-positivity biases. Nonetheless, the findings indicated that 42% of participants believed that eating disorder providers often have negative stereotypes about larger-bodied clients.

In a more recent investigation, Chen and Gonzales (2022) recruited former eating disorder clients in larger bodies to validate the scale for treatment-based experiences of weight stigma (STEWS) for a client-centered look at weight stigma experiences in eating disorder treatment environments. Findings supported the potentiality of providers to collude with the eating disorder by overlooking or disregarding symptoms and in fact supported eating disorder behaviors or attitudes in service of weight loss. The authors noted that nearly half of participants (46.4%) somewhat, moderately, or strongly agreed that their providers recommended dieting even when they did not come in to discuss weight loss. Future research should look at the impact of treatment and the significant implications of these clients' perceptions and their therapeutic relationship with the clinician.

How Weight Stigma Affects ED Diagnosis and Identification

Weight stigma can significantly impact the recognition and treatment of eating disorders. In traditional diagnostic frameworks, eating disorders like anorexia nervosa have been closely tied to body size (e.g., a key criterion for anorexia is being "significantly underweight"). This has led to a dangerous blind spot: individuals at higher weights who have serious eating disorders are often overlooked or misdiagnosed because of weight-biased assumptions. For example, an individual in a larger body who is severely restricting calories or compulsively overexercising might not fit the stereotypical image of anorexia, leading clinicians to underestimate the problem. In recent years, the diagnosis of atypical anorexia nervosa has been recognized—this refers to individuals who meet all criteria for anorexia (intense food restriction, fear of weight gain, distorted body image) except low body weight. Despite this medical recognition, weight stigma remains a hurdle to proper diagnosis.

Schmidt et al. (2025) found that clinicians often perceive individuals with eating disorders through stereotype-based lenses shaped by weight bias, which can influence diagnosis and treatment, particularly for those in larger bodies. Their findings highlight the importance of adopting a weight-inclusive perspective to reduce stigma and improve equitable care (Schmidt et al., 2025).

Georgia's Story: Weight Stigma in an ED Treatment Facility

During her first week in treatment, Georgia, a 24-year-old in a larger body, overheard staff referring to her as "our new binge eating client" despite never disclosing any binge behaviors. Her intake forms and medical records clearly documented severe food restriction, excessive exercise, and a recent 25-pound weight loss, yet the assumptions persisted. When she struggled to complete a meal, Georgia overheard a staff person comment that it should not be so difficult for her to finish. She felt she was disproportionately praised for joining movement groups. Georgia was battling atypical anorexia and felt unseen and invalidated. It caused her to question whether her eating disorder was real and if she "deserved" treatment because of her size.

Weight Stigma in Eating Disorder Treatment

There are several ways in which weight stigma and weight biases appear in eating disorder treatment. Weight stigma impacts the early detection and diagnosis of eating disorders, the establishment of weight goals in treatment, how clinicians evaluate their clients' food intake and behaviors. For clients in larger bodies, experiences of weight stigma may discourage them from getting the help they need and deserve. Weight bias can influence a client's or family's perception of a therapist's competence or credibility, and it can impact the ways in which providers approach clients. In these scenarios, weight bias weakens the therapeutic alliance, impacts relationships, and can reduce treatment engagement. Weight stigma in eating disorder treatment settings likely increases the risk for further internalized stigma, shame, and withdrawal from the ability to create and maintain authentic relationships.

A Weight-Centric Paradigm

Weight stigma, too often, permeates the treatment process for eating disorders. McEntee et al. (2023) argue that focusing on weight in ED treatment can intensify internalized weight bias among patients and providers, leading to increased shame and poorer outcomes. Current ED treatment guidelines and programs may inadvertently perpetuate a focus on weight that reinforces stigma. Weight-centric approaches (such as using weight as the primary measure of progress or health) can induce feelings of shame in patients, particularly those in higher-weight bodies. The continued use of the body mass index (BMI) is problematic and does not account for muscle mass, body composition, developmental stages, or cultural and genetic diversity in body size. Current systems that require regular weigh-ins and then the reporting of these numbers to third parties for determination of insurance approval for treatment is flawed. There is an increasing need to shift focus to behavioral assessments and measures of well-being versus weight and BMI.

Body Image and the Clinician

Clients with eating disorders often have complex relationships with weight, body image, and food. This can lead to heightened sensitivity to the weight and appearance of their clinician, sometimes affecting their willingness to engage in treatment (McEntee et al., 2023). Some clients may perceive clinicians in larger bodies as lacking authority on recovery, assuming that they do not "practice what they preach" regarding nutrition and health. Conversely, clinicians in thinner bodies may be seen as idealized figures, reinforcing weight-related anxieties and unrealistic body standards (Puhl et al., 2020). Overall, individuals with eating disorders may project their anxieties about weight onto their clinicians, particularly when the therapist's body size differs from societal ideals (Rothblum & Gartrell, 2019).

When two people are in a room together, they are inherently engaging in an assessment of each other. In eating disorder therapy, this is exponentially increased on how clients perceive the weight of their provider. Clients who struggle with body image concerns may project their anxieties onto their therapist, affecting their ability to trust recommendations or internalize treatment goals (Puhl et al., 2020). Existing literature suggests that both clients and their families may hold explicit or implicit biases about therapist weight, shaping their views on the therapist's credibility, empathy, and ability to support recovery (McEntee et al., 2023). These biases can influence the therapeutic alliance and, in some cases, create barriers to effective treatment.

A client in recovery from binge eating disorder or bulimia who is still in a larger body might sense that their providers are implicitly judging their weight, which could trigger feelings of failure or prompt relapse. Likewise, if a clinician assumes that a client's eating disorder is "less serious" because of their weight, they might not offer the same level of care (e.g., not referring to a higher level of care or nutrition counseling) as they would for a thinner patient with the same behaviors. Research demonstrates numerous examples of weight stigma in ED settings —from therapists expressing surprise at an ED diagnosis in a larger person to program materials that celebrate weight loss. Evidence of body sizing and judgments in treatment illustrate how pervasive and insidious the problem is.

In a powerful self-reflection of her inpatient treatment experience, Harrop (2019), a clinician, reflects on experiences of weight stigma from multiple providers, specifically recognizing the harm that was caused within the therapeutic dynamic after the clinician engaged in body-shaming, comparisons, misdiagnosis, and denial of the severity of illness based on size judgments. Harrop remarks that the interactions with the primary therapist

> disrupted the therapeutic alliance by body-shaming me, instead of embodying empathy for me. In her attempt to reassure me, my therapist argued that my body was less deserving of care and treatment because it was larger than my peers' bodies. I already carried immense shame about my body size, both because of sociocultural pressures to be thin and the internalized oppression of the eating disorder. This interaction deepened my sense of shame and lack of self-worth.

Individuals who have faced weight-based discrimination in the past may enter therapy with mistrust or apprehension, particularly if they have previously experienced judgment from healthcare professionals (Lee et al., 2021). This hesitation may cause clients to withhold personal experiences, limit self-disclosure, or disengage from therapy altogether. If therapists are unaware of their own weight biases, they may inadvertently reinforce stigma through microaggressions, assumptions about health and weight, or an overemphasis on weight loss as a measure of well-being (Rubino et al., 2020). These factors contribute to a relational dynamic in which clients do not feel fully seen or understood, further obstructing authentic self-expression in therapy.

The Impact of Weight Stigma Across the Lifespan

Reports of weight stigma are pervasive throughout our culture and continue to rise, having negative consequences across the lifespan in nearly all aspects of well-being including family, relationships, education, employment, and healthcare, which we have already discussed in detail. While weight stigma is the social devaluation of a person based on body size or weight, it can be expressed externally and experienced internally. External weight stigma involves behaviors such as experiencing verbal abuse, exclusion, and unequal treatment based on body weight. Internalized weight stigma occurs when societal stereotypes about weight are internalized, leading to negative self-perception and self-blame (Pearl & Puhl, 2018).

The Emotional Harms of Weight Stigma

There are several significant impacts to mental health as a result of weight stigma. Fears and concerns from those having experienced weight discrimination perpetuate individuals avoiding care to avoid further stigmatization. For example, because of embarrassment or fear of being shamed in fitness or medical environments, individuals who have previously been stigmatized are more likely to avoid exercise and experience increased emotional distress such as increased anxiety, depression, and low self-esteem (Rubino et al., 2020). As emotional distress rises, individuals may seek comfort in already established behaviors, including emotional eating, binge eating, or eating in secret, which ultimately creates and perpetuates a vicious pattern. In fact, studies have found that up to 79% of individuals report using food to cope with weight stigma, which can lead to consuming excess calories (Puhl & Brownell, 2006).

Weight stigma has profound effects on an individual's well-being. Being treated poorly or judged because of one's weight can lead to a host of psychological consequences. As mentioned, numerous studies have linked experiences of weight stigma to higher levels of depression, anxiety, and psychological stress (Papadopoulos & Brennan, 2015; Puhl & Suh, 2015). In one large survey, individuals who had been stigmatized due to their weight reported greater vulnerability to depression, heightened anxiety, body image dissatisfaction, low self-esteem, and even thoughts of suicide (Puhl & Suh, 2015).

The significant stress of stigma can also lead to social isolation and increased feelings of shame. Many people internalize the negative stereotypes, blaming themselves for the bias they encounter, which can worsen their self-image and mental health, again, perpetuating an ongoing cycle of shame. In a meta-analysis of 105 studies, Emmer et al. (2020) found a significant association between weight stigma and poorer mental health outcomes. On average, higher levels of weight-related stigma were correlated with greater psychological distress (indicating that as stigma increases, mental health worsens; Emmer et al., 2020). Significantly, this meta-analysis found that the link between stigma and mental health was stronger among individuals with higher BMIs. In other words, people in larger bodies—who likely experience stigma more frequently—suffer noticeable mental health impacts. This includes not only clinical depression and anxiety disorders but may lead to eating disorders and disordered eating behaviors. In fact, weight stigma often precipitates binge eating or cycles of dieting and weight regain, as individuals cope with negative emotions through food or develop an unhealthy relationship with eating (Friedman et al., 2008; Puhl & Heuer, 2009). These psychological and behavioral impacts can create a damaging feedback loop: stigma worsens mental health, which can lead to comfort eating or avoidance of exercise, potentially causing further weight gain and reinforcing the stigma.

The Physical Harms of Weight Stigma

Collectively, these concerns show how weight stigma directly and indirectly undermines mental and physical health. Individuals who feel unwelcome or shamed in healthcare settings may delay seeking care until problems become acute. They are also less likely to engage in healthy behaviors if those behaviors become associated with stigma or past trauma. In essence, weight stigma contributes to worse health outcomes such as higher rates of chronic illness complications, lower utilization of preventive services, and even increased mortality risk. Simply put, stigma itself becomes a barrier to effective healthcare and a driver of health inequities, independent of a patient's actual weight.

The Social Harms of Weight Stigma in Adolescence

Research shows that weight stigma in childhood can have long-term consequences, including low self-esteem, depression, social isolation, and increased weight gain due to stress and unhealthy coping mechanisms (Puhl & Latner, 2007). Weight can influence peer and friendship dynamics, particularly in childhood and adolescence. Youth in larger bodies often experience bias and exclusion from peers. Negative peer interactions, often driven by weight-based bullying, teasing, or "fat shaming" can take a toll on social and mental health, increasing risks of loneliness, low self-esteem, and depression. For example, a large social network analysis of US adolescents found that overweight students were less likely to be chosen as friends by their peers; nonoverweight youths were about 30% more likely to select another nonoverweight friend over an overweight friend (Schaefer & Simpkins, 2013). In fact, a headline from *Newsweek* touted "When Kids Are Fat, They are Less Likely to Have Friends" (2017).

In my own life, I have continued to struggle with the requirements of elementary schools to weigh children and report their BMI. This antiquated process raises serious concerns related to health, psychological well-being, and the perpetuation of weight stigma. BMI is a deeply flawed and overly simplistic measure of health; it does not account for muscle mass, body composition, developmental stages, or cultural and genetic diversity in body size. Using BMI to assess health in children can lead to misclassification and overlooks the broader determinants of well-being such as nutrition, physical activity, sleep, and mental health.

Even more so, school weigh-ins risk instilling shame and anxiety in young children at a formative stage of identity development. Public or semipublic weighing can trigger body dissatisfaction, increase the risk of disordered eating behaviors, and fuel bullying or peer ridicule, particularly among children in larger bodies. These practices reinforce the false notion that thinness equals health and moral worth, fostering a culture of body surveillance and social comparison. Instead of focusing on weight, schools should promote holistic, inclusive health education that supports physical and emotional development without singling out or pathologizing body size.

Beginning as early as elementary school, individuals in larger bodies are stigmatized. A meta-analysis that aimed to look at the link between "overweight or obesity and bullying behaviors among children and adolescents" reported that those with larger body sizes in this population had greater odds of experiencing bullying then other kids and teens (Cheng et al., 2022). In reviewing over 26 studies, as an update to a 2014 analysis, this meta-analysis further asserted that boys in larger bodies were at an increased risk of bullying in the school-aged population and that children and adolescents need protection from weight-based bullying.

In a study by Puhl et al. (2011), high school students perceived being overweight was a primary reason teens were victimized at school. This study reported "at least 84% of participants observed overweight students being teased in a mean way and teased during physical activities, and 65% to 77% of students observed overweight and obese peers being ignored, avoided, excluded from social activities, having negative rumors spread about them, and being teased in the cafeteria." Moreover, the authors asserted that when noticing these damaging behaviors, many teens remained "passive by standards" when these incidents occurred (Puhl et al. 2011).

The mental health impact on those perceived as overweight (whether by themselves or by others) can harm their relationship with themselves and with others in the long term. In adolescence, weight-based bullying is associated with higher rates of depression, anxiety, and low self-worth in adulthood (Hatzenbuehler et al., 2013). Additionally, when investigating the long-term impact of weight-based bulling in youth on longer-term health outcomes in a 15-year longitudinal study, researchers found that weight-based teasing in adolescence predicts "obesity" and adverse eating behaviors well into adulthood, especially for girls (Puhl et al., 2017). The research is consistent and clear: individuals who have been subjected to bullying as it relates to weight suffer negative mental health outcomes.

Weight-Related Harms in Adulthood

In adulthood, the initial picture of weight stigma is somewhat more encouraging than with children and adolescents. Carr and Friedman (2006) found that among US adults, BMI was not significantly associated with the quality of friendships, spousal relationships, or coworker relationships. This research suggested that by adulthood, individuals with a higher body weight can form supportive friendships or maintain friendships with those who are accepting of each other. In other words, while overweight individuals may face stigma in youth, those who navigate into adulthood often develop friend circles that offer mutual respect and positive interaction regardless of size. However, an exception was found in this study within family relationships; individuals identified as severely "obese" reported more strained and less supportive interactions with family members, and even more so when those persons had been overweight since adolescence (Carr & Friedman, 2006). Despite the results from Carr and Friedman (2006), we also know that adolescents who were teased about their weight (by peers or family) had higher odds of poor body image and disordered eating behaviors in adulthood (Puhl et al., 2017). This underscores that early peer relationship difficulties tied to weight can carry forward, even if adult friendships themselves become more supportive.

Relational Impacts of Weight Stigma

Most people maintain a variety of relationships in their life, and weight stigma can affect these differently. A clinician treating an ED client should consider the complexities of every relationship a client has when evaluating their treatment needs and forging an authentic relationship with them.

Romantic Relationships

Weight can play a complex role in romantic relationships, influencing both the formation of relationships and dynamics within them. Dating and partner selection can be challenging for individuals (especially women) with higher body weight. Existing research suggests that there is a negative impact of higher BMI and weight stigma in dating and marital relationships (Carels et al., 2022). Studies have shown that individuals with higher BMIs, particularly women, are often perceived as less attractive or desirable by their partners, which can contribute to feelings of inadequacy and self-doubt (Puhl et al., 2020). This perception may lead individuals to avoid emotional intimacy, fearing that their partner sees them as less worthy or valuable. The anticipation of stigma and rejection reinforces self-silencing behaviors, reducing emotional openness and trust within romantic partnerships. Over time, the cumulative impact of weight stigma on relationships can erode self-confidence and reinforce the belief that one must conform to unrealistic body standards to be loved and accepted (Pearl & Puhl, 2018; Montani et al., 2015).

Many individuals in larger bodies report experiencing weight-based prejudices from romantic partners or potential partners (Côté & Bégin, 2020). For example, partners may make critical comments about the person's weight or pressure them to lose weight. This type of weight-focused criticism from a partner has been linked to poorer personal relationship outcomes. Research has found that when one partner stigmatizes or criticizes the other's weight, it correlates with greater body dissatisfaction in the targeted partner, lower relationship satisfaction (and even lower sexual satisfaction), and a higher likelihood of disordered eating behaviors (Côté & Bégin, 2020).

Over time, these types of dynamics can erode relationship quality. In a comprehensive systematic review by Schmidt et al. (2021), the authors synthesized 32 studies on this topic and found a clear pattern: weight stigma within romantic relationships—most notably, a partner criticizing the other's weight—is consistently associated with worse relationship functioning. Additionally, couples dealing with weight-related disparagement show lower relationship satisfaction, reduced intimacy, less constructive communication during conflicts, and even higher relationship instability (Schmidt et al., 2021). Overall, weight stigma and weight-related comments and criticisms impact partner selection relationship well-being.

Family Relationships

Family relationships are another domain where body weight can have a significant impact. As Carr and Friedman (2006) observed, individuals with higher weight (especially those who are "severely obese") often experience more strained relationships with family members. Family strain can manifest as frequent weight-related comments, criticism, or differential treatment. Family members (parents, siblings, spouses, etc.) may consciously or unconsciously stigmatize an overweight relative, thinking it might motivate weight loss or out of misguided concern, though research indicates this usually does more harm than good. As indicated previously, the long-term effects of family weight criticism can be serious for an individual's mental and physical health. Additionally, these effects impact the ability to foster healthy relationships with others for fear of being mocked, made fun of, or misunderstood.

Workplace Relationships

The workplace is another interpersonal context where body weight can influence interactions and opportunities. A robust body of evidence shows that overweight and obese individuals often face weight-based discrimination or bias in employment settings. For instance, Carr and Friedman's (2006) research also noted that people with BMI in the obese range above 35 were significantly more likely to report experiences of job discrimination than those of average weight. Another analysis found an 84% higher likelihood of perceived job discrimination among the "severely obese" (Giel et al., 2010). These findings are congruent with numerous studies documenting bias in hiring, promotion, and wages. Individuals in larger bodies as job applicants are frequently judged as less competent, less disciplined, or less "professional" due to pervasive stereotypes (e.g., the false belief that higher weight individuals are lazy or lack self-control; Ruggs et al., 2018; Flint et al., 2024).

Weight stigma in the workplace contributes to meaningful inequities in both compensation and professional experiences. Research shows that individuals in larger bodies are more likely to experience discrimination in hiring, promotion, and evaluation processes, often driven by implicit and explicit weight bias (Ruggs et al., 2018; Flint et al., 2024). Beyond structural disparities, weight bias also affects daily workplace interactions, with employees reporting experiences ranging from subtle judgment about eating behaviors to overt stigmatization or bullying, which can negatively impact relationships, job satisfaction, and overall well-being (Ruggs et al., 2018; Flint et al., 2024).Unfortunately, unlike many other forms of prejudice, weight stigma remains socially acceptable in many workplaces. There have been efforts to shift this line of thinking, such as when Michigan introduced an anti-weight discrimination law (Sabharwal et al., 2020), but more could be done to destigmatize larger bodies in the workplace. Societal awareness of weight bias has lagged behind awareness of other biases. Notably, while biases based on race, gender, and sexuality have shown some decline in recent years, anti-fat bias has not decreased; large-scale implicit bias data from 2007–2016 showed that weight bias slightly worsened over that period (Alberga et al, 2016; Charlesworth et al., 2019).

Navigating Weight Stigma and Weight Bias While Building an Authentic Client–Clinician Relationship

For the clinician, acknowledging weight bias and stigma is important, but it is also crucial that the clinician understand how to bring this awareness to therapeutic practice in order to build authentic relationships with their eating disorder clients. Weight bias in eating disorder therapy is a complex and underexplored issue that can significantly impact the therapeutic process, treatment outcomes, and the client–therapist relationship. This section includes considerations for practitioners.

One way to build an authentic relationship with clients is to allow them to be their full selves in therapy. In *Fat & Queer: An Anthology of Queer and Trans Bodies and Lives* (Grimm et al., 2021), many of the contributing authors remark how authenticity is not just about self-expression but also about having space to exist without distortion or erasure. In the collection of stories, several of the authors describe how dominant mental health frameworks, including eating disorder treatment, have historically demanded conformity to thinness (as well as binary gender norms and White-centric ideals), which makes authenticity both unsafe and unsupported. Authenticity emerges from rejecting external demands and defying systemic oppression through storytelling, community building, and body liberation.

There are other factors related to weight bias and weight stigma that influence authentic relationships between the clinician and client. In further developing authenticity in the therapeutic relationship, it is necessary to explore how intersectional identities as discussed in the previous chapter overlay with weight stigma and weight biases. This will be included in the discussion that follows.

Asking Questions and Being Open to Conversations

As clinicians, it is critical to empower clients to build authenticity through insight and exploration, honoring their lived experiences. By asking clients to reflect on experiences of weight stigma, clinicians can begin to validate that their pain is real and systemic, not imagined or exaggerated. This combats the gaslighting and minimization many people face, allowing them to bring their whole selves into the room without editing or shrinking to fit provider expectations. Authenticity begins when clients feel they do not have to "perform wellness" or hide their suffering to be heard. Some examples of questions that clinicians could use to establish this honest environment include:

- "Can you recall a time when you felt judged or dismissed because of your body size in a medical, school, or therapeutic setting? What impact did that have on your willingness to seek support?"
- "In what ways have you had to advocate for yourself or correct misconceptions about your body?"

Exploring internalized weight bias can help clients name and examine the inherited, societal voices that shape their self-concept. This creates an opening to distinguish inherited beliefs from authentic self-perception, a critical step in reclaiming one's narrative. Some examples of questions to ask are:

- "What beliefs about your body have you internalized that might not actually be your own? Where do you think those messages came from?"
- "How do you talk to yourself about your body during moments of struggle or shame? Whose voice does that sound like?"

Inviting clients to explore their prior experiences in therapy or treatment signals that there is a potential for their new relationship with the clinician to be different. The conversation that comes from these questions may indicate that the clinician is willing to listen, repair, and co-create safety. This transparency supports a foundation of relational authenticity between clinician and client. Authenticity in therapy is a two-way street: clients can only show up fully when they sense the clinician is also real, humble, and attuned. Here are some more questions clinicians could use to continue establishing the authentic relationship:

- "Have you ever felt that your body made it harder to feel safe or understood in therapy? What would make this space feel more affirming to you?"
- "Do you feel like your providers have understood your relationship with food and body without blaming your weight?"
- "What has your experience with eating disorder treatment been like so far? Have you ever felt that weight change was prioritized over healing?"

Questions about embodiment, joy, and body connection move beyond symptom management toward a more expansive and inclusive definition of healing. This supports clients in aligning their behaviors, values, and emotions, which are hallmarks of authentic living. Authentic therapy doesn't ask "How can you fix your body?" but rather "How can we honor what your body already knows?" A clinician can broaden the conversation of embodiment with these questions:

- "What does safety in your body mean to you?"
- "Can you think of moments when you've felt connected to your body in a nonjudgmental or joyful way? What contributed to that feeling?"

In discussing needs, hopes, and values, the clinician returns the agency to the client. This shifts therapy from a top-down model to a collaborative process, which is essential for authenticity to flourish, especially for clients who have felt disempowered in healthcare. Clinicians can build authenticity by inviting clients to take ownership of their own care by guiding the conversation with questions like:

- "What would it look like for your recovery to not be centered around changing your body but honoring it?"
- "What kind of support do you need from me, from your support system, from the treatment team to feel seen and respected in this work?"

Re-Defining Goals

As discussed, for an intact therapeutic alliance, treatment goals must be mutually agreed upon. Lack of appropriate communication goals and interventions causes ruptures and breaks momentum for authentic relational healing. McEntee et al. (2023) provide recommendations for eating disorder treatment and research to foster a weight-inclusive paradigm. The recommendations below are for practitioners to use with clients as the therapeutic relationship evolves. Clinicians should tailor these steps with their clients based on the findings that come as the therapeutic work evolves.

- Develop the use of functional behavioral assessments versus a reliance on BMI and weight while re-examining the rationale for weigh-ins.
    - If the setting in which the clinician provides care necessitates weigh-ins, engage in an open dialogue around the unintended effects of weighing in ED treatment.
    - If weight goals are necessary in the treatment setting, ensure that the goals do not unintentionally reinforce fat-phobic attitudes through any promotion of weight loss.
- Demonstrate a commitment to care through active engagement in social justice across the weight spectrum and advocate for access to care. This can be evident to clients through marketing materials, what is available in the waiting room, and even in the artwork displayed in the treatment space.
- Develop treatment plans and goals that are rooted in increasing a client's flexibility in their relationship with food and people.
- Recognize that personal biases exist. Engage in supervision (peer or otherwise) to increase accountability and exploration of biases and stigmas, not just regarding weight, but through all intersectional identities.
- Engage clients with community to combat social isolation and historical shame while engaging in difficult conversations regarding body shape and size.
- Promote open dialogue by addressing weight stigma as an explicit part of a treatment plan.

BMI and Weights

The continued reliance on weight-based classification systems requires a paradigm shift; BMI is not a helpful measure for eating disorder treatment. BMI does not account for gender, ethnicity, or developmental history; moreover, research on BMI often is demonstrating correlation, rather than causation, despite how it is often represented. As McEntee et al. (2023) reported, "Mandated weighing can reinforce the false notion that weight is a stronger indicator of health than dietary habits, physical activity, and other health behaviors … to date, no dismantling studies have identified the utility of measuring weight in ED treatment" (p. 4). The paradigm shift that would need to occur to root out the BMI is not just at the provider level. Every treatment environment I have worked at for over 20 years has required regular intervals of weighing for clients with eating disorders. While as providers we had a significant reliance on this objective data point, it was also used for regular reporting to insurers for continued coverage. While I have had the experience of using many different types of weigh-ins—including blind weights, visible weights, or giving general feedback about weight changes—with clients, it is important to note that there is no clear evidence that this is impactful to treatment.

In the establishment of weight goals, providers must be mindful not to reinforce fat-phobic attitudes. In my role as a program administrator and clinical supervisor, I've frequently been called upon to navigate complex and emotionally charged conflicts related to weight restoration goals. One particularly difficult case involved a high-profile referral source who objected to a client's weight gain in residential care, despite extensive clinical justification grounded in growth charts, medical markers, and client-reported hunger cues. The treatment team's efforts to ground decisions in evidence-based care were overshadowed by discomfort with the client's potential body size. The situation escalated to leadership discussions, where the harmful and deeply entrenched bias was made explicit by a non-clinical leader stating, "no one wants a fat kid"—a moment that underscored how fatphobia can undermine ethical and compassionate treatment.

This experience was one of many that illuminated how deeply weight stigma is embedded not only in society, but within treatment settings that claim to be weight-neutral or health-focused. As a clinical leader, I found myself repeatedly having to advocate for decisions that were rooted in sound medical and psychological reasoning, only to face pushback when those decisions resulted in a client moving toward a weight that was culturally or socially undesirable. These conversations often became less about client well-being and more about appeasing referral sources or families uncomfortable with fatness, regardless of clinical evidence. I witnessed firsthand how this discomfort disrupted team cohesion, compromised therapeutic alliance, and ultimately risked reinforcing to clients the very fears and distortions treatment aimed to dismantle.

I have also repeatedly experienced providers attempting to reassure clients that they will not allow them to gain "too much" weight. As McEntee et al. (2023) concludes, statements like this continue to perpetuate the idea of fatphobia. "When fear of fatness is incorporated into treatment, it is often addressed only in the context of reality testing distorted cognitions rather than questioning the weight-centric practice of equating weight and fat with health." This quote highlights a critical limitation in many eating disorder treatments—the tendency to treat fear of fatness as a cognitive distortion to be corrected, rather than interrogating the broader societal and clinical assumptions that conflate weight with health. By failing to challenge weight-centric paradigms, treatment can inadvertently reinforce fatphobia and neglect the deeper cultural and systemic roots of body shame and stigma.

Being tasked with managing the fallout of these conflicts revealed how often clinicians and staff are pressured—implicitly or explicitly—to make treatment decisions based on optics rather than outcomes. It was especially painful to support frontline providers who were doing their best to uphold high quality care but felt disempowered by administrative or external demands. These moments highlighted for me the critical need for systemic training on weight bias, as well as courageous leadership willing to challenge fatphobic assumptions at every level of care delivery. They also reinforced why I remain committed to creating treatment spaces that do not equate thinness with health or morality, and that prioritize the dignity and autonomy of every client, regardless of body size.

Assessments and Instruments

There are various assessments that are designed to help explore weight stigma. These instruments vary in highlighting external sources of weight stigma, exploring interpersonal sources of weight stigma, and looking at different settings of application. Some assessments include the:

- Stigmatizing Situations Inventory (Myers & Rosen, 1999)
- Interpersonal Sources of Weight Stigma (Puhl & Brownell, 2006)
- Physical Appearance Related Teasing Scale (Thompson et al., 1991)
- Fat Microaggressions Scale (Lindloff et al., 2024)
- Weight Stigma Exposure Inventory (Ruckwongpatr et al., 2025)
- Anti-Fat Attitudes (Crandall, 1994)
- Weight Self-Stigma Questionnaire (Lillis et al., 2010)
- Perceived Weight Stigma Scale (Rafeh et al., 2019)
- Treatment-Based Experiences of Weight Stigma (Chen & Gonzales, 2022)

While it is beyond the scope of this chapter to dive into each of these instruments, it is important to use validated instruments along with engaging in thoughtful dialogues to best understand each person's experiences. Therapists should work to have conversations about potentially taboo topics, which certainly include body size, weight, and shape. In doing so, practitioners can help build relational interactions with clients while identifying the origins and experiences of weight stigma to aid in planning effective interventions.

Navigating Weight Biases with Families

It is additionally important to consider the extended therapeutic alliance perspective and weight stigma by considering how parental and familial biases about therapist weight can shape the treatment process. Some parents may express concerns that a therapist in a larger body is not a suitable role model for their child's recovery, particularly if the family holds weight-centric views of health (Phelan et al., 2015). This bias can undermine trust in the therapist's expertise and contribute to resistance in following treatment recommendations. Conversely, some families may prefer a therapist in a larger body, assuming they will be more compassionate and less likely to promote restrictive eating practices. However, this perception can also be problematic, as it places undue pressure on therapists to align with specific weight-related expectations rather than focusing on evidence-based care (McEntee et al., 2023). The weight bias held by families can either facilitate or hinder the effectiveness of treatment depending on how it aligns with their preexisting attitudes toward body size and health.

The Importance of Psychoeducation

Studies suggest that therapist weight can influence client expectations about treatment recommendations. For example, a therapist in a larger body who encourages a weight-inclusive approach may be met with skepticism from clients who have internalized societal anti-fat biases. They may question whether the therapist understands the desire for weight loss, even when weight loss is not a recommended goal in ED recovery (McEntee et al., 2023). On the other hand, a thin therapist may be perceived as reinforcing restrictive eating behaviors, even if their clinical stance is weight neutral (Rudolph et al., 2022).

Outside of providers and facilities, psychoeducation is critical for clients and families. Educating clients about weight-neutral approaches to eating disorder recovery can help shift focus from body size to behavioral and psychological well-being. Discussions about therapist weight should be addressed openly when it becomes a barrier to treatment progress (McEntee et al., 2023). Families should receive education on the role of weight stigma in eating disorders to prevent weight-based assumptions from interfering with treatment. Providers can introduce resources on the Health at Every Size (HAES) framework to reframe discussions around weight and health (Puhl et al., 2020).

Reflections and Questions for Clinicians to Use with Clients and Their Families

Here are some examples of educational prompts and reflection questions that clinicians can use in their work with clients and families. These examples are designed to increase awareness and challenge internalized beliefs while continuing to build rapport and expression of empathy with the continued goal of building authenticity.

Psychoeducation on Weight Stigma

- "Weight stigma refers to the negative attitudes and discrimination people experience because of their body size. It can come from the outside like from healthcare providers, media, and peers, or from within in the form of self-judgment."
- "Research shows that weight stigma, not weight itself, can lead to serious health problems—like stress, depression, disordered eating, and avoidance of medical care."

Normalizing and De-shaming

- "It's incredibly common to internalize weight bias because it's everywhere in our culture. You're not alone in holding those beliefs. We can explore where they come from and whether they still serve you."
- "We've been taught to see weight as a moral issue, but body size is not a reflection of character, health, or worth."

Family-Related Issues

- "How do you talk about weight, dieting, appearance, or health in your family?"
- "Are there unspoken (or spoken) expectations in your family about how people should look or eat?"
- "When someone in the family gains or loses weight, how is it talked about? How does that impact you emotionally?"
- "How do you think your family would respond if someone rejected dieting or pursued body acceptance instead?"

Systemic and Societal Influences

- "What do you notice about the kinds of bodies that are portrayed as desirable and successful in the media and celebrated in society? What about bodies that are deemed undesirable? How do you relate or not relate to these messages?"
- "How do you think those messages may have shaped your thoughts about your own body or others' bodies?"

Creating Spaces for All Bodies

Too often in healthcare settings, providers do not offer size-appropriate resources. These physical barriers can also prevent individuals in larger bodies from receiving needed care. Examples include ill-fitting hospital gowns and blood pressure cuffs as well as furniture that fails to fit someone's needs. In fact, Puhl and Brownell (2006) reported that 91% of facilities in their study did not have scales available for people over 350 pounds.

Despite the existing literature on the importance of creating inclusive environments, practitioners seem to struggle with putting this into action. When I was operating a nationwide treatment facility, the concerns on creating a weight-inclusive environment and reducing these physical barriers were top of mind at treatment center facilities and practitioner training. Despite the ongoing dialogues and best efforts, we often fell short of meeting the needs of all bodies. Exam tables, scales, blood pressure cuffs, chairs, and beds that supported individuals of higher weights often cost more than "standard" materials.

Even when we were unable to provide such resources for every space, we made sure there was a chair that could accommodate an individual at a higher weight. However, this practice ultimately led to even further perpetuations of weight stigma and experiences of weight-related discrimination for individuals. With only one piece of equipment that worked for a higher-weight individual, it was imperative to identify the piece of furniture when a client required it, including in group settings. Therefore, in order to comfortably receive much-needed eating disorder treatment, an individual had to be directed to the *one* chair they could sit in, in a room of 20 other chairs. This also assumed that only a single client would require the specialized chair. If there were multiple clients requiring the chair or if someone of a lower weight was using the chair, someone would have to "other" themselves and potentially face stereotypes that have contributed to a traumatic history of weight-shaming or choose another place to sit, even if the other options were uncomfortable or unable to fit a larger body.

Given that many ED practitioners work within practice environments, it is important to recognize that weight-inclusive care applies to the larger environment as well. This begins with an institutional commitment to weight-inclusive care, ensuring that environments are safe and welcoming for all bodies. This includes consistent and uniform furniture, medical equipment, and artwork that is inclusive to larger bodies. Treatment centers should incorporate anti-weight bias policies and ensure that clinical language, assessments, and treatment plans are free from weight-based assumptions (Phelan et al., 2015). Organizations and treatment centers should make a commitment to assess the facilities themselves in an ongoing manner as an evaluation tool for an inclusive environment. Furthermore, as it is important for clients to see diversity in providers regarding race and gender, it is also important for treatment programs to have staff with diverse body sizes to help normalize different body types and demonstrate that effective treatment is not dependent on a clinician's weight (McEntee et al., 2023).

Personal Reflections, Training, and Supervision

Clinicians should critically examine their own biases and how their body size may influence client perceptions. Engaging in training on weight stigma and implicit bias can improve awareness and intervention approaches (Phelan et al., 2015). Clinicians should work within teams and seek supervision to explore issues around weight bias. Clinicians can practice reflective, bias-aware care by actively questioning their assumptions about weight and health and ensuring that treatment plans, interventions, and relational development are pursued for clients, regardless of body size and shape.

Therapists themselves may struggle with internalized weight bias, influencing how they present treatment recommendations. Therapists in larger bodies may feel pressured to "prove" their credibility, leading them to overemphasize certain aspects of nutrition or exercise in ways that could be counterproductive to a weight-inclusive treatment approach (McEntee et al., 2023). Thin therapists may also feel pressure to downplay their own body size to avoid triggering clients, potentially limiting open discussions about body image concerns (Rudolph et al., 2022).

Self-Reflection for Clinicians

I have seen time and time again therapists struggling to feel confident about their own body size and shape while working in a treatment facility. Supervision and self-reflection for providers should include exploration of internalized ideas around weight and shape, including exploring personal thoughts on fatphobia, particularly within the framework as an eating disorder provider. Clinicians should consider the following self-reflection questions:

- What is your idea of "health"?
- How has thinness been perceived and/or prioritized in your own life?
- What does recovery look like for each client?
- How do you tailor treatment to be specific to your client's needs and not just based on a diagnosis?
- Do you use the same language, ask the same questions, and recommend similar treatments to clients in larger bodies regardless of your size as a practitioner?
- How do weight-based biases show up in your treatment environment?
- If you are a clinician in a smaller body, are you aware of your own thin privilege?
- If you are clinician open about your own recovery, how does your current weight represent recovery to individuals of different body sizes?
- How can the eating disorder field destigmatize weight bias and serve as better advocates for people in oppressed bodies?

Effecting Change

Common "anti-obesity" efforts are often unintentionally complicit in contributing to weight stigma (Tomiyama et al., 2018). Public health approaches need to move away from the blame and shame messaging that is pervasive in the discourse. Training and education are needed for providers to understand the shortcomings of BMI as an indicator of health (Rothman, 2008). A multilayer strategy is needed to tackle the pervasiveness of weight stigma that includes change throughout ecosystems including the macrolevel systems of healthcare and government.

Given the widespread nature of weight stigma, it is important to be aware of changing societal attitudes toward body weight. In recent years, public discourse has seen a growth in movements aimed at reducing stigma and embracing size diversity, chief among them the body positivity movement. The body positivity movement emerged from earlier fat-acceptance and feminist movements and has become prominent on social media over the past decade. Its core message is to promote acceptance of all body sizes, celebrate diverse body shapes, and challenge traditional beauty ideals that equate thinness with worth (Stevens & Griffiths, 2020). However, critics caution that body positivity is being co-opted by mainstream fashion and advertising media and could inadvertently reinforce an emphasis on appearance.

There are some early signs that social attitudes might be shifting alongside these movements, albeit slowly. A nationally representative survey in New Zealand tracked anti-fat attitudes over about a decade (2009–2017) and found weight bias remained relatively stable, but with a slight decrease in bias among the youngest generations, particularly young women. In that study, both men and women showed a marginal increase in "warmth" (positive feelings) toward people of higher weight over the 10-year period, suggesting a modest improvement in attitudes. The authors interpreted the small positive change among younger women as possibly reflecting shifting societal norms about the acceptability of weight stigma (Chivers et al., 2022).

Increased public awareness, spurred by advocacy groups, increased representation of larger bodies in the media, and campaigns like body positivity may be making overt weight-shaming less socially acceptable than before. Surveys in the United States have noted growing awareness that weight discrimination is a problem that should be addressed (though opinions vary on how to balance that with public health messaging). Despite this, it is important to recognize that any attitudinal changes are gradual and weight-based stigma remains pervasive. Some data suggest that weight bias actually increased during the late 20th and early 21st century as "obesity" rates rose. An analysis of US trends found a 66% rise in reported weight-based discrimination from the mid-1990s to mid-2000s (Puhl & Heuer, 2009).

Overall, social attitudes toward body weight are slowly evolving. There is growing public dialogue about weight stigma and early evidence of small improvements in attitudes among younger people. The body positivity movement has likely contributed to more positive interpersonal environments for some by promoting respect and inclusion regardless of size. Yet, meaningful reduction in weight-based biases on a broad scale remains a work in progress—many individuals with higher weight still encounter prejudice in their daily interactions, and eliminating the weight stigma requires continued cultural, clinical, and policy efforts.

Summary

Weight bias in eating disorder therapy is a complex issue that impacts client trust, family engagement, and treatment outcomes. Perceptions of therapist weight can create barriers to effective treatment, reinforcing harmful stereotypes about body size and health. Addressing these biases through therapist self-awareness, client and family education, and institutional policies can help foster a more inclusive and effective treatment environment. As weight stigma research continues to evolve, future studies should explore how therapist–client dynamics around weight can be optimized to enhance eating disorder recovery.

Weight stigma in healthcare is a pervasive problem that adversely affects quality care in many ways. It not only diminishes the quality of routine healthcare interactions but also leads to tangible negative health outcomes—from poorer mental health and heightened stress to inadequate treatment of physical illnesses and skewed diagnosis of conditions. Individuals subjected to weight bias may avoid the healthcare system or disengage from care, which exacerbates health issues in the long term. These impacts are heightened when we consider the complexities of eating disorder treatment. The research is clear: weight stigma itself is a health risk factor, independent of body weight, by driving unhealthy patterns of behaviors. Weight stigma has lasting effects on a person—from early childhood through adulthood—that is a social determinant of health and well-being. Addressing weight stigma requires an ongoing and conscious effort from providers and institutions that includes adopting weight-inclusive practices, facilitating trainings to recognize and counteract biases, and pursuing ongoing efforts to create clinical environments that respect and support people of all sizes. By doing so, we can move toward a more equitable healthcare system in which every individual, regardless of body size, receives the best possible care.

Key Take-Aways

- Weight stigma in healthcare is a pervasive problem that adversely affects quality care as well as leads to negative emotional, social, and physical outcomes across the lifespan.
- People may experience weight bias not just from the healthcare system but also within romantic and familial relationships as well as school and workplace environments.
- Experiences of weight criticism and weight bias are harmful, often impacting an individual's ability to foster healthy relationships with others, for fear of reenacting shameful experiences of the past.
- Weight bias exists within eating disorder (ED) therapy and is a complex and underexplored issue that can impact all processes of treatment, including the therapeutic process, treatment outcomes, and the client–therapist relationship.
- Providers and their employers should work to offer treatment that is consistent with inclusive care that includes a clear establishment of goals for treatment, foster open dialogue around weight stigma, take time for personal reflection regarding weight biases, create environments that are an inclusive space for all clients, engage in ongoing training, and provide education to clients and families on weight stigma.

- Given the widespread nature of weight stigma, it is important to be aware of changing societal attitudes toward body weight as well as policy decisions and laws that impact the perpetuation of weight stigma.
- Providers can be part of the solution through advocacy work not just with individual clients but through larger systemic approaches that include increasing access to care, increasing funding for research, and using measures of health outside of a reliance on BMI to promote weight-inclusive care.

References

Alberga, A. S., Russell-Mayhew, S., von Ranson, K. M., & McLaren, L. (2016). Weight bias: A call to action. *Journal of Eating Disorders, 4*, 34.

Carels, R. A., Miller, C., Hlavka, R., & Shonrock, A.M.T. (2022). *The interaction between BMI*, weight criticism, weight bias, and psychological and relational outcomes within marriage. Eating and Weight Disorders - Studies on Anorexia, Bulimia and Obesity. 27, 1887–1189.

Carr, D., & Friedman, M. A. (2006). *Body weight and the quality of interpersonal relationships.* Social Psychology Quarterly, 69(2), 127–149.

Charlesworth, T. E. S., & Banaji, M. R. (2019). Patterns of implicit and explicit attitudes: I. Long-term change and stability from 2007 to 2016. *Psychological Science, 30*(2), 174–192.

Charsley, J. S., Collins, S. C., & Hill, A. J. (2018). *The bigger picture: Young children's perception of fatness in the context of other physical differences.* Pediatric Obesity, 13(9), 558–566.

Chen, C., & Gonzales, L. (2022). *Understanding weight stigma in eating disorder treatment: Development and initial validation of a treatment-based stigma scale.* Journal of Health Psychology, 27(13), 3028–3045.

Cheng, S., Kaminga, A., Liu, Q., Wu, F., Wang, Z., Wang, X., Liu, X. (2022). *Association between weight status and bullying experiences among children and adolescents in schools: An updated meta-analysis.* Child Abuse & Neglect, 134, 105833.

Chivers, E. A., Yogeeswaran, K., Zubielevitch, E., & Sibley, C. G. (2022). *Change in weight-based bias over a decade: A longitudinal nationally representative survey.* The Lancet Regional Health. Western Pacific, 23, 100450.

Côté, M., & Bégin, C. (2020). *Review of the experience of weight-based stigmatization in romantic relationships.* Current Obesity Reports, 9(3), 280–287.

Crandall, C. S. (1994). *Prejudice against fat people: Ideology and self-interest.* Journal of Personality and Social Psychology, 66(5), 882–894.

Emmer, C., Bosnjak, M., & Mata, J. (2020). *The association between weight stigma and mental health: A meta-analysis.* Obesity Reviews, 21(1), e12935.

Flint, S. W., et al. (2024). Weight stigma and discrimination: Implications for workplace experiences and health. Current Obesity Reports.

Friedman, K. E., Ashmore, J. A., & Applegate, K. L. (2008). *Recent experiences of weight-based stigmatization in a weight loss surgery population: Psychological and behavioral correlates.* Obesity, 16, S69–S74.

Garcia Moreno, N., Walker, D. C., Gullo, N., & O'Dea, C. J. (2025). *Weight stigma's effects on misdiagnosis of eating disorders among laypeople and healthcare professionals.* International Journal of Eating Disorders, 58(4), 690–702.

Giel, K. E., Thiel, A., Teufel, M., Mayer, J., & Zipfel, S. (2010). *Weight bias in work settings – a qualitative review.* Obesity Facts, 3(1), 33–40.

Grimm, B. O., Morales, M. M., & Ferentini, T. J. (Eds.). (2021). *Fat & queer: An anthology of queer and trans bodies and lives.* Jessica Kingsley Publishers.

Hatzenbuehler, M. L., Phelan, J. C., & Link, B. G. (2013). *Stigma as a fundamental cause of population health inequalities.* American Journal of Public Health, 103(5), 813–821.

Harrison, S., Rowlinson, M., & Hill, A. J. (2016). "*No fat friend of mine*": Young children's responses to overweight and disability. Body Image, 18, 65–73.

Harrop E. N. (2019). *Typical-atypical interactions: One patient's experience of weight bias in an inpatient eating disorder treatment setting.* Women & Therapy, 42(1–2),45–58.

Hebl, M. R., & Xu, J. (2001). *Weighing the care: Physicians' reactions to the size of a patient.* International Journal of Obesity, 25(8), 1246–1252.

Lawrence, B. J., Kerr, D., Pollard, C. M., Theophilus, M., Alexander, E., Haywood, D., & O'Connor, M. (2021). *Weight bias among health care professionals: A systematic review and meta-analysis.* Obesity, 29(11), 1802–1812.

Lee, K. M., Hunger, J. M., & Tomiyama, A. J. (2021). *Weight stigma and health behaviors: Evidence from the Eating in America Study.* International Journal of Obesity, 45(7), 1499–1509.

Lehmkuhl, H. D., Nabors, L. A., & Iobst, E. (2010), *Factors influencing preschool-age children's acceptance of models presented as overweight.* International Journal of Pediatric Obesity, 5: 19–24.

Lillis, J., Luoma, J. B., Levin, M. E., & Hayes, S. C. (2010). *Measuring weight self-stigma: The weight self-stigma questionnaire.* Obesity, 18(5), 971–976.

Lindloff, M. R., Meadows, A., & Calogero, R. M. (2024). *Living while fat: Development and validation of the Fat Microaggressions Scale.* Journal of Personality and Social Psychology, 127(2), 335–362.

McEntee, M. L., Philip, S. R., & Phelan, S. M. (2023). *Dismantling weight stigma in eating disorder treatment: Next steps for the field.* Frontiers in Psychiatry, 14, 10126256.

Mellin, L. M., Irwin, C. E., & Scully, S. (1992). *Prevalence of disordered eating in girls: A survey of middle-class children.* Journal of the American Dietetic Association, 92, 7.

Mills, A. & Osborn, B. (2003). *Shapesville.* Gurze Books.

Montani, J. P., Schutz, Y., & Dulloo, A. G. (2015). *Dieting and weight cycling as risk factors for cardiometabolic diseases: Who is really at risk?* Obesity Reviews, 16, 7–18.

Myers, A., & Rosen, J. C. (1999). *Obesity stigmatization and coping: Relation to mental health symptoms,* body image, and self-esteem. International Journal of Obesity and Related Metabolic Disorders, 23(3), 221–230.

Papadopoulos, S., & Brennan, L. (2015). *Correlates of weight stigma in adults with overweight and obesity: A systematic literature review.* Obesity, 23(9), 1743–1760.

Pearl, R. L., & Puhl, R. M. (2018). *Weight bias internalization and health: A systematic review.* Obesity Reviews, 19(8), 1141–1163.

Phelan, S. M., Burgess, D. J., Yeazel, M. W., Hellerstedt, W. L., Griffin, J. M., & van Ryn, M. (2015). *Impact of weight bias and stigma on quality of care and outcomes for patients with obesity.* Obesity Reviews, 16(4), 319–326.

Puhl, R. M., & Brownell, K. D. (2006). *Confronting and coping with weight stigma: An investigation of overweight and obese adults.* Obesity, 14(10), 1802–1815.

Puhl, R. M., & Latner, J. D. (2007). *Stigma,* obesity, and the health of the nation's children. Psychological Bulletin, 133(4), 557–580.

Puhl, R. M., & Heuer, C. A. (2009). *The stigma of obesity: A review and update.* Obesity, 17: 941–964.

Puhl, R. M., Luedicke, J., & Heuer, C. (2011). *Weight-based victimization toward overweight adolescents: Observations and reactions of peers.* The Journal of School Health, 81(11), 696–703.

Puhl, R. M., Latner, J. D., King, K. M. and Luedicke, J. (2014), *Weight bias among professionals treating eating disorders: Attitudes about treatment and perceived patient outcomes.* International Journal of Eating Disorders, 47: 65–75.

Puhl, R. M., & Suh, Y. (2015). *Health consequences of weight stigma: Implications for obesity prevention and treatment.* Current Obesity Reports, 4(2), 182–190.

Puhl, R. M., Wall, M. M., Chen, C., Bryn Austin, S., Eisenberg, M. E., & Neumark-Sztainer, D. (2017). *Experiences of weight teasing in adolescence and weight-related outcomes in adulthood: A 15-year longitudinal study.* Preventive Medicine, 100, 173–179.

Puhl, R. M., Himmelstein, M. S., & Pearl, R. L. (2020). *Weight stigma as a psychosocial contributor to obesity.* The American Psychologist, 75(2), 274–289.

Rafeh, A. & Hanif, R. (2019). *Understanding perception of weight stigma: Development and validation of perceived weight stigmatization scale.* Pakistan Journal of Psychological Research, 34 (4), 869–897.

Rogers, C. (1951). *Client-centered therapy: Its current practice*, implications and theory. Constable.

Rothblum, E. D., & Gartrell, N. K. (2019). Sizeism in mental health training and supervision. *Women & Therapy, 42*(1–2), 147–155.

Rothman, K. J. (2008). *BMI-related errors in the measurement of obesity.* International Journal of Obesity, 32(3), S56–S59.

Richardson, S. A., Goodman, N., Hastorf, A. H., & Dornbusch, S. M. (1961). *Cultural uniformity in reaction to physical disabilities.* American Sociological Review, 26, 241.

Rubino, F., Puhl, R. M., Cummings, D. E., et al. (2020). *Joint international consensus statement for ending stigma of obesity.* Nature Medicine, 26(4), 485–497.

Ruckwongpatr, K., Chen, I. H., Pramukti, I., Huang, P. C., Latner, J. D., O'Brien, K. S., Wang, X., Chen, J. S., Üztemur, S., Lin, C. C., Chang, Y. L., Chin, W. L., Griffiths, M. D., & Lin, C. Y. (2025). *Assessing exposure to weight stigma: Development and initial validation of the Weight Stigma Exposure Inventory (WeSEI).* Journal of Eating Disorders, 13(1), 2.

Rudolph, A., Hilbert, A., & Herpertz, S. (2022). *The role of weight bias in eating disorder treatment: A systematic review.* Clinical Psychology Review, 91, 102113.

Ruggs, E. N., King, E. B., Hebl, M. R., & Fitzsimmons, M. (2018). Weight stigma in the workplace: A review and research agenda. Frontiers in Psychology, 9, 2206.

Sabharwal, S., Campoverde Reyes, K. J., & Stanford, F. C. (2020). *Need for legal protection against weight discrimination in the United States.* Obesity, 28(10), 1784–1785.

Schaefer, D. R., & Simpkins, S. D. (2013). *Using social network analysis to clarify the role of obesity in adolescent friends.* American Journal of Public Health 104, 1223–1229.

Schmidt, A. M., Jubran, M., Salivar, E. G., & Brochu, P. M. (2023) *Couples losing kinship: A systematic review of weight stigma in romantic relationships.* Journal of Social Issues, 79, 196–231.

Schmidt, A. M., Mensinger, J. L., Santos, R., & Brochu, P. M. (2025). Clinician perceptions of the stereotype content describing people with eating disorders: A weight-inclusive perspective. International Journal of Eating Disorders, 58(7), 1352–1366.

Stevens, A., & Griffiths, S. (2020). *Body positivity (#BoPo) in everyday life: An ecological momentary assessment study showing potential benefits to individuals' body image and emotional wellbeing*. Body Image, 35, 181–191.

Thompson, J. K., Fabian, L. J., Moulton, D. O., Dunn, M. E., & Altabe, M. N. (1991). *Development and validation of the Physical Appearance Related Teasing Scale*. Journal of Personality Assessment, 56(3), 513–521.

Tomiyama, A. J., Carr, D., Granberg, E. M., Major, B., Robinson, E., Sutin, A. R., & Brewis, A. (2018). *How and why weight stigma drives the obesity "epidemic" and harms health*. BMC Medicine, 16(1), 123.

Williams, J. (2017, June 9). When kids are fat, they are less likely to have friends, study finds. *Newsweek*. https://www.newsweek.com/overweight-kids-child-obesity-friends-623645

World Obesity Federation. (2023). https://www.worldobesity.org/what-we-do/our-policy-priorities/weight-stigma

Chapter 8

Beyond an Individual

Developing Authenticity with the Family System

Overview

- *Eating disorders do not exist in isolation, and family therapy provides a vital lens for understanding the relational contexts in which they develop and heal.* This chapter introduces family therapy approaches and lays the foundation for extending authenticity beyond the individual client.
- *Developing an integrative relational framework allows authenticity to become a shared experience within families.* Therapeutic authenticity is not confined to the therapy dyad but can ripple outward into the family system, shaping how members relate, support, and repair trust.
- *Family dynamics often mirror larger cultural forces, including weight stigma and body ideals.* Exploring how weight is discussed, judged, or silenced within families reveals powerful influences on identity, belonging, and authenticity.
- *Family work inevitably brings difficult conversations to the surface.* Long-standing conflicts, unspoken resentments, and painful histories can create turbulence, yet these ruptures also hold potential for deep relational repair when navigated with skill and authenticity.
- *The strain of caring for a loved one with an eating disorder cannot be ignored.* Authentic engagement requires naming caregiver stress, validating emotional burdens, and equipping families with tools that foster resilience and compassion.
- *Techniques such as meta-dialogue, addressing power dynamics, and navigating relational imbalances equip therapists to guide families through rupture toward repair.* By fostering authentic dialogue, families learn not only to support recovery but to build more honest, balanced, and enduring connections.

On her first day in residential treatment, Lorrin walked through the doors flanked by her parents, Roberta and Dave, all polished, polite, and ready to engage. They had recently received a call from the health center at Lorrin's Ivy League college: she had lost significant weight, was struggling academically, and

DOI: 10.4324/9781003632016-9

needed to withdraw to seek care. Within two weeks, her parents mobilized everything necessary to begin treatment.

Lorrin was the youngest of three children in a high-achieving family driven by excellence through academics, athletics, and social status. Her father was a respected physician; her mother managed the home. Both took pride in having created the kind of life they themselves never had and believed their children lacked for nothing. Perfectionism was worn as a badge of honor. When treatment began, they devoted themselves to the process with the same intensity: attending sessions, reading everything recommended, committing to coaching and webinars. They were determined to be "the best at treatment."

As Lorrin gained physical and emotional strength she expressed that she no longer wanted to play lacrosse or return to her college and instead planned to transfer to a state school. Lorrin used her growing knowledge of therapy as a weapon, explaining to her parents how she had been triangulated between them and how they were enmeshed. Her parents, once eager, became frustrated. Roberta felt displaced; Dave felt blamed.

Months into treatment, Roberta and Dave approached me unexpectedly at my place of worship, greeting me as I juggled balancing my young kids, one on each arm. The boundary breach felt intimate and intrusive. In our next session, I confronted them with tension and self-protection. I was aware how my tone shifted, my posture closed. The rupture was immediate. Only after supervision and reflection did I recognize what had happened: while I had challenged family roles and norms, I had not fully seen the parents' longing for affirmation, for respect, for guidance that didn't imply failure. They needed acknowledgment for their efforts and an invitation into new ways of relating that preserved their dignity. What I initially thought would be a straightforward case of eating disorder recovery became a lesson in the complex emotional architecture of families. The therapeutic alliance stretched beyond Lorrin, requiring attention to the voices, vulnerabilities, and needs of everyone in the room. Only then could change take root.

Eating disorders are often deeply rooted in family systems, where relational dynamics shape not only the onset and maintenance of disordered eating behaviors but also core beliefs about body size, shape, and self-worth. Family messages around food, weight, and appearance can reinforce disordered behaviors, particularly in environments that emphasize perfectionism or equate thinness with success and acceptance. These patterns often create a cycle in which the eating disorder becomes a symptom of family functioning. Effective treatment, therefore, requires addressing these underlying relational dynamics, helping families shift their communication, boundaries, and beliefs to foster recovery.

A (Brief) Overview of Family Therapy

Family therapy in the United States emerged in the mid-20th century as a response to the limitations of traditional psychoanalysis and individual-focused therapy. In the 1950s and 1960s, pioneers such as Murray Bowen, Salvador

Minuchin, Virginia Satir, and Carl Whitaker began exploring how family dynamics influence individual psychological functioning. Bowen developed family systems theory, which emphasized intergenerational patterns and differentiation of self, while Minuchin introduced structural family therapy, focusing on family hierarchies and boundaries. Around the same time, the Palo Alto Group, including Gregory Bateson and Jay Haley, developed strategic family therapy, which examined communication patterns and problem-solving strategies within families. These early movements created the foundation for viewing mental health issues not just as individual struggles but as manifestations of broader systemic dysfunctions.

During the 1970s and 1980s, family therapy gained recognition as an essential approach in clinical psychology and psychiatry. The field expanded to include a variety of models, such as the Milan systemic family therapy approach from Europe, which emphasized circular questioning and systemic interventions. In the United States, Virginia Satir's humanistic family therapy emphasized emotional expression and self-worth, while Carl Whitaker's experiential family therapy encouraged deep emotional engagement within families. Around this time, research on family therapy's effectiveness in treating mental health conditions including schizophrenia, substance use disorders, and eating disorders began to grow, further legitimizing the field. The integration of behavioral and cognitive strategies into family therapy approaches also became more common, bridging the gap between systemic models and evidence-based interventions.

Theories of family development provide a framework for understanding how families grow, change, and adapt over time. One model for understanding families is the family life cycle theory, which describes predictable stages families move through, from forming a couple to raising children and eventually adjusting to an empty nest. Each stage presents unique challenges and requires the family to reorganize roles, rules, and communication patterns. Meanwhile, attachment theory, pioneered by John Bowlby, highlights the lifelong impact of early relationships on emotional security and interpersonal connections, influencing how individuals form bonds within their family systems.

Minuchin's structural family theory focuses on family organization, hierarchy, and boundaries, emphasizing how dysfunction can arise from rigid or enmeshed relationships. Early therapy with eating disorder clients and their families was heavily influenced by structural family therapy. Minuchin and colleagues' research in the 1970s and 1980s identified common family dynamics in eating disorder cases, particularly enmeshment (overly close relationships with blurred boundaries), rigidity (resistance to change), and a tendency to avoid conflict. Their work suggested that disordered eating behaviors often function as a way to maintain family homeostasis, with the symptom serving as a distraction from deeper relational tensions. Early interventions based on structural family therapy focused on restructuring family roles, establishing clearer boundaries, and fostering healthier patterns of interaction. Studies from the 1980s demonstrated the effectiveness of these approaches, showing that families who engaged in therapy that addressed systemic dysfunction saw greater improvement in eating disorder symptoms than those who focused solely on individual treatment.

By the 1990s and 2000s, family therapy had become a well-established discipline within psychology, social work, and counseling. The rise of postmodern perspectives, such as narrative therapy and solution-focused therapy, shifted some focus toward how families construct meaning around their struggles and how reauthoring these narratives can lead to healing. Emotionally focused therapy, which is grounded in attachment theory, helps families create secure emotional bonds that support recovery. Family-based treatment, rooted in structural and behavioral principles, has been particularly effective for adolescent eating disorders, involving parents in meal supervision and weight restoration.

Family therapy is a central component of eating disorder treatment. It views the eating disorder not as an isolated issue within the individual, but as embedded in relational, emotional, and often intergenerational dynamics. Effective family therapy helps reduce blame, increase understanding, and mobilize the family as a resource for healing by addressing communication patterns, emotional expression, boundary-setting, and roles within the system. While models like family-based treatment offer structured frameworks, contemporary approaches increasingly emphasize flexibility, cultural responsiveness, and emotional attunement. When delivered with authenticity, family therapy can foster safety, trust, and collaboration, important elements in both disrupting eating disorder behaviors and supporting long-term recovery. Today, family therapies are currently the first line treatment for children and adolescents with anorexia nervosa as recommended by the National Institute for Health and Care Excellence (NICE, 2017).

Family Theories in Care

Early conceptualizations of eating disorders often implicated family dynamics as a causal factor, particularly during the 1960s and 1970s. Pioneering family systems theorists such as Minuchin, Bowen, and Satir emphasized the role of dysfunctional family structures in the development and maintenance of eating disorders. Minuchin and colleagues (1978a) described the "psychosomatic family," characterized by enmeshment, overprotectiveness, rigidity, and lack of conflict resolution—dynamics believed to contribute to anorexia nervosa. Minuchin & Fishman (1981) further identified patterns such as enmeshment, rigidity, and difficulty with conflict resolution as common characteristics in families of individuals with eating disorders, suggesting that the disorder serves a function within the family unit. Bowen's intergenerational theory highlighted the role of unresolved family-of-origin issues and emotional fusion, while Satir focused on incongruent communication and self-worth within the family system (Satir, 1991). These perspectives, though influential, often pathologized family functioning and inadvertently placed blame on parents, particularly mothers. Bruch (1973), in contrast, introduced a psychodynamic lens, framing anorexia as a struggle for autonomy and individuation from an overinvolved mother. Her work emphasized developmental factors, including disturbances in identity formation and body awareness (Rehavia-Hanauer, 2003), which added psychological nuance to family-based explanations.

About Family-Based Treatment

By the late 20th century, backlash against parent-blaming models gave rise to more collaborative approaches. The Maudsley model, or family-based treatment, emerged as a manualized, evidence-based intervention for adolescent anorexia nervosa. Developed in the United Kingdom in the 1980s, family-based treatment positioned parents as central agents in their child's recovery, actively supporting nutritional restoration while avoiding etiological blame (Lock & Le Grange, 2015). The recommended treatment typically offered to families of an adolescent with an eating disorder is family-based treatment due to the significant body of research that has concluded its successes. In a highly truncated explanation, family-based treatment is structured around three phases in which parents are put in the center of driving their child's treatment. The goals are weight restoration, restoring control of eating to the client, and returning to normal development (Lock & Le Grange, 2001). There are likely as many opinions about family-based treatment in the field of eating disorders as there are practitioners.

Relatively recently (2018) James Lock published an opinion article highlighting potential reasons for the confusions with family-based treatment. He rightfully purports that confusions in the field stem from a variety of factors including terminology, such as family-based treatment, family therapy–anorexia nervosa, "Maudsely method," Maudsley multi-family therapy, and a recent offshoot, parent-focused therapy for eating disorders. Unfortunately, if practitioners are confused, family members are often left to navigate the alphabet soup of a new language (treatment) rapidly without truly understanding the substance of the approach.

Let me be very clear: I am not a family-based treatment practitioner. I strongly value the tenets of family-based treatment and admire the longstanding empirical support for the model as well as the many adaptations that are evolving. I have, however, worked with many clients and families over the years that had less-then-stellar experiences with it. I recall one mom saying to me after her 20-year-old daughter was admitted to residential treatment, "Family-based treatment saved my daughter's life, but it destroyed our relationship." While this mom was grateful for the focus on weight restoration and meal compliance in that it likely saved her child's life, much of their work in residential treatment was then healing from the wounds that had developed in her younger years.

Despite its efficacy, family-based treatment has been highly critiqued. Some criticisms over the years of family-based treatment that are supported by my experiences include the rigidity of manualized-based approaches, the lack of attention to family diversity, and an overemphasis on behavioral symptom reduction. From a clinician perspective, concerns with family-based treatment in application have been therapist "buy-in" for certain presentations of family functioning, such as families who presented with marital discord, single-parent families, individual parental emotional struggles, or poor general family functioning (Astrachan-Fletcher, et al., 2018). Clinicians have reported a perception of family-based treatment as "traumatic" for an adolescent and/or family (Astrachan-Fletcher, et al., 2018).

There are emerging personal accounts of adolescents who have received family-based treatment. In a qualitative report of client experiences with family-based treatment, Conti et al. (2021) highlighted that specifically during the first phase of family-based treatment, clients struggled with the exclusive focus on weight restoration, which led to experiences of distress and "loss of voice." In another qualitative account, Nilsen et al. (2021) concluded that "our findings shed light on managing complexities and might suggest the need for a greater degree of tailoring and differentiation when providing family-based inpatient treatment, as there is no treatment program that fits all" (p. 7).

The limitations of family-based treatment have prompted a call for more tailoring treatment methods, which includes relational family therapy approaches that honor family lived experience, address emotional processes, and support authenticity and connection within the family system. Contemporary relational therapies focus less on control and symptom management and more on understanding meaning, attachment, and family dynamics in the broader cultural and developmental context (Gehart, 2017).

Developing an Integrative Relational Framework

Having completed my PhD in couple and family therapy in Philadelphia, I was entrenched in structural family therapy (SFT). I had the opportunity to learn from many who worked with Minuchin firsthand in his work at the Philadelphia Child Guidance Clinic. Additionally, another family approach was introduced during my doctoral studies that continues to shape my work. Ivan Boszormenyi-Nagy pioneered contextual family therapy, which focuses on relational ethics, fairness, and the "invisible loyalties" that have intergenerational impacts within families. Invisible loyalties can be conceptualized as characteristics and behaviors that impact our relationships with ourselves and others that are passed down through generations, unconsciously, and often detrimentally (Boszormenyi-Nagy & Spark, 1984). The concepts introduced to me through Nagy's work (although sometimes difficult to conceptualize) laid the groundwork for my understanding of the biopsychosocial framework on eating disorders. More recently, researchers have explored how transgenerational family relationship patterns further influence patterns in emotional expression and interpersonal relating, coping, and skill development and the intergenerational transmission of attitudes toward eating and weight (Cripps et al., 2024).

Early on in my family work, I merged concepts of structural family therapy, contextual family therapy, and other relational approaches along with cognitive–behavioral interventions to create an interpersonal style in my work. Even when I did not have the theory to understand why it was important, I instinctively knew that eating disorder treatment could not just be about the identified patient. We all play roles within our families of origin, and those roles play out in our romantic partnerships, relationships with friends, and in our workplaces.

Integrating family systems in relational therapy allows therapists to move beyond treating the eating disorder as an isolated individual issue and instead examine the broader family dynamics that contribute to its persistence. Lock and Le Grange (2015) emphasize that eating disorders often serve a function within the family system, whether by maintaining relational stability, expressing unspoken emotional distress, or reinforcing existing patterns of control and attachment. By addressing these systemic influences, therapists can help families recognize how their interactions, communication styles, and emotional responses may inadvertently sustain disordered eating behaviors. When combined with family systems interventions, interpersonal therapy fosters deeper emotional connections, strengthens healthy boundaries, and promotes open dialogue, allowing both the individual and their family to move toward long-term healing. This integrative approach shifts the focus from symptom management to transforming relational patterns, ultimately creating an environment that supports recovery and emotional well-being.

How Therapeutic Authenticity Is Extended to Families

The extended therapeutic alliance in eating disorder treatment requires therapists to build trust and rapport not only with the client but also with their family, ensuring that all members feel heard, understood, and actively involved in the recovery process. When families feel included in the therapeutic process, they are more likely to engage in meaningful behavioral changes, reinforce treatment goals, and provide consistent emotional support. A strong therapeutic alliance with the entire family creates an environment in which difficult conversations can take place, patterns can be restructured, and relational healing can occur through meaningful and authentic connections. By fostering trust at both the individual and family levels, therapists can enhance the effectiveness of treatment and promote long-term recovery outcomes. The concept of an extended therapeutic alliance is when the therapist must establish trust and rapport not only with the client but with the family as a whole.

In eating disorder treatment, this is particularly important, as family involvement is often critical for recovery, especially in adolescent cases. Building an extended therapeutic alliance requires therapists to navigate multiple relationships simultaneously, balancing support and challenge while ensuring that each family member feels heard and valued. Sprenkle and Blow (2004) highlight that therapists must foster a sense of collaboration, validating each person's perspective while gently restructuring problematic patterns. In the context of eating disorders, this means working with families to understand how their interactions influence disordered behaviors while empowering them to become allies in the recovery process. Sprenkle and Blow further argue that in family therapy, the therapeutic alliance must be multidimensional, encompassing not only the individual receiving treatment but also parents, siblings, and other key family figures. This extended therapeutic alliance recognizes that families play an active role in either maintaining or alleviating dysfunction, making their engagement in therapy essential for meaningful and lasting change. Without this broader alliance, therapy risks being undermined by family resistance, misalignment in goals, or unspoken relational dynamics that perpetuate distress. This approach also requires flexibility, as family members may have differing levels of motivation and readiness for change. By skillfully managing these dynamics, therapists can strengthen the family's ability to function as a cohesive support system rather than an unintentional barrier to healing.

Family alliance can be tricky; often in family-based treatment, parental involvement is key in facilitating the restoration of physical health in parents taking responsibility for feeding their child. As discussed earlier, this type of treatment that focuses on weight can be distressing to the family. Even in non-FBT settings, with anorexia nervosa, a weight-focused approached can be stigmatizing. Cripps et al. (2024) comments on alliance noting that a positive therapeutic relationship, in which families felt supported by their therapist, was important in providing containment during early stages of treatment.

Working with families is often both deeply meaningful and profoundly challenging. Families can be a tremendous source of strength, helping a young person rebuild their health meal by meal, sitting beside them through anguished tears, or holding hope when the patient cannot. At the same time, their involvement often brings fear, grief, and frustration to the surface. Asking parents to take responsibility for feeding their child, particularly when weight restoration is the focus, can feel like a judgment on their parenting or a threat to long-held beliefs about food, success, and control. I remember sitting with a mother who trembled as she plated her daughter's lunch, whispering, "I don't want to hurt her." Her daughter glared back, silently pleading with her not to make her eat. In that moment, their pain collided with my role to support, contain, and guide them through an unbearable scene. As Cripps and colleagues (2024) highlight, families need a strong, trusting relationship with their therapist to feel supported during these fragile early stages. Authenticity becomes essential: we must be honest about the challenges ahead, attuned to their emotional experience, and willing to walk with them, even when the path is messy and filled with resistance.

The Clinician Can Lead Families to Authenticity

Authenticity is often the foundation of building strong and successful therapeutic relationships with the entire family system. When clinicians model authenticity by being genuine, transparent, and emotionally present, they encourage family members to do the same, breaking through patterns of avoidance, defensiveness, or emotional suppression. Authentic interactions help uncover the underlying emotions, conflicts, and vulnerabilities that often drive dysfunctional family dynamics, allowing for deeper connection and healing. In the context of eating disorder treatment, authenticity can help family members recognize and address their own fears, anxieties, and beliefs about control, body image, and perfectionism, rather than projecting these struggles onto the individual with the eating disorder. By promoting honest, compassionate communication, clinicians can guide families toward more adaptive ways of relating to one another, ultimately creating an environment that supports both individual recovery and systemic transformation.

Exploring Weight Dynamics with the Family

In the case presented initially in this chapter about Lorrin and her family, another challenge that emerged during treatment was the consistent disagreement around Lorrin's goal weight. During treatment, the team quickly realized that Lorrin was hungry! At first, she would consistently ask for seconds as well as ask for the snacks that had been "forbidden" in her home. Her parents were concerned she was becoming "lazy" because she was not participating in sports or exercise. Lorrin called out Roberta in a session stating that her need for a 5:30 a.m. daily treadmill routine was "disordered," causing an intense moment. While Roberta and Dave were willing to explore "Lorrin's issues," they rejected the idea that the arrival of the eating disorder was something within their entire family system. When discussing weight goals, Roberta and Dave reported that they could not and would not be supportive of a weight goal that was higher than her weight at the time of her high school graduation.

Weight Stigma in Families

In cases where parents struggle with their own body image concerns or internalized weight stigma, their beliefs about body size, health, and self-worth may unconsciously shape how they engage with therapy and influence their ability to support their child's recovery. Addressing these dynamics requires therapists to navigate family resistance with sensitivity and skill, ensuring that the focus remains on creating a supportive, nonjudgmental environment for healing. The expanded alliance can be particularly challenging when parents or family members hold societal biases about body weight and size, projecting these beliefs onto the therapist, especially if the therapist's body does not align with conventional standards of health or beauty.

Research by Costin (2007) suggests that weight bias can significantly impact the therapeutic process, as parents may either overidentify with or reject the therapist based on their body size. If a therapist is in a larger body, parents who equate thinness with health may unconsciously question their credibility, while a thin therapist may be seen as either an aspirational figure or a source of intimidation. These biases can create resistance, distrust, or misalignment in therapy, ultimately interfering with the effectiveness of treatment. Recognizing and addressing these implicit beliefs is critical to maintaining a strong therapeutic alliance and ensuring that therapy remains focused on the client's well-being rather than societal weight norms.

The Therapist's Body

When I was pregnant with my first child, I was working as a primary therapist in an eating disorder program. Deep into my seventh month of pregnancy and beginning to experience discomfort with my growing body, I was facilitating a family meal. This was a group that I loved to run as it was an opportunity to break bread with clients and their family members in a community environment. I had become accustomed to clients and their families asking me questions about my changing body although never quite being comfortable with the attention my body was receiving. During this particular meal, the mother of my 15-year-old client asked me about the gender of my unborn child. I dutifully recited the answer I was now practiced in saying—that I was not finding out the gender of my unborn child. The mother then stated that it was obvious that I was having a girl. Her daughter, as she was attempting to navigate a container of yogurt, asked her mother why she said that. Her mom replied, "Because she's just so fat!"

Gender and birthing myths aside, this exclamatory statement shifted something in me. I had always considered myself in an "average" body size. I was not particularly accustomed to others judging or shaming my body size and weight. The unwanted attention to my own physical form not only ignited my own negative self-talk around weight during my pregnancy but significantly impacted how I interacted with this client and her family. I struggled with how to navigate the experience in the moment of a room of nearly 30 clients and family members, but more than that, it shifted my ability to be my full authentic self with this client.

Parents' perceptions of the therapist's body size may unconsciously influence how they perceive the therapist's competence, leading to potential disruptions in family-based therapy. Puhl and Heuer (2010) highlight the pervasive nature of weight stigma, showing that biases about body size affect judgments of intelligence, professionalism, and authority across various fields, including healthcare. In an eating disorder treatment setting, these biases can manifest as skepticism toward therapeutic recommendations, reluctance to fully engage in treatment, or misplaced focus on the therapist's personal habits rather than the client's needs.

Therapists must be aware of biases and address them directly when they arise, helping parents recognize how their own internalized beliefs about weight and health may be interfering with their ability to fully support their child's recovery. If a therapist is unable to align with the family due to unaddressed biases, such as the belief that a child must lose weight to be "healthy" or that eating disorders are purely a matter of willpower, the alliance may break down. In such cases, the therapist must navigate a delicate balance between educating the family and maintaining the therapeutic relationship without reinforcing harmful narratives. By openly discussing and challenging these perceptions, therapists can reinforce a more inclusive and health-centered approach to treatment that prioritizes emotional well-being over societal standards of appearance.

Therapists can help families restructure unhealthy patterns while simultaneously attending to the relational and emotional needs of both the individual and the family through relational approaches. This requires a balance of clinical expertise, self-awareness, and a willingness to engage in difficult conversations about bias, weight stigma, and family dynamics. When therapists acknowledge and address these barriers, they create an opportunity for deeper engagement, trust, and collaboration. Moreover, by modeling acceptance and neutrality around body size, therapists can help shift family attitudes toward a more compassionate and health-focused perspective. Ultimately, a strong and inclusive therapeutic alliance allows for more effective interventions, enhances family cohesion, and increases the likelihood of long-term recovery for individuals struggling with eating disorders.

When Family Treatment Gets Tough

There are instances in eating disorder therapy when a therapist may find it difficult (or even impossible) to align with the family due to deeply ingrained beliefs, resistance to change, or a lack of willingness to engage in the therapeutic process. Research by Lock and Le Grange (2015) on family-based treatment highlights that parental buy-in is crucial for the success of therapy, yet some families struggle to accept the level of involvement required. When parents deny the severity of the eating disorder, resist evidence-based interventions, or continue to reinforce harmful beliefs about weight and food, the therapeutic process can become strained. From a structural family therapy perspective, enmeshed or highly rigid family structures can create significant barriers, making it difficult for therapists to implement necessary interventions

(Minuchin et al. 1978a). In such cases, a therapist may have to shift the focus toward motivating the family toward change, but if resistance persists, the therapist may need to re-evaluate the best course of action, which could include recommending individual treatment or alternative family interventions.

Family therapy for eating disorders presents unique challenges, often requiring therapists to navigate complex relational dynamics, entrenched family roles, and resistance to change. Memoirs such as *Brave Girl Eating* (Brown, 2011) and *Goodbye Ed, Hello Me* (Schaefer, 2009) offer firsthand accounts of the difficulties families face in treatment. In *Brave Girl Eating*, Harriett Brown details the struggles of implementing family-based treatment (FBT) for her daughter's anorexia, highlighting the emotional toll on parents, the feelings of helplessness, and the tensions that arise when parents are tasked with refeeding their child. Similarly, in *Goodbye Ed, Hello Me*, Schaefer reflects on how family expectations and unspoken pressures contributed to her eating disorder, illustrating the ways in which familial environments—whether overly involved or emotionally distant—can reinforce disordered behaviors. These narratives align with clinical research that shows that family members often feel overwhelmed, guilty, or resistant to the therapeutic process, which can create additional roadblocks to recovery (Lock & Le Grange, 2015).

One major issue in family therapy for eating disorders is the challenge of shifting family perspectives on control, autonomy, and emotional expression. Books that are now seen as seminal influential texts such as *When Food is Love* (Roth, 1992) and *The Secret Language of Eating Disorders* (Claude-Pierre, 1999) highlight how family dynamics, particularly those rooted in perfectionism, high expectations, or unresolved trauma, can contribute to the development of eating disorders. Roth's work, seminal to many therapists now in mid-life, explored how parents' own relationships with food and self-worth are often unconsciously passed down to their children, complicating the recovery process. In therapy, these generational patterns must be addressed, so as not to continue to repeat themselves as Nagy would suggest. However, resistance from parents, likely stemming from fear, may be unconscious, as they are unable to recognize their own role in the disorder. This can make progress difficult.

Family interventions often require parents to confront their own fears and misconceptions about weight and health. This process can be uncomfortable, leading to conflict or disengagement from treatment. Without careful navigation of these challenges, family therapy can sometimes reinforce challenging dynamics rather than dismantle them, underscoring the need for skilled therapists who can balance empathy, structure, and education to facilitate real change.

When Family Therapy Brings Up Elephants in the Room

Family therapy often brings up deeply personal and emotionally charged topics that can be difficult to discuss. Some of the hardest conversations revolve around long-standing family conflicts, unspoken resentments, and traumatic experiences that have shaped family dynamics. Many families avoid discussing issues such as divorce, infidelity, addiction, or past emotional neglect because of the fear that addressing these topics will cause further division. However, leaving these issues unresolved can lead to ongoing dysfunction, with family members repeating patterns of avoidance, blame, or emotional withdrawal. Therapists often must guide families through these challenging discussions, helping them express feelings in a constructive way while preventing escalation into conflict or defensiveness.

In nearly every presentation I give for professionals or psychoeducational talks I do with families, I mention the elephants in the room. I even have a slide that is a hot pink elephant wearing a top hat that says, "Ready to talk?" I first began thinking about this concept after a case I had early on in my career, and I know many clinicians have similar stories from their clinical work.

Kayla and Kyla's Story: Uncovering Family Shame

I was assigned to work with a client, Kayla. Kayla was 18 years old, and it was the summer before she was scheduled to go away to college. She had been struggling with restriction of her intake for around two years. What made this case so interesting was that Kayla's identical twin sister Kyla was being treated for her eating disorder at the same time. The pair's eating disorders engaged them in ferocious comparison. Growing up, sharing a room as only two children of a middle-class family, the competition around physical beauty was significant. The twins' father, Steve, adored his daughters. After working long hours, he would come home almost desperate to hear about their days. He confided in the girls less like a father would and more like a friend. He talked to them about his troubles at work and his disappointing relationship with their mother. The girls' mother, Donna, did not attend in-person therapy sessions like Steve did. In the pre-Covid era, we would call her in on the phone to join rather than engage in a video call. Having never met or seen Donna, my understanding from the family was that she was committed to her work and had a very busy and demanding schedule.

During their early days of treatment, the team realized how difficult it was for Kayla and Kyla to see mirror reflections of themselves. They compared themselves to the other twin, counting their differences. At that point, staff at the treatment center decided that the girls should take a break from seeing each other in person. As a result, Kayla became homesick, this being the first time she'd ever been away from her house and her best friend, her twin. Although the girls could recognize that their eating disorders were competitive, they still loved and cared for each other and only wished the best for the other.

Around this time, we started having family sessions with each girl and the parents separately. I spoke with Donna to try to find time for an in-person session, feeling it would be helpful to see them interact in person. Kayla quickly responded that her mother worked from home. At the time, this was something most people did not do. I was struck by why this would be a reason she could not attend a therapy session and probed further. After reaching a dead-end with Donna, Kalya asked to talk after the phone session. It was during this conversation that I discovered that Donna did not leave the house—ever.

Donna had struggled with agoraphobia for many years. In addition, her anxieties had blossomed in more recent years to include significant hoarding behaviors. Their family home was so difficult to walk through that the girls would have to turn their bodies sideways to make it down the hallway to their bedroom. The house had stacks of newspapers, magazines, and other papers piled high on nearly every surface including throughout the kitchen and dining rooms, making it very difficult to prepare and eat meals. Steve's reliance on the twins was amplified because he struggled in knowing what to do with his wife while keeping the layers of secrecy around Donna's agoraphobia and hoarding. At that point, the four of them shared this deeply imbedded and shameful family secret, hiding it from friends and even other family members.

The team decided to have a family session with both girls and parents on the phone to talk about the elephants in the room. It was impossible to work on Kayla and Kyla's eating disorder treatment in a bubble; these significant dynamics within their family system had profound effects on the onset and continuation of their eating disorders. While the shift was not one day to the next and many painful conversations continued, Kayla and Kyla's acknowledgment of what was happening in their family system transformed their ability to stop keeping secrets, begin to explore relationships and dynamics openly, and finally begin to heal.

Family therapy often involves addressing the "elephants in the room": the unspoken tensions, painful histories, and deeply rooted conflicts that shape family dynamics but are rarely discussed openly. These unresolved issues may include past betrayals, unacknowledged trauma, favoritism, or long-standing patterns of emotional neglect. When these topics go unspoken, they create an undercurrent of resentment, anxiety, and avoidance, leading to dysfunctional communication and relational strain. Therapists play a crucial role in bringing these hidden issues to light, helping families recognize how avoidance perpetuates unhealthy cycles. Using techniques from structural family therapy (Minuchin, 1974) and emotionally focused therapy (Johnson, 2004), therapists can facilitate difficult conversations in a way that fosters understanding rather than blame. By creating a safe and structured space for dialogue, family therapy helps members confront the root causes of their struggles rather than merely addressing surface-level symptoms.

Common Elephants in the Room in ED Treatment

While there is not a one-size-fits-all approach to ED treatment and working with families, here are some of the more common situations that a clinician may experience along with some suggestions of how to navigate them. If left unaddressed, these elephants in the room may block an ED client from receiving treatment and make the clinician's job much more difficult.

Eggshells Everywhere

One of the biggest challenges for clients in family therapy is overcoming the fear that speaking openly will lead to conflict or emotional harm. Families often develop unspoken agreements to avoid discussing painful subjects, reinforcing patterns of silence and emotional distance. In the context of eating disorders, for example, parents and siblings may hesitate to talk about their own struggles with body image, dieting, or perfectionism, even when these issues significantly influence the client's disorder. Therapists must carefully guide these discussions, ensuring that all voices are heard while preventing conversations from becoming accusatory or defensive.

Resistance to discussing personal issues in family therapy often stems from discomfort, defensiveness, or a belief that therapy should focus solely on the client, who is often a child. Parents may view therapy as a place to "fix" their child's behaviors rather than as an opportunity for the whole family to grow and heal. This resistance can be particularly strong if parents have unresolved trauma, internalized weight bias, or a history of their own disordered eating, making it painful to acknowledge their role in shaping family attitudes toward food and body image (Costin, 2007). Puhl and Heuer (2010) further highlight that societal stigmas around weight and health can make these conversations even more difficult, as parents may struggle to separate their personal beliefs from what is actually best for their child's recovery. Therapists must navigate this resistance with care, validating parents' fears while also challenging them to engage in self-reflection. By helping parents recognize that exploring their own struggles does not equate to blame but rather provides an opportunity for healing, therapists can foster a more open, productive therapeutic environment that supports long-term recovery.

Parental History, Behaviors, and Attitudes

Another significant challenge in family therapy for eating disorders is when parents fail to recognize how their own issues contribute to the development and maintenance of the disorder. Many parents enter therapy believing that the eating disorder exists solely within their child, without considering how family dynamics, communication patterns, or their own relationships may be influencing the situation. Without addressing these underlying issues, therapy can become stalled, as the focus remains on symptom management rather than deeper systemic change.

Another particularly difficult topic in family therapy is discussing parents' or caregivers' roles in reinforcing harmful behaviors, particularly when it comes to eating disorders, mental health struggles, or generational trauma. Parents may feel guilt, shame, or denial when confronted with the idea that their behaviors—such as modeling disordered eating patterns, exerting excessive control, or prioritizing appearance over emotional well-being—have contributed to their child's struggles. This can lead to strong resistance, making it challenging for therapists to facilitate productive conversations. Additionally, discussing weight bias, body image expectations, and internalized societal pressures can be difficult, especially when parents and children have conflicting views on health and self-worth.

Weight Bias

Fear of weight goals is a common barrier in eating disorder family therapy, particularly for parents who struggle with their own anxieties around food, health, and body image. Many families, influenced by societal weight stigma and misinformation about nutrition, may resist the idea of weight restoration, believing that gaining weight equates to being "unhealthy" or "out of control" (Puhl & Heuer, 2010). Parents who have internalized cultural messages about thinness and self-discipline may unknowingly reinforce disordered beliefs, making it difficult for the client to trust the recovery process. Parents may worry that their child will gain "too much" weight, struggle with their own body image concerns, or feel uneasy about encouraging their child to eat beyond hunger cues—despite the medical necessity of doing so.

This fear can manifest in subtle ways, such as hesitancy to follow meal plans, discomfort with therapist-recommended weight goals, or an emotional reaction to their child's changing body during recovery. In some cases, parents may even unintentionally undermine progress by endorsing restrictive eating habits or expressing concerns about "overeating," reinforcing the eating disorder's grip (Costin, 2007). Therapists must address these fears directly by educating families on the biological necessity of weight restoration, the impact of malnutrition on cognitive and emotional functioning, and the importance of trusting the body's natural set point. Additionally, therapy must create a space where parents can process their own fears about weight gain and body image, helping them shift toward a more health-focused, rather than weight-focused, perspective. By reframing weight restoration as an essential part of healing rather than a threat, therapists can help families overcome their resistance and support their child's full recovery.

The Strain of Caring for Someone with an ED

Carers, often but not limited to being parents, are a critical part of treatment. For carers, EDs are often associated with burden and stress. As a result, intense emotions can arise and inadvertently create maintaining factors of the eating disorder (Treasure et al. 2017). From a meta-analysis of carer interventions, Hannah et al. (2022) found that small group interventions for carers, away from the client themselves, could be beneficial, particularly for families with high levels of maternal criticism and clients who have been unwell for less than a year. From my experience, carer-only process groups are an incredible source of strength for carers to express authentic emotional experiences—including frustrations and concerns—for their loved one, while relating to others.

Tools for Authentic Engagement in Eating Disorder Family Work

Lock and Le Grange (2015) emphasize that healing in families requires honesty. Families must be willing to address not only the eating disorder itself but also the relational patterns that sustain it. When handled with sensitivity and skill, confronting the elephants in the room allows families to break free from cycles of avoidance, repair fractured relationships, and develop healthier ways of supporting one another. Addressing these topics requires a therapist to create a safe and nonjudgmental space where honesty is encouraged, and change can begin without fear of blame or rejection.

There are several ways therapists can engage clients and family systems authentically, including building congruence with the extended family members, honoring the family's lived experience, working through power dynamics and imbalances, and navigating ruptures—all through a lens of use of self and transparency.

Therapist Use of Self and Transparency

Authenticity in systemic work often requires the therapist's use of self. This approach incorporates the therapist's self as carefully considered therapeutic responses that deepen connection, repair ruptures, or model vulnerability. For example, in eating disorder treatment, families often project moral judgments around weight, food, or body image onto the therapist. Therapists who can acknowledge the impact of these projections, especially if related to their body, gender, or cultural identity, enhance authenticity. Clinicians should also be aware of their own identities including body size, race, gender, and parenthood to help remain grounded and nondefensive. Harry Aponte's person-of-the-therapist model (Aponte & Kissil, 2016) explicitly encourages therapists to use their lived experience to empathize with family pain, while maintaining boundaries and therapeutic clarity. Clinicians can model authenticity through inviting feedback, practicing reflexivity, and engaging in collaboration with family members. Example statements of how to do this include:

- "I want to acknowledge that some eating disorder frameworks don't always fit all families, especially when weight or food have different meanings culturally."
- "I'd like to check in; how is this conversation aligning with your experiences and values?"

Systemic Congruence and Presence

Congruence and presence can be difficult to build within family work. Congruence refers to a therapist being real: their authenticity and genuineness while presence is about being with the client in the moment. Therapists who model congruence help clients and families feel safe to do the same, promoting deeper emotional honesty. Geller and Greenberg (2012) emphasize that therapist presence enhances empathy and client responsiveness, especially in emotionally complex systems. Presence allows for attunement to subtle cues including shifts in tone, body language, or relational dynamics. This type of presence is particularly important in high-conflict or emotionally charged family environments. In family therapy, how clients are physically positioned, which includes where and how they sit in the room, can reveal a great deal about relational dynamics, emotional alliances, power structures, and boundaries. Several well-established family therapy approaches use seating arrangements and spatial techniques as tools for assessment and intervention including structural, strategic, Bowenian, and experiential family therapy approaches.

The Physical Space

Satir (1991) uses family sculpting techniques to make visible the emotional experience of each family member through posture, space, and proximity to explore nonverbal truths and to encourage emotional congruence, a key aspect of authenticity (Rogers, 1961; Jordan, 2017). In this example, the clinician would have a family member arrange the others in the room to represent how they experience a specific family dynamic such as closeness, isolation, power imbalances. The clinician would ask questions such as "can you place each family member where they feel emotionally close or distant from you" or "how much space do you need to feel honest and safe in this family".

From a structural approach, Minuchin (1974) would suggest that seating becomes a symbolic intervention that encourages direct connection, clearer emotional boundaries, and less scripted roles, which are foundations for authentic relational engagement. Some prompts and questions from a structural perspective might include: "sit in the chair where you think your sibling would sit if they were being fully honest" or "if a corner of the room represented your true self, where would you go."

Honoring Lived Experiences

Historically, traditional family therapy could sometimes pathologize or oversimplify complex family dynamics, particularly when cultural, generational, or trauma histories are at play. When therapists engage families with curiosity, cultural humility, and respect, they can help foster trust, vulnerability, and relational healing. Here are some examples that honor a family's experiences.

Therapeutic Letter Writing

White & Epston (1990) developed the concept of therapeutic letters as a narrative tool to re-author relationships and honor lived realities. This is a technique very often used in eating disorder treatment in a variety of ways. In this context, letter writing can enable emotional truth-telling with safety by slowing down reactive patterns from family members. This ultimately helps to further develop vulnerability. Additionally, it can demonstrate a commitment to the therapeutic process for all family members by the assignment of a between-session task. In this example, family members each write a letter to express how the eating disorder has impacted them, what they miss, and what they wish could be spoken without fear. Letters should be reviewed with the therapist and either read aloud in session or shared privately with therapeutic support.

Relational Genograms

One of the first groups I regularly led on an eating disorder inpatient unit was "the genogram group." Each week, I watched patients gather around a large sheet of butcher paper, slowly sketching their family histories that included names tangled with memories, connected by lines of closeness, conflict, or loss. Genograms, first developed by Murray Bowen (1978), offer more than a traditional family tree; they illuminate patterns that repeat across generations. Later, Monica McGoldrick and colleagues (2016) expanded the practice to include cultural narratives and emotional histories, deepening our understanding of how families transmit beliefs, roles, and meaning. I remember one young woman drawing a circle around her grandmother's name, noting how she had survived famine and passed down strict rules around food that still shaped her family's meals decades later. Moments like that often opened the door for families to reflect on the stories they carried about nourishment, shame, achievement, and belonging. To support authenticity and insight, clinicians might ask questions such as: "How has food shown up as a source of love, stress, or survival in your family's story" or "were there times when members of your family had to hide parts of themselves to fit in or stay safe?"

Power Dynamics and Relational Imbalances

Addressing power dynamics and relational imbalances is ongoing in family work. It can be difficult to address while fostering truthful, attuned, and emotionally honest connections within the family system. The clinician should stay attuned to these issues as they treat the client to foster an authentic therapeutic relationship.

Collaboration and Power-Checking

As relational cultural theory outlines, it is important that people in treatment coauthor their recovery. This also extends to the family system and is particularly important for those historically marginalized to feel seen and ensure that treatment is aligned with their experiences and truths, not just the clinician or team's expectations. Mutual authenticity can be built through working together on therapy goals and openly reflecting on power within the environment. Statements and questions that clinicians could use with their clients to evaluate the power balance include:

- "I want to check if how we're working together feels fair and respectful to everyone."
- "Does this space allow for honesty from each of you, or do some voices feel louder than others?"
- "I want to name that our approach (or model) doesn't always fit every family's experience. What feels authentic to your family?"

Power, Voice and Silence

Naming silences and encouraging emotional risk-taking supports deeper, more congruent communication. When clinicians validate marginalized voices in the family system (often the identified client or a quieter caregiver), it opens the space for shared collaboration in the recovery process. From a narrative therapy and collaborative lens, clinicians can name and reflect on who holds voice, who defers, and what is left unsaid in family conversations, paying particular attention to topics around food, feelings, and body image. Prompts to navigate this include:

- "When hard things come up, for example treatment decisions, whose feelings tend to take up space? Whose get quiet?"
- "Who feels they must be strong or loud to be heard? How does that impact family meals?"
- "What would it take for everyone's experiences to be welcome here?"

Navigating Family Therapy Ruptures

I began this chapter describing a family rupture that I experienced with my client Lorrin. That example was just one of many I can recall. Gehart (2017) notes that ruptures are inevitable in relational systems work and that owning mistakes deepens therapeutic integrity. Owning mistakes is difficult to do in any circumstance and yet is a significant part of being authentic in the relationship with oneself. Here are some examples of how to do this as a clinician.

Acknowledgment without Defensiveness

Authenticity begins with recognizing and taking responsibility for the impact of our words or actions, even when our intent was neutral or caring. In family work, this often means pausing to name what is happening in the room before moving forward. A clinician might say, "I'd like to pause for a moment. I'm noticing that something I said may not have landed well. I want to check in about how you're feeling and understand what came up for you." This type of acknowledgment communicates openness rather than defensiveness, reinforces collaboration, and invites families to share their emotional experience in real time.

Transparency to Model Boundaries

Rather than rigidly asserting authority or withdrawing, a clinician can model clear, emotionally regulated boundary-setting that honors the family's lived experience. This might sound like: "You're right to speak up. I realize I asked about something that might feel private or sensitive. My intention was to understand, not to intrude." Naming the tension without defensiveness communicates safety and respect, while clarifying intent keeps the therapeutic frame intact. In doing so, the therapist demonstrates that boundaries are not barriers but structures that support connection. When families witness a clinician respond with curiosity instead of reactivity, they often feel more willing to stay in the conversation, even when it is uncomfortable. Over time, these small moments lay the groundwork for honest exploration of the underlying fears, loyalties, and grief that drive family patterns, ultimately strengthening the alliance and modeling relational repair.

Cultural and Familial Meanings of Boundaries

What might appear as a rupture in therapy may simply reflect differing cultural or generational understandings of safety, privacy, and connection. Some families equate emotional openness with disrespect or disloyalty, while others view sharing feelings as a sign of trust. Naming these differences can create space for curiosity rather than judgment. A clinician might say, "I'm noticing that talking about feelings in front of one another seems uncomfortable, or maybe even disrespectful. Could we explore what privacy and openness mean in your family?" This kind of invitation affirms that no single approach is "right," and it helps families situate their patterns within broader cultural narratives, allowing therapy to honor identity while gently expanding what is possible within the relationship.

Meta-Dialogue

Hargens and Grau (1994) identified the concept of meta-dialogue in family therapy. Meta-dialogue is a process where therapists share their thoughts and observations about the family's interactions, creating space for reflection and new perspectives. In using this technique, therapists discuss their internal processes, perceptions, and potential interpretations of the family's communication patterns, encouraging both the family and the therapist to consider multiple viewpoints. For example, this could occur in a session when one parent becomes defensive after the therapist gently reflects on how comments about food might impact the client. The therapist might experience how the room shifts: tension rises, eye contact drops, and a sibling goes silent. The therapist senses a rupture has occurred. In using meta-dialogue, the therapist starts a conversation about the process itself as a way of naming and exploring what's happening in the room to restore authenticity, trust, and connection. Examples of how a clinician may bring this into a session could include:

- "I want to pause for a moment, not to move away from what we're talking about, but to slow down and check in on how we're talking together right now. I noticed when I brought up how comments about food might be experienced, something shifted in the room. There was a change in energy."
- "It's important to me that this space feels safe enough for honest conversations, even when they're hard. I may have missed something or stepped too far too soon. Can we take a moment to explore how that landed for each of you?"
- "This isn't about blame. We are here to make sure that everyone's voice and experience is honored, including the ways we protect each other or pull back when things get vulnerable. What was that moment like for you? And how can we move forward in a way that feels more respectful and authentic for everyone?"

Building Alliances

Sprenkle et al. (2009) highlighted that collaborative alliance-building is more effective than top-down authority in systemic therapy. Authentic repair requires that therapists acknowledge their own power in the room and remain open to feedback without needing to control the outcome. To address the power dynamics in the sessions, a clinician could say:

- "I know I'm in a role here where I guide the conversation. I also know that means I might miss something important. I want to make space for us to slow down if needed."

Summary

Family therapy in eating disorder treatment builds authenticity by creating a space where each member can express their lived experience, emotional truths, and relational needs without fear of judgment. When therapists model authenticity it encourages family members to do the same. The extended therapeutic alliance is developed through open dialogue and mutual vulnerability. Through exploration of the elephants in the room, clinicians can help family members recognize and address their own fears, anxieties, and beliefs about food and body image, rather than leaving recovery strictly to the individual with the eating disorder. Clinicians should keep in mind that in most settings there will come a point when family therapy gets tough, but there are resources, including supervision and training, to help navigate difficult situations.

Key Take-Aways

- Family therapy is a central component of eating disorder treatment and views the eating disorder not as an isolated issue within the individual but as embedded in relational, emotional, and often intergenerational dynamics.
- Establishing an extended therapeutic alliance can be complex, as family members may bring their own biases and anxieties into the therapeutic space.
- In cases where parents struggle with their own body image concerns or internalized weight stigma, their beliefs about body size, health, and self-worth may unconsciously shape how they engage with therapy and influence their ability to support their child's recovery.
- Authentic therapy with families, especially those navigating eating disorder treatment, requires the therapist to be self-aware, emotionally attuned, and open to relational complexities.

References

Aponte, H. J., & Kissil, K. (Eds.). (2016). *The person of the therapist training model: Mastering the use of self.* Routledge.

Astrachan-Fletcher, E., Accurso, E. C., Rossman, S. et al. (2018). *An exploratory study of challenges and successes in implementing adapted family-based treatment in a community setting.* Journal of Eating Disorders, 6, 44.

Boszormenyi-Nagy, I., & Spark, G. M. (1984). *Invisible loyalties: Reciprocity in intergenerational family therapy.* Brunner/Mazel.

Bowen, M. (1978). *Family therapy in clinical practice.* Jason Aronson.

Brown, H. (2011). Brave girl eating: A family's struggle with anorexia. Harper Collins.

Bruch, H. (1973). *Eating disorders: Obesity,* anorexia nervosa, and the person within. Basic Books.

Claude-Pierre, P. (1999). *The secret language of eating disorders: The revolutionary new approach to understanding and curing anorexia and bulimia (1st Vintage book ed.).* Vintage Books.

Conti, J., Joyce, C., Natoli, S., Skeoch, K., & Hay, P. (2021). "*I'm still here, but no one hears you*": A qualitative study of young women's experiences of persistent distress post family-based treatment for adolescent anorexia nervosa. Journal of Eating Disorders, 9, 1–17.

Costin, C. (2007). *The eating disorder sourcebook: A comprehensive guide to the causes,* treatments, and prevention of eating disorders (3rd ed.). McGraw-Hill.

Cripps, S., Serpell, L., & Pugh, M. (2024). *Processes of change in family therapies for anorexia nervosa: A systematic review and meta-synthesis of qualitative data.* Journal of Eating Disorders, 12(1), 104.

Gehart, D. R. (2017). *Mastering competencies in family therapy: A practical approach to theories and clinical case documentation (3rd ed.).* Cengage Learning.

Geller, S. M., & Greenberg, L. S. (2012). *Therapeutic presence: A mindful approach to effective therapy.* American Psychological Association.

Hannah, L., Cross, M., Baily, H., Grimwade, K., Clarke, T., & Allan, S. M. (2022). *A systematic review of the impact of carer interventions on outcomes for patients with eating disorders.* Eating and Weight Disorders, 27(6), 1953–1962.

Hargens, J., Grau, U. (1994). *Meta-dialogue.* Contemporary Family Therapy, 16, 451–462.

Johnson, S. M. (2004). *The practice of emotionally focused couple therapy: Creating connection (2nd ed.).* Brunner-Routledge.

Jordan, J. V. (2017). *Relational–cultural therapy.* American Psychological Association Handbook of psychotherapy, 3, 221–239.

Lock J. (2018). *Family therapy for eating disorders in youth: Current confusions,* advances, and new directions. Current Opinion in Psychiatry, 31(6), 431–435.

Lock, J., & Le Grange, D. (2001). *Can family based treatment of anorexia nervosa be manualized?* Journal of Psychotherapy Practice & Research, 10(4), 253–261.

Lock, J., & Le Grange, D. (2015). *Treatment manual for anorexia nervosa: A family-based approach (2nd ed.).* The Guilford Press.

McGoldrick, M., Gerson, R., & Petry, S. (2016). *Genograms: Assessment and intervention (3rd ed.).* W. W. Norton.

Minuchin, S. (1974). *Families & family therapy.* Harvard University Press.

Minuchin, S., Rosman, B., & Baker, L. (1978a). *Families and Family Therapy.* Cambridge, Harvard University Press.

Minuchin, S., Rosman, B. L., & Baker, L. (1978b). *Psychosomatic families: Anorexia nervosa in context.* Harvard University Press.

Minuchin, S., & Fishman, H. C. (1981). *Family therapy techniques.* Harvard University Press.

National Institute of Care Excellence. (2017). *Anorexia nervosa: Treatment for children and young people.* Information for the public. Eating disorders: Recognition and treatment. Guidance NICE.

Nilsen, J. V., Hage, T. W., Rø, Ø., Halvorsen, I., & Oddli, H. W. (2021). Family-based inpatient treatment for adolescent anorexia nervosa: A thematic analysis of former patients' post-treatment reflections. *Eating Disorders, 29*(4), 390–407.

Puhl, R. M., & Heuer, C. A. (2010). *Obesity stigma: Important considerations for public health.* American Journal of Public Health, 100(6), 1019–1028.

Rehavia-Hanauer, D. (2003). *Hilde Bruch's insight into the inner world of eating disorders: A review and retrospective.* Eating Disorders, 11(2), 101–119.

Rogers, C. R. (1961). *On becoming a person: A therapist's view of psychotherapy.* Houghton Mifflin.

Roth, G. (1992). *When food is love: Exploring the relationship between eating and intimacy.* Plume.

Satir, V. (1991). *The Satir model: Family therapy and beyond.* Science and Behavior Books.

Schaefer, J. (2009). *Goodbye Ed,* Hello Me. McGraw Hill-Ascent.

Sprenkle, D. H., & Blow, A. J. (2004). *Common factors and our sacred models.* Journal of Marital and Family Therapy, 30(2), 113–129.

Sprenkle, D. H., Davis, S. D., & Lebow, J. L. (2009). *Common factors in couple and family therapy: The overlooked foundation for effective practice.* Guilford Press.

Treasure, J., Smith, G., Crane, A. (2017) *Skills-based caring for a loved one with an eating disorder* (2nd ed., pp. 125–128). Routledge.

White, M., & Epston, D. (1990). *Narrative means to therapeutic ends.* W. W. Norton.

Chapter 9

Authenticity Through Rupture and Repair

Overview

- *Therapeutic ruptures are inevitable and must be understood as part of the process rather than as failures.* Breakdowns in the relationship often take the form of either confrontation or withdrawal, both of which require careful recognition and response.
- *Repair work is the heart of authenticity in therapy.* Shifting treatment goals, revisiting trust, and recommitting to collaboration transform ruptures into opportunities for deeper connection and resilience in the alliance.
- *Even in the best of circumstances, building an authentic therapeutic relationship can feel out of reach.* This chapter examines how cultural forces, technology, and eating disorder symptoms themselves create barriers to connection, authenticity, and trust.
- *Eating disorders often interfere directly with authentic relationships, fueling secrecy, resistance, and ambivalence.* Techniques such as motivational interviewing help navigate these challenges, honoring client autonomy while inviting collaboration and openness.
- *Clinicians bring their own humanity into these obstacles.* Self-awareness, reflection on bias, countertransference, and the thoughtful use of self-disclosure highlight how the therapist's presence shapes both ruptures and repairs.
- *Transference and countertransference are fundamental dynamics that mirror the very ruptures and repairs central to therapeutic work.* In eating disorder therapy, these processes can manifest as projections of past wounds, client resistance, or clinician reactivity. When approached with self-awareness, supervision, and reflective dialogue, they become powerful opportunities to deepen authenticity, model relational repair, and strengthen the therapeutic alliance.

Introduction

The first time I met Abby, I sensed I was stepping into complicated territory. She was late for her intake, and after searching nearby offices, I returned to find her

DOI: 10.4324/9781003632016-10

curled beneath the desk, 28 years old, folded into the fetal posture of someone trying to disappear.

This was her eighteenth admission. Her history was heavy: childhood sexual assault followed by disbelief, layers of family silence, multiple traumas, chronic depression, and years of disordered eating. Abby had survived more than most could imagine, and yet she walked through the world profoundly alone. In that first session, and many after, she barely spoke.

I tried to meet her with consistency: same time each day, clear boundaries, quiet presence. Our sessions were marked mostly by silence. Sometimes that felt like connection; sometimes it felt like absence. One afternoon, I was called to my supervisor's office. Abby had filed a complaint: I had ended a session six minutes early. To her, this confirmed what she had always believed—that people leave. That she was not worth the full hour.

I was stunned. I remembered offering to end early only after she spent most of the session in silence. But what I framed as respectful, she experienced as abandonment. My instinct was to defend myself, but the truth was simpler: her reaction made perfect sense. The rupture was real.

When we met again, I acknowledged what had happened. I told her I could understand how that moment felt like I was pulling away, even if that wasn't my intention. We talked. Very slowly and awkwardly about what trust meant to her, what she needed from me, what it was like for her to risk staying in the room. It wasn't a tidy resolution, but it was a step. And she stayed.

Insurance cut that first round of treatment short. She left before she was ready. I assumed that was the end.

But over the next eight years, Abby returned four more times to the same treatment facility. Two of those times, she asked specifically to work with me. I was surprised; I thought the early rupture had defined us. Instead, she told me the opposite: what mattered most was that I hadn't tried to push her or interpret her silence as failure. I had stayed. Even when she pulled away, I didn't.

Still, I struggled. I sought trainings, read everything I could, consulted widely. At times I felt I had nothing new to offer. Working with Abby was profoundly humbling; not because I had the answers, but because I so clearly didn't.

Eventually, I tried something different. I suggested we meet outside. The change was immediate. Fresh air disrupted old dynamics. The "patient" identity softened. We took short walks, sat under trees. She talked more, sometimes about grief, sometimes about possibility. She even laughed.

Over time, Abby made bold choices. She moved to a warmer climate, returned to school, and slowly rebuilt her life. Years later, I ran into her at a coffee shop. I didn't recognize her at first. She had healthy hair, clear eyes, surrounded by people. She told me she was finishing her PhD in psychology.

Her transformation didn't come from any single intervention. We had tried nearly every treatment modality and model. What made the difference was the relationship: messy, imperfect, and challenging that was built through rupture and repair. The turning point was not a technique, but a choice we made together: to keep showing up.

Rupture is inevitable. Repair is not. Abby taught me that the most healing thing we sometimes offer is our willingness to stay, even when someone is not yet ready to come close.

Managing Ruptures in Therapy: Understanding Breakdowns in the Relationship

A "rupture" in a therapeutic alliance refers to a significant breakdown or strain in the relationship between a clinician and client marked by a loss of trust, communication difficulties, or a sense of disconnect (Safran & Muran, 2000). A rupture typically signals a moment in therapy when the therapist receives feedback, whether direct or indirect, that the therapeutic process is "off" and requires adjustment (Eubanks-Carter et al., 2015). This may involve the clinician misinterpreting a client's emotions, failing to provide enough empathy, or overlooking critical aspects of the client's experience (Ackerman & Hilsenroth, 2003). Ruptures can also emerge when treatment goals clash with a client's readiness for change. For example, a therapist might encourage weight restoration in a client with anorexia before they have emotionally processed their fears about weight gain, leading to feelings of coercion and resistance. Particularly in eating disorder treatment, a client may withdraw or feel invalidated if they feel the therapist is overly focused on medical stability or behavioral change while neglecting emotional struggles, such as body image distress or trauma (Simpson & Mazzeo, 2017, Treasure et al., 2020).

In eating disorder and body image therapy, where issues of control, vulnerability, and self-perception are central, ruptures can be particularly disruptive. Clients with eating disorders often have histories of invalidation or strained interpersonal relationships, making them more sensitive to perceived misunderstandings or breaches in trust (Geller et al., 2010). These disruptions can hinder therapeutic progress, increasing the likelihood of treatment resistance, emotional disengagement, or premature termination.

Clients may experience ruptures as personal rejection, intensifying beliefs around not being worthy or being "too much" to be cared for. Common causes of ruptures in therapy include misinterpretations of a client's feelings, perceived judgment from the therapist, disagreement about treatment goals, or significant life events that disrupt the client's emotional engagement (Zaitsoff & Taylor, 2009a). Ruptures can result in decreased engagement, increased resistance, and a heightened sense of mistrust. If unresolved, these issues may lead to therapy dropout, which is a common challenge in eating disorder treatment (Duffy & Henkel, 2016).

It is essential for therapists to recognize and address ruptures promptly to prevent long-term damage to the therapeutic relationship. Addressing ruptures effectively is crucial for rebuilding the therapeutic alliance and fostering a safe space for healing.

Two Types of Ruptures: Confrontation and Withdrawal

Ruptures can manifest in two primary forms: confrontation ruptures and withdrawal ruptures (Eubanks-Carter et al., 2015). A confrontation rupture occurs when a client expresses direct anger or disagreement with the clinician. In eating disorder therapy, this might happen if a client feels pressured to adopt a meal plan they are not ready for or if they perceive the clinician as dismissive of their struggles with body image. While confrontation ruptures can feel challenging, they also provide opportunities for deeper therapeutic work if addressed constructively. Clinicians can use validation, reflective listening, and collaborative problem-solving to acknowledge the client's concerns and recalibrate treatment goals (Norcross & Wampold, 2018).

In contrast, a withdrawal rupture occurs when a client becomes emotionally distant or disengaged from the therapy process (Safran et al., 2011a). This form of rupture is particularly common in individuals with eating disorders, as avoidance and emotional suppression are central features of these conditions (Schmidt & Treasure, 2006). A client may appear compliant in sessions while internally disengaging, making it difficult for the therapist to assess their true level of participation. Recognizing withdrawal ruptures requires therapists to attune to subtle cues, such as decreased verbal expression, avoidance of difficult topics, or a shift toward appeasing rather than engaging in meaningful dialogue (Treasure et al., 2020). Gentle inquiry and increased emphasis on emotional safety can help reestablish connection and trust.

Ruptures Do Not Always Signal the End of Treatment

Ultimately, ruptures in therapy are not necessarily negative; when handled effectively, they can lead to stronger therapeutic relationships and deeper engagement in the healing process (Safran & Muran, 2000). Repairing a rupture requires therapists to acknowledge the client's feelings, validate their experience, and collaboratively explore ways to move forward. In eating disorder therapy, where trust is often fragile, addressing ruptures with empathy and flexibility can make the difference between disengagement and meaningful progress.

Repair Work and Shifting Treatment

Ruptures can provide opportunities for deeper therapeutic work and relationship strengthening when effectively addressed (Safran & Muran, 2000). Effective repair strategies include fostering open communication, rebuilding trust, enhancing cultural competence, emphasizing collaboration, and encouraging clinician self-awareness.

Navigating Resistance in Therapy

Resistance in therapy is a significant challenge that can impede the development of an authentic therapeutic alliance, particularly in the treatment of eating disorders. In a therapeutic context, resistance refers to a client's conscious or unconscious behaviors that hinder the therapeutic process, such as avoiding difficult topics, minimizing their struggles, or directly opposing the therapist's guidance (Miller & Rollnick, 2013). These behaviors often stem from deep-seated fear, ambivalence, or a need for control, especially in eating disorder therapy, where clients may feel that their disordered behaviors are essential to their identity or coping mechanisms (Fairburn, 2008). When resistance arises, it can create tension in the therapeutic relationship, making it difficult for the therapist and client to establish mutual trust and engagement in the healing process (Zaitsoff & Taylor, 2009a).

A Relational Approach to Resistance

The impact of resistance on relationship-building in therapy is profound. An essential component of effective therapy is the establishment of a strong therapeutic alliance, built on trust, openness, and collaboration (Norcross & Wampold, 2018). However, when a client exhibits resistance, whether through disengagement, noncompliance with treatment recommendations, or reluctance to explore emotions, it can disrupt the rapport between therapist and client. In eating disorder therapy, where control and autonomy are often core issues, clients may resist interventions that threaten their sense of agency (Treasure et al., 2020). They may perceive the therapist as an authority figure imposing unwanted change rather than as a supportive guide, which can lead to feelings of frustration on both sides, potentially reinforcing the client's avoidance behaviors and creating a therapeutic stalemate (Geller et al., 2010).

Resistance can often be misinterpreted as non-compliance in treatment. In examining alliance with individuals with anorexia specifically, research suggests that resistance often reflects the client's struggle to trust and rely on others for support, necessitating therapists to adopt empathetic and client-centered approaches to foster trust and collaboration (Lev Ari et al., 2024). While both therapists and clients may share a mutual desire to build a close therapeutic relationship, the semi-structured interviews conducted by Lev Ari et al. (2024) indicated that this desire is complicated by individuals' deep-seated fear of disappointment and emotional pain, often arising from past relational trauma. These researchers urge therapists to see resistance as a symptom of the eating disorder itself, and therefore part of the treatment needed.

Me Ambivalent? No. Yes? I don't know!

Resistance in eating disorder therapy is often rooted in ambivalence about recovery. Many individuals struggling with eating disorders experience a conflicting desire to both recover and maintain their disordered behaviors, as these behaviors often serve as coping mechanisms for deeper emotional distress (Schmidt & Treasure, 2006). When therapy challenges these patterns, clients may resist by rationalizing their eating behaviors, avoiding discussions about body image and food, or downplaying the severity of their condition (Vitousek et al., 1998). This resistance can prevent the clinician from addressing core psychological issues, such as low self-worth, perfectionism, or trauma (Simpson & Mazzeo, 2017).

By addressing resistance and ambivalence with empathy and patience, clinicians can create a space where clients feel safe enough to lower their defenses, engage more openly in therapy, and ultimately work toward lasting recovery. To navigate resistance effectively, clinicians must prioritize relationship-building strategies that foster trust and collaboration. This includes adopting a nonjudgmental, client-centered approach that validates the client's fears and ambivalence while gently encouraging exploration of change (Miller & Rollnick, 2013).

Motivational Interviewing

Motivational interviewing is a technique commonly used in many settings, including eating disorder therapy, to help clients resolve ambivalence by exploring their own motivations for change rather than imposing external pressure (Treasure et al., 2020). Prochaska and DiClemente's (1983) stages of change model highlights the importance of tailoring interventions to the client's motivational stage, particularly in eating disorders, where denial or ambivalence about the need for change is common and can impact alliance development.

Additionally, the therapeutic alliance can be strengthened through the use of motivational interviewing by emphasizing autonomy and choice, helping clients feel empowered rather than coerced (Geller et al., 2010).

In *Motivational Interviewing: Helping People Change* (2013), Miller and Rollnick highlight a collaborative, client-centered counseling approach designed to enhance intrinsic motivation for change by resolving ambivalence. The book emphasizes empathy, reflective listening, and the importance of honoring autonomy, making it especially effective in addressing behavioral issues.

Many years ago, I had the opportunity to attend an extended training on motivational interviewing. Although I had not named my work as being informed by motivational interviewing, through more training, I realized I had been using these skills and what a powerful technique it was in my direct work with clients and as a clinical supervisor. Jordan's case highlights how I have incorporated motivational interviewing in my work as a supervisor.

Jordan's Case: Introducing Motivational Interviewing in the Clinical Setting

As a clinical supervisor, I was overseeing Jordan, a recent master's degree graduate and new to eating disorders. Jordan was working with Chris, who entered treatment after their third relapse with bulimia nervosa. Though physically present, Chris was hesitant to engage in treatment. Jordan struggled with Chris's ambivalence in treatment, believing that early behavioral change was needed for Chris's recovery. I introduced Jordan to the spirit of motivational interviewing, which includes collaboration, evocation, and autonomy. We brainstormed and role-played dialogue from a motivational interviewing approach.

ME: (as therapist): "It seems like part of you wants things to change, but another part isn't so sure. Would it be okay if we explored that together?"

Jordan shrugged.

ME: (as therapist): "You mentioned last week that you're tired of the secrecy and guilt that comes with purging, but also that it feels like the only way to cope when things feel out of control."

Jordan and I discussed the use of simple reflection that was nonjudgmental and compassionate to create space.

JORDAN: (as client): "Yeah. I hate what it does to my body, but it also … numbs things."

Rather than steering toward a solution, we stayed with the ambivalence.

ME: (as therapist): "Sounds like it serves a purpose. And you're starting to wonder if there might be other ways to manage those feelings."

We discussed that idea of using a decisional balance technique.

ME: (as therapist): "On one hand, what are the things you feel you gain from the eating behaviors? And on the other hand, what are some of the things you feel you've lost or missed out on?"

We discussed how to use open-ended questions and affirmations. Jordan offered examples: "What would being free from this cycle look like for you?" In another example, Jordan tried, "You've already shown so much strength by talking about this—what's helping you stay in the room today, even though this is hard?"

Jordan continued to use this type of approach with Chris, and Chris appeared to (slowly) trust Jordan more. Jordan focused on Chris developing their own voice, recognizing that they were the expert on their own life. In time, Chris moved beyond talking about ED behaviors and opened more about their fears of being "too much" for their family through their gender identity exploration and later ED challenges.

Motivational interviewing techniques including reflective listening, rolling with resistance, and honoring ambivalence created the conditions for authenticity to emerge organically. As Chris began to speak more freely, they stopped editing what they thought Jordan wanted to hear. The therapeutic relationship became a rehearsal space for self-compassion and congruence.

Obstacles to Creating an Authentic Therapeutic Relationship

As discussed throughout this text, the therapeutic alliance is built upon trust, empathy, and collaboration between the clinician and client. Barriers in creating authentic relationships are factors that fundamentally block treatment progress that are more rooted in our systems and culture. While the therapeutic relationship is the foundation of effective therapy, various obstacles can impede the development of a strong, authentic alliance between therapist and client. These can stem from both client-related challenges, therapist-related issues, or external factors that make therapy less accessible or effective. In eating disorder therapy, where trust, vulnerability, and openness are crucial for progress, these obstacles can be particularly significant (Zaitsoff & Taylor, 2009b). Identifying and addressing these challenges is essential for fostering a meaningful and effective therapeutic relationship.

Client Factors

The common factors approach, explored earlier in this book in depth in Chapter 4, highlights client factors, such as readiness for change, resilience, and support systems, as influential in alliance formation. Several of these client-related factors can also hinder the development of an authentic therapeutic alliance. Many clients enter therapy with resistance to change, fearing that addressing their eating disorder will mean losing a coping mechanism they rely on for emotional regulation (Treasure et al., 2020).

Trust

Trust is foundational to a client's ability to be authentic with a clinician, as it creates a sense of emotional safety where vulnerability feels possible rather than threatening. When a client trusts that their clinician will respond with empathy, nonjudgment, and consistency, they are more likely to share honest thoughts, feelings, and experiences, especially those marked by shame, fear, or ambivalence. A lack of trust in the clinician is a common issue in alliance formation, particularly for individuals with eating disorders who may have experienced invalidation, stigma, or control in past relationships (Geller et al., 2010).

Past Therapy

Past negative experiences in therapy, such as feeling misunderstood, dismissed, or judged, can significantly impact a client's willingness to engage in future therapeutic relationships (Duffy & Henkel, 2016). These experiences can foster distrust, increase emotional guardedness, and reinforce internalized beliefs that vulnerability is unsafe or will be met with invalidation. For individuals with eating disorders or complex trauma histories, prior experiences of being pathologized or not feeling seen by a clinician may contribute to further disconnection and resistance in subsequent therapeutic settings (Zilcha-Mano, 2017). Cultural or religious differences between the client and therapist may create additional barriers if the therapist is not attuned to the client's values or background, leading to misunderstandings and discomfort (Becker et al., 2010).

Clinician Factors

Clinicians, despite their best intentions and clinical training, can and do contribute to relational ruptures in therapy—moments where the therapeutic alliance is strained or broken. These ruptures often occur through subtle or overt misattunements, unexamined countertransference, or enactments of power, privilege, or avoidance. While rupture is a natural and sometimes necessary part of therapy, it is the therapist's responsibility to recognize, repair, and reflect on their role in these dynamics.

Misattunement

One of the most common clinician contributions to rupture is empathic mismatch or misattunement. Even subtle moments when a clinician misses or minimizes a client's emotional experience can feel profoundly invalidating, especially for clients with attachment wounds or histories of betrayal. Safran and Muran (2000) note that such moments can evoke feelings of being unseen or dismissed, leading to withdrawal, compliance masking disconnection, or overt confrontation. A lack of empathy or understanding from the clinician can quickly erode trust and create emotional distance (Norcross & Wampold, 2018). If a clinician dismisses or minimizes a client's experiences, especially in eating disorder treatment, where body image and food-related distress are deeply personal, clients may disengage from therapy altogether (Geller et al., 2010).

Power and Privilege

In some cases, clinicians may enact power dynamics that echo oppressive experiences from clients' pasts, especially when working with clients from marginalized identities. Over-pathologizing, dismissing cultural experiences, or rigidly enforcing treatment protocols can feel coercive and controlling, contributing to rupture (Comas-Díaz, 2012). This is especially pertinent in eating disorder care, where weight-focused metrics and compliance-based language can replicate external systems of surveillance and judgment (Zaitsoff & Taylor, 2009a). Unconscious biases or judgments about the client's background, body size, or cultural identity can also create a significant disconnect if not addressed (Becker et al., 2010). Additionally, poor communication skills, such as failing to pick up on client cues or using invalidating language, can weaken the alliance (Eubanks-Carter et al., 2015).

External Factors

Beyond client and therapist dynamics, external factors can also pose significant obstacles to building an authentic therapeutic relationship. Financial constraints are a major issue, as the cost of therapy can prevent individuals from accessing care consistently, leading to interruptions that weaken the therapeutic bond (Duffy & Henkel, 2016). Scheduling conflicts, whether due to work, school, or other responsibilities, can also make it difficult for clients to attend sessions regularly, reducing continuity and making it harder to build trust (Norcross & Wampold, 2018). A lack of a support system outside of therapy may further hinder progress, as clients struggling with eating disorders often benefit from reinforcement from family or friends in addition to their therapist (Treasure et al., 2020). Finally, geographical distance can limit access to specialized eating disorder therapists, particularly in rural or underserved areas. While teletherapy has helped bridge some of these gaps, virtual sessions can sometimes feel less personal and make relationship-building more challenging (Simpson & Mazzeo, 2017).

Open Communication

One of the most crucial steps in repairing a rupture is creating space for open communication. Clients may feel hurt, misunderstood, or invalidated, and addressing these feelings directly allows for clarification and resolution (Eubanks-Carter et al., 2015). Clinicians should invite clients to express their concerns, acknowledge any mistakes or misinterpretations, and validate the client's emotions. Active listening and reflective statements can help clients feel heard and respected, reducing the risk of further disengagement. Encouraging a gentle and open dialogue without pressure or defensiveness can help clients begin to communicate more effectively.

I recall a session with a 16-year-old client who abruptly became withdrawn after I made a comment about her progress that she experienced as minimizing her struggle. Instead of pushing forward with the planned agenda that I was "supposed to" cover that day, I paused and invited her to share what she was feeling in that moment. She hesitated at first but eventually expressed that my words made her feel unseen, as though her ongoing pain had been dismissed.

Acknowledging my misstep and reflecting back to her the significance of her experience shifted the atmosphere in the room: she sat forward, her voice steadied, and we were able to rebuild trust by making the rupture itself part of the therapeutic work.

Building Trust

Trust is a fundamental component of the therapeutic alliance, and once a rupture occurs, restoring trust requires intentional effort. Clients with eating disorders often have histories of broken trust in relationships, making them more sensitive to perceived betrayals or misunderstandings in therapy (Treasure et al., 2020). To rebuild trust, clinicians should demonstrate consistency, reliability, and a nonjudgmental stance. Acknowledging the client's concerns and showing a willingness to adapt the therapeutic approach fosters safety and strengthens the bond (Duffy & Henkel, 2016). Trust-building also involves setting clear expectations, respecting boundaries, and ensuring that the client feels in control of their recovery process. Here are examples of how to build (and re-build) trust that reflect a nonjudgmental stance, collaborative spirit, and commitment to creating a safe environment.

Respecting Boundaries and Reinforcing Client Autonomy

CLINICIAN: "I want you to know that you're in control of what we explore here. If there's ever a topic you're not ready to talk about, I'll respect that. We can go at your pace, and I'll check in with you along the way so you always feel supported, not pushed."

Adapting Interventions Based on Client Feedback

CLIENT: "Sometimes the worksheets feel overwhelming. I don't think they're helping right now."

CLINICIAN: "Thank you for telling me that. It's helpful to know what's not working. Let's adjust our sessions to focus more on talking things through together instead, and if something else starts to feel more useful down the line, we can revisit it. This is your space, and I want it to feel right for you."

Cultural Competence

Cultural competence plays a vital role in rupture repair, as misunderstandings may arise due to differences in cultural perspectives, values, or lived experiences (Becker et al., 2010). If a rupture stems from a client feeling unseen or misunderstood regarding their cultural background, the therapist must take responsibility for learning about the client's unique perspective and avoiding assumptions. In eating disorder therapy, cultural factors influence body image ideals, attitudes toward food, and perceptions of mental health treatment (Zaitsoff & Taylor, 2009a). Therapists should engage in ongoing education about diverse cultural narratives around eating and appearance while inviting clients to share their perspectives openly. By demonstrating cultural humility, therapists can foster inclusivity and reduce the likelihood of ruptures caused by cultural misunderstandings. Here are some examples of dialogue that could occur between a clinician and a client.

Repairing After a Cultural Disconnect Around Body Ideals

CLINICIAN: "Last session, I mentioned mainstream body image pressures without asking how those messages show up or don't in your community. That might have made you feel unseen."

CLIENT: [Nods silently.]

CLINICIAN: "I'd like to better understand your cultural lens on body, beauty, and food. What messages have you received growing up? Your experiences matter, and I want to make sure they shape how we do this work together."

Responding to a Cultural Misstep with Humility

CLIENT: "When you said my parents were being controlling about food, it felt like you didn't understand our culture. That's just how we show care."

CLINICIAN: "Thank you for telling me that. I can see how my comment may have come across as judgmental or dismissive. I realize I made an assumption without fully understanding your family's values. I'd really appreciate it if you're open to helping me learn more about how food and caregiving work in your culture so I can better support you."

Collaboration

Repairing a rupture requires a collaborative approach, where both therapist and client work together to navigate the difficulty and find solutions (Norcross & Wampold, 2018). This involves aligning treatment goals, incorporating the client's input, and allowing them to take an active role in shaping their therapeutic journey. In eating disorder therapy, collaborative care models, such as the Maudsley method, emphasize shared decision-making and client empowerment (Treasure et al., 2020). When clients feel they have agency in the therapeutic process, they are more likely to remain engaged and invested in treatment. Clinicians can reinforce collaboration by asking for feedback regularly, being flexible in their approach, and encouraging the client to express preferences regarding treatment strategies. Here are examples to show how inviting the client into the decision-making process, validating their expertise in their own experience, and adjusting treatment collaboratively can repair ruptures and strengthen engagement.

Collaborative Goal Reassessment After a Rupture

CLINICIAN: "I know last week felt tough, and I want to make sure we're still on the same page about where we're headed. Can we take a moment to revisit your goals and see if anything feels different or needs adjusting? Your voice in this process matters, and I want to be sure the work we're doing feels aligned with what you need right now."

Encouraging Client Input After Feeling Unheard

CLIENT: "I felt like you didn't really understand why I didn't want to do the meal plan this way."

CLINICIAN: "I appreciate you telling me that. Let's talk through what's not working for you about the current plan and explore options together. You know your experience better than anyone, and I want us to find a strategy that feels supportive, not overwhelming."

Self-Awareness

Clinician self-awareness is critical in rupture repair. Clinicians must reflect on their role in the rupture, examining whether countertransference, unconscious biases, or miscommunication contributed to the breakdown (Safran et al., 2011b). In eating disorder therapy, clinicians may unknowingly project their own beliefs about food, weight, or body image onto the client, which can lead to ruptures if not carefully managed (Geller et al., 2010). Engaging in supervision, seeking peer consultation, and practicing mindfulness can help therapists remain attuned to their own reactions and biases. A clinician's ability to acknowledge their own limitations and grow from ruptures models self-compassion and emotional resilience for the client, reinforcing a therapeutic environment of mutual respect and growth. Here are examples of how a therapist can demonstrate self-reflection, openness to feedback, and humility to turn ruptures into opportunities for repair and authentic relational modeling.

Acknowledging Personal Bias and Repairing with the Client

CLINICIAN (IN SUPERVISION): "I NOTICED I FELT UNUSUALLY FIRM WHEN WE DISCUSSED WEIGHT RESTORATION TARGETS. I WONDER IF SOME OF MY OWN BELIEFS ABOUT BODY SIZE AND HEALTH INFLUENCED HOW I PRESENTED THAT.":

Later in session with client:

CLINICIAN (CONTINUED): "I've been reflecting on our last conversation, and I'm concerned that how I talked about weight may have felt rigid or disconnected from your experience. I want to make sure we approach this in a way that respects your voice and values—can we talk about how that felt for you?"

Recognizing Countertransference and Modeling Growth

CLINICIAN: (after a session where the client shut down): "I felt a strong urge to 'fix' things quickly, which might have come across as pressure. That reaction may be more about my discomfort with your distress than what you actually needed."

In next session:

"I want to acknowledge that I may have responded more from my own anxiety than from really tuning in to where you were. I'm committed to slowing down and listening more closely—I'd appreciate your feedback as we move forward together."

Externalization of the Eating Disorder

In many therapeutic approaches, clinicians have identified the value of the externalization of the eating disorder as a separate entity. This type of strategy can foster collaboration, helping clients and clinicians address resistance in a less confrontational manner (Ramjan & Fogarty, 2019). Research supports this concept of externalization in an effort to repair ruptures and deepen alliance by providing a non-judgmental approach to exploring the client's perspectives in their voice, which validates them and aids in relational connection. As discussed earlier in this chapter, Jenni Schaeffer personifies her eating disorder as "Ed." I have worked with many clients who relate to this externalization, offering a name to their eating disorder to better understand this externalization.

One client I worked with shared that she had started calling her eating disorder "The Critic." We used this externalization to separate her sense of self from the disorder's voice. When she said, "The Critic told me I didn't deserve lunch," we explored how that voice had protected her but was also holding her back. Naming the disorder gave her power to push back with more compassion and clarity while shifting our work from confrontation to collaboration.

Clinician Self-Disclosure

Clinician self-disclosure, when used thoughtfully and ethically, can play a meaningful role in repairing ruptures and strengthening the therapeutic alliance in eating disorder treatment. In the context of a rupture where a client may feel misunderstood, judged, or disconnected, appropriate self-disclosure can serve to humanize the therapist, reduce power imbalances, and re-establish trust. For example, a clinician acknowledging their own struggle to fully understand the complexity of body image in a particular cultural context can validate the client's experience and invite open dialogue (Hill & Knox, 2002). This transparency, when offered without shifting the focus away from the client, can model authenticity and emotional resilience—key elements in repairing relational breaks (Safran & Muran, 2000).

Thoughtful clinician disclosures, such as sharing a moment of uncertainty or reflecting on the clinician's learning process, can help normalize imperfection and foster collaboration (Zur, 2007). However, self-disclosure must be used with intention, guided by clinical judgment and an understanding of the client's needs, stage of treatment, and relational history. It is essential that disclosures serve the client's therapeutic goals and not the clinician's emotional needs.

Lev Ari et al. (2024) found that clients described feeling more valued and secure when clinicians disclosed genuine affection or adapted traditional boundaries, such as extending session times or maintaining contact between sessions. These actions reinforced clients' trust and sense of safety. However, clinicians should be cautioned to maintain boundaries and find the balance between flexibility and structure.

Clinicians should continually reflect on their motivations for disclosing and remain open to feedback about how their communication is received. Engaging in supervision and maintaining cultural humility are critical in ensuring that self-disclosure strengthens rather than complicates the alliance (Brown & Landry, 2021). When used skillfully, clinician self-disclosure in the context of rupture and repair can deepen authenticity in the therapeutic relationship and support clients in reclaiming agency and trust in relational spaces.

Transference and Countertransference in the Therapeutic Relationship

As we are closer to the end of this book, it is important to note that I have not deeply explored transference and countertransference, although these terms have appeared in this text. While not explicitly named previously, the concepts of transference and countertransference are similar to many other terms in therapy that have been discussed including *ruptures and repairs, relational enactments, attachment re-enactments, therapeutic mirrors, reactivity, projections, projective identification.*

Transference and countertransference are fundamental dynamics in the therapeutic relationship that can either enhance or hinder treatment progress. Transference occurs when clients project past feelings, expectations, or relational patterns onto their clinician, often unconsciously replaying unresolved emotions from early relationships (Freud, 1912). In the context of eating disorder therapy, transference can manifest in several ways. For example, a client with a history of critical or controlling parental figures may perceive their clinician as judgmental or overly directive when discussing meal plans or weight restoration (Geller et al., 2010). These projections can create resistance in therapy, as clients may struggle to separate their past relational wounds from their present therapeutic experience. Recognizing and working through transference is essential in helping clients develop healthier relational patterns and improve their emotional awareness.

In therapy, the concept of "projection" is often used interchangeably with transference, as both involve the redirection of past emotions onto present relationships. Clients with eating disorders frequently project feelings of shame, inadequacy, or perfectionism onto their clinician expecting criticism or rejection even when none is present (Zaitsoff & Taylor, 2009a). Countertransference, on the other hand, refers to the clinician's emotional reactions to the client's projections. This occurs when therapists, consciously or unconsciously, respond to clients based on their own unresolved emotions or biases (Hayes et al., 2011).

In eating disorder therapy, countertransference can arise when therapists experience frustration with clients' resistance to treatment or feel personally impacted by discussions of body image and food. For example, a clinician with a personal history of disordered eating may find themselves overly invested in a client's recovery or, conversely, hesitant to challenge harmful behaviors for fear of imposing their own past struggles (Simpson & Mazzeo, 2017). Or a client who has struggled with societal beauty standards may unintentionally reinforce a client's fear of weight gain by overemphasizing body neutrality rather than directly challenging weight-related distortions. If not carefully managed, countertransference can lead to boundary blurring, emotional disengagement, or even reenactments of harmful relational patterns. Awareness of these dynamics is crucial in preventing therapeutic ruptures and maintaining a supportive, client-centered approach.

Working Through Transference and Countertransference in Eating Disorder Therapy

Effectively managing transference and countertransference in eating disorder therapy requires therapists to maintain strong self-awareness, engage in regular supervision, and practice reflective listening.

Clinician Self-Awareness

Clinicians should recognize personal triggers. Being attuned to emotional reactions that may stem from the clinician's own history or unconscious needs is an important aspect of awareness. Techniques for this include:

- Using journaling, mindfulness, or structured self-review after sessions to process internal reactions (Geller & Greenberg, 2012).
- Using embodiment cues and noticing somatic sensations (tightness, agitation, calmness) during sessions as information about emotional undercurrents (Porges & Furman, 2011; Geller & Greenberg, 2012).

Clinical Supervision and Consultation

Here are some ways that clinical supervision and consultation may help a clinician manage transference and countertransference:

- Seeking regular supervision to explore emerging relational dynamics (Aponte & Kissil, 2016).
- Participating in group case consultation. This can help therapists gain external perspectives on how relational patterns might be playing out across the therapeutic dyad.
- Using person of the therapist (POTT) work to trace the roots of emotional reactivity and build capacity to differentiate the clinician from the client's needs (Aponte & Kissil, 2016).
- Recognizing and tracking any parallel processes in therapy and supervision. Notice if dynamics in supervision resemble those with the client, indicating unresolved countertransference (Falender & Shafranske, 2004).

Reflective Listening and Relational Repair

Other approaches to managing transference and countertransference involve reflective listening and relational repair. Here are some strategies a clinician could use:

- Inviting discussion of misunderstandings, misattunements, or discomfort in the therapeutic relationship to model emotional safety (Safran & Muran, 2000).
- Using relational language and acknowledging the "here and now" experience between the clinician and client to deepen authenticity and trust (Norcross & Lambert, 2019).
- Monitoring implicit biases, which is especially important when working with clients of different body sizes, races, or gender identities, where projections may be shaped by social constructs (Puhl & Heuer, 2010).
- Using metacommunication (speaking about the process) when appropriate to acknowledge a shift in the relationship. For example, "I noticed that when I offered that suggestion, you looked away and got quiet. I wonder if something shifted between us?"

Summary

This chapter focused on the essential and often uncomfortable reality that relational ruptures are part of therapy. Abby's story demonstrates this truth. She entered treatment after years of trauma, disconnection, and broken trust. When a session ended a few minutes early, she experienced it as rejection rather than flexibility. What seemed like a small moment carried the weight of her history. Her reaction taught us that ruptures are rarely about the moment itself. They reflect deeper wounds that clients bring into the therapeutic space.

Ruptures in eating disorder treatment often appear as anger, silence, resistance, or withdrawal. The goal is not to avoid these moments but to recognize them and move toward repair. Repair means slowing down, naming what happened, inviting conversation, and reestablishing safety. Over time, this process builds a more resilient relationship. Abby returned to treatment several times, and each time she asked to continue working with her therapist. She said what mattered was not flawless technique but that someone stayed with her, listened, and did not give up when things felt difficult.

This chapter also explores how therapists bring their own reactions, fears, and hopes into the work. When reflected on with honesty and curiosity, these reactions can deepen the relationship rather than hinder it. Transference and countertransference are not problems to avoid. They are information that can guide repair and strengthen the alliance.

The lesson from Abby's story is simple. Healing rarely happens because therapy goes smoothly. It happens because both people stay engaged when it does not. Repair becomes the work. Through presence, humility, and patience, clinicians help clients experience a new kind of relationship, one in which rupture does not mean abandonment but becomes an opening for trust and growth.

Key Take-Aways

- Ruptures are inevitable and often appear as confrontation or withdrawal; recognizing them early is essential.
- Repair happens through empathy and openness. Naming the rupture, inviting dialogue, and adjusting course can deepen trust and connection.
- Shame, secrecy, and resistance common in eating disorders can block authenticity and strain the alliance if unaddressed.
- Clinicians must meet barriers with humility, using skills like motivational interviewing, cultural sensitivity, and self-reflection to rebuild collaboration.
- Obstacles to authenticity such as mistrust or power dynamics can become turning points when named and explored together.
- Countertransference requires ongoing reflection; when processed thoughtfully, it offers insight that can strengthen the therapeutic relationship.

References

Ackerman, S. J., & Hilsenroth, M. J. (2003). *A review of therapist characteristics and techniques positively impacting the therapeutic alliance.* Clinical Psychology Review, 23(1), 1–33.

Aponte, H. J., & Kissil, K. (Eds.). (2016). *The person of the therapist training model: Mastering the use of self.* Routledge/Taylor & Francis Group.

Becker, C. B., Franko, D. L., Speck, A., & Herzog, D. B. (2010). *Ethnicity and differential access to care for eating disorder symptoms.* International Journal of Eating Disorders, 43(5), 422–428.

Brown, C. A., & Landry, M. J. (2021). *Therapist transparency and the therapeutic alliance: A clinical review.* Journal of Contemporary Psychotherapy, 51(1), 15–25.

Comas-Díaz, L. (2012). *Multicultural care: A clinician's guide to cultural competence.* American Psychological Association.

Duffy, M. E., & Henkel, K. E. (2016). *The impact of therapeutic alliance on treatment outcomes in eating disorder therapy: A meta-analysis.* Eating Disorders, 24(2), 99–116.

Eubanks, C. F., Muran, J. C., & Safran, J. D. (2019). Repairing alliance ruptures. In J. C. Norcross & M. J. Lambert (Eds.), *Psychotherapy relationships that work: Evidence-based therapist contributions* (3rd ed., pp. 549–579). Oxford University Press.

Fairburn, C. G. (2008). *Cognitive behavior therapy and eating disorders.* The Guilford Press.

Falender, C. A., & Shafranske, E. P. (2004). *The practice of clinical supervision.* In C. A. Falender & E. P. Shafranske (Eds.), Clinical supervision: A competency-based approach (pp. 3–35). American Psychological Association.

Freud, S. (1912). *The dynamics of transference.* The standard edition of the complete psychological works of Sigmund Freud, Volume XII (1911–1913): The case of Schreber, papers on technique and other works (pp. 97–108). Hogarth Press in London in 1953–1974.

Geller, J., Cockell, S. J., & Goldner, E. M. (2010). *Eating disorders and the therapeutic relationship: Developing skills to work with resistance and ambivalence.* Routledge.

Hayes, J. A., Gelso, C. J., & Hummel, A. M. (2011). *Managing countertransference.* In J. C. Norcross (Ed.), Psychotherapy relationships that work: Evidence-based responsiveness (2nd ed., pp. 239–256). Oxford University Press.

Hill, C. E., & Knox, S. (2002). *Self-disclosure.* Psychotherapy: Theory, Research, Practice, Training, 39(4), 413–417.

Lev Ari, H. S., Gur, E., Lotan-Wohl, M., Bernstein, Z. L., & Tuval-Mashiach, R. (2024). *Facilitators and obstacles to therapeutic alliance among patients with anorexia nervosa: A qualitative dyadic research.* Counseling & Psychotherapy Research, 24(1), 136–153.

Miller, W. R., & Rollnick, S. (2013). *Motivational interviewing: Helping people change (3rd ed.).* Guilford Press.

Norcross, J. C., & Wampold, B. E. (2018). *Relationships and responsiveness in the psychological treatment of eating disorders.* International Journal of Eating Disorders, 51 (2), 132–140.

Norcross, J. C., & Lambert, M. J. (2019). *Evidence-based psychotherapy relationships: The third task force.* In J. C. Norcross & M. J. Lambert (Eds.), Psychotherapy relationships that work: Evidence-based therapist contributions (3rd ed., pp. 1–23). Oxford University Press.

Porges, S. W., & Furman, S. A. (2011). *The early development of the autonomic nervous system provides a neural platform for social behavior: A polyvagal perspective.* Infant and Child Development, 20(1), 106–118.

Prochaska, J. O., & DiClemente, C. C. (1983). *Stages and processes of self-change of smoking: Toward an integrative model of change.* Journal of Consulting and Clinical Psychology, 51(3), 390–395.

Puhl, R. M., & Heuer, C. A. (2010). *Obesity stigma: Important considerations for public health.* American Journal of Public Health, 100(6), 1019–1028.

Ramjan, L. & Fogarty, S. (2019). *Clients' perceptions of the therapeutic relationship in the treatment of anorexia nervosa: Qualitative findings from an online questionnaire.* Australian Journal of Primary Health, 25(1), 37–42.

Safran, J. D., & Muran, J. C. (2000). *Negotiating the therapeutic alliance: A relational treatment guide.* Guilford Press.

Safran, J. D., Muran, J. C., & Eubanks, C. F. (2011a). *Repairing alliance ruptures.* Psychotherapy, 48(1), 80–87.

Safran, J. D., Muran, J. C., Samstag, L. W., & Winston, A. (2011b). *Evaluating an alliance-focused treatment for personality disorders.* Psychotherapy Research, 21(6), 682–689.

Schmidt, U., & Treasure, J. (2006). *Anorexia nervosa: Valued and visible.* A cognitive-interpersonal maintenance model and its implications for research and practice. British Journal of Clinical Psychology, 45(3), 343–366.

Simpson, C. C., & Mazzeo, S. E. (2017). *Calorie counting and fitness tracking technology: Associations with eating disorder symptomatology.* Eating Behaviors, 26, 89–92.

Treasure, J., Schmidt, U., & Macdonald, P. (2020). *The clinician's guide to collaborative caring in eating disorders: The new Maudsley method (2nd ed.).* Routledge.

Vitousek, K., Watson, S., & Wilson, G. T. (1998). *Enhancing motivation for change in treatment-resistant eating disorders.* Clinical Psychology Review, 18(4), 391–420.

Zaitsoff, S. L., & Taylor, A. (2009a). *Factors related to the continuation of eating disorder treatment.* Eating Disorders, 17(1), 42–57.

Zaitsoff, S. L., & Taylor, S. (2009b). Factors related to the therapeutic alliance in the treatment of eating disorders: A systematic review. *Clinical Psychology Review*, 29(5), 545–554.

Zilcha-Mano, S. (2017). *Is the alliance really therapeutic?* Revisiting this question in light of recent methodological advances. European Journal of Clinical Psychology, 23(2), 170–181.

Zur, O. (2007). *Boundaries in psychotherapy: Ethical and clinical explorations.* American Psychological Association.

Chapter 10

Living Authentically Through Endings

Lessons from Therapy and Life

Overview

- *Termination is never just the end of therapy; it is itself a rupture, a process, and a profound relational experience.* This chapter explores the complexities of treatment endings, where grief, relief, fear, and gratitude often coexist.
- *Navigating endings in therapy mirrors the endings we face in life.* By confronting closure with honesty and presence, therapists and clients alike can practice authenticity in the face of loss, change, and transition.
- *Endings offer unique opportunities for reflection and growth.* Self-reflection questions invite clinicians to consider their own responses to closure, helping them recognize patterns of attachment, avoidance, and meaning-making that emerge in these moments.
- *Authenticity extends beyond the therapy room into every dimension of life.* When therapists embody presence, congruence, and empathy, they not only guide clients toward healing but also model a way of living marked by integrity, vulnerability, and connection.
- *Looking back across the book, a core lesson emerges: authenticity is not a technique but a way of being.* From body image to intersectionality, from systems to systems of oppression, from ruptures to repair, the most enduring tool in therapy is the courage to be real.

Introduction

From the beginning, Avery was the kind of client clinicians hope for. She was engaged, intelligent, and eager to do the work. We built a strong alliance early on, and her treatment trajectory was promising. She met milestones with consistency, opened up in individual therapy, and offered rich insights about herself and her recovery. As we approached discharge from residential care, we began planning for next steps. That's when everything shifted.

Almost overnight, Avery began struggling in ways she never had before. She began leaving food uneaten, lashing out behaviorally, and becoming distant in our sessions. At

DOI: 10.4324/9781003632016-11

first, I was confused. This was a 180-degree turn from the client I had come to know. I brought my confusion into the room with her. Gently but honestly, I shared what I was observing and expressed how much I had valued our work together. I invited her to help me make sense of what was happening.

Avery paused, then offered something that struck me deeply. She said she had grown to care about me, about the staff, and about the structure of the program. These relationships had come to mean something real to her. And now that we were talking about discharge, it felt like all of her experiences—our relationship, her progress, the connections she made—were being erased. "If it could just end," she said, "maybe it was never real to begin with."

Her words mirrored what research has increasingly illuminated: for clients with eating disorders, especially those with attachment wounds or long-standing illness, termination can stir profound grief, abandonment fears, and questions of authenticity (Ulven et al., 2025); *Fernández-Aranda et al., 2021*). *What therapists view as termination, clients may experience as betrayal, especially when the therapeutic alliance has been one of the few secure relational bonds in their lives* (Vinchenzo et al., 2022). *In Avery's case, the very success of the therapeutic relationship paradoxically made the prospect of ending intolerable.*

I was left reflecting on how termination is not simply a clinical task to complete but a deeply relational process to navigate. It requires preparation, mutual meaning-making, and an attuned awareness of how endings are interpreted through the lens of past wounds. For Avery, the shift in behavior wasn't sabotage, it was protest. Her sudden regression was a response to anticipated loss, a last effort to keep something that felt safe from disappearing.

Her story reminds me that in eating disorder treatment, termination must be approached not as a final step, but as a continuation of the therapeutic work itself that honors the relationship, validates the client's experience, and affirms that what was built together was, in fact, real.

Termination as a Rupture, a Process, and a Relational Experience

The research is clear: when termination approaches, the therapeutic process often shifts in powerful ways. Clients and therapists experience endings differently, and for individuals with eating disorders, the close of treatment can feel less like a celebration of progress and more like a rupture (Marmarosh, 2022; Vinchenzo et al., 2022). Feelings of grief, fear, uncertainty, and even abandonment may surface as clients face the loss of a consistent relational anchor. For some, the therapeutic relationship has been one of the few safe spaces where their inner world felt seen and held. As that space begins to close, old patterns of self-protection can re-emerge: restricting emotions, disengaging, clinging, regressing, or anticipating disappointment. Clinicians, too, carry their own emotional responses including pride, sadness, worry, and hope, all of which can shape how endings unfold. When approached with intention, transparency, and collaborative planning, termination becomes more than an ending. It becomes a meaningful chapter in the story of recovery, offering clients a chance to internalize the relationship, reflect on their progress, and step forward with a strengthened sense of agency and connection.

The Words We Use

Even with the best of intentions, therapists can carefully structure the course of treatment by collaboratively setting goals, offering authentic presence, and implementing thoughtful interventions, and yet still miss something essential when it comes to how therapy ends. Relationally, therapy is not simply about how we begin or what interventions we do but also about how we say goodbye. For many of us—both clinicians and clients—endings stir deep emotional currents. They touch early attachment wounds, echo past losses, and awaken fears of abandonment. And while we place great importance on building rapport, navigating ruptures, and guiding change, we don't always give the same attention to the closing chapter of therapy. How we move toward an ending can leave an imprint as lasting as any insight or breakthrough along the way.

Personally, the word "termination" has always felt jarring; for me it evokes something abrupt, cold, or transactional. It conjures images of being fired, ending a lease, or the finality of a severed connection. But therapy, at its best, is anything but impersonal. So instead of termination, I invite clinicians to think in metaphors that more accurately reflect the relational essence of therapy: a graduation, where a client steps into life with new tools and insight; a bridge crossing, where the clinician walks partway but not the whole journey; or the planting of a seed, with the understanding that growth continues long after the final session. For now, let's call it moving on—a process that honors both the relationship and the resilience it fostered.

The Complexities of Treatment Endings

Therapy termination is a pivotal phase of the psychotherapeutic process, marked by a mix of clinical, ethical, and emotional challenges. For both clinicians and clients, it can evoke a range of responses including grief, anxiety, accomplishment, and unfinished business. While many scholars advocate for planned and collaborative termination, the reality is often more complicated, particularly in work with adolescents and individuals with eating disorders.

West and Torrico (2021) emphasize that termination is often underemphasized despite its significant impact on therapeutic outcomes. They advocate for a relational, phased approach that allows for the processing of loss, celebration of growth, and exploration of future supports. Additionally, Goode et al. (2017) advocate for a collaborative model of termination, emphasizing shared decision-making and goal review as central to ethical closure. For clients with eating disorders, whose treatment often navigates ambivalence, attachment insecurity, and chronicity, termination may reactivate fears of abandonment or relapse, making early and ongoing discussion about how treatment ends essential. Collaborative and relationally phased treatment can help counteract the power struggles and feelings of control often embedded in treatment while offering strong relational support. In my own clinical experience, I have found that naming the inevitability of endings early in treatment not only reduces anxiety but also helps clients internalize that therapy can be both a secure base and a place to practice letting go. I recall working with a young adult who, upon hearing in our second session that we would eventually talk about how therapy might end, immediately teared up and said, "No one's ever said that in therapy before. It makes me feel like you won't just disappear." That moment grounded the work for us both, making termination not a looming threat but a shared process we would navigate together.

Abrupt Decisions

From my work with Avery, I learned more about the complex experience treatment transitions bring on for both clients and clinicians. One type of treatment ending that I have found challenging over the years is when a client makes a decision to leave treatment abruptly. Schaeffer and Kaiser (2019) explored the complexities of unilateral termination, in which clients leave therapy without notice. This phenomenon can be especially common among clients with eating disorders, who may drop out due to shame, fear of change, or conflict around autonomy. The authors propose a structured framework to address such terminations retroactively and proactively, emphasizing the importance of rupture repair work and therapist self-reflection. This highlights the importance of continuously engaging in a meta-dialogue around the therapeutic process, checking in with clients.

I still remember a young woman who, after months of steady progress in residential treatment, suddenly left against medical advice. We had been doing deep work around family dynamics, and it became clear later that the intensity of that exploration felt overwhelming for her. One day she went on a pass and simply didn't return. I received a call from her mother informing me that she wasn't coming back. In those moments, I was flooded with self-doubt, wondering whether I had pushed too hard or missed the subtle signs of her ambivalence. Another time, a college student abruptly stopped attending outpatient sessions after a conversation about increasing meal plan structure. She later emailed me to say she felt "too exposed" and needed to retreat, though she also admitted she regretted not saying goodbye in person. These experiences have taught me that unilateral termination is rarely just about "noncompliance." Instead, it reflects the client's ongoing struggle with trust, autonomy, and the vulnerability of being in treatment. For me, they have underscored the need to check in regularly not only about symptoms and behaviors, but also about how clients are experiencing the therapy itself including naming tensions, exploring fears of dependency, and making space for honest dialogue before rupture becomes exit.

Over time, I have come to see these abrupt endings as part of my own growth process, too. Each instance has stretched my ability to tolerate uncertainty and sit with the discomfort of not having closure. They have forced me to examine my countertransference: my desire to "save" clients from leaving, my own fear of being abandoned, and the sting of not being able to prevent their pain. While these endings are never easy, they have shaped me into a more patient and self-aware therapist, reminding me that even ruptures and sudden departures can carry meaning and, if processed thoughtfully, can inform how I show up more authentically in future therapeutic relationships. For me, abrupt endings have taught me to sit with the discomfort of unfinished therapeutic processes and to accept that closure is not always possible. These experiences heightened my awareness of my own fears of abandonment and the pull to "rescue," helping me approach future ruptures with more clarity and balance. Each termination reminded me of the importance of inviting honest conversations about ambivalence and dependency, allowing me to show up more openly and authentically in the therapeutic relationship

Early Treatment Endings

Premature treatment termination remains a significant barrier to effective eating disorder treatment, with both clients and clinicians acknowledging its emotional, relational, and systemic roots. Often cited as "dropout" both in clinical practice and literature, research highlights the complexity of early treatment endings beyond individual motivation or resistance, pointing to issues of misattunement, systemic constraints, and the chronicity of the disorder. In a systematic review and qualitative synthesis, Vinchenzo et al. (2022) analyzed patient-reported reasons for premature termination, finding that clients often leave due to feeling misunderstood, judged, or disempowered in treatment. Many reported a lack of individualized care, rigid treatment protocols, and inadequate attention to their emotional and relational needs. These findings challenge the assumption that dropout is merely a sign of patient resistance or ambivalence; instead, clients frequently described termination as an act of self-protection when the therapeutic environment felt invalidating or misaligned with their lived experience.

From a clinician perspective, Ulven et al. (2025) conducted a qualitative study exploring clinicians' experiences with premature termination. Clinicians often attributed dropout to clients' avoidance, denial, or fear of weight gain but also acknowledged systemic challenges such as insurance limitations, unrealistic recovery timelines, and treatment models that prioritize symptom reduction over relational engagement. Therapists expressed ambivalence, guilt, and concern about their own ability to connect authentically with clients, especially when pressured to produce short-term outcomes. This mismatch between client needs and treatment demands can exacerbate ruptures, particularly when emotional safety and therapeutic alliance are not sufficiently prioritized.

Specific Populations

Treatment experiences, and therefore endings, vary by population, age, and diagnosis. Marmarosh (2022) underscored the importance of understanding clients' emotional experiences around endings. She found that clients often feel ambivalent about termination, expressing both pride in progress and anxiety about losing the therapeutic relationship. These dynamics are magnified in adolescent populations, where identity development and individuation are still in progress. Adolescents may experience termination as a rupture rather than a rite of passage, especially when therapy has been mandated or connected to family conflict, as is often the case in eating disorder treatment.

Fernández-Aranda et al. (2021) acknowledge the "enduring eating disorder" model by showing that longer illness duration is a strong predictor of treatment nonresponse and dropout. Chronicity correlates with entrenched cognitive and behavioral patterns, poorer therapeutic alliance, and increased medical and psychosocial complications. These clients often require longer, more relationally attuned care models yet are at higher risk of being prematurely discharged when short-term outcomes are not met. It is essential not to label eating disorder clients as "chronic." Rather, it is important to understand longer-term eating disorders as a distinct clinical entity rather than as treatment failure. This perspective can help reduce stigma and improve long-term engagement.

Therapy endings are a multidimensional process that demand clinical sensitivity and relational care. Developmentally, adolescents may view endings through a lens of dependency, loss, or rebellion, while adults may wrestle with themes of completion, regression, or self-efficacy. For clients with eating disorders and across age groups, transitions and endings often elicit fears of losing a secure attachment figure, concerns about relapse, or unresolved identity and control issues. Effective termination should be planned early, revisited often, and addressed explicitly in a collaborative, relationally attuned manner.

The "how" of the ending also impacts therapist's experiences around termination. Just as a client's experience of therapy will differ in treatment completion versus premature termination or treatment dropout, so will a clinician's. Theory can offer insight into the process of termination; for example, from a cognitive behavioral perspective, a therapist is likely to process termination by tapering sessions, continuing to review progress gained, and encouraging clients to use gained skills in their own process. Other orientations, such as a psychodynamic perspective, include an interpersonal dimension of termination that includes processing of the therapeutic relationship. Norcross, Zimmerman, Greenberg & Swift (2017) recruited 65 "prominent North American psychotherapists of six theoretical orientations (psychoanalytic/psychodynamic, experiential/humanistic, cognitive/cognitive–behavioral, systemic/interpersonal, multicultural [including feminist], and integrative/eclectic)" (p. 67) to identify termination tasks and behaviors. Their findings suggest that regardless of background or orientation, therapists should routinely speak with their clients about termination and come to an agreement around timing. They also suggest that as that time approaches, therapy can focus on the growth that has occurred as well as feelings of loss (Norcross et al., 2017).

Navigating Endings in Therapy

The process of moving on—whether from therapy, relationships, or life transitions—can evoke a wide range of emotional responses for clients and clinicians alike. For many clients, especially those navigating themes of attachment, abandonment, or identity, the idea of "moving on" is not merely a milestone but is the very material of therapy. In these cases, the anticipation of an ending may trigger grief, fear, or resistance, making it essential that we approach termination not as a logistical endpoint but as a dynamic, relational process.

Because of the emotional weight endings can carry, it is critical to introduce the idea of termination early in treatment and revisit it throughout. Regardless of whether the clinician is working in a managed care facility with time-limited services or in outpatient settings without fixed session caps, the therapeutic relationship will eventually shift or conclude. Therapy is meant to be finite, even with the nonlinear nature of healing. Clients may return for "tune-ups," brief re-engagements to support stability or address new challenges, but the core goal remains empowerment and internalization of therapeutic tools.

The findings suggest that therapists should engage clients in open and ongoing conversations about termination, working collaboratively to reach agreement on its timing. As the end of treatment approaches, practitioners can acknowledge both the feelings of loss and the progress that has been achieved, helping clients hold these experiences together. Establishing a mutually agreed-upon closure date can provide structure and offer guidance on how to navigate this important phase. A termination checklist, built upon consensus-based tasks, could serve as a practical tool for clinicians, ensuring consistency and thoughtfulness in how endings are managed. These results also highlight the need to intentionally cultivate termination-related skills in clinical training, preparing students to handle treatment closure with confidence, sensitivity, and authenticity. In my own clinical work, I have found that openly naming the complexity of endings deepens trust and models authenticity, showing clients that closure itself can be a practice of honesty, courage, and connection.

That said, how clinicians manage endings deeply influences how clients experience them, often in ways that are felt more than spoken. Below are self-reflection prompts for clinicians to consider through journaling and self-reflection. With these prompts in mind, clinicians could bring questions to their supervisors to further reflect on and engage with the topic of therapeutic endings.

Clinician Self-Reflection

- How do you respond to endings and transitions in your life?
- Consider your own experiences of moving on from friendships, jobs, or life phases. What emotions arise for you when relationships change or conclude? How might these experiences influence the way you navigate termination in therapy?
- Do you find yourself subtly avoiding conversations about termination with clients?
- If so, what might that reflect about your own relationship to loss, completion, or professional identity? When you anticipate an ending with a client, do you lean more toward avoiding discomfort or embracing openness? What does this reveal about your own authenticity?
- What messages have you received regarding goodbyes and relationships growing up?
- Reflecting on your developmental history can shed light on your unconscious enactments in the therapy room. In what ways do you invite clients to express their feelings about ending therapy, and how do you respond when those feelings are different from your own based on your experiences?
- Does your nonverbal communication reinforce safety and clarity, or might it unintentionally signal avoidance or discomfort? How can you use the process of termination as an opportunity to model honesty, vulnerability, and authentic connection with your clients?

Modeling Healthy Closure

Clients are often watching more than they are listening; the way we end relationships can leave as deep an impression as how we begin them. Thoughtful, attuned termination offers a lived experience of boundaries, care, and acknowledgment, especially powerful for clients and families whose histories are marked by abrupt endings, avoidance, or unresolved conflict. When clinicians explore their own reactions to separation and change, they are better able to stay present during endings, rather than rushing the process or disengaging. A mindful approach might include reflecting on the work accomplished, naming emotions that surface, and articulating hopes for the client's continued growth. In doing so, clinicians provide not only insight but also a model of respectful, mutual closure, an experience that can help re-write internal narratives about loss and support clients in navigating future transitions with clarity, confidence, and compassion.

Key Take-Aways

- Endings in therapy are not merely administrative; they are emotionally complex, relationally charged processes that can evoke grief, fear, relief, and growth for both clients and clinicians.

- Early, ongoing, and authentic dialogue about termination strengthens therapeutic safety, reduces the risk of premature endings, and helps clients internalize the relationship as a secure base rather than fear an abrupt loss.
- Premature or abrupt terminations often reflect deeper struggles with trust, autonomy, and vulnerability, not "noncompliance." Attuned conversations about ambivalence, attachment, and the client's experience of therapy can prevent rupture from turning into exit.
- The therapist's own attachment history, comfort with goodbyes, and countertransference shape the quality of endings. Self-reflection is essential for managing transitions ethically, relationally, and authentically.
- Termination is ultimately a practice of authenticity: holding progress and loss together, honoring the relationship, and modeling the courage to move on. It becomes a meaningful part of recovery rather than an afterthought.

References

Fernández-Aranda, F., Treasure, J., Paslakis, G., Agüera, Z., Giménez, M., Granero, R., et al. (2021). *The impact of duration of illness on treatment nonresponse and drop-out: Exploring the relevance of enduring eating disorder concept.* European Eating Disorders Review, 29(3), 499–513.

Goode, J., Park, J., Parkin, S., Tompkins, K. A., & Swift, J. K. (2017). *A collaborative approach to psychotherapy termination.* Psychotherapy, 54(1), 10–14.

Marmarosh, C. (2022). *Clients' experiences of therapy ending.* In J. N. Fuertes (Ed.), The other side of psychotherapy: Understanding clients' experiences and contributions in treatment (pp. 351–378). American Psychological Association.

Norcross, J. C., Zimmerman, B. E., Greenberg, R. P., & Swift, J. K. (2017). *Do all therapists do that when saying goodbye?* Psychotherapy, 54(1), 66–75.

Schaeffer, J. A., & Kaiser, E. M. (2019). *A structured approach to processing clients' unilateral termination decisions.* Journal of Clinical Psychology: In Session, 75(12), 2103–2112.

Ulven, O., Stige, S. H., & Danielsen, Y. S. (2025). *Premature termination of eating disorder treatment – a qualitative study of therapist perspectives.* Journal of Eating Disorders, 13(1), 76.

Vinchenzo, C., Lawrence, V., & McCombie, C. (2022). *Patient perspectives on premature termination of eating disorder treatment: A systematic review and qualitative synthesis.* Journal of Eating Disorders, 10(1), 39.

West, W., & Torrico, B. (2021). *Terminating the therapeutic relationship.* In D. Murphy (Ed.), Counselling psychology: A textbook for study and practice (2nd ed., pp. 333–348). Wiley.

Epilogue

Living the Work

Endings are never simple, but they are meaningful. Termination in therapy is not merely the last session on a calendar; it is a process, a turning point, and a deeply relational experience. It carries the same emotional textures as the endings we encounter in life including grief and gratitude, loss and renewal, fear and hope. In therapy, as in life, endings are not about erasing what came before but about carrying forward what was learned, lived, and shared. As I close this book, I find myself holding the same mixture of emotions I have so often witnessed in my clients: the reluctance to let go, paired with the recognition that the work has given us something enduring.

Clients are often watching more than they are listening; the way we engage in endings can leave as deep an imprint as how we begin. Thoughtful, attuned closure offers a lived experience of boundaries, care, and acknowledgment, especially for clients and families whose histories include abrupt separations or unresolved ruptures. When we reflect together on what has been felt and accomplished, name the emotions that surface, and articulate hopes for the path ahead, we model an ending rooted not in abandonment but in connection. This form of closure becomes not just a conclusion, but an embodied experience of respect that helps re-write internal narratives about loss and strengthens the capacity to navigate transitions with clarity, confidence, and compassion.

Looking back, the threads of authenticity have woven through every chapter of this journey. We began with a question: What does it mean to be real? Drawing on Carl Rogers and others, we explored authenticity as not merely a philosophical concept but a lived practice measured moment by moment, relationship by relationship. We saw how congruence, presence, and attunement invite clients into deeper connection with themselves and with others, cultivating healing beyond symptom reduction.

We widened the lens to understand how eating disorders emerge within a broader biopsychosocial–spiritual ecology. Culture, body image, and social pressure can fracture a person's sense of self, while social media and dominant cultural scripts intensify shame and disconnection. Authenticity can feel not only challenging but dangerous. This context matters because no one develops an eating disorder in a vacuum.

DOI: 10.4324/9781003632016-12

Exploring the treatment landscape affirmed both the value and the limitations of manualized care. Cognitive-behavioral and family-based models offer important structure, yet too often fail to capture the full humanity of clients. Healing requires a more expansive toolkit, one that weaves together relational, somatic, psychodynamic, expressive, and culturally responsive modalities. Authenticity asks us to adapt our frameworks and to hold space for both evidence and lived experience.

The common factors literature reminded us that what unites all therapies is ultimately more powerful than what distinguishes them. The therapeutic alliance—rooted in trust, collaboration, and authenticity—is the most consistent predictor of positive outcomes. In eating disorder treatment, where secrecy and ambivalence are common, this alliance can be fragile. But when cultivated with patience and presence, it becomes the strongest bridge toward lasting change.

We also named what is too often left unsaid: culture, identity, and systemic inequities shape every therapeutic encounter. Intersectionality, cultural humility, and the minority stress model demonstrated how authenticity is influenced by forces larger than the individual. Weight stigma revealed itself as both a societal wound and a therapeutic barrier, distorting how clients see themselves and, too often, how we see them. Recognizing these forces is essential; ignoring them risks reinforcing harm.

Expanding our frame to include families deepened our understanding of authenticity as a systemic endeavor. Families bring love, loyalty, conflict, and history into the therapeutic space. Patterns around food, body, achievement, and communication are often intergenerational. Supporting families through these complexities requires tools like meta-dialogue, power awareness, and structured boundaries, all tools that stretch both therapists and families. At its best, this work allows families to re-write roles, repair wounds, and reclaim narratives that have shaped them for generations.

Of course, no authentic relationship is free of rupture. Therapy is not linear; it is punctuated by misattunements, misunderstandings, and mistakes. But it is precisely in these moments that authenticity is tested and forged. Repair requires humility, curiosity, and the willingness to acknowledge impact, even when intent was benign. It asks us to examine our own countertransference and cultural lenses, recognizing that our humanity is not an obstacle but a vital instrument of healing.

Again and again, this book has underscored that authenticity is not a technique, it is a way of being. It asks us to meet shame with empathy, resistance with curiosity, stigma with courage, and difference with humility. It invites us to bring our full selves into the room, not as flawless models but as fellow travelers shaped by our own histories, identities, and vulnerabilities. In my roles as therapist, leader, supervisor, parent, and partner, I continue to relearn that authenticity is not a destination but a daily practice: leaning into discomfort, embracing imperfection, and choosing connection.

If there is one truth I carry forward, it is this: authenticity heals not because it is perfect, but because it is honest.

It is what sustains therapy, fortifies the therapeutic alliance, supports families through crisis, and restores dignity in the face of shame. It is what makes life, and relationship, worth engaging in fully. Like my clients, I am still learning.

As you finish this book, my invitation is simple:

Take authenticity with you.

Let it shape how you listen, how you speak, how you show up in your relationships, and how you care for yourself. Authenticity will not always feel easy; at times, it will ask you to sit with discomfort, ask difficult questions, or reveal vulnerability. Yet it will always be worth it. My hope is that these pages serve as both compass and companion, reminding you that living authentically is not about perfection, but about presence, honesty, and connection.

This ending is not a goodbye, but a beginning.

The work continues within you, between us, and in every brave, imperfect act of showing up with your whole self.

Index

Note: Page numbers in **bold** indicate tables

For Product Safety Concerns and Information please contact our EU representative GPSR@taylorandfrancis.com
Taylor & Francis Verlag GmbH, Kaufingerstraße 24, 80331 München, Germany

www.ingramcontent.com/pod-product-compliance
Lightning Source LLC
LaVergne TN
LVHW010635300926
849161LV00005B/951

* 9 7 8 1 0 4 1 0 5 2 5 5 5 *